THE TRUTH
ABOUT
TRUDEAU

BOB PLAMONDON

great river media inc.

The Truth About Trudeau
Bob Plamondon

Great River Media

Copyright © 2013 by Bob Plamondon

Library and Archives Canada Cataloguing in Publication

Plamondon, Bob, author
The Truth about Trudeau / Bob Plamondon.

Includes bibliographical references and index.
ISBN 978-0-9868242-1-0 (bound)

1. Trudeau, Pierre Elliott, 1919-2000. 2. Canada - Politics and government -
1968-1979. 3. Canada - Politics and government - From 1980 to 1984.
4. Prime ministers - Canada - Biography. I. Title.

FC626.T7P53 2013 971 064 '4092 C2013-902814-5

Great River Media Inc
Suite 500 - 250 City Centre Avenue
Ottawa, ON
K1R 6K7
www.greatriver.ca
For inquiries about the book, or to contact the author, visit:
www.truthabouttrudeau.ca

Book design: Carole McLachlin Design
Printed and bound in Canada

*To Nathaniel, Charlotte,
Megan and Michael*

TABLE OF CONTENTS

PREFACE

We must concern ourselves with politics, as Pascal said, to mitigate as far as possible the damage done by the madness of our rulers.
Pierre Elliot Trudeau

THERE IS MUCH to admire about Pierre Trudeau. He espoused a clear and consistent vision. He demonstrated exceptional intellect and toughness. He charmed a nation with his irreverence and charisma. And he led our country through a rocky period of rising Quebec nationalism when politicians from English Canada struggled in their dealings with *la belle province.*

Our fascination with Canada's third-longest-serving prime minister has sustained a large catalogue of bestsellers. Many are flattering reflections by his friends and others of like mind and persuasion. Trudeau himself authored or co-authored 11 books covering his time in office. As Winston Churchill reportedly said, "History will be kind to me for I intend to write it."

This literary blitzkrieg paid off. In the 2006 nationwide populist search conducted by the CBC for the *Greatest Canadian* of all time, Trudeau ranked number three, above all other prime ministers.

But Pierre Trudeau is not universally admired. Critics deemed his vision too centrist and his style too arrogant. Pirouettes behind the Queen were not cute, but condescending. Flipping his middle finger at voters in Salmon Arm was not irreverent, but insulting. Yes, Quebec remained in Canada during Trudeau's tenure, but its nationalist forces grew in response to his intransigence, leading to the near loss of the 1995 Quebec referendum. And Western alienation established deep roots as a consequence of Trudeau's National Energy Program. When *Beaver Magazine* (now *Canada's History*) conducted an online poll in 2007 to name "Canada's worst person," after the 15,000 ballots were counted, Pierre Trudeau topped the list.

Being a great prime minister is about more than winning and losing popularity contests. More important is what a prime minister accomplishes for current and future generations. When we periodically re-examine Macdonald's vision for Canada, Robert Borden's wartime policies, R.B. Bennett's management of the Depression, William Lyon Mackenzie King's handling of Conscription, and Brian Mulroney's leap on Free Trade, we are not simply deciding if they were correct in their time, but whether their wisdom and judgment has stood the test of time.

As for Trudeau, surely the passions for and against the man have cooled to the point where Canadians can objectively assess how he changed Canada, for better and for worse. Did he leave the nation stronger and more united, or weaker and more divided? Did he prove to be a transformative leader with enduring accomplishments, or a prime minister whose actions have been undone by his successors?

When 117 academics and other experts were asked by *Maclean's* magazine in 2007 to rate our prime ministers, Trudeau ranked number five out of the nine who held office for more than a single term. That's the middle of the pack, and far below the rating that Trudeau receives in public opinion surveys in which he is consistently rated among the very best prime ministers. But even a cursory review of the record reveals that Trudeau's critics have a point:

- The discrepancy between the strong economic position Trudeau inherited from his predecessor and the calamity he left to his successor could not be more stark. The accumulated deficit under Trudeau rose tenfold, from $19.4 billion to $194.4 billion, or from 25.5 percent of GDP to 43.2 percent. The unemployment rate was 4.5 percent in 1968 versus 11.2 percent in 1984. The annual budgetary deficit was 0.9 percent of GDP in 1968 and 8.3 percent in 1984. Total annual federal spending was $12.9 billion when Trudeau became PM and was $109.2 billion when he quit, leaping from 17 percent of GDP to 24.2 percent. Trudeau's record on inflation, fueled by government spending that rose an average of close to 15 percent over his 15.5 years in office, was the worst among developed nations. Under Trudeau, our currency fell 17 percent against the American dollar, 47 percent against the Japanese Yen, and 68 percent relative to the German Mark.

- While poverty for seniors declined under Trudeau, the general income gap between rich and poor Canadians remained unchanged. When he left office, 42.7 percent of unattached seniors lived in poverty, as did one in six children, and 42.5 percent of households headed by women — compared with just 13.2 percent in the early 1960s.
- It is a myth that Trudeau opened up the country to scores of new immigrants. When he left office, the relative immigration rate was one-third what it was in 1968.
- In world affairs, Canadians say they were proud to have had a strong intellect representing their country. But Trudeau undermined our alliances, pointlessly annoyed our major trading partners and cozied up to communist dictators. His panache and flair got attention, but did not advance Canadian interests. His talk about North-South, a Third Option, and his peace initiative were ridiculed. As one American observer commented, Trudeau did not have enough country to satisfy his ambitions.
- While Trudeau defiantly opposed Quebec separatists and implemented official bilingualism, no prime minister did more damage to national unity. More than 30 years later, the West has not forgiven Trudeau for his National Energy Program. While Trudeau helped win the 1980 Quebec referendum for the NO side, he did so by misleading the people of Quebec — and then implemented constitutional reform that their government opposed. Along the way he made life difficult for many federalists on the ground in Quebec who were trying to win hearts and minds.
- Trudeau's major judicial achievement, the Charter of Rights and Freedoms, is not the panacea its proponents assert. While far from revolutionary, over time the Charter Americanized our constitution, made our culture more litigious, enabled judicial activism, and gave parliamentarians an excuse to duck sensitive issues.
- On matters of personal freedom, Trudeau was at best inconsistent. He presided over the most serious suspension of civil liberties since World War II — on false pretenses. Rather than responding to a provincial request, the invocation of the War Measures Act in October 1970 was Trudeau's idea. And for all his purported love of liberty, during his reign Trudeau restrict-

ed the ability of Canadians to choose their own health care, their music, and the television shows they wanted to watch.

- Far from being a "green" prime minister, Trudeau let Canada fall behind the United States on environmental protection. He subsidized the price of oil, invested in the oil sands, and opened the far north for exploration.
- Politically, while Trudeau won four of five federal elections, after 1968 he lost every contest outside of the province of Quebec. In his wake, the Liberal Party of Canada has struggled as a national political force.
- Even in retirement Trudeau left his mark. When Mulroney and all provincial premiers agreed to a constitutional package at Meech Lake in 1987, Trudeau used his influence to scuttle the deal. Gordon Robertson, a former clerk of the Privy Council who served under Pearson and Trudeau, concluded that nothing in Canadian history rivaled the irresponsibility of Trudeau in helping to destroy the only prospect of an agreement that would bring Quebec into willing acceptance of the Constitution.

Pierre Trudeau was certainly an intriguing, intelligent, charismatic, visionary and fearless leader. But on the fundamental question of whether he advanced and strengthened the nation, he fell well short of the mark. Canadians may have admired his personal qualities, but we should have been wary of a man with a radical past whose ideas had never been tested.

So let us, as Trudeau liked to say, be coolly intelligent and follow reason over passion. Let us examine the evidence, review the record, and learn the truth about Pierre Elliot Trudeau.

SECTION I

INTERNATIONAL RELATIONS AND NATIONAL DEFENCE

CHAPTER 1

THE TRUDEAU DOCTRINE

Personally, I tend to discount the weight of our influence in the world.

PIERRE TRUDEAU ONCE said that everything he needed to know about foreign affairs he could read in the New York Times.[1] More than a colourful quip, it embodied Trudeau's liberation from the Department of Foreign Affairs and its more structured approach to diplomacy. Rather than ground foreign policy in our economic and security interests, Canadian foreign affairs became Trudeau's personal domain. While he produced a few bold ventures and the occasional triumph, more often than not his indulgent forays around the globe infuriated our friends and allies.

Derek Burney, who worked at Foreign Affairs in the 1970s, and would go on to serve as our ambassador in Washington under Mulroney, thought Trudeau had panache and flair but was often oblivious or indifferent to Canadian interests. "Trudeau was a consummate actor. He got attention on the world stage, but few results."[2]

Many Canadians took pride in how Trudeau could hold his own with world leaders, both intellectually and stylistically. But we have to ask ourselves what we got in return for his displays of bravado.

WHEN TRUDEAU BECAME prime minister, he downplayed foreign policy as an area of interest. As a middle power, Canada, Trudeau suggested, should not extend its reach or exaggerate its importance. He harbored no ambitions of Canada punching above its weight.

When the Commonwealth conference came up in 1969, the first such international meeting with Trudeau at the helm, he initially refused to attend, calling it a waste of his time.[3] Trudeau had once observed that the monarchy was less important to Canada than skiing and snowshoeing, but he didn't consider its abolition a priority.[4]

When his officials pointed out that Canada's foreign minister could not very well sit at the table with heads of government at the conference, Trudeau relented. But after one of the lengthy formal sessions, he made his dissatisfaction known by sliding down a banister with photographers at the ready. The Queen, however, was not amused, calling the stunt "rather disappointing."

Trudeau initially claimed that he had little choice but to get involved in foreign-policy issues, "if only because of the various summits, personal exchanges, and visits that inevitably occur." In one sense, he did take a passive approach, believing that Canada had no right to interfere in the affairs of another country regardless of how oppressive and offensive their reality might be. Before entering politics, he thought South Africa's problems so complex and difficult that an outsider could sympathize but not criticize or recommend what course should be pursued.[5] In this context, he said that Canada was "not an important nation."[6] "We should be trying to make our own country a good place. Personally, I tend to discount the weight of our influence in the world."[7] But the evidence suggests that he was either being insincere or had changed his mind once he occupied high office. The record shows that when given the opportunity, he made dramatic changes in Canadian foreign policy and made his mark on the world stage. Mark MacGuigan, a foreign affairs minister under Trudeau, captured the reality of his boss's desire: "Whenever things got interesting, Trudeau pushed me out of his way."[8]

Trudeau distanced Canada from our traditional allies and undermined our relations with countries upon whom we relied for trade and national security. At the same time, he cozied up to the enemies of freedom and democracy, thereby lending credibility to brutal regimes that practiced oppression, torture, and imprisonment for political beliefs. When he visited dictators, he made little effort to raise the issue of human rights.

His fascination with socialism, even communism, made him unique among western leaders. It proved a lifelong enthrallment, grounded by Trudeau's socialist inclinations and his many treks to communist countries while a private citizen, places where most foreigners did not often tread. He preferred civility and diplomacy with those operating behind the Iron Curtain to confrontation or estrangement.

While Trudeau followed Lester B. Pearson, a Nobel Peace Prize winner and seasoned diplomat, he showed anything but deference to his predecessor. In his early days as prime minister, he launched a comprehensive foreign policy review, which led to the publication of six booklets under the title *Foreign Policy for Canadians*. Under Trudeau's new blueprint, Canada would give diplomatic recognition to China, put our commitment to NATO on notice, and pledge that we would substantially increase assistance to third world countries. Canada, under Trudeau, would distance itself from its allies to become an increasingly neutral nation.

The policy review proposed new initiatives, and attempted to circumvent the Foreign Affairs department and the Canadian diplomatic core. The prime minister's office, under the watchful eye of his chosen guru Ivan Head (who was seen internationally to speak for the prime minister), became the centre of foreign policy thinking and action. It was Head who co-wrote a book with Trudeau: *The Canadian Way: Shaping Canada's Foreign Policy, 1968–1984*.

Perhaps the most unusual aspect of Trudeau's early foreign policy work was the extent to which he diminished the importance and value of Canada's relationship with the United States. In his comprehensive foreign policy review, America barely rated a mention.

CHAPTER 2

LOSING AMERICAN FAVOUR

*By and large, the Canadian corporate sector clearly had little
interest in pursuing a third option.*

WHEN ADDRESSING AN American audience at the National Press Club in 1969, Trudeau quipped, "Living next to you is in some ways like sleeping with an elephant. No matter how friendly and even-tempered is the beast, one is affected by every twitch and grunt."[1] While this remark had a humorous intent, the reference to America as a *beast* spoke to much more than the differential in size between our countries. Trudeau intended to keep his political distance from the United States, if not antagonize them outright.

WHEN TRUDEAU CAME to power, Richard Nixon occupied the White House. Despite six face-to-face meetings, the neighbouring leaders were never on friendly terms (although the personal relationship was no worse than what Canadians had experienced during the Kennedy-Diefenbaker era). Henry Kissinger once observed, "It cannot be said that Trudeau and Nixon were ideally suited for one another."[2]

The first test of Canadian-American relations in the Trudeau-Nixon era involved Arctic waters. With the discovery of oil in Alaska, the U.S. wanted to determine if tankers could travel the Northwest Passage year-'round to supply oil to the Atlantic seaboard. So began the mission of the 145-thousand-ton Humble Oil company tanker, the *SS Manhattan*.

But military purposes loomed large, and may have trumped shipping as the more important impetus behind navigating the Northwest Passage. The U.S. government vigorously defended freedom of the seas. Long-held Canadian claims over the Northwest Passage threatened the U.S Navy's ability to patrol the globe freely. When the American administration indicated it would resist Canadian efforts to hinder passage of the *SS Manhattan* through the Northwest Passage, John Diefenbaker challenged Trudeau in the House of Commons to defend Canadian interests. Rather like drawing a line in the ice, Canada asserted its dominion by offering to "escort" the ship, principally with the help of the Canadian Coast Guard icebreaker *John A. Macdonald*. Canada also provided aerial surveillance, and a Canadian official boarded the *SS Manhattan* to act as an observer and technical advisor.

While, militarily speaking, Ottawa could not stop the Americans from traversing the Northwest Passage, it could offer up the pretence that Canada "condoned" and "oversaw" the mission. Recognizing the limits of our military capacity, Trudeau's clever positioning on the American-led voyage never put the question of our territorial control to the ultimate test.

It turned out the Americans were grateful to have the *John A. Macdonald* on the expedition, since its ice-breaking capabilities came in handy on multiple occasions to free the U.S.-flagged ship. While America cooperated with Canada on the journey, it conceded nothing from a sovereignty perspective.

Beyond tagging along on this mission, Trudeau determined that Canada would assert its sovereignty by extending its offshore border from three miles to twelve, which had been emerging as an international norm among non-shipping nations. This unilateral extension of the Canadian border narrowed the list of navigable routes through the Northwest Passage, an outcome the Americans opposed.

Trudeau followed the advice offered by Ivan Head to frame the boundary extension in the context of the environmental protection of Arctic waters rather than domestic sovereignty. Trudeau proposed that Canada would seek to establish an "international legal regime" through the United Nations and its agencies to combat pollution in international waters. He promised to raise the matter with the Secretary General of the United Nations.[3]

The Americans were prepared to accept the twelve-mile limit provided that it was subjected to a treaty with widespread international recognition. They also stipulated that the wider limit could not impede freedom of navigation through and over international straits.[4]

Despite American objections, Trudeau went ahead with domestic legislation in the form of the Arctic Waters Pollution Prevention Bill. In response, the American administration said it would defy the bill, and possibly send submarine excursions through self-proclaimed Canadian territory. An outraged Trudeau phoned the U.S. Secretary of State William P. Rogers: "Mr. Rogers, if you send up a tin can with a paper-thin hull filled with oil, we'll not only stop you, we'll board you and turn you around. And if we do so, Mr. Rogers, we'll have the world on our side."[5]

Trudeau told Rogers to convey his views to President Nixon. We can imagine the laughter in the Oval Office when Nixon was confronted with the threat that an American submarine would be stopped, boarded, and rebuffed by the Canadian Navy. But that did not deter Trudeau, who had good reason to think international sentiment would favour Canada.

The official American response was that they did not recognize coastal jurisdiction over their vessels on the high seas, including the right of any state to establish unilaterally a territorial sea of more than three nautical miles, or exercise more limited jurisdiction in any area beyond twelve nautical miles. Nonetheless, Canadian legislation received Royal Assent on June 26, 1970.

The United States eventually got what they wanted, but Canada scored some points as well. The matter of sovereignty on the high seas was resolved in an international forum at the UN Law of the Seas Conference held in 1973. Trudeau claimed that many of the elements adopted at the conference could be traced to the principles he established in the Canadian legislation. After ratification of the international treaty in 1982, Canada withdrew its Arctic amendment and accepted the jurisdiction of the International Court of Justice in 1985.

Trudeau's determination not to surrender to American excursions won him domestic political points and advanced Canada's claim to Arctic waters. But it did little to warm relations with Richard Nixon. While Trudeau admired Nixon's key foreign policy initiatives, such as opening up a dialogue with the Soviets and forging diplomatic relationship with China, Trudeau did not hesitate to offend the American president, even when there was no upside to doing so.

Trudeau decided to stake middle ground for Canada between the U.S. on one side and the Soviet Union on the other. It seemed of no great consequence to Trudeau that one superpower constituted a communist dictatorship that brutalized many of its citizens, and the other an open democracy and our biggest and most reliable trading partner. Trudeau's approach implied a moral equivalence between the two superpowers, a stance that understandably aggravated the Americans. In Trudeau's view, Canada was not so much a friend to America, but rather a nation that happened to be "strategically placed between the two great nuclear-armed adversaries."[6] Mark MacGuigan, Canada's foreign affairs minister from 1980–82, wrote that Trudeau believed in the "evils" of both American militaristic capitalism and the Soviet system.[7]

It was difficult at times for the Americans to know if Canada could be trusted as an ally. According to an entry in the official Canadian government web site for Foreign Affairs, "Trudeau was too much of a pacifist and a leftist for the Americans, some of whom considered him little more than a communist."[8] To confirm their suspicions, the Americans had only to open the CIA file on Trudeau to learn about his state-sponsored excursions to the Soviet Union and China before he entered public life.

NIXON, ALONG WITH his Secretary of State Henry Kissinger, wondered if Canada was friend or foe after Trudeau told the Soviets that America's presence so close to Canada posed "a danger to our national identity from a cultural, economic and perhaps even military point of view."[9] The Americans already looked askance at Trudeau's public misgivings about Canada's commitment to NATO and NORAD. For him to suggest to a communist government at an international meeting that America represented a military threat to Canada was even more disturbing, if not downright radical.

At about the same time as Canada asserted itself with new defence policies and unilateral claims over Arctic sovereignty, the United States announced an across-the-board 10-percent import surtax. Washington also mused about cancelling the auto pact between the U.S. and Canada. The combined impact of such policies would have devastated the Canadian economy.

Given his rhetoric on defence and NATO, Trudeau had placed Canada in a weak and vulnerable position to respond to American protectionism. Nixon may not have fully understood the impact his August 1971 bombshell would have on Canada, since he thought Japan was America's largest trading partner. Given the importance of our trading relationship with America, Trudeau might have made the issue a priority in his meetings and phone calls with Nixon, but he did not. While the import tax did not represent direct retaliation for Trudeau's foreign policy manoeuvres, those had irritated Nixon, and diminished the traditional goodwill between Canada and the U.S. that could have been used to countermand the import surtax quickly.

Trudeau, who was vacationing on the Adriatic when Nixon made his trade announcement, thought America had made a simple error by not exempting Canada from its protectionist measure. But it was not an oversight. In fact, when Nixon arranged to discuss his import tax with world leaders, he intentionally chose not to call Trudeau.[10] It took Trudeau four months before he could meet with Nixon, when they ultimately came to terms.

When visiting Ottawa in 1972, Nixon confirmed the drift that had come to characterize Canadian-American relations. He told our Parliament that Canada and the United States had separate identities, characterized by significant differences, and that "nobody's interests are furthered when these realities are obscured."[11] What this statement meant was that the United States would no longer give Canada special treatment. This pleased Trudeau, but it also represented an enormous risk to our economic interests.

NOT ONLY DID Nixon dislike Trudeau, he didn't understand him. After one meeting, Nixon remarked to his staff: "That Trudeau, he's a clever son of a bitch. What in the Christ is he talking about?" After another meeting, Nixon told his staff that Trudeau was "a pompous egghead." Nixon took note of every disparaging remark Trudeau made of the United States. "You've got to put it to these people for kicking the U.S. around after what we did for that lousy son of a bitch."[12] Nixon had negative stories about Trudeau planted with the press, telling his aide H.R. Haldeman "Play it hard, find a way goddammit. Give it to somebody around here."[13] In a moment of frustration he told Kissinger, "I'll never go to that country while he's there,"[14] although he did visit in April 1972, a trip Nixon said was a waste of his time and something he needed "like a hole the head."[15] Kissinger confided to his friends his own perception that Trudeau was "foppish" and "a mother's boy."[16]

Although Trudeau came to office saying that Canada had no right to intervene in the affairs of other countries, that position did not stop him from introducing a motion in Parliament in January 1973 that condemned the prolongation of the war in Vietnam. Trudeau had a point, but Canada had little to gain by publicly admonishing the

Americans. The U.S. would not change course because of statements in Canada's Parliament. But the resolution managed to sour relations between the two countries further. The last Canadian prime minister dressed-down for commenting on the Vietnam War was Lester Pearson. Lyndon Johnson famously grabbed Pearson by the shirt collar, lifted him off the floor and shouted, "You pissed on my rug!"

Before his resolution in Parliament, Trudeau had avoided commenting on Vietnam, although he considered the war abhorrent and American actions repugnant. Canada was involved in Vietnam to the extent that it participated in the International Commission for Supervision and Control, an international inspection mechanism that became engaged when a peace treaty was negotiated in 1973. Henry Kissinger named Canada a member of the commission under terms that Trudeau believed "bore no chance of success."[17] Trudeau said that Canada would not be a "public dupe" in a flawed process. Ultimately Canada withdrew from the mission, prompting Nixon to call Trudeau an "asshole" privately, revealed when secret Oval Office recordings were made available to the public. When Trudeau learned of the remark, he pithily responded, "I've been called worse things by better people." On the international peace mission, Canada was replaced by Iran.

Towards the end of Nixon's first term, the New York Times observed, "Despite three cordial official visits with President Nixon, [Trudeau] has still not found an effective way of dealing with the country with which Canada does most of her trading."[18]

TRUDEAU DEVELOPED A stronger and more constructive relationship with Nixon's successor, Gerald Ford. Although Ford held office for only 29 months, he arranged for Canada to gain entry into what is now known as the G8. But Ford did not particularly intend on doing Trudeau or Canada any favours. Including Canada in the world's leading economic club represented his response to France inviting Italy to the World Economic Conference in 1975. The Americans objected to this larger European voice and wanted a counterweight. At the time, France had opposed Canadian involvement in this club of nations. Trudeau wisely decided not to take the role of *demandeur* and waited for a resolution, without Canada having to grumble in public that it had been slighted. When the Americans hosted the conference in 1976, Ford included Canada as a full participant.

Canada had one skirmish with the Ford administration when Canada refused to allow Taiwan to call itself the "People's Republic of China" at the 1976 Olympics. When the government in Taipei boycotted the games, Ford briefly considered keeping American athletes out as well.

On a social level, the Ford-Trudeau friendship included a skiing holiday in Vail, Colorado in 1977, a rare opportunity for a Canadian prime minister to get the ear of an American president.[19]

IF TRUDEAU EVER had a kindred spirit in Washington, it was Jimmy Carter. Inaugurated in January 1977, Carter declared that under his watch America would pursue a "moral foreign policy," which aligned with Trudeau's sensibilities. Carter asserted that the U.S would promote human rights, seek measures to counter nuclear proliferation, and end the American practice of sustaining friendly dictatorships. Canada also had an important friend in Vice President Walter Mondale, who hailed from the bordering state of Minnesota and knew of our interests and issues.

While the one-term Carter never visited Canada while Trudeau was in office, Trudeau was granted the rare privilege of addressing a joint session of Congress on one of his four visits while Carter was president. Trudeau spoke of a "new world order" and highlighted the importance of tolerance and diversity around the world. In speaking before Congress, Trudeau had come a long way since the 1950s, when the Americans had blacklisted him and denied him entry as a security risk.[20]

Carter was receptive to Trudeau's request for American support of a united Canada. Carter had no need to make a specific reference to Quebec, since the intent of the message was clear. Carter signed agreements with Canada on acid rain and an East Coast fisheries treaty, but he could not get them ratified by the American Senate.

After the Soviet Union invaded Afghanistan in 1979, the Canadian government, then under Joe Clark, determined that Canada would boycott the 1980 Moscow Olympic Games. When Trudeau returned to office in February 1980, the issue landed on his desk. Unlike President Carter, who led the call for a boycott, Trudeau believed it would have no impact on the Soviets and refused to sustain Clark's policy until the athletes themselves endorsed the measure.

Carter had to deal with something far more important than the Soviet invasion of Afghanistan or the Olympic games: the Iran Hostage Crisis. Iranian rebels, with government support, took over the American embassy in Iran in November 1979. In the mêlée, the Canadian embassy became a refuge for six U.S. diplomats.

When the Canadian portion of the caper played itself out, Trudeau was opposition leader. Unaware that our diplomats were providing refuge for the Americans at great personal risk to embassy staff led by ambassador Ken Taylor, Trudeau berated the Clark government for not helping the Americans at a time of crisis.

Fearing for the safety of our diplomats and their American houseguests, and seeking to downplay the Iran issue, Clark wanted the questioning to stop, so he secretly briefed Trudeau on the mission on the floor of the House of Commons. To Clark's dismay, Trudeau's questioning on Iran continued in Parliament with a tone that Clark found distressing.[21] Once Trudeau was back in power, he quickly restored trading relations with Iran for all but military equipment.

It was expected that Trudeau would appoint Taylor, who had been awarded the United States Congressional Gold Medal in 1980, as Canada's ambassador to the United States, but instead he got the lesser job of consul general in New York City. Those familiar with the appointment concluded that Taylor did not receive the top diplomatic post because he was perceived to be a Tory. He was also an Albertan, which raised suspicions in the PMO. Trudeau, who had Allan Gotlieb in mind for the post, was not prepared to change course, despite the opportunity created by Taylor's heroic efforts. (It is noteworthy that when Mulroney became prime minister, he kept Gotlieb as our ambassador in Washington.)

While Canada suffered little harm and gained marginal benefit during the Carter-Trudeau years, the closeness of their relationship was evident when Trudeau died and Carter attended the funeral, serving as an honorary pallbearer.

WHILE TRUDEAU AND Carter were well-matched, Ronald Reagan was anything but Trudeau's ideological soul mate. Trudeau acknowledged Reagan's infectious optimism, writing that the American president was "constitutionally incapable of personal animosity." But Trudeau also saw Reagan as an intellectual lightweight, a bumbler, a throwback, a grade-B actor and a danger to world peace. He wrote that Reagan was incapable of firm adherence to any concept, "no matter how simple," and was limited to "brilliant repetitions of a familiar script supplied to him by someone else."[22] On the matter of how to end the Cold War, Trudeau thought Reagan misguided by trying to win the contest rather than come to terms with its adversary. According to Conrad Black, an intimate of many world leaders, Trudeau was "thunderstruck" when the Soviet Union collapsed.[23]

Reagan was proven correct, putting Trudeau on the wrong side of history.

In assessing Reagan, Trudeau wrote that it was hard to conceive of someone less able to understand issues and make responsible decisions. Yet when Americans are asked to rate their most accomplished presidents, Ronald Reagan usually makes the top five. But Trudeau considered Reagan a reckless and dangerous simpleton.

The styles of the two leaders could not have been more different. Trudeau incarnated the zeitgeist of the 1960s and 1970s, earning the praise of cultural icons John Lennon and Yoko Ono. As for Reagan, he once humorously declared of the hippie generation, "They dress like Tarzan, have hair like Jane, and smell like Cheeta."[24]

Reagan and Trudeau met face-to-face on four occasions, including at the G7 summit at Montebello, Quebec in 1981. While Trudeau claimed that the American delegation cared more about physical arrangements than the summit's content, it was Trudeau who, at the last minute, insisted that the Americans be relocated from a choice wing of the hotel overlooking the river so that the Canadian and West German delegations, led by his friend Helmut Schmidt, could have the best views.

When Trudeau invoked the nationalistic and confiscatory National Energy Program the American business community raised the roof, and the Reagan administration went on the offensive. American complaints only stiffened Trudeau's resolve to pursue his intended policies vigorously.[25] Reagan understood that he could not change Trudeau's mind, so he decided to wait him out and hope for a change in administration.

Trudeau determined that Reagan's "peace through strength" approach with the Soviets was destabilizing, unsophisticated, and "downright dangerous." At international summits, Trudeau would chide Reagan, publicly and privately. Some American officials told Canada's ambassador to the U.S., Allan Gotlieb, not to worry too much, because Reagan was a secure man and did not take the insults personally. Richard Darman, Reagan's deputy chief of staff, informed Gotlieb that "[t]he president was not really upset by the fact that Trudeau said he was an imbecile." Gotlieb wrote in his diary that he could not believe his ears. He told Darman, "That's impossible. Trudeau would never say a thing like that. It would be totally out of character — he is respectful of fellow leaders." Gotlieb was later asked by his wife, "'Do you really think Trudeau would be indiscreet enough to call Reagan an imbecile?'" "'Never,' I replied. 'He may think it, but he wouldn't say it.'"[26]

But Trudeau did insult Reagan in public. At a meeting in Bonn, a reporter shouted a question at President Reagan while world leaders posed for a group picture. Suggesting that Reagan was incapable of formulating a coherent answer, Trudeau directed the reporter to "[a]sk Al," as in Secretary of State Alexander Haig.

Gotlieb warned Trudeau about the damage caused by his interventions: "Every time you express exasperation with the Americans or utter some criticism, (American) scribes immediately telephone around town, intimidating people, telling them that Trudeau was in a terrible snit about the Yanks and so we officials better be tough as nails in dealing with them."[27]

After a 1982 summit meeting, Canada's foreign minister, Mark MacGuigan, told Gotlieb that a self-indulgent Trudeau "'constantly contradicted, refuted, and needled Reagan ... and he was the only one to do it.'"[28] Gotlieb concluded, "Trudeau must really have been kicking his heels on that trip. The question is what will be the costs."[29]

Reagan was an avid reader of the *National Review*, a respected conservative publication. It did a cover story on Trudeau, calling him a "communist dupe." Michael Deaver, a key White House figure, told Gotlieb that the article had made an impression on Reagan.[30] Rounding out the portrait, Undersecretary of State Robert Hormats testified before a Senate hearing that Canadian policies under Trudeau were those of a third-world country, on a par with leftist dictatorships in Latin America.[31]

American resentment toward Trudeau reached a fever pitch, causing West German Chancellor Helmut Schmidt to warn Trudeau in July 1982 to "back off." Schmidt told Trudeau that his anti-business and anti-American views had become a major irritant. At a dinner with Schmidt, Trudeau offered a spirited defence of his policies, saying he would not be pushed around. Schmidt thought some American politicians disliked and even abused Trudeau because of his self-confident independence. Trudeau was someone who could not be dominated from the outside.[32]

With Reagan in the White House, Trudeau abhorred American foreign policy and longed for the days of Richard Nixon. He admired Nixon for his détente with the USSR, for arms control, and for relations with China. Trudeau told Gotlieb that he wanted Reagan to act more like Nixon, something that surprised and disappointed American liberals.[33]

Trudeau offended American leaders by both his policies and his manner. In October 1982, he showed up one hour late for a small working lunch in Ottawa with Secretary of State George Schultz. He had been treated to a flight on a CF 18 by the Canadian military and did not apologize for his tardiness. After the luncheon, Allan Gotlieb wrote in his diary, "A decade ago Trudeau was preaching 'the national interest' as the basis for Canadian foreign policy. Now his foreign-policy activity is directed less and less by Canada's interests and seems increasingly a matter of personal will and whim."[34]

So distrustful was the Reagan administration of Trudeau that it did not inform the Canadian government in advance of the 1983 American invasion of Grenada. It did not consult Trudeau because it considered him a security risk who might not keep the operation a secret.[35]

When it came time for Trudeau to make our case in Washington for a treaty on acid rain, Canada had no goodwill left on the table. While Canada's lakes and forests were being destroyed, Reagan's team classified two National Film Board productions on acid rain as political propaganda. Canadian protests fell on deaf ears.

There was a stark difference in tone, and in results, when Mulroney became prime minister. He saw Trudeau as shortsighted and wrong-headed, and correctly assessed that Canada would gain more from the Americans by being a trusted friend and ally. Even though Republican presidents and officials doubted the science of acid rain, their sentiment changed after George H. W. Bush told his White House staff, "We have to do this for Brian." Bush was following Reagan's lead. At one summit, Reagan's defence minister, Frank Carlucci, asked Derek Burney, "What is Mulroney's position on acid rain, free trade and Arctic sovereignty?" Burney responded, "Why do you want to know that?" Carlucci replied, "Because they are our positions now."[36] Mulroney said simply, "When you have access to the president you can energize the system."[37]

AFTER EXPERIENCING THE scare of Nixon's 10 percent surtax on all imported goods, and the declaration by Nixon that the special relationship between Canada and the U.S. was a thing of the past, Trudeau considered three options. The first was status quo. Second was to try to forge closer ties to the U.S. Third was to diminish Canadian economic dependence on the United States. Trudeau chose the "third option."

The stated goal of this option was to "develop and strengthen the Canadian economy and other aspects of its national life and in the process to reduce the present Canadian vulnerability." This change in direction for Canada coincided with Trudeau's personal views that our country should be wary of American influence and that Canadians should move toward being "citizens of the world."

At a high level, the third option involved increasing Canadian ownership of our economy, protecting Canadian culture, and diversifying Canada's trade abroad. The policy may have sounded good politically, especially to Canadian nationalists who opposed American influence, but Ottawa had attempted it before, and failed. John Diefenbaker famously attempted to wave a magic wand to shift our trade towards Europe, without success. Trudeau had always been wary of nationalism, so it required some flexibility on his part to change his bearings.

The third option was inspired in part by Liberal MP Herb Gray's eponymous 1972 report on foreign direct investment in Canada. *The Gray Report* concluded that Canada had insufficient control over its economic future. Trudeau sent out a clarion call to all ministers and departments for ideas and techniques that would diminish Canada's economic dependence on the United States.[38] Opposition leader Robert Stanfield labeled the initiative a "bag of fog" for its lack of detail and substance.

While Great Britain embraced Trudeau's proposals to increase European trade, continental nations did not. France's Gaullist government seemed reluctant to deal with Canada;[39] West Germany also proved surprisingly standoffish. As our ambassador to the European Economic Community put it, "Canada should not expect favours from Europe if it is not prepared to shoulder its defence burden."[40] A friend, West German Chancellor Helmut Schmidt, explained his country's hesitation directly to Trudeau: "A German farmer ... recognizes the maple leaf on tanks and infantry vehicles ... These vehicles are reassuring and important." West Germany was also concerned about Canadian restrictions on uranium exports, which undermined Canadian reliability as a trading partner.[41]

While the Canadian government poured money into trade promotion overseas, and bolstered the capacity of our missions abroad to facilitate trade, Trudeau inevitably had to face the reality that business is conducted by businesses. Profits, not politics, drove their bottom line.

When Trudeau became prime minister, 67 percent of Canadian exports went to the United States.[42] When he left office that number was 76 percent, and rising. The percentage of imports coming from the United States remained virtually unchanged over Trudeau's fifteen-and-a-half years in office.

In his memoirs, Trudeau admitted that Canadian business pursued no novel business arrangements and made no discernible shift in investment patterns during his tenure. "By and large, the Canadian corporate sector clearly had little interest in pursuing a third option and had joined forces with American complaints about the structure of Canadian laws and regulations that were designed to ensure net benefit to Canadians."[43]

It would have been prudent for Trudeau to discuss his third option with Canadian business leaders *before* launching it, to gauge its chances of success. In the end, Trudeau engaged in a futile effort to countermand the responsive forces of free enterprise. Third-option policies — the Canada Development Corporation, the Foreign Investment Review Agency, Petro Canada, National Energy Program — did little to reduce our overall exposure to American influence, but did much to harm the Canadian economy.

WHILE TRUDEAU SOUGHT closer trade ties with Europe, he stood at odds with the French government owing to their "encouragement" of Quebec's separatist elements.[44] One French project that Trudeau stifled was the creation of an association of French speaking nations, ultimately known as *La Francophonie*.

France began to promote the idea of a French-speaking commonwealth in the late 1960s. An initial meeting took place in Gabon in 1968, on matters related to education. Since the meeting agenda fell within the constitutional jurisdiction of Canadian provinces, conference organizers invited the government of Quebec to attend. International relations, however, constituted a federal responsibility. Trudeau, then justice minister, objected, and attempted to thwart the organizers. He claimed that allowing Quebec to represent itself internationally set a precedent, comparable to when Great Britain gave Canada the right to conduct its independent foreign policy in 1931. Canada broke off diplomatic relations with Gabon over the incident.

When more formal efforts were made to establish an association of francophone states, Trudeau made it clear that "Canada would not condone it if 'L'Agence' was employed as a tool to divide Canada or for the resurrection of the French Empire."[45] At one point in 1979, Trudeau threatened to cut off diplomatic relations with France if it didn't butt out of internal Canadian affairs vis-à-vis Quebec.

Trudeau's principal secretary, Tom Axworthy, alleged that from 1967 to 1971 the French secret service employed agents to undermine the Canadian government and finance Quebec separatists. "De Gaulle went whacko in his later years," said Axworthy, who claimed that France worked with African francophone nations, encouraging them to invite Quebec separatist delegations to international meetings, while ignoring the federal Canadian government.[46]

Trudeau told his cabinet that he called a Canadian official in Paris on an unprotected phone line, hoping that French officials had tapped the line. The cabinet minutes read, "The prime minister... had told him the government did not want France interfering in Canadian domestic matters and the Canadian government was serious. If the French interfered, it might be necessary to break relations with France."[47] More covertly, Trudeau gave the RCMP permission in 1970 to spy on French diplomats. Trudeau told the RCMP commissioner that he would deny any knowledge of the operation if it were detected by the French government.[48]

It was not until Trudeau left office and Ottawa set conspiracy theories aside that francophone nations established a formal network. At the first meeting, held in Quebec City in 1987, provincial representatives (Quebec and New Brunswick) participated in preliminary subject-matter sessions, while Canada sat at the table for the "international summit." To this the inflexible Trudeau lamented, "And thus does creeping separatism continue when the guard is not maintained by the Canadian government."[49] From a different perspective, one would observe that Quebecers become more confident and feel more respected when they can express themselves and their language in international fora.

Trudeau's position on *La Francophonie* demonstrated his resistance to even the slightest hint of compromise or conciliation when it came to giving additional status to the province of Quebec. He believed that adding even minimal powers or influence to Quebec would help beat a sure path to separation. But given Canada's history and the bargain struck at Confederation, it was hard to see how compromise, respect and realignment in the relationship between the federal and provincial governments would lead to Canada's destruction.

MANY AMERICANS, FRENCH and British were happy to see the last of Trudeau. Allan Gotlieb wrote that when Mulroney took office, expectations ran very high in Washington that he would change almost all of Trudeau's policies.[50] Trudeau's initiatives had soured the in-

ternational investor community on Canada. Trudeau pointlessly antagonized our most important foreign customer and pursued a futile
international trade initiative. He marginalized us from our allies by
failing to invest in our common defence and by making friends with
communist dictators. His antics may have made headlines, but didn't
advance Canadian interests.

CHAPTER 3

A FRIEND TO COMMUNISTS

Viva Cuba – Viva Castro

T RUDEAU EXPRESSED OVERT fascination with communism and socialism during his academic training and in his early writings. His incomplete doctoral thesis explored the relationship between Christianity and Marxism. And while it was unusual during the 1950s and 1960s for Westerners to travel behind the Iron Curtain, go to China, and visit post-revolutionary Cuba, as a private citizen Trudeau toured and studied all three countries. After becoming prime minister, his curiosity with communism endured.

AT THE AGE of 32, Trudeau accepted an invitation from the Soviet government to attend a propaganda conference with an "economic agenda." The other five members of the Canadian delegation included prominent members of the Communist Party of Canada.[1] It was there that he remarked to the wife of U.S. chargé d'affaires, Hugh Cumming, that he was a communist and a Catholic and was in Moscow to criticize the U.S. and praise the Soviet Union.[2] In a two-page memorandum dated May 7, 1952, the U.S. State Department assessed Trudeau's allegiances, noting that he evinced "an infantile desire to shock."[3] Canadian diplomats informed the Americans that Trudeau was young and adventurous, with a desire to travel "but did not possess much common sense." The Americans were reassured by our diplomats that

Trudeau, who had recently held a position in the Privy Council office, was a minor player who had not been given access to classified information when he roamed the Canada's corridors of power.

While the Americans had boycotted the Moscow conference, Trudeau saw merit in defiance: "It was important to show that not all capital, not all markets, are controlled by the United States ... I would hate people to say, rightly, that we are the ones keeping the Iron Curtain shut tight."[4] If the trip represented an attempt at détente, Trudeau went for the gusto, even visiting the grave of Lenin's mother.[5]

Trudeau worried that being labelled a communist would derail any hopes he had to run for public office someday. But he justified his trip with the thought that "[p]eace perforce involves negotiating with enemies. It was not by demonizing them or spreading lies about them, as Pearson did, that war would be avoided. On the contrary." He signed this particular manifesto "Comrade Trudeau."[6]

In his writings about the trip, Trudeau reflected his admiration for Soviet methods. "At least the Soviet economists have resolved the problem of inflation without producing unemployment ... without doubt, the country is progressing tremendously ... even if that's not what the people might want."[7]

Contrasting the evils of capitalism with communism, Trudeau wrote of his Soviet hosts, "From a material point of view your system can be excellent for countries such as yours ... and I add that in your country I never saw opulence displayed, which was an insult to a great many people [sic] like I have often seen in countries on the other side of the Iron Curtain."[8] Beyond shocking the Americans, Trudeau showed off his "infantile" tendencies, provoking his sponsors by throwing snowballs at a statue of Lenin.

Despite his attempts to rationalize his trip, Trudeau was indeed labelled a communist in his home province, in particular by Father Leopold Braun, who had once been a priest in Moscow.[9] In 1960 another priest, Abbé Gérard Saint-Pierre, referred to Trudeau in *Le Nouvelliste,* the daily newspaper in Trois-Rivières, as "the Canadian Karl Marx." When Trudeau sought permission from the Church to sue, the bishop replied that, given Trudeau's writings, "I hesitate to consider this libel."[10]

Together with travelling companion Jacques Hébert (appointed to the Senate by Trudeau in 1983), Trudeau sojourned for six weeks through China in 1960.[11] The trek resulted in a book, "Two Innocents in China," first published in 1961. They described their journey as an opportunity to tell Canadians more about China, a country they clearly admired. Hébert said that China was desperate for political recognition, and had approached about 100 people before they found the two Canadians willing to take the state-sponsored trip.

Trudeau, already labeled in Quebec as a troublemaker and outcast, had little positive reputation left to lose. Hébert and Trudeau admitted this in the preface to their book:

> It must be said that ... the authors of the present volume were pretty well immune to reprisals by this time. Since both of them had been generously reproved, knocked off and abolished in the integralist and reactionary press in consequence of earlier journeys behind the Iron Curtain, the prospect of being assassinated yet again on their return from China was hardly likely to impress them.[12]

This early investment in Trudeau by the Chinese government paid off in spades after he unpredictably became prime minister within a decade of his state-sponsored visit.

After touring much of the world in 1948, one of last countries Trudeau visited that year was capitalist Cuba. He said he wanted the experience of cutting sugarcane to test his strength and endurance. In April 1960 Trudeau attempted a return trip to Cuba, this time setting out from Florida in a canoe with two companions hoping to paddle their way to the communist island. They wanted to prove a canoe to be a sea-worthy vessel and got halfway across before strong winds and faulty equipment ended the trek some 19 hours and 50 miles after it had begun.[13] Thousands of Cubans attempting to flee the island dictatorship would later die sailing in the opposite direction.

In 1964 Trudeau took a more conventional route to Castro's Cuba to witness the results of the revolution firsthand. Trudeau remarked to a friend that when a country has an immense job to do, and do rapidly, it's almost impossible to accomplish without making fanatics out of the people. Trudeau said he could feel a revolutionary fervor: "There were no elections in Cuba, but when you see mass rallies with Fidel Castro speaking for 90 minutes in 100 degree heat you wonder what is the need for elections."[14]

Such was Trudeau's assessment of communism, and his variable commitment to democracy. Upon becoming prime minister, Trudeau rekindled whatever feelings of affection he had for these three communist regimes he had visited.

WHEN VISITING THE Soviet Union in May 1971, Trudeau wanted to establish a friendship. He gained favour by telling the Soviets that American presidents did not care much for solving problems, and then reminded them that he had reduced Canadian troops in Europe by fifty percent. (When he cut our NATO commitment, he told our allies the reduction would not be noticed by the Soviets, so perhaps he felt the need to draw it to their attention).

While signing a new protocol on consultations with the Soviets, Trudeau commented, "Canada has found it important to diversify its channels of communication because of the overpowering presence of the United States, and that is reflected in the growing consciousness amongst Canadians of the danger to our national identity from a cultural, economic and perhaps military point of view."[15] Warnings of that nature about America, particularly with military overtones, had not emanated from Canada since the War of 1812.

Trudeau openly admired how the Soviets built the Siberian city of Norilsk, lamenting that no comparable Canadian city existed. It was a Soviet dissident who later reminded Trudeau that Norilsk had been built by prisoners. "When he praised it, he praised this thing built on human bones," said Vladimir Bokovsky, a man who spent 11 years under Soviet lock and key.[16]

During the visit, Trudeau pointed to the similarities he saw between the Soviet and Canadian styles of government.

> Those of your countrymen now in Canada, Mr. Chairman ... find themselves living within a constitutional framework with a formal structure similar to that in the Soviet Union. Each of our countries has chosen a federal system of government ... its very complexity is its strength, for it permits the necessary degree of flexibility ... We have a great deal to learn from the Soviet Union ... a country from which we have a great deal to benefit.[17]

But there was no evidence that Trudeau's personal comradeship with the Soviets enjoyed much support in Canada, nor that many Canadians thought the two systems of government had much in common.

Within six months of Trudeau's 1971 visit to the Kremlin, Soviet Premier Kosygin travelled to Ottawa, an unusually short gap between official visits, indicating his country's desire to cement good relations. At an official function Trudeau said, "Canada and Canadians want very much to look to the north, as they have looked long to the south, and see friends in each direction."[18] The concept of putting the United States and the Soviet Union on the same plane troubled many Canadians, not to mention Americans. Trudeau remained loathe to criticize the Soviets, even when they behaved oppressively and violated the human rights he allegedly held dear.

Trudeau's affinity for things Russian was not based just on a philosophical connection but a personal one as well. Trudeau's son Alexandre, born in 1973, gained his common nickname "Sasha," because it is the short form of Alexander to Russians. The name was also linked to the Soviet ambassador to Canada, Alexander Yakovlev, who was a Trudeau family friend.[19]

As mentioned, the USSR's 1979 invasion of Afghanistan failed to convince Trudeau of the merits of a Canadian boycott of the 1980 Moscow Olympic Games. Pressure from Canadian athletes and the American administration persuaded him that Canada should stay home. But unlike the Americans, he refused a full trade embargo and continued with the sale of Canadian wheat to the USSR.[20]

Under the watchful eye of the Soviet Union, Poland imposed martial law in 1981. General Wojciech Jaruzelski banned the Solidarity Movement and arrested union leader Lech Walesa, who would later become Poland's president. Trudeau expressed his sympathy, not with the oppressed, but with the General. Standing in the House of Commons on December 18, 1981, Trudeau declared, "If martial law is a way to avoid civil war and Soviet intervention, then I can say it is not all bad."[21] He added that he hoped the military regime would be able to keep Solidarity from making excessive demands.[22] In contrast, Ronald Reagan labeled the Polish government brutally oppressive and the authors of "'a dark night of tyranny'."[23] Rather than defend the forces for democracy, Trudeau stood down. "It is not for us to say how [the end of martial law] should be accomplished ... we have always held that the Polish people should be free to settle their own problems in their own ways." The Polish communists could happily quote Trudeau to justify their actions. Incredibly, Trudeau had shrugged off the Soviet occupation of Eastern Europe as merely a "straight sphere-of-influence question."

Trudeau also showed little sympathy for Soviet dissidents. He referred to Jewish human rights activist Anatoly Shcharansky and the Nobel Prize-winning physicist Andrei Sakharov as "hooligans." While other western leaders pleaded with the Soviets to release its political prisoners and to allow dissidents to leave the country, if only just for medical leave, Sakharov's children claimed their pleas failed to move Trudeau. "'If Trudeau had been more interested in (our case) and less preoccupied with his role as a mediator between the U.S. and the Soviet Union he could have accomplished much.'"[24]

When accepting an honorary degree at Notre Dame University in 1982, Trudeau proclaimed the Americans and Soviets equally "hazardous" to world security.[25] In 1983, Trudeau told the House of Commons that he simply couldn't believe the Soviets knowingly destroyed a brightly lit commercial airliner, Korean Air Flight 007, after it inadvertently ventured into Soviet air space on September 1, 1983, killing all 369 on board, including 10 Canadians. Trudeau excused Soviet leaders and called the downing a tragic accident. Urging calm, Trudeau told the House of Commons, "At this stage we won't get more from the Soviet Union by treating them as murderers. We might get some de-escalation in the cold war by treating them as human beings."[26] Trudeau called the denunciations of the Soviets "hysterical."[27]

Opposition leader Brian Mulroney called Trudeau an interpreter for the mentality of the Kremlin. Margaret Thatcher said that what liberal leftists like Trudeau seemed unable to grasp was that "such acts of brutality as the shooting down of a civilian aircraft were by no means uncharacteristic of the communist system itself."[28] The Soviets ultimately admitted that they knew it was a passenger plane, but felt justified in shooting it down because it had veered into their air space and was deemed to be spying.

After leaving office, Trudeau maintained his good relations with the Soviets, taking his sons on a tour of Siberia. He told the Soviet Novosti Press that he wanted to show his boys the Soviet north because it was "where the future is being created." He also said he wanted to help dispel the myth about this northern habitat, "about which so many prejudices are held in the West."[29]

On trips to the Soviet Union with business leaders, Trudeau astonished members of the Canadian delegation by offering political advice to his communist hosts. He told them to disregard President Reagan and wait for his successor. Canadian observers judged the sentiment of these remarks highly disloyal to NATO and our allies.[30]

The Soviets lavished Trudeau with exceptional hospitality. In 1986, while travelling with Senator Leo Kolber, a Trudeau appointee, and Canadian businessmen Bernard Lamarre and Paul Desmarais, Trudeau secured Soviet permission to visit the closed city of Vladivostok. Rather than relegate their guests to the "cattle cars" used by Russian residents, the Soviets ensconced Trudeau's entourage in new train cars equipped with luxurious dining and sleeping compartments, and provided a staff of four to handle their needs. Trudeau had a full car to himself and enjoyed an endless supply of caviar, a delicacy he favoured.[31]

When the USSR crumbled under the weight of its own oppression and economic decline in the late 1980s, Trudeau criticized western countries for facilitating the Soviet break-up by "playing footsy with the independentists ... recognizing every Tom, Dick, and Harry Republic that decided to proclaim its independence." Trudeau did not see the deterioration of the USSR as progress. He did not celebrate the innate desire of humanity for freedom and democracy, but called it "chaos (and) something which I think we will eventually regret."[32]

IF TRUDEAU WAS fascinated by the USSR, he was positively euphoric about China. Trudeau is properly remembered for having the confidence and foresight to extend diplomatic relations with China, although he won no favour from Nixon and Kissinger, who would have preferred that America do so before Canada.[33] Trudeau, who was not about to play second fiddle to an American president, was on relatively safe international ground in recognizing China, since he had followed the diplomatic stance already taken by Great Britain, France and the Netherlands.

Early in his first mandate, Trudeau decided to recognize the People's Republic of China; acting on a view he had held since his private visits there in 1949 and 1960. Many western nations at the time recognized Taiwan as the legitimate seat of the Chinese government. However, recognizing the government responsible for one billion lives was a prudent thing to do. Canada gave its formal recognition to the People's Republic of China in October 1970, less than a year before Nixon announced he would visit China, which he ultimately did in February 1972.

Trudeau travelled to China in October 1973, where Chairman Mao honoured him with an audience in the Forbidden City. While impressed with Mao, Trudeau declared that Chou En Lai a fascinating personality, and the most impressive leader he had ever met.[34] When he returned to Canada, Trudeau defended Mao's policies in Parliament, seemingly unconcerned about their responsibility for the rape, torture, imprisonment and deaths of millions of people. Trudeau's fascination with China included urging Canadians to explore acupuncture, a technique he called a medical breakthrough of "momentous consequences."[35]

While the Chinese appreciated Trudeau, once they received diplomatic recognition from the United States, Canada faded into relative insignificance. The first visit to Canada by a Chinese premier, Zhao Ziyang, did not occur until 1984. Nonetheless, the benefits of being ahead of the United States, and building upon the positive image of Canadian doctor Norman Bethune's benevolent work in China, gave Canada a privileged position in the eyes of the Chinese government. Trudeau's leadership on China made it that much easier for Canadian businesses to open up trading relationships.

Mulroney believed Trudeau was correct to initiate diplomatic relations. "It was farsighted," Mulroney said, but then added, "It was also consistent with his own point of view and his sympathies"[36]

In retirement, Trudeau visited China with his children shortly after the 1989 Tiananmen Square massacre. Trudeau had retained his celebrity status, and the Chinese government feted him as an official visitor with a full complement of banquets, speeches and an array of toasts. His son Sasha recalled that when his father was called to speak, he would invariably refer "very delicately" to the "difficulties" that China had recently faced. Nonetheless, the Chinese government appreciated the public relations value of a former Canadian prime minister visiting so soon after the international community had condemned China for brutalizing its citizens. He later told his sons that China was an ancient land with its own internal imperatives. "Outsiders simply cannot know what is best for China or how it needs to travel down its chosen path."[37] Few other westerners resumed relations so quickly with the Chinese.

ON JANUARY 1, 1959, Fidel Castro and 800 guerrilla fighters triumphantly entered Havana. Having overthrown the government of military strongman Fulgencio Batista, Castro's grip on power held firm until for over 50 years until his health began to fail. Under Castro, Cuba quickly aligned itself with the Soviet Union to secure an economic, military and ideological lifeline. Richard Nixon once said Castro couldn't go to the bathroom unless the Soviet Union put the nickel in the toilet.

In the years following the overthrow of Batista, Cuba repelled an American-backed invasion at the Bay of Pigs and then allowed the entry of Soviet nuclear missiles, later removed at the insistence of President Kennedy. While the U.S. broke off diplomatic relations with Cuba, under Pearson Canada maintained its ties, although not in a manner that offended the Americans.

Trudeau's first official contact with Cuba came in 1970, after Castro agreed to accept the FLQ terrorists who had kidnapped James Cross and sought asylum. In thanking Castro for his cooperation, Trudeau wrote:

> Dear Mr. Prime Minister,
> On behalf of the Government of Canada I wish to express to you our sincere thanks for the co-operation extended by your government in the arrangements leading to the safe release of Mr. James Cross ... I also understand that in keeping with the good relations between our two countries, the individuals who have been given safe-conduct will not, while in Cuba, undertake any activity directed against Canada.[38]

On January 26, 1976, some seventeen years after the Castro coup, Pierre Trudeau became the first Canadian leader, and the first NATO leader, to visit Cuba. Castro made international news at that time, not only for receiving the Canadian prime minister but also for sending his troops to fight in a civil war in Angola at the behest of the Soviet Union. Trudeau ignored American suggestions that he cancel the trip, although Ottawa issued a meek condemnation of the Angola intervention just prior to his visit.

When Trudeau arrived in Havana he received a hero's welcome, with 250,000 Cubans lining the streets, cheering wildly upon Castro's command. Giant posters of Trudeau were plastered over the Cuban capital.

In private meetings, Trudeau asked Castro about Angola. Castro told him Cuba was assisting the "legitimate" government of Angola with a small number of troops to help protect against "guerrillas" backed by South Africa and some NATO powers. Trudeau, who had limited fondness for NATO, quickly dropped the matter.

Beyond Angola, the world's main problem with Cuba was its oppressive regime, which would not allow Cubans to leave the country or exercise fundamental democratic rights. Rather than highlight and admonish the oppression, Trudeau publicly honoured the communist dictator with proclamations of "Viva Cuba" and "Viva Castro," and "Long live prime minister and commander-in-chief, Fidel Castro." A former Canadian ambassador described Trudeau as a "mentor" to Castro. Trudeau was overheard by reporters saying how much easier governing would be if things were run "the Cuban way."[39]

Castro and Trudeau enjoyed each other's company and took a mini-vacation together, holidaying on the beach with their families in tow. This visit may have pleased Trudeau, but it caused consternation in the U.S., which had maintained a trade and travel boycott of the island dictatorship. When Trudeau returned to Canada, he defended his boisterous enthusiasm for Cuba by claiming his "viva" salutations were simply how the locals said "good morning." The Cubans thought it meant friendship and encouragement. Trudeau urged his friend to call him Pierre or Pedro, "as long as I can call you Fidel."

When Trudeau discovered that Castro had lied to him about the number of troops Cuba sent to Angola, he cut off Canada's "non-humanitarian aid" to the country. The type of aid, however, was unspecified. And the estrangement did not last long. To help celebrate the patriation of the Canadian constitution, Castro attended a concert at the Canadian ambassador's residence in Havana.

In 1981 the Trudeau government worked out a deal with Cuba whereby the Cuban government paid a final settlement of $850,000 to Canadians whose property was seized in the 1959 coup. Investors claimed they received a pittance compared with their original investments.[40] At one point in the negotiation, Cuba offered to pay the 50 companies who had made claims against the Cuban government with tobacco leaves and sugar.[41] All this to say Canadian companies with assets in Cuba during the revolution did not realize much benefit from the Castro-Trudeau friendship.

After Trudeau left office, he and Castro maintained their friendship, with Trudeau visiting Cuba on three occasions. Castro reciprocated by participating in the filming of a CBC documentary based on Trudeau's memoirs where the men convivially conversed in Spanish.

The Canadian ambassador to Cuba, Mark Entwistle, hosted many of the Trudeau-Castro soirees in the 1990s. After witnessing almost one hundred hours of repartee between Trudeau and Castro, Entwistle described the pair as intellectual soulmates.

When Trudeau died, Castro declared three days of official mourning. The flags on government buildings in Cuba flew at half-mast, as they would for a native hero. In a public decree Castro observed, "At all times, [Trudeau] showed friendship and sympathy toward Cuba, by openly and firmly maintaining his position against the hostile imperialist policy toward our country." In other words, by thumbing his nose at the Americans on Canadians' behalf. Castro called Trudeau a world-class statesman and a close personal friend whom he greatly admired. "I always considered him a serious political leader ... He was an upright and brave man who, regardless of difficult circumstances, fostered his country's relations with Cuba."[42]

While Trudeau gained an honorary pallbearer in Castro, nothing in their friendship tangibly benefited Canada. What it did was annoy our closest ally and best customer.

The coziness between Canada and Cuba ended with Trudeau. Mulroney made a point of not travelling to the country while prime minister. Jean Chrétien visited Cuba in 1998, but displayed fortitude and integrity by raising the plight of four political prisoners, displeasing Castro in the process. In 1999, Castro declared Canada the "second enemy in the north" after 13 Cuban athletes defected during the Winnipeg Pan-American Games.

CHAPTER 4

AT WAR WITH THE CANADIAN MILITARY

Europe can defend itself

THE CANADIAN ARMED Forces have earned respect around the world for their toughness and discipline. But they proved no match for Pierre Trudeau. In his battle to emasculate the Canadian military, Trudeau took few prisoners. For those who believed in peace through unilateral disarmament, Trudeau was their man. For those who believed in peace through strength, Trudeau was at best naïve, at worst outright dangerous.

TRUDEAU WAS NO pacifist. In his personal life he almost never turned the other cheek. In his political life he almost always met force with overwhelming force. His father had taught him to box. When the young Trudeau boasted of his prowess to his friends, they quickly found him adversaries, whom he wouldn't refuse to fight for fear of losing face.[1] He battled ferociously during WWII, not against the Germans, but with the Canadian government. He had learned in school to shun imperialistic conflicts.[2] When not campaigning against the war and conscription, he concocted a plan to overthrow the government and take Quebec out of Confederation in the process.

While Trudeau did not avoid confrontation, he brushed off fears of the military threat posed by the Soviet Union and its allies in the 1950s and 1960s. He was fascinated with Marxism, believing there was much to be learned from the Soviets and the Chinese. Trudeau did not take any military threat from the Warsaw Pact countries seriously. Since he saw no reason to fear the Soviets, he concluded that there was no need for the West to maintain an overwhelming deterrent of nuclear weapons. Such was his view that he set aside plans to join the Liberals in 1963 after Lester Pearson decided to accept American nuclear weapons on Canadian soil.

When Trudeau was serving Pearson as his parliamentary secretary, Ottawa announced it was transforming the Canadian military by uniting its constituent parts (navy, armed forces and air force) into a single force. The unification officially occurred just a few months before Trudeau became prime minister. This controversial decision had a pervasive, deleterious impact on the morale of the military.

When campaigning in the 1968 general election, Trudeau said little of Canada's defence policies. In his first speech on foreign policy as prime minister in May of 1968, he declared that the overwhelming threat to Canada came not from foreign interests, ideologies or nuclear weapons, "but from the two-thirds of the people of the world who are steadily falling farther and farther behind in their search for a decent standard of living."[3] In establishing this doctrine, Trudeau set in motion a constant decline in military spending for much of the following 16 years, starting with a freeze of the defence budget in 1969.

TRUDEAU HAD LONG been wary of Canada's commitment to NATO. In his early days as prime minister, Trudeau launched a series of "policy seminars" within his cabinet on national defence. Its most contentious agenda item? The withdrawal of Canada from NATO.

NATO, a club of originally twelve (28 nations in 2013), offers significant benefits to Canada, a charter member. Since we possess neither the wealth nor the capacity to defend our massive territory independently, we rely on our NATO partners for assistance when necessary. NATO members treat an attack against any one of them as an attack against all of them, best illustrated when NATO invoked article 5 of the Washington Treaty the day after September 11, 2001.

Canada can rest easy knowing that it has the power of the American military, and other member states, at its disposal should our territory be threatened. But to remain a respected member of the club, every member has to do its part. Trudeau thought Canada not only didn't have to do its part, it didn't even need to belong to NATO. He summed up his view in 1968:

> Canada is in the extraordinarily fortunate position of not having to defend itself because we know darn well that the United States will defend us. They won't let a hostile nation take over Canada to wage war on the United States. So, in a sense, we are much freer that other nations, and I believe we should use that freedom to explore … ways in which the middle-sized nations can move the world toward peace, in a way in which many European countries cannot.[4]

During the Cold War, the Soviet Union presented the main threat to NATO countries. Western Europe felt most under threat, which is why Canada and the United States stationed troops in West Germany after WWII. Trudeau came to office with the view that Western Europe was not under threat, that it could defend itself if it was, and that Canada should butt out.

When vying for the Liberal leadership, Trudeau told a Calgary audience that he would "tend to withdraw somewhat from NATO." On a day when the Red Army and police tear-gassed anti-Soviet protestors in Prague, Trudeau shrugged that he was less worried about happenings on the other side of the Berlin Wall than on Canadian soil.[5] In his first press conference as prime minister, he spoke of the need for a complete reassessment of Canadian foreign policy, including our participation in NATO.[6] At the cabinet table, Trudeau advocated for a withdrawal from NATO to make Canada a "neutral" nation, akin to Switzerland and Sweden. Paradoxically, while the logical consequence of "going it alone" would be a serious investment in Canada's military forces, Trudeau froze the defence budget.

Cooler heads prevailed. The official *Defence Review* concluded that Canada should sustain its NATO and NORAD commitments, a view that Trudeau found unacceptable. He told the responsible cabinet ministers, Mitchell Sharp and Léo Cadieux, to reconsider their positions before any of their reports were circulated to cabinet. The duo resisted Trudeau's command. John Turner, then minister of justice, was against withdrawing from NATO, and so were most of his friends in cabinet.[7]

Trudeau then asked Ivan Head to prepare and submit secretly an alternative submission to cabinet from a so-called non-group of four policy specialists. Sharp threatened resignation, but Trudeau persuaded him to stay by diminishing the status of the non-group report to an unofficial document. Cabinet minutes report Trudeau saying that an observer would find it strange that Canadian troops contributed to the defence of Europe to impress our friends while leaving exposed our vast coastline, our territorial seas, and air space.[8]

Trudeau's broader views took center stage in a new Canadian defence policy unveiled on April 3, 1969. In order of importance, Canada's four defence priorities were: surveillance of Canadian territory and coastlines; defence of North America in cooperation with the United States; NATO commitments; and international peacekeeping. Funding for priorities three and four came only after the first two priorities were fulfilled. This left open the question of whether Canada would continue to send troops to Europe as part of its NATO commitment. When asked if all of our troops might come home, Trudeau flippantly responded, "Maybe, or maybe not."[9] He added that 20 years after NATO had been established, Europe could defend itself. Our NATO partners had reason to be worried.

The tiered priorities, combined with a three-year spending freeze, represented a clever way for Trudeau to diminish the Canadian military and pull back from our NATO commitment at the same time.

On September 19, 1969 Ottawa cut Canada's NATO force in half, from 10,000 to 5,000 men. The reduction formed part of a larger overall reduction of our forces by 16,000 troops, bringing the planned complement of our uniformed Canadian military to 82,000 troops. A few years previous, the defence minister, Paul Hellyer, had claimed that we could go no lower than 100,000 soldiers to maintain an effective military. Policy advisor Ramsay Cook wrote that Trudeau would have pulled out of NATO entirely, but it would not have been worth the political grief at home and abroad.[10]

In downplaying the significance of his plan, Trudeau told his cabinet that NATO was unnecessary because the Soviet Union, which had recently crushed the Prague Spring in Czechoslovakia, did not pose a threat requiring a deterrent force in Europe.[11] Trudeau believed that NATO and NORAD's existence was predicated on the Soviet Union being "untrustworthy, unpredictable, and either desperately unstable or demonically self-disciplined."[12] Trudeau demonstrated his naiveté about the Soviets by suggesting that Czechoslovakia and Poland would respond to the change in Canadian policy by reducing the troops they had committed as part of the Warsaw Pact. Unlike other western leaders, Trudeau held a more favourable view of Soviet intentions.

Canada's fleet thereafter spent more time on domestic duties and less time monitoring the movements of Soviet ships and submarines. Trudeau infuriated his defence minister when he spoke at the cabinet table about our military forces building highways and solving problems of pollution as cadres for social development.[13] Trudeau wanted Canadian military investments, meagre as they were, to focus on Canadian sovereignty and domestic infrastructure, rather than on maintaining bases for combat troops in West Germany.

Our allies criticized the withdrawal of our troops from European soil as emboldening to the members of the Warsaw Pact. Trudeau responded by claiming that Canada was so insignificant that the Soviets would hardly notice our decisions.[14] But to Canada's allies it looked like we wanted a free ride, and would not invest appropriately in joint security.

A FOE OF NATO and a fan of unilateral disarmament, Trudeau attracted the attention of John Lennon and Yoko Ono, who dropped by the prime minister's office for a visit on December 23, 1969. When the rock stars emerged, they declared themselves smitten: "He was more beautiful than we expected," said Ono. "If all politicians were like Mr. Trudeau there would be world peace,"[15] added Lennon. Tellingly, there was not another politician prepared to undermine alliances and obliterate defences in the hopes that peace would envelop the world.

To highlight this hope as a strategy, Trudeau boasted that Canada was the first country in the world to choose to divest itself of nuclear weapons. He said he would invest the money saved in developing nations.[16] To a domestic audience, this message sounded politically powerful at a time when the Americans remained mired in the Vietnam War. But it also entailed risks. In 1969 Trudeau opined, "I am not interested in protecting a few Canadian cities if this means we will be consenting to a kind of policy which we think is dangerous to the world."[17] That was cold comfort to the people actually living in the Canadian cities that might be targets of Soviet missiles.

While meekly maintaining our membership in NATO, our ever-shrinking defence budget made us a poor contributor to the alliance. Relative to our population, Canada's military contingent was about one-third the size of those of our NATO partners in 1982. Our per-capita spending on defence that year clocked in at less than half the NATO average, and about 28 percent of what the U.S. invested. As a percent of GDP among NATO countries, Canada's defence spending exceeded only that of Luxembourg.[18]

ON AUGUST 24, 1971 Ottawa issued its first and only white paper on defence. Titled "Defence in the 70s," in it the government declared that it would not reduce Canada's troop complement to 82,000, as had previously been announced in 1969, but to 83,500. This still represented a cut from the 87,500 troops that were in place at the time. The government also indicated that it would lift the freeze on military spending, although its minuscule one percent increase meant that the defence budget could not keep pace with inflation, which was running at five percent and rising.[19]

The white paper highlighted the need to maintain the military for domestic security, noting the possibility that "emergencies will again arise which will necessitate the Canadian Forces coming to the aid of the civil power." The paper reminded Canadians of the role our forces had already played in the Montreal police strike of 1969, and a riot at the Kingston Penitentiary. Of course, Trudeau had not hesitated to deploy troops on domestic soil in response to the FLQ crisis in October 1970.

In the immediate post-World War II environment, it was understandable that Canadian military investments would decline. But during the 1960s, the threat emanating from the Cold War was real and substantial. While military spending in both the USSR and the United States spiked upwards, Canada's trended in the other direction. While the Soviets funneled close to 10 percent of their GDP into the military, Canada squeezed out less than two percent.

Trudeau starved the military into submission. During his first term in office alone, he slashed the portion of the federal budget devoted to defence by about one-third, from 15.4 percent to 10.7 percent. Capital spending in the military was cut almost in half.

When Trudeau became prime minister, our total forces numbered about 100,000. When he left office, they were down to about 80,000. Had the size of the military increased with population growth during the Trudeau era, our forces would have expanded to 125,000, which means the relative troop reduction worked out to 36 percent.[20] Ironically, while the number of active servicemen and women declined, the number of civilians working at National Defence increased.

Even more so than manpower, Canada's military infrastructure deteriorated under Trudeau. When most NATO countries allocated between 25 percent and 30 percent of total military spending to capital costs, Canada laid out less than 10 percent. After spending $18 million to refit the HMCS Bonaventure in 1966-67, a Majestic class aircraft carrier, Ottawa sold her for scrap in 1972 for $850,000.[21]

The government got rid of four destroyers because it had insufficient manpower to keep them operational.[22] During his final years in office, Trudeau made efforts to revive Canada's languishing shipyards by investing in the construction of six frigates, on the books for the better part of a decade.[23] But this investment had more to do with regional economic development than rebuilding Canada's defence capacity.

Our military leaders did not take the assault on their budgets lightly. Within earshot of reporters, Admiral Boyle bluntly told a parliamentary delegation in 1975 that Canada did not have the resources to do the job required of it. "If we can't put up then we should shut up and surrender our sovereignty to the Americans." The admiral told the MPs that because of a lack of money for fuel, our ships could sail for only 90 days that year instead of the planned 120. Air force flying hours were reduced by about 16 percent to stay within budget.[24] "Every time I go down to the United States I hang my head in shame," lamented Boyle. Within two years he was forced to retire on orders from the Prime Minister's Office.[25]

The following year, in another bold challenge to his political masters, Vice Admiral J. C. O'Brien declared, "Of all the governments we've had, the one that has mentioned the word priorities most, and considered Canada's defence least, is the Trudeau government."[26] While Trudeau made the bulk of his military cuts in his first term as prime minister, the decline never abated. The portion of the federal budget devoted to defence dropped from 15.4 percent in 1968, to 10.7 percent in 1972, to 7.2 percent in 1983.

THE ONE AREA in which Trudeau did equip the military was its capacity to operate in both official languages. Even there, the methods of execution proved sloppy, divisive and expensive. Experts on the ground advised creating predominantly French-speaking and English-speaking units, while Trudeau preferred a fully bilingual military. When new bilingual units were created, English-speaking regiments were disbanded. In 1972 Major General C. Vokes remarked, "I know of nothing more calculated to destroy morale than to have chances of promotion stifled by inability to speak another language. If we are to stifle military merit on the order of bilingualism the present high quality of our armed forces will surely deteriorate."[27]

Trudeau remained undeterred, and ultimately achieved many of his bilingualism goals. After ten years of Trudeau government, the proportion of French-speaking officers in the Canadian military nearly doubled, from 10.6 percent to 19.2 percent.[28] This was achieved through quotas and mandating promotions for "qualified personnel" who could exercise their duties in French.[29] But this meant the best officers spent time in language training, rather than with their troops, to ensure a rise in rank. Francophones promoted because of language skills often faced troops skeptical of their leadership abilities.

French power did not express itself only in raw numbers, but also in military awards. When one round of selections for the Order of Military Merit was forwarded to the oversight committee, the response was that there were "not enough Francophones. Find more."[30] The concern was that the Governor General, Jules Leger, would not sign the list unless he saw sufficient recognition of French speaking recruits.

ONE OF CANADA'S leading historians on military matters, Jack Granatstein, posed this provocative question as the title for his 2004 book, *Who Killed the Canadian Military?* Granatstein, Distinguished Research Professor of History Emeritus at York University, author of over 60 books, and once head of the Canadian War Museum, titled the chapter on Trudeau's contribution to the military's demise "Malign Neglect." Not only was Trudeau "anti-military," he treated our forces as if they came from an "alien nation." Granatstein concluded that, among others, "[w]ithout a doubt, Pierre Trudeau killed the Canadian Forces."[31]

While Canada endured the Trudeau years without a substantive compromise of our territory, we gutted our capacity to defend ourselves and diminished our influence in world affairs. Trudeau had no real sway with our allies on defence or other matters because Canada did not uphold its part of the bargain for joint security. Worse, we undermined our friends with whom we had fought wars, and tendered support to the enemies of freedom and democracy. For a country that bravely fought for freedom in two world wars, it was not Canada's finest hour.

CHAPTER 5

A NEW WORLD ORDER

There are third-level and third-rate pipsqueaks who say
I can't talk about peace. Baloney.

T RUDEAU WANTED A world in which wealth was equitably shared among people and nations. He also wanted a world without nuclear weapons or much military strength. Not only did he fall far short of his goals for utopia, he made no progress whatsoever.

WHILE TRUDEAU INITIALLY upped Canadian overseas assistance, he felt loathe to leverage our investments against improving human rights or democratic freedoms in developing countries. His did not want to intervene in other states' affairs, but rather to influence a new economic order, which sought to resolve issues of hunger, disease and poverty. He also desired an alternative means of sharing global wealth in the form of international socialism.

Trudeau befriended leaders like Julius Nyerere of Tanzania. Trudeau seemed unconcerned that Nyerere was a radical who repressed his own people. To Trudeau, Nyerere's socialist ideals were his saving grace. That Nyerere displaced nearly 10 million peasants from their land and imposed a one-party state did not trouble Trudeau so long as he advanced the "collective good."

When the world clamoured for a humanitarian response in Biafra, a self-declared secessionist Christian-dominated state carved out of the southeastern region of Nigeria, Trudeau expressed reluctance to get involved. While millions starved and rock stars put on relief concerts, Trudeau fretted that if Biafra could claim its independence from Nigeria, then why not Quebec from Canada? When pressed by reporters on what Canada would do to help the close to one million people starving half a world away, Trudeau flippantly replied, "Where's Biafra?"

Despite his insensitivity to this particular situation, world poverty and health remained close to Trudeau's heart throughout his term as prime minister. When Canada hosted the G7 at the rustic Montebello resort in July 1981, Trudeau chose as its theme issues of "North-South," with a half-day of the agenda dedicated to the subject. In preparing for the summit, Trudeau restated that the world failed to share its wealth equitably, that developing nations needed a more direct and powerful voice in international institutions, and that the world's richest nations should contribute more money to developing ones. In response, UK Prime Minister Margaret Thatcher and U.S. President Ronald Reagan proposed free enterprise, rather than socialism, as the preferred solution, and Trudeau's pitch went nowhere. Thatcher made her point again when addressing the Canadian House of Commons in 1983, where she observed that her remarks more powerfully defended values and principles (of freedom and free enterprise) than did those of Canada's own government.[1]

When Trudeau became prime minister Canadian foreign aid represented 0.34 percent of our GDP. By the time he left office, this assistance had squeaked up to 0.37 percent of GDP,[2] far short of the .7% target his government had set for itself during the 1970s.[3] His biggest change was bureaucratic, as he transferred much of the foreign aid dossier away from the bureaucrats at the External Affairs Aid Office and into a new agency called the Canadian International Development Agency (CIDA). (In the March 21, 2013 federal budget, Finance Minister Jim Flaherty announced that CIDA would be amalgamated with the Department of Foreign Affairs and International Trade, effectively unwinding Trudeau's restructuring).

Trudeau acknowledged that after five terms as prime minister, all he had achieved regarding developing nations was to give their concerns a higher profile. Without significant investments or positive outcomes, Trudeau could only take credit for what he called a constancy of dedication.[4] Put another way, he could talk the talk, but not walk the walk.

AFTER THE PATRIATION of the constitution, Trudeau's mind drifted to what else he might complete in his final term in office before stepping down. He recalled his opposition to the introduction of nuclear missiles on Canadian soil in the early 1960s, including his insults of the then Liberal prime minister. But except for weakening the Canadian Forces with funding cuts, Trudeau had done little to rid the world of military might. He worried about an escalation of American anti-Soviet rhetoric, as well as Reagan's obsession with ending communism.[5] Trudeau thought our American ally, and not the Soviets, had escalated the tension he would seek to resolve.[6]

At the May 1983 G7 meeting, Trudeau spoke out against the buildup of nuclear weapons by the superpowers. Margaret Thatcher ridiculed Trudeau for his timidity so ferociously that Ronald Reagan thought she was going to order Trudeau to "go stand in the corner."[7] Trudeau worried about Thatcher, who once told him, "things [i.e. plant life] were growing again one year after Hiroshima."[8]

Trudeau knew Thatcher considered him to be hopelessly "wet" and that she could not be budged.[9] He had purposely annoyed Thatcher by speaking French at international conferences in private conversations when in her presence.[10] At one summit meeting she chaired, she would not give Trudeau the floor. Reagan wrote in his memoirs that Trudeau's rudeness to Thatcher "and his insulting way" horrified him. Thatcher told Reagan that Trudeau was being childish and could be easily ignored.[11]

Trudeau did not see much point in debating the Iron Lady, since her approach, as he discerned it, was to hector without much of an exchange of views. In other words, Thatcher and Trudeau had similar debating styles. Thatcher's view of Trudeau is best illustrated by a remark she made while attending the funeral of Soviet leader Konstantin Chernenko in March 1985. She was in the "safe room" at the British embassy, in the company of two of her ministers, Mulroney, and two Canadian officials, Bob Fowler and Bill Fox. When the British foreign secretary, Sir Geoffrey Howe, asked, "What's happening to Pierre Trudeau now?" Mulroney replied that he was practicing law, adding that he had gone to Washington to pick up some big international prize. Thatcher lifted her eyes from her papers, then demurred, "It must have been the Lenin Prize," one of the Soviet Union's most prestigious awards.[12] In fact, Trudeau had won the annual Albert Einstein peace prize, but Thatcher had made her point.

Canada's ambassador to the United States, Allan Gotlieb, in his detailed diary, wrote that he could not see the point of Trudeau picking fights with world leaders where little could be won:

He is battling not just Americans, but the British and French
— and even the Germans, although I'm not sure he fully ap-
preciates this. Maybe he thinks he is just tweaking the nose
of the negotiator, Uncle Sam. But in fact he's telling the European leaders what is good for their national interests and
public opinion. He is playing a rather immodest role and
one that doesn't seem to be grounded in Canadian interests.
There is so much in his performance that now smacks of personal indulgence.[13]

Trudeau thought of former politicians and military leaders who
spoke out about peace only *after* leaving office, often expressing regret
that they did not make better use of the levers of power at their disposal.
As the summer of 1983 came to an end, Trudeau took his stand: "I
was for peace before I entered politics, and I'm not going to wait until
I'm out before speaking out and trying to get things changed."[14]

The women in Trudeau's life encouraged him to act on his instincts
for nuclear disarmament. Margaret Trudeau wrote of her husband's
ability, as leader of a "neutral" nation, to bring opposing countries
together.[15] Actress Margot Kidder also had Trudeau's ear. She
attended diplomatic functions with Trudeau where he would squeeze
her thigh under the table whenever she berated American officials
and "scored a point."[16] Kidder thought it was "weird to mix politics
and romance," but she took the opportunity to inspire her lover to
become a world champion for peace.[17]

Liberal party brass also encouraged Trudeau to pursue his passion.
Senior strategist Keith Davey thought that Trudeau's position in the
forefront of middle-power nations made him ideally suited to take a
message of peace to world leaders.[18] This would presume that, for some
unknown reason, world leaders were opposed to the concept of peace.

Trudeau had other motivations for wanting to appear anti-nuclear
and pro-peace. In the 1970s, as part of a foreign aid package, Canada
had supplied India with plutonium and nuclear technology to produce
energy. But India abused our generosity and detonated an atomic
device in 1974 under the codename "Smiling Buddha." Canada
became implicated in the first-ever test of a nuclear weapon outside
the five permanent members of the United Nations Security Council.
The test also violated a 1971 agreement between India and Canada.

There was something else that bothered Trudeau. In 1983
Washington asked Ottawa to permit testing of the cruise missile in
our far north, in part because the terrain mimicked that of the Soviet

Union. Trudeau was reluctant to approve the testing, but his friend Helmut Schmidt persuaded him that Canada would be a poor partner in NATO and NORAD if it refused such a request. "Pierre," he said, "you have reduced your troops and your budget, but if you are part of a club you must support the club ... That's the least you can do"[19]

Canada's cruise missile announcement came at the dinner hour on a Friday afternoon in July, a time when many Canadians were embarking on summer vacation. With Trudeau out of sight and Parliament not in session, Defence Minister Gilles Lamontagne and Foreign Affairs Minister Allan MacEachen told the press that Canada was prepared to do its share by permitting up to 30 tests of the guidance system of the unarmed cruise missile. The ministers unsuccessfully attempted to evade protestors by leaving through the back door of the press theatre, located across the street from Parliament Hill.

In an open letter to Canadians on May 9, 1983, Trudeau brought out a big gun to justify his decision to allow missile testing. Quoting from Pope John Paul II, Trudeau noted, "'In current conditions, deterrence based on balance, certainly not as an end in itself, but as a step toward a progressive disarmament, may still be judged morally acceptable.'"[20] Agreeing to test the cruise missile on Canadian soil was the right decision for national defence purposes and showed a minimal commitment to our allies, but it flew in the face of Trudeau's position of neutrality and disarmament, which rankled him. Trudeau also had to stand up to opposition in his cabinet, including that of Lloyd Axworthy, who threatened to quit over the matter.[21]

TRUDEAU FORMALLY ANNOUNCED his "Peace Initiative" on October 27, 1983 at the University of Guelph. He proposed a comprehensive nuclear test ban, a ban on the testing of high-altitude weapons, a five-nation conference on nuclear arms control, and a mechanism to enhance consultations between NATO and the Soviets. Trudeau visited leaders of the five nuclear powers, plus 18 other government leaders, but, predictably, he delivered no concrete results. Observers thought him naïve for thinking he could have any impact or sway on the five nuclear powers. The Russians were enemies of the Chinese and the Americans. And the French, British and Americans had long been wary of Trudeau.

Trudeau was ridiculed in the media for his misplaced initiative. When he travelled to Washington to argue for "peace," White House staff leaked damaging stories about him. Trudeau responded to bad press by saying there were "third level and third rate pipsqueaks who say I can't talk about peace. Baloney."[22] Most saw this remark as being directed at Lawrence Eagleburger, the State Department official responsible for Canada, who was heard to say, "whoever thinks we would agree to [Trudeau's proposals] must've been smoking something pretty funny."[23]

The White House correspondent for *Newsweek*, Eleanor Clift, and syndicated columnist and former Nixon advisor Patrick Buchanan, appeared on CBC television to assess Trudeau's meeting with Reagan. "Nothing serious went on today," remarked Clift. She noted that senior White House officials told her that Trudeau's initiative represented nothing more than rhetorical schmoozing to score PR points with the Soviets. Buchanan was more blunt. "The Reagan administration will entertain this proposal with all seriousness as if it had come from Boys Nation [the annual civic training event run by the American Legion in Washington for junior high school students]." He called Trudeau a comic figure who was playing a game without having invested in the defence spending necessary to be taken seriously. Clift added this clever insight: "Trudeau does not have enough country to support his ambitions."[24]

Just before retiring, Trudeau proposed a permanent bureaucratic initiative for peace. Announced in the December 1983 Throne Speech, the Canadian Institute for International Peace and Security intended to reflect Canada's concern about current international tensions by gathering, collating, and digesting information already available on defence and arms-control issues. The Mulroney government shut down the Institute in 1992 and laid off its 40 staff, saving taxpayers $5 million per year. The closure constituted part of a broader program of expenditure restraints that axed 46 government agencies, many created by Trudeau.

Outside Canada, Trudeau's peace initiative was regarded as lacking substance and credibility. But inside the country the Liberals proudly proclaimed his peace plan to restore the luster Trudeau had lost after approving American cruise missile testing. Like so many of Trudeau's forays into international relations, the "peace initiative" concerned Trudeau's personal image more than Canada's place in the world. Indeed, Trudeau personally claimed the $50,000 Albert Einstein Peace Prize in the fall of 1984 for his efforts.

TRUDEAU WAS AN international media star who slid down a banister and pirouetted behind the Queen to gain attention. But his playing the court jester did Canada little good on the world stage. At a time rife with global tension, this type of pantomime distanced us from our allies. They saw through Trudeau's charade of strength and virtue, to the reality of Canada's underperforming economy and crumbling military.

Many domestic observers did as well. Conrad Black has nothing positive to say about what Trudeau did for Canada in international matters, especially his infatuation with communist dictatorships:

> The notion that Trudeau was a respected world statesman is utter bunk. Nixon and Zbig Brzezinski thought he was intelligent, as they both told me, but also that he was erratic and that most of what he said was nonsense. There is no doubt that Trudeau preferred the Russians to the Americans ... he had nonsensical ideas about the legitimacy of the Soviet occupation of Eastern Europe, and despite his claims to being a civil liberties advocate, had a very weak record of raising such points with left wing, as opposed to right wing dictatorships ... Robert Ford, our long-serving and very respected ambassador in Moscow, and Michel Gauvin, our well-regarded member of the International Control Commission in Vietnam, both thought Trudeau an unmitigated jackass. Ford thought his truckling to Russia contemptible (and he actually met Stalin) and Gauvin thought his flirtations with the Asian Communists an outrage.[25]

Black saw Trudeau's interventions on the world stage as not only wrong-headed but ineffectual:

> I used to see him in New York some times [sic], and he was awed by the U.S. star system and by the scale of the country. He was completely intimidated by the presence of Nixon, as was clear from one of those news-documentaries of a visit to the White House, where he was tongue-tied. Nixon said he was "smart as a whip" but Nixon was convinced that he was taking a position that most Canadians would not agree with, but that there was never any need for him to research the matter, as Trudeau didn't figure much in these things, that is he was irrelevant and ineffectual. Zbig told me that what he said was always worth listening to, but that much of the time what he said was very eccentric and fey. And his arms control initiatives were a complete fiasco.[26]

In December 1972, the same month he passed away, Lester Pearson met with John Turner, then minister of finance. "He knew he was dying," recalled Turner, "He was very, very distressed about Trudeau's foreign policy and attitude to the alliances."[27] Pearson advised Turner to wait Trudeau out. When Turner was asked to elaborate further on the conversation he replied, "I will keep that to myself."[28] But in effect, Turner confirms that our Nobel Peace Prize winning prime minister had declared Trudeau to be a disappointment on the world stage.

For a man of great intellect, Trudeau was remarkably inconsistent and enigmatic. He claimed to be an anti-nationalist, but pursued policies that isolated Canada economically. He championed the cause of the developing world, but delivered little more than speeches and platitudes. He instituted a Charter of Rights and Freedoms for Canada, but bolstered authoritarian regimes abroad. He became a friend to the Soviets, and a foe to NATO. He loved the company of a Hollywood star, yet held America in disdain. He was a man of peace, but did not believe in peace through strength. He dismissed Ronald Reagan as an imbecile, yet failed to credit him for his role in dismantling the Berlin Wall and ending the Cold War.

Trudeau deserves credit for showing leadership on the establishment of diplomatic relations with China and the defence of Canadian sovereignty in the far north. But his own ministers count themselves among his harshest critics on international relations. Mitchell Sharp, a foreign affairs minister under Trudeau, wrote that his grandstanding and speeches, eloquent as they were, "did more to enhance the reputation of the prime minister than to influence the content of Canadian foreign policy."[29]

In their 477-page examination of Trudeau's foreign policy record, historians Jack Granatstein and Robert Bothwell remark in wonderment at the "on-and-off nature of his interest, the lack of follow through, the peripatetic nature of his concerns."[30] They conclude that "sporadic" is the best way to describe Trudeau's foreign policy.

Derek Burney contends that Trudeau was ridiculed and perceived to be naïve on the world stage, about the most damning epithet one can give in diplomatic circles. Allan Gotlieb, Canada's ambassador to the U.S. under Trudeau, wrote that when a leader sought to perch himself on high moral ground through "a solemn international mission to save the world," then it was time for that leader to step aside.[31]

Canada became better-known than it had been in the developing world due to Trudeau's rhetoric on international development. To pacifists, Trudeau shone as a beacon of light. He asserted Canadian neutrality by awarding moral equivalency to our allies and the communists. Only in retirement did he express worry to a former diplomat that he may not have been "hardline enough with those guys in Moscow."

Perhaps the most telling judgment came at Trudeau's funeral. Only Fidel Castro and Jimmy Carter served as honorary pallbearers. Important world leaders who followed Trudeau did not pay their respects, nor did they express their admiration.

SECTION II

THE NATION

CHAPTER 6

THE OCTOBER CRISIS

You mean you would let them kill me, rather than agree to terms?
Margaret Trudeau (then Sinclair)
Pierre Trudeau: *Yes, I would.*

IN OCTOBER 1970, Canada needed a prime minister with nerves of steel — and it got one. While some Canadians had dismissed Trudeau as a peacenik and pacifist, he proved to be the exact opposite: an authoritarian and political opportunist. Rather than protect civil liberties, as was his expressed passion, he suspended habeas corpus, which landed nearly 500 people in jail without a warrant or charge. While he showed that the federal government could and would play rough, Trudeau's real focus was not with the kidnappers who sparked the crisis, but Quebec separatists. He used the War Measures Act (WMA) as much to quell separatism as he did to quash terrorism.

CHARLES TRUDEAU WANTED his son to be able to take care of himself intellectually and physically. The young Pierre was scrawny, but a program of exercise and strength training enabled him to face much larger foes. After his father gave him a pair of boxing gloves and some lessons as a present, Trudeau learned to use his fists to great effect. He bragged about his pugilistic prowess, so it didn't take long before his friends eagerly offered Trudeau up to foil any bully troubling the neighborhood. When pressed into action, he would never back down for fear of losing face.[1] Pierre Trudeau liked a good fight.

During his academic studies, Trudeau did not reject violence as a means to an end. "Terrorism," he wrote as a student, "though it constitutes violence in regard to the life of the person being assassinated, does not constitute political violence if it is absolutely needed to attain the accepted political end of a given nation."[2] He also defended the right of a government to keep the peace, arguing that fighting oppressors might require the suspension of some civil liberties.[3]

When tough measures were required, Trudeau the student espoused the "shock-and-awe" approach. "If a fight is unavoidable, strike hard and first. If a race has been singled out as the only plausible one in the circumstances, it is sheer stupidity to begin belly-aching over its illegality, the superstitious fear of illegality has made more than one great man tremble and spoil his aim."[4]

Even in his twenties Trudeau sought confrontation over conciliation. When addressing striking miners in Schefferville, Quebec, he inflamed an angry mob, shocking even union bosses with his incendiary rhetoric. Jean Marchand, who represented the workers, remarked that miners are not like schoolchildren. "While students might steal pencils, the miners steal dynamite ... when Trudeau urged physical resistance by the strikers, I got a little worried."[5]

It should be no surprise that when confronted with the radical elements of Quebec's so-called "Quiet Revolution," Trudeau the Prime Minister came out swinging.

Of course, Quebec and Canada had seen political violence before. One of the first periods of unrest occurred in 1837-38 when armed combatants in both Upper and Lower Canada demanded responsible government. In 1849, rioters in Montreal, then the capital of the Union of Canada, burned the Parliament buildings. Quebecers protested violently after the hanging of Louis Riel, and against the imposition of conscription during the two world wars. In 1919, a six-week general strike in Winnipeg culminated in "Bloody Saturday," when the Royal Canadian Mounted Police (RCMP) killed two demonstrators.

But none of this was as sustained or impactful as the turbulence roiling *la belle province* during the 1960s, courtesy of the province's separatist movement and its violent defenders, the Front de Libération du Québec (FLQ).

On a single day in 1963, the Federal Tax building, the Montreal train station, and a CN rail line were bombed in a coordinated attack. In the same year, terrorists tossed Molotov cocktails at an English-language radio station and bombed both a military barracks and an RCMP detachment. Police discovered twenty-four sticks of dynamite underneath a Radio-Canada transmission tower. An explosion killed Wilfred O'Neil, a night guard at the Canadian Forces Recruiting Centre. During this less-than-quiet revolution, Canada Post became a favorite FLQ target. Dynamite sticks appeared in mailboxes overnight. And when the FLQ could not steal explosives, ammunition, and weapons from construction sites or armories, they robbed banks to finance their criminal activities.

The police infiltrated the FLQ, leading to the arrest and conviction of dozens of terrorists. To FLQ operatives and their supporters, those in jail were not criminals, but political prisoners. This spurred them to terrorize the population further — and the English-speaking population in particular — as a means of securing the release of their incarcerated comrades. Bombings targeted statues of English military heroes, members of the monarchy, English banks and retailers, Liberal party conventions, and even the United States consulate in Montreal.

Despite the imprisonment of many FLQ terrorists, the violence intensified. There were 52 explosions reported in 1968 and 1969, including a blast that ravaged the Montreal Stock Exchange, causing 27 injuries. During a protest at the Murray Hill transport company in Montreal in 1969, a private security guard fired on the crowd and killed a non-uniformed police officer. A bomb was even discovered in a toilet at the home of the mayor of Montreal, Jean Drapeau.

On October 5, 1970 at 8:15 a.m., a group of armed members of the Libération cell of the FLQ kidnapped James Cross, the British trade commissioner in Montréal, from his home. Five days later, the FLQ struck again, when members of the Chénier cell kidnapped Quebec's Deputy Premier and Minister of Employment and Labour Pierre Laporte, from his own front yard.

Despite a decade of violence, and the FLQ already having taken responsibility for six murders, Trudeau called the events "highly unforeseeable," and claimed to be "completely stunned" by the abductions. He admitted his government was badly prepared and poorly equipped to respond, adding that there were no laws in the Criminal Code to give police the special powers they needed to deal with such "exceptional circumstances."[6]

But the methods employed by the FLQ were not new. Five months earlier, in March of 1970, Jacques Lanctôt had been charged with the failed kidnapping attempt of an Israeli diplomat. He skipped bail and joined the crew who abducted Cross. Lanctôt was already known to police; he had met fellow FLQ kidnapper Paul Rose in a police van after both were arrested for their participation in a violent protest at the 1968 St. Jean Baptiste parade, the night before the federal election; Rose credited this event with turning him into a terrorist.[7] Trudeau was at the same parade, but was seated on the viewing stand from which he famously refused to budge despite being pelted with rocks and bottles.

Trudeau blamed the RCMP for Ottawa's poor state of readiness for the October Crisis. He claimed in his memoirs that he had instructed the force to take the terror campaign seriously prior to the abductions. In December 1969, Trudeau, along with members of a cabinet committee, met with RCMP officials to discuss the Quebec situation. He gave the Mounties official instructions to "gather information on the sources of financing for the separatist movement in Quebec, on separatist influence within the government of Quebec, the public service, political parties, universities, unions and professions, and on the political troubles in Québec."[8]

Trudeau's instructions to the RCMP trained their focus on his ideological and political opponents, not on violence and criminality. Trudeau wrote that what he *really* meant to tell the RCMP was that they should become better educated about the very nature of separatism, and understand that "violent separatists could come from and find support in good, middle-class Québec."[9] What he meant to say is difficult to reconcile with his actual instructions.[10]

Trudeau had once dabbled in anarchism himself. In one high-school essay, he fantasized about his role in a 1976 revolution, foretelling the year the sovereignist Parti Québécois (PQ) came to power:

> If I have the good fortune to get my hands on a war I will manage to blow up the enemy's munitions factories and I will win the war for my side. I return to Montréal sometime around the year 1976: the time is right to declare Québec's independence. The Maritime Provinces join with us, and so does Manitoba. I take command of the troops and lead the army to victory. I now live in a country that is Catholic and *canadien*.[11]

In the summer of 1942, at the age of 22, he, along with a few co-conspirators, wrote a manifesto that called for an independent Quebec that would be Catholic and French and Laurentian. The Quebec nation Trudeau envisioned was to have a social and economic constitution that was hierarchical, familial and corporatist.[12]

DURING THE OCTOBER Crisis, Trudeau claimed to have taken the principled path of "no negotiations" with the FLQ. The reality was that the government did meet some of the terrorists' demands, including granting a public reading of the FLQ manifesto and arranging safe passage to Cuba for the Cross kidnappers. But on balance, Trudeau's instinct was to meet terror with the maximum force the government could muster. He would brook few limits to defeat terrorism — and separatism.

Even before becoming prime minister, Trudeau had thought about how he would deal with such a situation. There would be no negotiation, not even to obtain the release of a hostage. He told his girlfriend (and future spouse) Margaret that were she or any of their children ever to be abducted, he would not meet any ransom demands. "You mean you would let them kill me, rather than agree to terms?" Margaret asked incredulously. "Yes, I would," he replied.[13]

Thus, at the outset of the crisis he told his cabinet that he would not give the terrorists an inch.[14] But members of the Quebec government, and the editor of Le Devoir, Claude Ryan, advocated otherwise. In the days after the Cross kidnapping, Mitchell Sharp, the Secretary of State for Foreign Affairs, acceded to the FLQ demand that their manifesto be broadcast to the public. In the rambling and convoluted manifesto the FLQ sought the release of 23 FLQ members from prison and referred to Trudeau as "la tapette, c'est des peanuts," meaning that Trudeau was a "faggot" and a "peanut politician."

Trudeau did not flinch when Pierre Laporte was kidnapped on October 10, one week after Cross. Trudeau had been Laporte's classmate in high school, although they differed on politics.[15] Before the 1968 convention at which Trudeau became prime minister, Laporte had warned of a political catastrophe if the next leader of the Liberal party hardened his attitude towards Quebec.[16]

Although Trudeau had no evidence or intelligence to suggest a conspiracy beyond the kidnappings, in order to protect politicians and defend federal buildings Canadian soldiers were dispatched to Ottawa on October 12. The province of Quebec called in the army on October 15, using the provisions of the National Defence Act. Many Canadians felt unsettled at the sight of armed troops on the streets. Two journalists, Peter Reilly and Tim Ralfe, confronted Trudeau on the grounds of Parliament Hill to question him on the military deployment in Canada's capital.

Most Canadians are familiar with at least one part of the exchange between Trudeau and CBC reporter Ralfe: the Prime Minister's famous quip "Just watch me," his response when Ralfe asked him how far he would go to defeat the terrorists. But there was far more to the conversation than this. In fact, the CBC edited the interview to remove its more argumentative aspects and reprimanded Ralfe for breaching journalistic standards by engaging in active debate.[17]

The exchange with Ralfe[18] exposes not only Trudeau's thinking on the terrorist situation, but also his confrontational character and debating style, his habit of answering questions with questions, of demeaning and belittling his opponents with insults and epithets, and of exaggerating their positions to the point of absurdity.

As soon as Ralfe asked his first question, Trudeau understood he was under attack. Just as when he muttered to a 12-year-old protestor in Saskatoon that he would "kick his ass" if the boy didn't stop pitching kernels of wheat at him, Trudeau's instinct was not that of the statesman, but the street fighter. No one pushed Trudeau to do anything — not a neighborhood bully, not a gang of terrorists, and certainly not a CBC reporter.

When Ralfe asked Trudeau about the presence of guns on the streets of Ottawa, the Prime Minister responded, "What's your worry?," challenging Ralfe to defend his own position first. Trudeau made the issue a stark choice: either you stand up to the kidnappers or you are a weak-kneed bleeding heart; either you have a society where armed soldiers walk the streets, or you live with kidnappings.

Trudeau asked more questions than he answered during the interview. Why not protect the state against blackmail? Why not protect against kidnapping? And why, even with hindsight, would it have been improper to protect Mr. Laporte and Mr. Cross from abduction?

Trudeau did not just challenge Ralfe's questions, but his motive in asking them. "You're going to make a big news item of this I am sure," warned Trudeau. "The more recognition you give to them the greater the victory is, and I'm not interested in giving them a victory," essentially accusing Ralfe of aiding the FLQ in his pursuit of a hot story.

Ralfe then criticized Trudeau for calling imprisoned FLQ members "bandits," accusing him of inflaming the situation. Trudeau again pointed fingers at journalists: "You people should stop calling them political prisoners. They're not political prisoners, they're outlaws. They're criminal prisoners, they're not political prisoners, and they're bandits. That's why they're in jail."

When Ralfe expressed his distress about living in a "police state," Trudeau called him "silly." Ralfe said it was about choices, and that living in a free and democratic society means that you don't have people running around with guns even if there is the chance that the prime minister may be kidnapped. At that point, Trudeau went in for the kill.

> Sure, but this isn't my choice, obviously. You know, I think it is more important to get rid of those who are committing violence against the total society and those who are trying to run the government through a parallel power by establishing their authority by kidnapping and blackmail. And I think it's our duty as a government to protect government officials and important people in our society against being used as tools in this blackmail. Now, you don't agree to this but I am sure that once again with hindsight, you would probably have found it preferable if Mr. Cross and Mr. Laporte had been protected from kidnapping, which they weren't because these steps we're taking now weren't taken. But even with your hindsight I don't see how you can deny that ... well there are a lot of bleeding hearts around who just don't like to see people with helmets and guns. All I can say is, go on and bleed, but it is more important to keep law and order in the society than to be worried about weak-kneed people ...

Ralfe pressed the point: "At any cost? How far would you go with that? How far would you extend that?" Showing his mettle Trudeau famously replied, "Well, just watch me."

As far as most Canadians are concerned, the interview ends there. But there was much more. Ralfe asked about the possibility of wiretapping and the extent of the erosion of civil liberties. Again, Trudeau did not flinch. "The government [will] use every means at its disposal to defend itself against the emergence of a parallel power which defies the elected power." Tough talk for certain, but to call a group of kidnappers a parallel power was like calling a lit match a forest fire. As to the bleeding hearts, Trudeau cabinet minister Don Jamieson was convinced Trudeau had in mind Claude Ryan, then-editor of *Le Devoir*.[19]

THE CONVENTIONAL THINKING is that Quebec premier Robert Bourassa made the determination that led to Trudeau invoking the War

Measures Act (WMA). The reality is that the WMA was inspired by Trudeau and not Bourassa, and certainly not by the RCMP.[20]

The WMA was passed in 1914 to give exceptional powers to the government in times of war. The National Defence Act obliged the federal government to comply with any request from a province for an armed military presence on the streets.[21] In assessing the situation, and the limits of his actions, Trudeau said that it was not the kidnappings that worried him most, but how eminent Quebec officials responded to FLQ demands. He described it as a turning point when people of influence in Quebec, including Ryan, had "shamefully" signed a manifesto that appeared in *Le Devoir* on October 15 urging his government to negotiate and give in to the demands of the terrorists to negotiate the release of "political prisoners."

This enraged Trudeau: "We can't give in, but we've got to show that democratically elected governments are the governments ... and that terrorists will not govern in this land."[22] That those urging "appeasement" were university professors, leaders of a political party, labour-union leaders and opinion leaders suggested to Trudeau that he needed to shock the province out if its "extremely disordered state."[23]

Trudeau saw disorder on October 15, 1970, when 3,000 people assembled at the Paul Sauvé Arena in Montreal in support of the FLQ. Their sympathies lay not with kidnapping and terrorism, however, but the separatist cause itself. That was the real political issue Trudeau sought to confront, even if he required the army and the suspension of civil liberties to do it.

Trudeau had argued for the WMA in cabinet before it had been discussed with the governments of Quebec or Montreal. The cabinet settled on a strategy whereby the law would be invoked in response to a request from another government.[24] Although Trudeau "passed the buck" to Bourassa and Montreal mayor Jean Drapeau by having them make the request, the evidence unearthed in a book edited by University of Montreal professors Guy Bouthillier and Édouard Cloutier is that Trudeau's principal secretary, Marc Lalonde, actually drafted the request and personally delivered the letter that Bourassa signed.[25] Lalonde admitted to having a hand in drafting the request, but claims it was more as an editor than originator.[26]

Eric Kierans, Trudeau's minister of communications, described a fateful cabinet meeting on October 15 as one of the strangest sessions he ever attended.[27] While ministers were given little information and no concrete evidence of an insurrection, it was clear to Kierans that the fix for the WMA was in. Marc Lalonde, who controlled the agenda, said, "things look very bad, very bad indeed." He added that Quebec was ready to explode, and that without swift and stern action there would be riots and political assassinations. Jean Marchand claimed that the terrorists had infiltrated every strategic place in Quebec and that theirs was an organization with "thousands of guns, rifles, machine-guns, bombs, more than enough [dynamite] to blow up the core of downtown Montréal."

Kierans was prepared to oppose the WMA in cabinet, but Richard Gwyn, his executive assistant, and Allan Gotlieb, his deputy minister, advised him not to break ranks with Trudeau. When Kierans gave his support, Trudeau raised one hand, "in a sort of gesture of triumph." Kierans followed the government line that if Canadians generally "knew what we knew," they would understand the need for drastic action. John Turner reiterated the same point in the House of Commons: "It is my hope that someday the intelligence upon which the government acted can be made public, because until that day comes, the people of Canada will not be able fully to appraise the course of action which has been taken by the government."[28] That day has yet to come. Turner would later say that while there was support to invoke the WMA from Bourassa and Drapeau, the real force behind invoking the Act came out of the prime minister's office. Turner had opposed the WMA in cabinet discussions until Trudeau agreed to limit its tenure to six months.[29]

Trudeau addressed the nation on October 16 on a matter of "grave crisis." He claimed violent and fanatical men were attempting to destroy the unity and freedom of Canada. He admitted that the FLQ constituted "a few misguided persons" who threatened liberty, but that our "fragile democratic society" must be prepared to defend itself. Having endured two world wars it stunned the nation to hear their prime minister refer to the country's state of democracy as "fragile."

To dramatize and personalize the terror, Trudeau said the identity of the hostages was immaterial. "The kidnappers' purposes would be served equally well by having in their grip you or me, or perhaps some child."

Trudeau reiterated the kidnappers' demands, including claims for money and the release of 17 criminals who had been convicted of murder, manslaughter and robbery. These men, Trudeau reminded us, had not been imprisoned for their political beliefs but for the crimes they had committed against society. The release of these bandits, Trudeau argued, would only invite more terrorist attacks and more kidnappings. The safety of the hostages was the kidnappers' responsibility, not the government's.

The WMA permitted the full weight of the state "to be brought quickly to bear on all those persons advocating or practicing violence as a means of achieving political ends." Trudeau argued that taking away individual freedom during a crisis would protect life and liberty in the future.

Despite the fact that bombings and murders had plagued Quebec for a decade, Trudeau concluded that it had suddenly became "crystal clear" that the criminal law system could not deal with organized terrorism. Through the WMA, he gave the police the powers to search and arrest without warrant, detain suspected persons without laying specific charges, and detain persons without bail. Restrictions were also imposed on what the press could report about the FLQ.

Trudeau argued that, during this crisis, the WMA was the only tool at his disposal; he was worried that special legislation would alert the terrorists as to the government's plans and those of law enforcement agencies.[30] In the heat of the moment, these statements went publicly unchallenged. Trudeau admitted to the House of Commons that the authority granted in the WMA was not meant for a domestic disturbance and was broader than what was required. Trudeau said that after the crisis passed he would look at legislation that gave less invasive powers to the police and military than those required during a large-scale war.[31]

What this statement ignores is the possibility, even likelihood, that he could have passed suitable legislation in a matter of days. The country wanted a strong response, and the scattering of opposition voices in the House of Commons could have quickly been silenced. Indeed, the WMA had been similarly enacted at the outset of the First World War.

However, Trudeau was not interested in a diminished or a delayed response. His intent was to crush both the uprising and separatism. The WMA was as much a political statement as it was a tool to restore law and order and free the hostages. To Trudeau's authoritarian mind, there was no point in using half measures.

Progressive Conservative leader Robert Stanfield initially opposed the WMA, but came on side when the majority of his caucus sided with Trudeau. Mulroney, then vice chair of the Progressive Conservative Election Committee, urged Stanfield to support the government. Recalls Mulroney, "When the PM and Minister of Justice stand up in Parliament before the House of Commons and say that they have incontrovertible evidence of the existence of a major conspiracy to undermine the government of Canada — that's a big deal. I spoke with Stanfield and urged him to tie his support to Trudeau and Turner's statements in the House of Commons about an insurrection. It turned out there was no insurrection. They made the whole thing up."[32]

NDP leader Tommy Douglas said in debate that Trudeau was "using a sledgehammer to crack a peanut."[33] Trudeau responded, "This criticism doesn't take the facts into account. First, peanuts don't make bombs, and don't take hostages and don't assassinate prisoners. And as for the sledgehammer, it was the only tool at our disposal." As a parliamentarian, all Douglas asked of the government was evidence of an apprehended insurrection, failing which he refused to give the government carte blanche to do whatever it wanted. Despite pockets of NDP resistance, the motion to invoke the WMA passed by a vote of 190 to 16.[34]

Trudeau learned from the October Crisis that it was "absolutely essential to have, at the helm of state, a very firm hand, one that sets a course that never alters."[35] Despite protesting the authoritarianism of Maurice Duplessis in the 1950s, in his moment, and facing somewhat different circumstances, Trudeau trumped even Duplessis in bringing down the heavy arm of government on the people. Invoking the WMA was as much a political operation as a police operation. Two of Trudeau's cabinet ministers, Pelletier and Marchand, were personally involved in vetting a list of those to be arrested.[36]

Within hours of the WMA being invoked, 497 people had been arrested, many of them poets, writers, artists, and legitimate political activists. They were not, of course, tossed into dark dungeons and abused; for some, having been detained was a badge of honour that came with a lifetime of rather enjoyable notoriety. But this does not diminish the fear and anxiety experienced by those imprisoned without any legal rights, facing an uncertain outcome. An account of the crisis by Bourassa cabinet minister William Tetley provided evidence that, out of the large number detained, only 62 people were charged and 32 were held without bail.[37]

Certainly at the time the exercise was anything but amusing. When the police sought out Nick Auf der Maur, then a left-wing storyteller and host of a CBC television program, they went to his former apartment by mistake and arrested the new occupants – South Vietnamese students – who just happened to be in the right place at the wrong time.[38] The police eventually caught up with Auf der Maur and threw him in jail for a few days. Beyond the arrests, some 10,000 homes were searched without warrant, and 12,500 troops were deployed on the streets of Québec.[39]

But the more immediate shock came the day after the invocation of the WMA. The FLQ directed journalists to an abandoned car at the St. Hubert airport parking lot, the trunk of which contained the body of Pierre Laporte. The note, as translated, read, "Faced with the arrogance of the federal government and of its lackey Bourassa, faced with their obvious bad faith, the FLQ has decided to take action."[40] We know now that Laporte had severely injured himself trying to escape by jumping out of a main-floor bedroom window. The kidnappers, who acknowledged the execution, then strangled him with brute force, although there were subsequent claims by the terrorists that the killing was accidental. We do not know the extent to which the invocation of the WMA was a factor in Laporte's murder.

Margaret Sinclair (who became Margaret Trudeau on March 4, 1971) was with Trudeau when he received the news, recalls tears streaming down his face. He was a shaken man who was growing old before her eyes. "It gave him a new bitterness," wrote Margaret, "and a hard sadness I had never seen before."[41] Trudeau met with the media at 3:00 a.m. to make a brief statement. "I can't help feeling as a Canadian, a deep sense of shame that this cruel and senseless act should have been conceived in cold blood and executed in like manner."[42]

On November 2, 1970, John Turner introduced the Public Order Act into the House of Commons to modify certain aspects of the WMA. The Public Order Act had a sunset clause of April 30, 1971.[43]

Despite reaffirming that he would not give in to the kidnappers' demands, Trudeau nonetheless was prepared to negotiate with the FLQ, offering them safe passage to a country of their choice in return for the delivery of the hostages. Trudeau justified the offer of safe conduct on the grounds that the hostages might be able to identify their captors and the government did not want the kidnappers to have an incentive to murder them. Trudeau also noted that the government of Quebec was prepared to recommend parole for the five prisoners on the FLQ list who were eligible for it, yet another instance in which FLQ demands were partially addressed.

On December 3, James Cross was located and freed by the police. Trudeau permitted his captors to fly to Cuba. Upon returning to Montreal years later, they were given light sentences, most of which were suspended.[44]

On December 28, Laporte's kidnappers were arrested and subsequently convicted for their crimes. Ottawa pulled the army out of Quebec in January 1971. The emergency powers under the WMA expired on April 30.

Turner later admitted that the WMA had been "substantial overkill." He doubted that there had been an "apprehended insurrection," and felt that the criminal code was adequate for dealing with most aspects of civil disorder.[45] He acknowledged the federal government had incomplete and inadequate information about the extent of the crisis and that political motivation played a part in the response.[46] For his part, Trudeau expressed no regrets about how he handled the crisis that resulted, among other things, in one dead Quebec cabinet minister.

IT IS IMPOSSIBLE to say what shocked Quebec back to its senses — the actions of a steely prime minister or the death of Laporte. Even the most ardent separatist-anarchists lost their will when they saw their ideals turn murderous. Onetime radicals, like Pierre Vallières, denounced violence and advocated a political and democratic path to separation through the Parti Québécois.

Historian Jack Granatstein, who was initially critical of Trudeau for his handling of the October Crisis, has since changed his mind, not because the WMA helped liberate Cross, but because it instilled awareness that the state would use its full powers to restore order and public confidence. Senior bureaucrat Gordon Robertson, who has been generally critical of Trudeau's attempts at nation-building, said that his actions that October were "probably the most important single contribution he made to the preservation of peace and democracy in Canada during his time as prime minister."[47]

Reg Whitaker, Distinguished Research Professor Emeritus at York University and a specialist in security and intelligence issues as well as politics, examined all the available evidence and concluded that Trudeau and his cabinet deliberately exaggerated the crisis to obtain emergency powers to intimidate Quebec separatists. What the police really needed and wanted was to pursue the kidnapping with patient and deliberate investigative work.[48] According to Whitaker, the RCMP never asked for the WMA, and if their opinion had been sought, they would have advised against invoking it.[49] Don Jamieson recalled that then-RCMP Commissioner William Higgitt confirmed that the WMA had produced nothing of any consequence to their investigations.[50]

A national poll conducted soon after the crisis revealed that four out of five Canadians supported Trudeau's actions.[51] While most people in Canada agreed with Trudeau, many in the media and on university campuses did not. Months after the crisis had peaked, Trudeau was invited to a private gathering of journalists who complained that because of emergency measures they had faced editorial censorship. Trudeau replied that "an honourable person would have resigned in protest."[52]

Yet Trudeau himself had been far from honourable. He had wildly overestimated or purposely exaggerated the threat to society imposed by the FLQ. James Cross concluded, "It was a case of six kids trying to make a revolution."[53] This was a far cry from Jean Marchand's purported brigade of 3,000 strong-armed revolutionaries.[54] But the October Crisis gave Trudeau the possibility of killing two birds with one stone: terrorism and separatism. He mostly succeeded with the former, but not the latter.

Based on his private conversations with Trudeau, author Peter C. Newman debunked the notion that a manifesto signed by many Quebec intellectuals represented an attempt to form a provisional government, calling it a "meticulously concocted lie." Before the WMA had been invoked, Lalonde summoned Newman to a meeting in the prime minister's office. "I have called you here to discuss a matter of utmost seriousness, but first I must warn you that I will deny this conversation took place. We believe that a group of prominent Québécois is plotting to replace the province's duly elected government. The conspirators are Rene Lévesque, Jacques Parizeau, Marcel Pepin, and Claude Ryan. This move towards a parallel power must be stopped ... There is nothing speculative about this." A short while later, Trudeau called Newman to confirm and amplify Lalonde's warnings. It was a conversation that Trudeau also told Newman he would deny had ever taken place. When Newman challenged Trudeau to back up his assessment that a credible conspiracy was in the works, Trudeau replied, "I acted on information I've been accumulating since I was three years old."[55]

Perhaps the most comprehensive review of the October Crisis came forty years after the event in a book entitled *Trudeau's Darkest Hour*. The editors of this collection of essays, scholars Guy Bouthillier and Edouard Cloutier — both Quebec sovereignists — concluded that the October Crisis revealed Trudeau to be authoritarian, totalitarian, dictatorial and a fascist.[56]

Not all political violence in Quebec ended in October of 1970. In the years that immediately followed, bombs were detonated at the Brink's Company in Montreal and the Montreal Post Office. And as the RCMP became more engaged with the separatist threat, they did not hesitate to break the law themselves. They opened people's mail and stole the membership lists of the Parti Québécois in a 1973 Watergate-style burglary. A Royal Commission was ultimately called over the force's conduct.

The evidence today tells us that the imposition of the WMA was more a political statement than a law enforcement mechanism. It was Trudeau's version of "shock and awe."[57] He was prepared to jettison his belief in individual rights and liberties to achieve his true priority: thwarting separatism.

While the October Crisis put support for Trudeau at an all-time high, public approval did not last long. Within two years, his government was reduced to a razor-thin minority in the House of Commons.

Despite promises by Trudeau to repeal the WMA, it was not until 1988 that the Mulroney government passed the Emergencies Act. It required that a declaration of an emergency must be reviewed by Parliament and that any temporary laws made under the Act would be subject to the Charter of Rights and Freedoms, and therefore must be justified as reasonable in a free and democratic society.[58]

To judge Trudeau's response to the October Crisis fully, we must ask one last question: Did his conduct strengthen or weaken the nation? Given the election of the PQ government in Quebec in 1976, the rise of the Bloc Québécois in the 1990s, and the results of the 1995 Quebec referendum, Trudeau's actions clearly did not squelch separatist forces. Even separatism's violent side did not subside solely because of a fear of the Canadian army and a brass-knuckled prime minister. It is more likely, as William Tetley observed in his insider account of the October Crisis, that Laporte's brutal murder explained the collapse of the FLQ.[59] Ironically, Trudeau's heavy-handed tactics may well have inspired many Quebecers to support the "democratic" arm of separatism, the Parti Québécois, which came to power within six years of the event.

Another way to assess Trudeau's actions is to consider what would have happened had he not invoked the WMA. While we don't know if it had any influence on the murder of Laporte, we know that freeing Cross and arresting the kidnappers and murderers resulted from investigative work that required no special legislative measures.

And while the WMA had popular support at the height of the crisis, it did nothing to enhance the attachment of Quebecers to Canada. Quebec was never going to leave Canada by way of force, only by democratic means — means which separatists have pursued with vigour ever since.

CHAPTER 7

A CONSTITUTIONAL OBSESSION

Today, at long last, Canada is acquiring full and complete national
sovereignty. The Constitution of Canada has come home. The most
fundamental law of the land will now be capable of being amended
in Canada, without any further recourse to the Parliament of the
United Kingdom.

TRUDEAU OFTEN SAID he was loath to open up what he called
the "constitutional can of worms." But in truth he was
obsessed with patriating the Canadian constitution from
Great Britain and enacting a charter of rights and freedoms. While
Trudeau's Charter has enjoyed broad public support, no government
of Quebec ever endorsed the fruits of what Trudeau described as a
federal "coup d'état." While a constitution is intended to inspire and
unify, the reality is that, some thirty years after Queen Elizabeth II
proclaimed ours into law, Trudeau's creation remains a subject of
controversy.

MOST CANADIANS REMEMBER Trudeau as an avid federalist, a supporter
of a strong central government, a proponent of a bilingual Canada
and a champion of individual rights. However, Trudeau's private papers reveal that during his youth he was an anti-democratic separatist

revolutionary. Québec's destiny, thought Trudeau, was as an independent country.

To preserve and protect the French language and culture, he wanted Québec to turn inward. He saw the Church as the cornerstone of French society, and advocated limits on immigration. At the age of 18 Trudeau took part in an oratorical contest on the historic reality and survival of the "French Canadian Nation." He argued that "[n]o one denies that [the French Canadian nation] has the will to live collectively, and has their own proper territory and political organization ... To maintain our French mentality, what we must do is to preserve our language and to shun American civilization."[1]

Trudeau was prepared to take up arms for an independent Quebec and worked to develop parameters to guide a post-revolutionary society.[2] This revolution, only revealed by Trudeau friends Max and Monique Nemni in their 2006 book *Young Trudeau: Son of Quebec, Father of Canada*, was to serve the French in Quebec while abandoning those in the rest of Canada. "On the subject of the solidarity of the French minorities, we do not think it appropriate to take a stand ... Let us remember, however, that we cannot at the same time withdraw from the federation and propose to exercise a control there."[3] Separating Quebec from the rest of Canada was an explicit goal, to be declared when the time was right. Sovereignty constituted a necessary condition of such a revolution. Trudeau's vision for Quebec turned not on fundamental values and principles, but on blood and language. Among the tactics suggested to carry off the revolution was kidnapping.[4]

The constitution of the Laurentian state Trudeau envisioned would be "at one and the same time authoritarian and the guardian of freedoms," with an emphasis on strong leadership. Though it cannot be said conclusively whether Trudeau was a fascist sympathizer in his youth, he certainly condemned parliamentary democracy and liberalism, while promoting dictatorship on the basis that the state could not pursue the common good of the nation unless it answered to a single leader.[5]

During World War II, Trudeau dismissed the BNA Act as a fraud. He wrote that at Confederation, the leaders from Canada East entered into a partnership, a compact, with other provinces, which had effectively been dissolved after its terms were changed without consulting Quebec. Trudeau never provided evidence of this alleged change. Nevertheless, dismissing the BNA Act allowed him to endorse the separatist objective because the BNA act could be considered an unjust law passed by the *British* Imperial Parliament, and could only be amended in Great Britain.[6]

WHILE TRUDEAU TOOK offence at Canada's ongoing legislative connection to Great Britain, most Canadians did not give it a second thought. Canada had existed within that relationship from 1867 to 1982 without hindering our development. When a new province entered Confederation, or Parliament was restructured, or when federal and provincial governments sought to shift jurisdictions — such as when Ottawa was given authority over unemployment insurance in 1940 and Old Age Security in 1951 — the Brits were only too happy to accede to requests from Canada for enabling legislation. In 1949 the Canadian Parliament was given limited authority to pass constitutional amendments within exclusive federal jurisdiction. One such homegrown initiative was to establish the mandatory retirement age of senators at 75, which came into force in 1965. To most Canadians, having the country's constitution kept offshore was of little consequence to their day-to-day lives

The constitutional flaw that irritated Trudeau was thus more symbolic than substantive. It only required the consent of the Queen's representative to Canada, the Governor General, for legislation passed in the House of Commons and the Senate to become the law of the land, as is the case today.

At Confederation, it made sense for our fledgling nation to make the British Parliament the trusted caretaker of our constitution. Canada earned its independence over time, not by amendments to the BNA Act, or even the patriation of our constitution, but by developing our economy, establishing our institutions of governance and earning respect in the international arena through the sacrifices of our people during the Great War. It was inevitable that one day Canada would sever its constitutional link to Great Britain, but only when the time was right.

TRUDEAU THOUGHT THE BNA Act a rather bland piece of legislation. Unlike the American Declaration of Independence, which begins with noble and principled statements — *that all men are created equal, endowed by their Creator with certain unalienable Rights, that among these are Life, Liberty and the pursuit of Happiness* — the BNA Act spoke not of principles and rights but of a desire simply to form a union "under the Crown of the United Kingdom of Great Britain and Ireland, with a constitution similar in principle to that of the

United Kingdom." Rather than freedoms, the BNA Act referred to "interests," such that the Union would "conduce to the welfare of the Provinces and promote the interests of the British Empire." The operating objective for the federal government under section 91 of the BNA Act was to make laws for the peace, order, and good government of Canada.

Trudeau wanted a constitution that spoke to high-minded values rather than precedent and good governance. And Trudeau wanted those values ultimately to be protected by the courts rather than the people's elected representatives. For Trudeau, democracy provided insufficient defence for citizens who might be oppressed by a capricious government.

But the evidence did not support the notion advanced by Trudeau in the 1970s and 1980s that the state inherently threatened individual rights. Indeed, Canadians inherited the entirety of British legal tradition at Confederation, including the Magna Carta (1215), the Habeas Corpus Act (1679), the Petition of Right (1628), and the Bill of Rights (1689). These, along with other instruments such as court judgments, parliamentary conventions, royal prerogatives, and international conventions, were available to Canadians, even though they were not listed in the BNA Act.

Trudeau wasn't the first prime minister to advance the cause of individual rights and freedoms. In light of abuses against Canadians of German and Japanese descent during the First and Second World Wars, John Diefenbaker urged repeal of the War Measures Act (WMA), which he claimed constituted an invitation to any government to declare an emergency to the detriment of the rights of the people. The powers in the WMA were so broad, some said, that it was like that old joke about your grandmother's nightie: it covered everything. Based on Trudeau's own use of the WMA, Diefenbaker's warning was prescient.

When Diefenbaker introduced the Bill of Rights on September 5, 1958, he knew that failing to put it into a constitutional amendment limited its application. Critics called the narrow applicability of the bill a timid and tepid affirmation of a political and social tradition. Nevertheless, the bill was proclaimed law on August 10, 1960. Diefenbaker considered the bill an expression of Canadian values, rather than a raw legal instrument. Years later, he reflected on its meaning: "Those law professors and politicians who condemned it had closed their eyes to what was happening. All the laws of this Dominion were made to conform to it. It became the standard and the pattern for those Canadian provinces that wished to enact their own provincial Bill of Rights." Trudeau was of the view that Diefenbaker's Bill of Rights did not go far enough, since it was just a law like all the others — one that could be amended by a single and simple vote of Parliament.

THE FIRST SERIOUS effort to patriate our constitution from Great Britain to Canada took place in 1927. Another attempt was made in 1931 when the British Parliament passed the Statute of Westminster, giving Canada, and other self-governing colonies, legislative independence from Great Britain. However, at Canada's own request, the BNA Act remained in force because our federal and provincial governments could not agree on an amending formula. For the provinces in particular, the British Parliament played an important role as the trusted caretaker of our constitution, something akin to a referee who would not let the rules of the game be changed without the consent of the main players.

While Britain continued its benign hold over our constitution, it also held the upper hand in terms of Canada's Supreme Court. Decisions rendered by Canadian courts could be appealed to the Privy Council in Great Britain until 1933 for criminal matters, and until 1949 for civil appeals. While it might seem preposterous that Canada could not manage its own judiciary, we should remember that in 1929, it was left to the Privy Council of Great Britain to overrule Canada's own Supreme Court judgment that women were not "persons." In 1927 that same Council ruled that Newfoundland, and not Quebec, owned Labrador.

Through the 1950s and 1960s, attempts to make our constitution a purely Canadian document failed because of a lack of unanimous support among the federal and provincial governments. They also foundered on the divisions within French Canada on the subject, rifts as old as Confederation itself.

Housing our constitution in Great Britain understandably annoyed anti-monarchists, especially francophone Quebecers like Trudeau who objected to swearing allegiance to the Crown. But French Canadians who lived in Canada East when the BNA Act was passed in 1867 claimed it as a victory. By dissolving the Union of Canada in which French and English Canadians were bound together in a single legislature, Confederation gave Quebec control of its destiny. Editors at *La Minerve*, a Montreal newspaper published in French and tied to George Étienne Cartier, wrote: "As a distinct and separate nationality, we form a state within a state. We enjoy the full exercise of our rights, and the formal recognition of our national independence ... In giving ourselves a complete government we affirm our existence as a separate nationality." Confederation gave Quebecers their own government that could pass legislation irrespective of the wishes of their neighbors to the west.

While Quebec now had a legislature to defend the interests of the majority French-speaking population, francophones living outside Quebec depended on provincial legislatures that often discriminated against their interests. Despite guarantees on French-language education and denominational schools in Manitoba passed in 1871, the Manitoba government abandoned those undertakings in 1890. Liberal Prime Minister Sir Wilfrid Laurier, a francophone Quebecer like Trudeau, declined to intervene and refused to use the federal power of disallowance to remedy the situation.

For its part, Quebec took some comfort in believing that the federal government could not intervene in areas of provincial jurisdiction. Be it health, education or the use of language, the BNA Act established the rules of governance for Canada. Before entering politics, Trudeau felt that the central government should never unilaterally modify the jurisdiction of the provinces.[7] Changing the rules without the consent of the Quebec government was akin to the unilateral rewriting of a prenuptial agreement.

TRUDEAU'S INTELLECTUAL FORMATION changed course during the decade that followed the Second World War. During his university studies, Trudeau shed his authoritarian and separatist sentiments and accepted democratic socialism and liberalism. In doing so, he departed from the path of many Quebec intellectuals of the day.

Trudeau also altered his professional course. He now wanted to make statesmanship his profession.[8] In his memoirs he wrote that during his high school and university years he did not read newspapers or listen to the news on the radio. Instead, he preferred to read the classics, poetry, and philosophy, or to engage in personal adventure.[9]

Towards the end of World War II (1944), having already completed a law degree in Quebec, Trudeau furthered his education at Harvard. His academic specialty was the organization of society, political science, and the laws that governed the economy. While at Harvard, Trudeau concluded that his native Quebec was parochial and a backwater of intellectual, economic and social development. Quebec, he surmised, would not assure its future by becoming insular and shielding itself from external influence, but by bravely welcoming and embracing the best that the world had to offer.

Trudeau abandoned his separatist ideals, but he bypassed what was then the natural alternative: Canadian federalism. Instead, he famously declared his personal motto by pinning a sign to the door of his dorm room that read simply, "Pierre Trudeau, Citizen of the World." He went from separatist to multi-nationalist in one fell swoop.

After completing his written and oral exams for a doctorate at Harvard, he pursued further studies in Europe at L' École des sciences politiques and the London School of Economics. While studying in Paris he explored two related topics for his dissertation, both grounded in Canada's constitutional dilemma: "Liberties embodied in the Canadian Constitution" and "Bill of Rights not in BNA but in reality."[10] This was early evidence of a constitutional fixation to come.

Ultimately Trudeau chose the interplay between Christianity and Marxism as the topic of his uncompleted dissertation. This led Trudeau to travel extensively through Eastern Europe, the Middle East, and Asia, including China.

Without completing his PhD. Trudeau officially entered the work force in the summer of 1949, at the age of 30. Under the supervision of respected civil servant Gordon Robertson, Trudeau found a home in the Privy Council Office (PCO) in Ottawa where he focused his time on the challenges of developing a "made-in Canada" constitution. He even turned down an offer from the Finance department because he preferred the nation-building focus of the PCO.[11]

Trudeau saw the virtues of federalism as a means to steer Quebec away from the path of ethnic nationalism, a position he had previously espoused. In a letter to a friend, Trudeau writes optimistically about Canada: "I have so far been mainly occupied with research on constitutional reform, and on major economic policy issues: you know how passionate I am about these two subjects. One thing is for sure: some moves are underway in Ottawa that will leave their mark in history."[12]

Intellectually he saw federalism as a superior form of government because it was more pluralist than monolithic. It respected the diversity among people and groups.[13] He also believed that federalism was the best system from which to launch radical socialism in Canada:

> Indeed that superb strategist Mao Tse-tung might lead us to conclude that in a vast and heterogeneous country, the possibility of establishing socialist strongholds in certain regions

is the very best thing. Federalism must be welcomed as a valuable tool, which permits dynamic parties to plant social- ist governments in certain provinces from which the seed of radicalism can slowly spread.[14]

Trudeau ended his two-year stint as a public servant with the view that the federation should be grounded by a bill of rights and that the federal government should surrender its power of disallowance.[15]

He then returned to Montreal to engage in intellectual discussion about Quebec's place in Canada and the world. The main instrument he used to advance and expose his thinking was the influential, yet thinly circulated, intellectual journal, *Cité Libre*. He flirted with left- wing political causes and advocated on behalf of various unions. After Trudeau chided striking workers by saying that if they had guts they would rise up in arms, union leader Jean Marchand wondered what Trudeau, who was 30 at the time, was going to do whenever he grew up.

Trudeau's ideas about the organization of society had become clear by his 30s and varied little for the remainder of his life. His opposition to nationalism was heightened by what he perceived as a period of "Great Darkness" that he considered the hallmark of the regime of Quebec premier Maurice Duplessis. Trudeau called nationalism regressive and poisonous to society, warning that it stirred passions and feelings that prevented people from tackling problems rationally. He blamed nationalism for the worst wars in history and for the suppression of individual human rights. "I'm opposed to any political system based on race and religion," he wrote. "All such politics are reactionary, and for the past 150 years, nationalism has been an anachronistic notion." Indeed, Trudeau opposed any form of sovereignty based on nationalism or ethnic identity:

> Man has done very well without nations ... the tiny portion of history marked by the emergence of the nation-states is also the scene of the most devastating wars ... What worries me about the fact that five million Canadians of French origin cannot manage to share national sovereignty with seven mil- lion Canadians of British origin, beside whom they live and who they know, in general, have no fleas, is that this leaves precious little hope that the several thousand million Ameri- can, Russians and Chinese... will ever agree to abdicate their piece of sovereignty in the realm of nuclear arms ... The very

idea of the nation-state is absurd. To insist that a particular nationality must have complete sovereign power is to pursue a self-destructive end. Because every national minority will find, at the very moment of its liberation, a new minority within its bosom which in turn must be allowed the right to demand its freedom.[16]

Constitutionalism was his preferred governance structure: a means by which a civilized society could achieve polyethnic pluralism in a multinational state with entrenched individual rights to thwart "the tyranny of the majority." He saw federalism as the ideal structure to balance conflicting interests. Trudeau saw in Canadian federalism a governance system that put us ahead of the rest of the world, and an example that others should follow.[17]

Trudeau's philosophy of protecting individual rights put him on a collision course with the emerging political views of leading Quebec intellectuals, who embraced nationalism as the means to protect the French language and culture. Trudeau responded bluntly and caustically to his critics: "The ultimate tragedy would be in not realizing that French Canada is too culturally anemic, too economically destitute, too intellectually retarded, too spiritually ossified, to be able to survive more than a couple of decades of stagnation, emptying herself of all her vitality into nothing but a cesspit, the mirror of her nationalist vanity and dignity."[18]

In an August 1958 essay published in the *Canadian Journal of Economics and Political Science,* Trudeau wrote that French-Canadians have historically not believed in democracy for themselves. "In all-important aspects of national politics, guile, compromise, and a subtle kind of blackmail decided their course and determined their alliances. They appear to discount all political or social ideologies, save nationalism."[19]

While he credited the Liberal Party of Canada for preventing the growth of a nationalist Quebec party on the federal scene, he viewed federal Liberals as exploitative, incompetent and corrupt. Hurling insults at the Liberal clan came easily to Trudeau, who claimed that "[t]he shameful incompetence of the average Liberal MP from Quebec was a welcome asset to a government that needed no more than a herd of performing donkeys to file in when the division bell rang. The party strategists have but to find an acceptable stable master ... and the trained donkeys sitting in the back benches could be trusted to behave."[20]

With the exception of Laurier, Trudeau could point to no federal French-Canadian cabinet minister who made significant contributions to Canada, "except at election time, of course, when the tribe always invokes the aid of its witch doctors."[21] Trudeau's praise is surprising, considering that Laurier had fatefully decided to mollify the Anglophone majority in 1896 by abandoning French minority language rights in Manitoba. This decision persuaded many francophones in Canada that their rights would only be protected within the borders of Quebec, where they were in the majority. It is ironic that Trudeau, who wanted to protect the French language outside Quebec, kept a bust of Laurier in his prime ministerial office.

Trudeau vehemently opposed the view that Quebec was the sole protectorate of the French language and culture. He berated Duplessis's nationalistic government as intolerant, discriminatory and totalitarian because it did not pursue the good of all its citizens.[22] Trudeau contended that if a state were defined by single ethnicity (a common language and established customs), the identity and rights of the individual, and in particular minorities, would inevitably be repressed.

In his memoirs, Trudeau reflected with concern on the Quiet Revolution stirring in Quebec in the late 1950s. He believed that after a decade of fighting for all Quebecers, the mantra "maîtres chez nous" promoted the cause of only French Quebecers, or as he called them, "old stock Quebeckers."[23] Though he recognized the concept of a French Canadian nation as a social identity, Trudeau expressly rejected the idea that such a nation required or deserved its own sovereign state.

Ultimately, Trudeau believed Quebec's nationalist government desired nothing less than political independence. "If we were to promote the political independence of every sociological nation around the world, the planet would soon be torn by countless conflicts among ethnic and linguistic groups, each demanding sovereignty in the country in which it constitutes a minority."[24] While opposing sovereignty for Quebec, Trudeau nonetheless stood against incursions into areas of provincial jurisdiction by the federal government. When Duplessis refused federal funds offered up for post-secondary education in Quebec, Trudeau sided with his premier by saying that such an intervention required a constitutional amendment.

Trudeau was distressed that the youth of the 1960s were embracing separatism, claiming they were shriveling up intellectually rather than opening themselves to a world of knowledge and opportunity. The two courses Trudeau taught at the University of Montreal between 1962 and 1965 were "Constitutional Law and Administrative Law" and "Civil Liberties."[25] His students would later remark that what he talked about in his lectures was precisely what he implemented as prime minister in 1982.[26]

Trudeau relished bucking the trend of rising Quebec nationalism, and standing up for federalism. According to his long-time friend Gerald Pelletier, Trudeau loved the role of contrarian. When invited to a black tie affair, he would show up in jeans, saving his formal attire for when others were in casual dress.

Trudeau's work antagonized Quebec nationalists. He faced down opponents who wanted either a more autonomous Quebec or a more flexible federalist arrangement with the province. While Trudeau was quick to hurl insults at Quebec nationalists, he also blamed English Canada for using its size and wealth to humiliate and oppress French Canadians. He saw the federal public service, the Canadian armed forces, and the financial services industry as oppressive bastions of anglo privilege.[27] Ironically, at the time Montreal, Quebec served as the banking hub of Canada; Toronto, Ontario had yet to become its location of choice.

WHEN TRUDEAU ENTERED federal politics in 1965, the nation was gripped by disunity. The Royal Commission on Bilingualism and Biculturalism, which had been established in 1963, concluded that Canada had entered the worst crisis in its history. It was more than an academic political discussion: terrorists detonated bombs, committed murder, and sowed anxiety in the streets.

Initially, as parliamentary secretary to Prime Minister Lester B. Pearson, Trudeau assumed a low profile in Ottawa, seeking to learn the political ropes before speaking out. However, when given the Justice portfolio in April of 1967, it was not long before he used his position to advance his ever-present ideas on constitutional change.

After only a few months in cabinet, Trudeau opened his proverbial "can of worms" by giving a visionary speech at the annual meeting of the Canadian Bar Association. On September 4, 1967, Trudeau declared that the federal government was ready to discuss constitutional change. At the meeting, Trudeau argued for patriation of the constitution, with an entrenched bill of rights (binding on both the federal and provincial governments) and an amending formula. Trudeau wanted to protect human rights, but also protect and enhance the French language to ensure that francophone Canadians had an equal opportunity to participate in the political, cultural, economic, and social life of the country.

Under Pearson's chairmanship, the Liberal Party held a constitutional conference in February 1968. Pearson had already announced his resignation as party leader, so it was an opportunity for Trudeau to showcase to the nation how he would handle the Quebec question.

As prime minister, Pearson had practiced the art of "cooperative federalism," which he described at the opening of a 1963 federal-provincial conference as "the mutual respect for the jurisdictions and the responsibilities of Canada and of the provinces."[28] He spoke of timely and reliable consultation as the basis for coordinating action by Ottawa and the provinces on matters of common and overlapping interest.

Trudeau, who had been pondering a run at the leadership, decided to delay any announcements about seeking the top job until after the conference. He wanted to avoid appearing to link his high-minded interventions to his personal ambitions.

For its part, the federal government advanced constitutional discussions by raising the issue of a charter of rights, including language rights, while leaving aside the question of the division of powers between the federal and provincial governments. That's when Trudeau and Quebec Premier Daniel Johnson Sr. clashed. "Your problem, Mr. Johnson, is not with the federal government. It is with federalism." Johnson dismissively addressed Trudeau as "Lord Elliott." Trudeau countered by calling the Quebec premier "[t]he member for Bagot," Johnson's riding.[29]

It was good theatre, but the content of the exchange mattered less than the exchange itself. Trudeau emerged on the national scene and demonstrated that Quebec politicians could not bully him. And he showed he could speak to Quebec nationalist politicians in ways that no politician from English Canada could dare dream of doing.

The conference concluded with an agreement to give priority to patriating the Constitution with an amending formula. The recommended formula required the consent of any province containing at least 25 percent of Canada's total population, from two Atlantic provinces, and from two western provinces containing together at least 50 percent of the total population of the western provinces. The First Ministers also agreed to incorporate language rights into the Constitution, while providing the provinces with some say over the appointment of Supreme Court justices.

In advance of the Liberal leadership campaign, Trudeau published a selection of his writings under the title *Federalism and the French Canadians*. In the foreword, Trudeau wrote:

> We French-Canadians are terribly lacking in tenacity. Rather
> than devote all our efforts to the real improvement of our in-
> tellectual, social, and economic condition, we let ourselves be
> carried away by legal superstructures without even inquiring
> whether they will work ... I have had the same ideas on our
> Constitution for a long time [so] ... if the party does not agree
> with my opinions, it can repudiate me; if my constituents do
> not, they can elect someone else. To "ready-made" or second-
> hand ideas, I have always preferred my own.[30]

The book played better in English Canada than in Quebec. French
President Charles de Gaulle sniffed, "[W]e have no concessions
and no friendly gestures to make to Monsieur Trudeau, who is
the opponent of the French fact in Canada." Nonetheless, a strong
francophone federalist from Quebec was just what the Liberal Party
of Canada wanted in a leader.

The 1968 federal election campaign was not a battle of ideas,
but of images. Who best incarnated the zeitgeist of the 1960s — the
vibrant, charismatic, intellectual and flamboyant Liberal Trudeau, or
the dour, stiff, earnest, unexciting Progressive Conservative Robert
Stanfield? The *London Spectator* described Trudeau as Canada's
saviour: "It was as if Canada had come of age, as if he himself single-
handedly would catapult the country into the brilliant sunshine of
the late twentieth century from the stagnant swamp of traditionalism
and mediocrity in which Canadian politics had been bogged down
for years."[31] There was also a sense in the nation that this wild-eyed,
philosophy-quoting counter-nationalist from Quebec might just hold
the answer to our growing unity crisis.

As prime minister, Trudeau immediately signaled the importance
of the constitution when forming his cabinet. Upon making John
Turner his minister of justice, Trudeau stripped from the portfolio
the constitutional file, and reserved it for himself.[32]

Other than the introduction of official bilingualism, Trudeau's first
opportunity to remake the nation came at a constitutional conference
in 1971 at Victoria, the location chosen to mark the 100th anniversary
of British Columbia's entry into Confederation. The conference
aimed to achieve a simple patriation of the constitution, "with such
other changes as can be agreed upon quickly" by the federal and
provincial governments, including an amending formula whereby
any province *then* containing at least 25 percent of the population

of Canada would enjoy a veto over constitutional amendments. This formula effectively gave Quebec and Ontario perpetual vetoes.

There had been a nominal agreement hammered out between federal and provincial governments prior to the conference that included a basic charter of rights, three Quebec justices on the Supreme Court (appointed after provincial consultation), recognition of French and English as official languages of the federal government, and a veto for provinces with 25 percent of the population. In supporting the Victoria proposal, Trudeau said he had accepted the terms that had been stipulated by Quebec premier Robert Bourassa.[33] But just before the conference, Bourassa expressed concern over federal funding of social programs in areas of provincial jurisdiction. Trudeau claimed not to have been forewarned. In his memoirs he wrote of his shock that Quebec had developed a bad case of "cold feet." However, senior federal advisor, Gordon Robertson, noted that Quebec had signaled its apprehensions a few weeks prior to the conference.[34] At the conference, Bourassa informed the prime minister and his provincial counterparts that he needed two weeks to consult his cabinet colleagues before he could commit Quebec to the Victoria Charter.[35]

In those two weeks Bourassa came under attack, in particular from Claude Ryan, the editor of Le Devoir, for not protecting provincial jurisdiction in the area of social policy. Ryan, who had long known Trudeau, considered him to be formalistic, idealistic, arrogant and dangerous, and no friend to Quebec.[36] Bourassa, who had been advised by Trudeau that the Victoria Charter was a take-it-or-leave-it agreement, took a pass, handing Trudeau a major defeat on the national stage. This held an element of political payback by Quebec nationalists, whom Trudeau had insulted over much of the previous decade. All sides in Quebec's National Assembly applauded Bourassa.

To the English media Trudeau said he was not greatly concerned about the collapse of the Victoria Accord. To the French media he said that the separatists would take advantage of the failure.[37] But the demise of the accord hardened Trudeau's resolve to achieve his constitutional goals, even if that meant undermining federalists in Quebec and taking great risks with the fabric of the nation.

Trudeau did not hide his disdain for Bourassa. Despite the fact that the alternative to Bourassa in Quebec politics was PQ leader René Lévesque, Trudeau damaged the federalist leader by calling Bourassa "politically stupid."[38] In 1974, Bourassa's government passed Bill 22, making French the official language of Quebec, which ran counter to what Trudeau sought to accomplish in Ottawa by declaring the federal government officially bilingual. By making the Quebec government French, in the same way that Ontario was English, Bourassa not only upset the federal government, but also Quebec's English-speaking minority, who thought they were being treated like second-class citizens. On their end, French-speaking sovereignists thought the legislation timid.

Meanwhile, constitutional talks continued. In April 1975 the federal and provincial governments agreed in principle on the timing of patriation of the constitution and reaffirmed the Victoria amending formula, but many items remained unresolved. In March 1976 Trudeau met Bourassa in Quebec City to discuss progress on the constitutional file. At the airport Trudeau noticed a magazine cover featuring a picture of Bourassa eating a hot dog. When the press asked him what they were going to have for lunch, Trudeau condescendingly remarked, "Everybody knows the premier likes to eat hot dogs." Whatever Trudeau's intention, this remark was interpreted to mean Bourassa was a weakling with no guts.

Over lunch, Bourassa told Trudeau that in the next round of constitutional talks Quebec would seek a substantial transfer of federal powers. In other words, the province would not cooperate on patriation without getting something in exchange.[39] To Trudeau, Bourassa had waved a red flag. Trudeau, who was seeking to strengthen the federal government, saw Bourassa's pitch as a naked power grab, not something that should be "dignified" with names like "special status" or "distinct society."

By 1976 Trudeau was fed up. He wrote to the provincial premiers about three possible constitutional options: simple patriation with unanimous consent for amendments until an amending formula could be agreed upon; simple patriation with the Victoria amending formula; or, the Victoria charter plus new provisions on protection of the French language and culture. The premiers responded that patriation should be deferred until the parties could agree on an expanded role for the provinces. An annoyed Trudeau responded that the federal government might *unilaterally* patriate the Constitution.

For the better part of a century, the prospect of constitutional renewal without unanimous federal and provincial support had never been considered. Now Trudeau was proposing going solo, with unimagined consequences. The man who thought federalism put Canada in the vanguard of good governance was contemplating an action as if he were the leader of a unitary state. Trudeau, who had once suspended civil rights by imposing the WMA, now wanted to override democratic rights by imposing a constitution without the consent of the provinces or the people. To decouple patriation of the constitution from a rebalancing of powers, Trudeau was prepared to cut provinces out of the equation altogether. As he put it, "I had begun to despair of the possibility of negotiating a settlement without paying much too high a price in terms of federal power."

Trudeau was so confident that he was on the right path that in May of 1976 he declared that separatism in Quebec was dead. Before an international audience, he claimed the independence movement as the evil fruit of the unbalanced treatment of a minority of the country.[40] In berating and belittling Bourassa, musing about unilateral patriation, and then taunting separatists that their cause was lifeless, Trudeau set the scene for political upheaval in Quebec. Bourassa called an election earlier than required to stop the "unilateral Trudeau threat." Yet, when the votes were counted, Quebecers thought that the best person to stop Trudeau was not Bourassa, but René Lévesque and the Parti Québécois. On November 15, 1976, the first separatist provincial government since Joseph Howe led the Nova Scotia Party in 1868 was duly elected.

Most prime ministers might have seen the election of the PQ government as a sobering day for Canada. But Trudeau relished the chance to fight the separatist movement out in the open.[41] Trudeau had known Lévesque for many years and did not respect him, believing him to be a disorganized and confused prima donna.[42] Trudeau and Lévesque were dissimilar in much more than their views on federalism. While Trudeau spent the Second World War contemplating ancient philosophers and protesting, Lévesque preferred to witness history in the making. He volunteered for the U.S. Army in the War Information Office, marking the beginning of his career in journalism.

After the Quebec election, Trudeau dismissed the pending threat to the Canadian union and ignored the PQ promise to hold a referendum on the question of sovereignty. He insisted that the provincial election revolved around economic and administrative issues, not the constitution. He declared that the federal government would uphold the spirit and the letter of the constitution and that Mr. Lévesque would be welcome at an upcoming constitutional conference.

In response to the PQ victory, Trudeau established the Task Force on Canadian Unity, also known as the Pépin-Robarts Commission after its chairs, John Robarts, a former premier of Ontario, and Jean-Luc Pépin, a past and future Trudeau cabinet minister. The Commission's report recommended the creation of a new constitution with an entrenched charter of rights, including minority language rights, and an amending formula that included a Canada-wide referendum. The Commission also concluded that Canada needed a structural makeover to address duality and regionalism. It recommended increased power to the provinces in the areas of taxation and immigration; limitations on federal spending in areas of provincial jurisdiction; and the elimination of the federal power to disallow provincial statutes. Residual powers (all powers not otherwise assigned in the constitution) were to be given to the provinces rather than to the federal government, the opposite of what was provided for in the BNA Act. The Supreme Court would include five Quebec judges out of a total of eleven who would be appointed by the federal government following provincial consultation. The provinces would appoint senators and proportional representation would be used to populate the House of Commons. Finally, Quebec would receive "special status" to help preserve its distinctiveness and to enhance its French heritage.

Trudeau saw most of the commission's key recommendations as non-starters, especially special status for Quebec. Pépin-Robarts certainly overreached in calling for proportional representation and making recommendations on the composition of the Supreme Court, although it's not clear that these proposals were Trudeau's primary objections. The reality was that the Commission had been a federal stalling tactic, established to distract the public without committing the federal government to a particular course of action. Trudeau knew he could adopt whatever recommendations agreed with his intentions, and just as easily ignore those that did not.[43]

IT IS EVIDENT that Trudeau invited Lévesque to the constitutional bargaining table in bad faith. In his memoirs, Trudeau explained that because the aim of the PQ was to break up Canada, there never was a realistic chance of persuading a separatist party to renew the country's constitution. Trudeau's real battle was to prepare Canadians, and especially Quebecers, "for the day when the federal government might have to break convention and make an appeal to London without having gained unanimous provincial consent, and perhaps even unilaterally."[44] This ignored the fact that Lévesque had indicated in writing, and by agreement with his provincial counterparts that he was prepared to sign a patriated Canadian constitution. Of course, Lévesque may have believed that a common front of provinces would inevitably fail and that Quebec would win if the provinces stuck together, and also win if he could prove that federalism didn't work.

Trudeau was not just prepared to isolate the separatist Quebec government, but those of all provinces. No prime minister before Trudeau had contemplated such a divisive and risky strategy as unilateral patriation. But Trudeau had a history of being a risk-taker to the point of recklessness. It did not bother him that he may have been going against the grain: "It is wonderful to be despised," he wrote in his youth, "if, deep down, we know we are right."[45]

Trudeau enjoyed confrontations of almost any sort, whether in politics, sports, or tests of will. He would boast that when others portaged, he would shoot the rapids. While adventuring in the far north, he proclaimed that life was most beautiful, "when his food began to run out, the rapids were the most dangerous, the rain oppressive, the storms unrelenting." When travelling as a student, he forged a document in order to cross restricted borders, and was deported from one country after a day of detention and a warning that he could have been charged with espionage and put to death if convicted.[46] In 1961 he ran with the bulls in Pamplona.[47] Trudeau was not one to back down in the face of danger.

On June 12, 1978, the Trudeau government took its first unilateral step toward patriation by tabling a white paper titled A Time for Action, while also introducing a constitutional reform bill (C60) in the House of Commons. The bill proposed replacing the Senate with a house of the federation that gave greater weight to the regions. Under the draft legislation, one-half of the upper chamber would be elected by the House of Commons after each federal election, and the other half would be appointed by provincial assemblies after their own general elections. Provincial premiers disapproved of the plan, and the Supreme Court ruled it unconstitutional.

Later that fall, Trudeau showed some willingness to compromise at a first minister's conference where he agreed to study seven provincial demands. Trudeau said he would look at limits on federal spending power, consider allowing provinces to levy indirect taxes, clarify shared jurisdiction over natural resources, and include equalization and regional development within constitutional discussions. Trudeau added that a fair share of the benefits from natural resources should accrue to the people of the province in which they are found, without depriving other Canadians of a reasonable cut. Even Lévesque was impressed. But Trudeau ultimately had second thoughts about these compromises, saying to reporters, "I've almost given away the store." Trudeau opined that the more he offered, the more provincial appetites grew.

WHILE TRUDEAU TALKED about a constitutional deal, minority language rights steadily eroded in Quebec. Trudeau did and said little when Quebec Liberals passed Bill 22 in 1974, and when the Parti Québécois passed the more stringent Bill 101 in 1977. In his memoirs Trudeau explained, somewhat ironically, "I had no intention of using the Constitution to disallow the legislation. The way to change bad laws was to change the government, rather than using Ottawa to coerce a province."[48] Yet he saw nothing wrong with Ottawa forcing constitutional change on the provinces, against the will of their duly elected governments.

When Trudeau faced the voters in 1979, he told 16,000 party faithful at Maple leaf Gardens in Toronto at a key campaign rally that he would meet the provincial premiers one more time to seek a consensus on patriation, "and failing that, we will bring the constitution back and consult the Canadian people in a referendum," bypassing the provincial governments. He called it a "shame" and an "embarrassment" that Canada's constitution was in the hands of the British Parliament. The throng of Liberals at Maple Leaf Gardens dozed off. It was the speech Trudeau wanted to give, but Liberal strategist Keith Davey wrote that his insistence on talking about the constitution "was bad news for us."[49] The 1979 vote was the only general election Trudeau lost.

In his concession speech on election night, Trudeau stood his ground:

> The important thing is that we haven't given up an inch on our principles as Liberals. We stood for minority rights ... we fought for equality of opportunity ... a strong national government ... and I want to say for those of you who were perhaps surprised to see me talk in the last weeks of the campaign about having a Canadian constitution made by Canadians, in Canada, for Canadians. I still think, I believe this was the right course. I knew that when I took that course we took the risk of failing greatly and perhaps we did in the short run, but I am absolutely certain, that in a medium and longer term, this is the course that Canada will have to follow.[50]

After the defeat Trudeau told Keith Davey he was giving up, that he did not have the heart or the will to carry on as leader of the party, and that he "just couldn't go on being a performing seal."[51] Trudeau announced his resignation as Liberal leader three weeks *after* the Quebec government announced its plan for a referendum on sovereignty association. It was then unclear what role, if any, Trudeau would play in that vote. But, unexpectedly, the Tory government of Joe Clark lost the confidence of the House of Commons in December 1979, and Trudeau rescinded his resignation and returned to lead the Liberals in the 1980 election.

While Trudeau could not stop talking about the Constitution in the 1979 campaign and lost, he said next to nothing about it in 1980, and won. Trudeau agreed to keep silent after he was told that public opinion polls indicated voters were fed up with the constitutional question,[52] a fact he reiterated when asked by an interviewer for Radio-Canada about why he stopped talking about the constitution. As *Globe and Mail* columnist William Johnson observed at the time, "Constitutions are rules, and rules are boring, except for lawyers and referees ... Mr. Trudeau tried riding the constitution in last year's election campaign, but it didn't get him very far. No one was interested. This time, he clearly feels he can get far more mileage out of the 18 cents a gallon of gasoline in the Tory budget."[53] As a former Saskatchewan premier once said, "if I had 100 problems, the constitution was number 101."[54]

The voters elected Trudeau in 1980, but did not give him a mandate to undertake constitutional renewal. In fact, the voters had rejected that proposition in 1979. And after the 1980 election Trudeau did not have a truly national mandate to govern, holding only two of the 77 seats west of the Ontario border. His Quebec MPs represented 50 percent of the Liberal caucus, at a time when Quebec was home to only 27 percent of the nation's ridings.

MANY OF TRUDEAU'S supporters believe federalists won the 1980 Quebec referendum because of the prime minister's interventions. While that claim cannot be proven, what we do know is that Trudeau misled Quebecers about what a No vote would mean for their future.

Despite leading a government with minimal representation from western Canada, Trudeau did not govern cautiously, deciding in 1980 to focus on the Quebec referendum, the energy issue, and the Constitution. Not expecting to be in office for very long, Trudeau was determined to take great risks to achieve the results he wanted.[55] But first he needed to win the referendum, held on May 20, 1980, just three months after the federal election. Trudeau was judicious and strategic in his interventions, and spoke out on only four occasions: on April 15 in the House of Commons; on May 7 to the Montreal

Chamber of Commerce; on May 9 at a rally in Quebec City; and most importantly, on May 14 at the Paul Sauvé Arena in Montreal.

In the early stages of the referendum campaign, the outcome was far from certain. But the separatists made two decisive mistakes. First, PQ cabinet minister Lise Payette insulted women supporters of the No side by calling them Yvettes (the name of a submissive young girl in a well-known Quebec school text). Second, René Lévesque questioned Trudeau's French heritage, arguing that he was too English because of his mother's blood: "His name is Pierre Elliott Trudeau and this is the Elliott side taking over, and that's the English side, so we French Canadians in Quebec can't expect any sympathy from him." This divisive and obviously racist sentiment was a political gift to Trudeau, which he readily exploited.[56]

At the Paul Sauvé Arena, a symbolically important location since it was where Lévesque addressed his followers after the PQ win in 1976, Trudeau exposed the ethnic prejudice inherent in the Premier's insult:

> I was told that no more than two days ago Mr. Lévesque was saying that part of my name was Elliott and, since Elliott was an English name, it was perfectly understandable that I was for the NO side, because, really, you see, I was not as much of a Quebecer as those who are going to vote YES. That, my dear friends, is what contempt is. It means saying that there are different kinds of Quebecers. It means ... saying that the Quebecers on the NO side are not as good Quebecers as the others and perhaps they have a drop or two of foreign blood, while the people on the YES side have pure blood in their veins. That is what contempt is and that is the kind of division which builds up within a people, and that is what we are saying NO to. Of course my name is Pierre Elliott Trudeau. Yes, Elliott was my mother's name. It was the name borne by the Elliotts who came to Canada more than two hundred years ago. It is the name of the Elliotts who, more than one hundred years ago, settled in Saint-Gabriel de Brandon, where you can still see their graves in the cemetery. That is what the Elliotts are. My name is a Quebec name, but my name is a Canadian name also ... All Quebecers have the right to vote YES or NO ... regardless of the name of the person voting, or the colour of his skin.[57]

In the same 40-minute speech, Trudeau made a solemn commitment meant to assuage the soft nationalists who were dissatisfied with the status quo. He proposed that if Quebec voted No, the federal government would take action to renew the constitution. He told the crowd that a No vote meant change:

> If the answer to the referendum question is NO, we have all said that this NO will be interpreted as a mandate to change the Constitution, to renew federalism ... I can make a most solemn commitment that following a NO vote, we will immediately take action to renew the Constitution and we will not stop until we have done that. And I make a solemn declaration to all Canadians in the other provinces, we, the Quebec MPs, are laying ourselves on the line, because we are telling Quebecers to vote NO and telling you in the other provinces that we will not agree to your interpreting a NO vote as an indication that everything is fine and can remain as it was before. We want change and we are willing to lay our seats in the House on the line to have change. This would be our attitude in the case of a NO vote.

> If the answer to the referendum is YES ... Mr Lévesque will be welcome to come to Ottawa, where I will receive him politely, as he has always received me in Quebec City, and I will tell him that there are two doors. If you knock on the sovereignty-association door, there is no negotiation possible ... It is like saying to Mr. Lévesque, "The people of Newfoundland have just voted 100 percent in favour of renegotiating the electricity contract with Quebec. You are obliged, in the name of democracy, to respect the will of Newfoundland, are you not?" The wishes of Quebecers may be expressed through democratic process, but that cannot bind others — those in other provinces who did not vote to act as Quebec decides ... On the other hand, if Mr. Lévesque, by some miracle, and it truly would be a miracle, knocked on the other door, saying: I have a mandate to negotiate, and would like to negotiate renewed federalism then the door would be wide open to him, and I would say: "You did not have to go to the trouble of holding a referendum for that; if it is renewed federalism you want, if that is what you wish to negotiate, then you are welcome.[58]

Trudeau was not precise about what being wide open to Lévesque meant in reality, but the implication of what he meant when he said everything was not well was clear: that suggestions for change coming from Quebec would be respectfully received. In practical terms, it was reasonable for Quebecers to expect that Trudeau would offer powers enabling the Quebec government better to protect the French language and culture. This is what Trudeau's speechwriter, André Burelle, believed. Certainly constitutional reform advocated by Trudeau that night was not expected to diminish Quebec's powers.

Recall that the head of the No side in the referendum, Quebec Liberal leader (and former head of Le Devoir) Claude Ryan, had released a beige paper prior to the referendum that spoke of the need to preserve the rights of Canada's "two founding peoples." It called for a Quebec veto over constitutional amendments as well as an independent review of all acts of the federal Parliament dealing with language and culture. The beige paper was introduced at the outset of the campaign, and many in Quebec concluded that Trudeau was open to this sort of reform. Indeed, the day after Trudeau's speech, Ryan told reporters that his beige paper proposals for renewed federalism had been warmly welcomed in Ottawa, countering reports of their lukewarm reception.[59]

The No side won the referendum in decisive fashion with 60 percent of the vote. In defeat, Lévesque said Quebecers had cleanly given federalism another chance. He expected that Trudeau would honour his promises of constitutional reform. On referendum night, Trudeau responded by saying, "We have all lost a little in this referendum ... we must try to heal in the days and weeks to come." Returning to his basic philosophical defence of anti-nationalist federalism, in his prepared statement Trudeau added, "To those who may wish to recreate in this land those old nationalistic barriers between peoples — barriers of which the world has been trying to rid itself — I say we Canadians do not have to repeat the mistakes of the past ... All of us have the opportunity to show the whole world that we are not the last colonials on earth, but rather among the first people to free themselves from the old world of nation-states."[60]

In victory Trudeau gave full credit to Ryan for leading the No side and congratulated him for his skills and tireless effort. But with victory Ryan issued a caution: "While the essential principles of federalism will be preserved we must not underestimate the importance of [constitutional] changes that must be made so that federalism becomes more acceptable and more broadly based."[61]

Although they lost the referendum, the PQ was re-elected in the Quebec general election held on April 13, 1981. In effect, Quebecers were sending Lévesque back to the constitutional bargaining table to negotiate with Trudeau.

IF EVER THERE was a prime minister who was prepared to roll the dice over Canada's future, it was Trudeau. Sensing he had only a few years left in office, Trudeau declared that he was not in much of a mood for bargaining. "I decided that enough was enough ... I'm convinced, and I hope the people of Canada are convinced, that there are some things you have to do decisively, without cooperative federalism. You've got to do it alone, otherwise it will never be done ... It's obvious we will never have a constitution of our own if we don't do it alone."[62]

The end of cooperative federalism? Trudeau had not prepared himself for negotiation, but for an all-out war: "There had been a hell of a lot of nice guys since 1926 and the constitution was never patriated. Maybe it took a nasty guy ... People said I was arrogant. I never was with nice people. Only with those who goaded me. But I was still spoiling for a fight. I still had something of a Cyrano temperament."[63] No other prime minister before him had so recklessly pursued a policy objective that, in reality, mattered so little to Canadians.

After the referendum, Trudeau summoned his populist Quebec minister, Jean Chrétien, to go through the motions of canvassing the provincial premiers to see what kind of deal they might accept. At about the same time, *The Globe and Mail* issued an editorial asking Trudeau, "What's the rush on the constitution?" In reality, the clock that was running out was not Canada's, but Trudeau's. He had one final term to achieve what has been called his magnificent obsession.

Trudeau invited the first ministers to 24 Sussex Drive on June 7, 1980, for a day of private talks. The premiers wanted to pick up on the agenda that had been on the table prior to the Liberal defeat in 1979, the one about which Trudeau mused that he had "given away the store."[64] But Trudeau no longer believed that he needed to cooperate with the provinces. He was prepared to proceed unilaterally, and had no reason to compromise. Trudeau suggested constitutional negotiations in two stages: First, a "people's package," including patriation and a charter of rights, and second, the "politician's package," including the division of powers between the federal government and the provinces. He even mused about decentralizing in some areas in exchange for strengthening the Canadian common market by removing provincial barriers to the free movement of goods and people.[65] While a sound economic idea, it was, regrettably, not a Trudeau priority.

This strategy meant that Trudeau would get what he wanted first, and then the provinces, having surrendered their leverage, could have a go at persuading the public and some future federal government to engage in further constitutional reform. This plan removed the power of having a seat at the constitutional table, which the provinces had enjoyed since 1867. It established a new federal doctrine of unilateral patriation. Trudeau proposed to make a nation of compromises into the fiefdom of a strongman.

Explaining his actions, Trudeau confirmed in 1986 that he had declared war against the provinces: "Let's just say that in this last stage I felt one needed almost a *putsch, a coup de force* ... I didn't need advice. At that point I knew exactly what I wanted."[66] That's why he cut out the senior bureaucracy from the constitutional strategy planning sessions, and in particular senior civil servant Gordon Robertson who, according to Trudeau, was too much of a gentleman. It was going to be a rough-and-tumble affair, and there was no place for, as Trudeau put it, a mandarin, concerned with the common weal, afraid of irreparable damage to the fabric of society. Robertson was out as the key advisor, replaced by Senator Michael Kirby, a mathematician. Kirby embraced the role, calling himself Trudeau's son of a bitch.[67]

While the economy was in recession and Canadians were suffering from its ill effects, Trudeau remained preoccupied with the constitution. "I went ahead and took away [the provinces'] god damn chips. It was not without doing violence to myself ... that I decided to deliver the knockout punch."[68] The boxing metaphor was quintessential Trudeau, recalling the sport his father insisted he master in his youth. Trudeau enjoyed a fight even if the odds were stacked against him. He famously stood his ground on a reviewing stand during the 1968 St. Jean Baptiste parade when, as prime minister, he was pelted with bottles and debris, refusing to leave as he was urged to do by his security detail. He had been forewarned of the danger and ignored the pleas that he stay away. "If you didn't want me to come," he told the parade organizers, "you shouldn't have invited me. Now that I have accepted, I'm certainly not going to admit, by backing down, that the prime minister of Canada can't watch the festival of Saint-Jean in his own hometown. I've been watching this parade since I was six years old."[69] Standing his ground, even taking a swing, came naturally to Trudeau.

It was one of Trudeau's many contradictions. While he claimed to detest violence, he could dish it out himself. Victor Irving was a member of Trudeau's RCMP security detail in 1969 and recalls a violent incident involving the prime minister:

> A young man, wearing an NDP ski cap, came upon Trudeau's right side and yelled at him "You're a mother fucking creep" ... I saw the guy's head snap back. The next day Pierre Trudeau was charged with assault. My evidence was the following ... I was the closest person to the prime minister when the complainant was hit. I did not see the PM throw the punch. As I was pushing people out of the way, I may have accidentally been the culprit myself. If the prime minister had actually hit the guy, I should have seen him do it. What I didn't tell them was that I believed Trudeau did punch the guy in the nose, but I was never asked what I believed. The guy got what he deserved, I thought. The case was dismissed.[70]

In his memoirs, Trudeau tells the story of being persecuted by an upperclassman:

> One time, during lunch, one of these older students decided to provoke me by throwing a banana in my soup. I immediately fished it out and flung it into his soup ... "Right," said my persecutor, in a rage, "if that's the way you want it, we'll settle this outside as soon as we leave the lunchroom." "Okay — if you want," I said. I was acting confident; there was no question in my mind of backing down. But deep down I didn't have the slightest wish to fight it out with this older guy, because I wasn't at all sure I would have the upper hand. He too had done some boxing. So I didn't push it any further while waiting for dessert. At the end of the meal, we both stood up. We stared at each other in the eye for a long moment. "Okay," he said. "Just this time, I'll give you a break." He walked away, to my great relief. But I have learned you can win some confrontations just by acting confident.[71]

No one ever doubted that Trudeau was tough. When Rex Murphy was making the case on CBC that Pierre Trudeau was "The Greatest Canadian," he remarked, "The rose has steel petals." When Trudeau told the premiers he was going to deliver a knockout punch, he meant it.

Because Canada's constitution still remained with Britain, Trudeau needed to bring that country's political leadership onside. Trudeau gambled that the desire of a Canadian prime minister would trump the objections of provincial premiers. Trudeau met with British Prime Minister Margaret Thatcher at 10 Downing Street on June 25, 1980 to inform her of his constitutional strategy. While Thatcher gave indications of support, Trudeau had failed to inform her of his plans to include a charter of rights in the patriation package, or of the likely provincial resistance. Later she remarked, "How can you expect me to be enthusiastic about your charter when we are against one?"[72] The British government was not amused and leaked news of its displeasure to *The Globe and Mail*. The Westminster Parliament Committee on Foreign Affairs under Sir Anthony Kershaw warned that the British Parliament was under no obligation to pass legislation requested by Ottawa *unless* there was agreement from the Canadian provinces.

Trudeau went to his cabinet to seek their views on his plans before the September 1980 first ministers' meeting. He told his colleagues he was in for a hell of a fight. "The premiers will be against us. The British will be nervous. The media will be critical. The [anglophone] academics won't say anything, as usual. We could tear up the goddam country by this action but we're going to do it anyway."[73] It is hard to imagine a Canadian prime minister, before or since Trudeau, saying that his actions may tear up the country, but no bother, he would go ahead regardless.

Had Trudeau gone back to the agreement reached in Victoria that Bourassa had rejected, or the proposals he made to the premiers in 1978, he might not have faced as much opposition. But now that he was going it alone, he was determined to put in place the constitution that he wanted.

Joe Clark, the leader of her Majesty's Loyal Opposition, thought Trudeau wrong-headed to ignore the provinces. "Because a constitution is so basic to a country it must be the product of the broadest possible consensus. It cannot be arbitrarily imposed on this nation by any one individual or government. Nor can it be achieved through threat, ultimatum or artificial deadline. That kind of constitution making does not serve Canada."[74]

Trudeau did not believe he would get a deal with the provinces, but he went through the motions of seeking an agreement so that he could justify unilateral patriation when the time came. In September of 1980 Trudeau met with the ten premiers for a constitutional conference in Ottawa. Prior to the formal session, at a Sunday night dinner hosted by Governor General Ed Schreyer, Trudeau was in a sour mood, not wanting to deal with his provincial counterparts.

When it was proposed to him that a provincial leader should co-host the formal conference, he recoiled. "Okay, you propose that on television tomorrow and you'll see what my answer is. I'm ready to do battle ... so let's have the debate on television tomorrow."[75] The premiers declined the offer to duke it out over chairing the conference on television.

The next day, the conference got off to a provocative start with Newfoundland premier Brian Peckford's opening statement during the televised portion of the proceedings. Reflecting on the dinner conversation from the previous evening, he said that his view of Canada was closer to that articulated by Lévesque than it was to the centralist, rigid and authoritarian vision of Trudeau. In response, Trudeau said Lévesque's vision had been rejected by the people of Quebec in a referendum.

Trudeau had isolated himself. He had none of the skills or charm of Sir John A. Macdonald, who had overcome a far greater challenge, "herding cats," in his words, to cobble a country out of rancorous and disparate colonies. Trudeau acted more like a Machiavellian Prince than a nation builder.

After the premiers submitted a list of issues they wanted to discuss, Trudeau once again threatened unilateral patriation. "I'm warning you gentlemen, I've been warning you since 1976 that we could introduce a resolution in the House of Commons patriating the Constitution, and if necessary we'll do this unilaterally. So I am telling you now, we're going to go it alone. We're going to introduce a resolution, and we'll go to London, and we won't even bother asking a premier to come with us." Premier Sterling Lyon of Manitoba responded abruptly, "If you do that, you're going to tear the country apart." Trudeau was defiant: "If the country is going to be torn apart because we bring back from Britain our own constitution after 115 years of Confederation and after more than 50 years of fruitless discussions, and because we have asked for a Canadian charter of rights, when most of you already have provincial charters, then the country deserves to be torn up."[76]

Trudeau would later write, "I was convinced that the time had come for Canada to choose to be or not to be."[77] Trudeau was alone in making such a dire assessment. National security and national unity have always been key priorities of every prime minister since Confederation, but Trudeau's warnings about the dissolution of the nation over an issue that barely registered in the minds of most Canadians sounded absurd.

To bolster his argument on the need for a charter, Trudeau repudiated the long-held British principle that Parliament, and not the courts, should reign supreme. He claimed that the British Parliament could be trusted to protect minorities because it was a unitary state, but that a federal state such as Canada required a charter to ensure the same result.[78] This argument went unchallenged at the time. But what Trudeau really meant was that the provinces could not be trusted to protect minority rights. Of course, most provinces already had charters that bolstered individual rights.

Trudeau contended that creating the charter did not constitute a federal power grab, since it would restrict the legislative sphere of both the federal and provincial governments.[79] But unlike Diefenbaker's Bill of Rights, the charter would apply to provincial laws, giving the courts the power to strike down statutes passed by any level of government. The charter's minority language education rights, which had not been a provision of the constitutional proposals advanced in 1971 at Victoria, meant that Québec would lose some sovereignty over education. That did not mean Trudeau was completely unprepared to make any compromises, as long as those compromises did not matter to him personally. For example, to gain the support of the federal NDP, Trudeau agreed to their demands for increased provincial powers over natural resources. This converted NDP leader Ed Broadbent to a charter advocate, and he was enlisted to help gain the support of the NDP premiers.[80] Compromising on natural resources and economic management was far different to Trudeau from compromising on language.

Trudeau appeared on television on October 2, 1980 to announce his plans to proceed unilaterally to bring a new constitution to Canada consisting of three parts: patriation, a charter of rights and freedoms with minority language and education rights, and an amending formula. Plans for a free trade agreement within Canada were dropped. Trudeau said that anyone who opposed his plans would look foolish in the eyes of the world.

He proposed that an amending formula requiring unanimous support be in place for the first two years, to be replaced with the Victoria formula, which had always been the federal preference, or, alternatively, a formula that had the acceptance of eight provincial governments representing at least 80 percent of the population. A referendum would be held to choose between the two competing formulas.

Two Trudeau ministers flew to London days after the announcement to brief the Thatcher government on patriation plans. Trudeau had gained the support of Ontario premier Bill Davis, but western premiers took a different view. "We will fight back any way we can devise," declared Alberta premier Peter Lougheed. Manitoba's Sterling Lyon called the plan a fundamental invasion of provincial jurisdiction and a repudiation of the parliamentary system. Meanwhile, Lévesque kept his options open, suggesting the economy and not the constitution was his priority, adding, "People don't eat constitutions." At the same time, he told reporters that a PQ government would not hold another referendum during its second term if his government were re-elected. In other words, the country was not in jeopardy.

Eight premiers responded to Trudeau's plan by presenting a united front and an alternative plan. Lévesque, having won re-election the previous week, stood as a prominent member of the "gang of eight." By joining with his fellow premiers, he answered the question of whether there were a constitution that a sovereignist government would accept.

The gang of eight's April 16, 1981 accord countered Trudeau's contention that the premiers would hold patriation hostage in exchange for some grab bag of additional powers. The eight premiers called for patriation of the constitution without a charter of rights and with a provision that allowed provinces to opt out of constitutional amendments that infringed upon provincial power. To cement the partnership, and in recognition of the opting-out provision, Lévesque agreed to an amending formula whereby Quebec would not have a veto. It was a historic concession. Quebec would be a province just like the others, with no special status.

The gang of eight also proposed the Alberta amending formula that required the support of seven provinces representing fifty percent of the population. Lévesque challenged Trudeau by saying, "I hope this agreement would encourage Mr. Trudeau to renounce his *coup de force* and compromise in good faith."

Trudeau dismissed the proposal as a victory for those who wanted Canada to disintegrate slowly. "The (separatists) can't get out right away but they can get out bit by bit and that is written clearly in the agreement today ... a confederation of shopping centres ... is not my kind of Canada."

But Trudeau's hyperbole was unfounded. The only point of clarity that the gang had asserted was that if the federal government invaded provincial jurisdiction, a province could opt out with compensation. This demand did not represent the undoing of Canada, but rather did little more than confirm the four corners of the BNA Act. But to Trudeau, flexibility in the federation would inevitably lead to national dissolution. This was certainly not the stance taken by the Fathers of Confederation, or by any prime minister before Trudeau.

The premiers thought Trudeau's plan not only wrong for Canada, but also illegal. Quebec, Manitoba and Newfoundland launched legal challenges to the scheme. On March 31, a Newfoundland court declared the federal government had no authority to request an amendment that would directly alter provisions of the British North America act affecting federal-provincial relations without first obtaining provincial consent.[81] Representing the federal government at the hearing was future Newfoundland premier Clyde Wells, who argued unsuccessfully that the proposed charter rights did not limit provincial powers.

The Supreme Court of Canada (SCC), with six of its nine members appointed by Trudeau, ultimately decided the matter by means of a reference.[82] Court observers had noted that Trudeau's appointees had tended to side with the federal government on previous disputes with the provinces.[83] But this ruling had far deeper implications. If it found for the federal government, the court would no longer simply be determining the jurisdictional lines between federal and provincial authority, but would be asked to rule on the constitutionality of all laws and the administration of justice with reference to a charter. In other words, the SCC was ruling on a matter in which it was potentially a chief beneficiary of power and influence.[84]

It was revealed in a 2013 book titled *Bataille de Londre* by Frédéric Bastien, professor of history at Dawson College, that Supreme Court justice Willard Estey and Chief Justice Bora Laskin were in contact with both the Canadian and British governments while the court was contemplating the reference. At the very least, this communication represented a fundamental violation of the independence of the judiciary.

The Supreme Court ruled that the federal proposal did affect the rights and powers of the provinces, and that constitutional convention required substantial provincial consent for amendments affecting their powers. However, there was no legal requirement preventing the federal Parliament from asking the United Kingdom to amend the BNA act without the consent of the provinces. Trudeau interpreted the ruling as a call to try to play nice, at least.

Trudeau then agreed to try one more time to negotiate with the provinces, failing which he would seek unilateral patriation. "It was important," he wrote in his memoirs, "for us to be seen making the effort."[85] If he was rejected by the British Parliament, he said he would put the matter to the Canadian people in a referendum as a declaration of independence for a sovereign Canada. He did not say what threshold would constitute acceptance, or whether he needed the acceptance of only seven provinces representing 50 percent of the population (including Ontario and Quebec, as per the Victoria Accord). Given that Quebecers had just elected a PQ government, support for Trudeau's plan in his home province was unlikely.

GOING INTO THE fateful November 1981 constitutional conference, Trudeau had just two allies at the conference: Bill Davis from Ontario and Richard Hatfield from New Brunswick. The gang of eight came to the conference intact and united.

With little progress at the conference and Lévesque scheduled to leave, Trudeau made an offer that he thought might fracture the gang of eight. Turning to Lévesque he said, "Rather than break up in disarray and continue our fight on the doorstep of the British Parliament, why don't we get patriation first — nobody can object to that — and give ourselves two years to solve our problems over the amending formula and the charter, and failing that consult the people in a referendum? You're the great democrat, you're the great believer in referendums. You can't be opposed to one ... or are you afraid to take me on?"[86]

Lévesque felt taunted. Instinctively, and without thinking what his fellow gang members would say to the idea, he took the bait. He wanted to fight a charter he was sure would be rejected in Quebec.

Trudeau gloated to the press that a new alliance had been formed between the government of Canada and the government of Quebec. "This is a triumph. There is suddenly a Quebec-Ottawa alliance. You are all surprised, gentlemen. Too bad for you. The cat is among the pigeons."[87]

The seven other premiers from Lévesque's gang were not interested in fighting a referendum on a charter of rights. Lévesque quickly realized that he had fallen into a trap, and after lunch he retracted his acceptance of Trudeau's proposal. Trudeau wanted to end the conference, but Jean Chrétien, his point man on the constitution, sensed an opening and urged Trudeau to give him some time to try to make a deal behind the scenes.

Building upon ideas and a document that came from Newfoundland premier Brian Peckford, representatives from Ontario and Saskatchewan cooked up a proposal with Chrétien for the charter of rights Trudeau wanted, but with a legislative override that the provinces could invoke: the notwithstanding clause. The 7/50 Alberta amending formula was proposed, meaning Ontario and Quebec would not have a veto over constitutional amendments and there would be no fiscal compensation for provinces that opted out of programs in areas of provincial jurisdiction. It is noteworthy that Quebec had accepted the Alberta amending formula, but only if it could opt out of federal programs with compensation. And Trudeau had always supported a veto for Ontario and Quebec.

Trudeau initially refused the deal because of what he called the mealy-mouthed notwithstanding clause, which violated his sense of justice. The tide turned at about 10:30 p.m., when Trudeau received a phone call from Bill Davis, who indicated that Ontario would not support patriation without this compromise.

With the prospect of Ontario opposing him in London, Trudeau worried that Britain would drag its feet until his time in office came to an end. Trudeau relented, fearing that he would have no patriation and no charter. In time, Trudeau tried to blame Chrétien for the notwithstanding clause, which Chrétien refuted in his memoirs: "I recommended it, but [Trudeau] gave it."

Lévesque was oblivious to this turn of events. Unbeknownst to him, his gang members had abandoned him. He later said the other premiers had a vision of politics that could easily be turned by a couple of cocktails. Afterwards, Saskatchewan negotiator Roy McMurtry claimed that the positions taken by the gang before the conference were simply a stance from which they would bargain. That came as news to Lévesque, and revealed a flaw in his negotiating strategy. Once he signed on with the gang of eight, he could not move. For him it was all or nothing, while for the others it was the opening gambit in a longer bargaining process.

The next morning, after Trudeau had secured a five-year sunset clause on any provincial override against the charter, and a guarantee that his cherished minority language rights would be exempt from the notwithstanding clause, he turned to Lévesque and said, "Come on, surprise me. Make some kind of gesture now that you've lost this inning. Come along and we'll all do this together."

But there was nothing on the table for Lévesque. Even Quebec's historical constitutional veto had been taken away. Quebec had lost some control over education, notably over who could access it in the English language. And there was no compensation when the federal government intervened in areas of provincial jurisdiction. The deal was far worse for Quebec than what Trudeau had proposed in Victoria in 1971.

Thus, the Quebec government refused to sign the constitution. In wrapping up the conference, Trudeau did not want to celebrate a grand nation-building moment. Sensing the risk and fragility of the deal, Trudeau sheepishly said, "We better grab the signatures and run before anyone changes their mind."

For Lévesque, it was a total betrayal. He called it "the night of the long knives," the expression commonly used to describe Adolf Hitler's purge of his political opponents in 1934. Trudeau had little sympathy for Lévesque, but the man who concocted the deal behind the scenes, Jean Chrétien, was more contrite. In his first autobiography, *Straight from the Heart*, Chrétien wrote:

> It was one of the saddest moments in my career to see Québec so isolated, particularly when Lévesque asked, "Won't you please give me back my right of veto?" Personally I felt it was a proper request, not for Québec as a province but for a minority population with unique concerns in linguistic and cultural matters, but it was too late. Lévesque had given up Québec's veto when he made a deal with the gang of eight and now he had to pay the price.[88]

Chrétien, who had served as a loyal soldier to Trudeau, acknowledged the significance of the fact that our constitution was amended without the support of a major province. We are left to wonder what Trudeau would have done had Ontario, rather than Quebec, been the lone holdout.

Recognizing the implications for national unity, in the weeks that followed, Chrétien persuaded Trudeau to accept a modest amendment giving Quebec fiscal compensation when it opted out of amendments that affected culture and education, and control over the circumstances under which immigrants would have minority education rights.[89/90]

Upon leaving the government conference centre in Ottawa, Lévesque remarked, "Maybe second thoughts and further events will make them understand that this will have incalculable consequences." He later used stronger language, saying, "Trudeau m'a fourré" — "Trudeau fucked me." Lévesque committed to use any means necessary to block any limits on Quebec's established authority.

Trudeau scoffed at opposition from Quebec, noting that 71 out of 75 federal MPs from Quebec voted in favour of the constitutional deal in the House of Commons. In his memoirs, he used convoluted logic to combine these votes with those cast against the accord in Quebec's National Assembly to suggest that a clear majority of all elected members from Quebec voted for the patriation package.[91] The reality was that the Liberal MPs in Ottawa under his wing, bound by party discipline, had no mandate to implement a constitutional deal, let alone one that stood opposed by the Quebec government.

In December 1981, Senator Ernest Manning, an appointee of Pierre Trudeau, predicted dire consequences for Canada stemming from patriation without the government of Quebec on board:

> Where does Québec stand on this matter today? She stands ... more isolated than ever from the rest of Canada, more polarized, more angry, and more resentful because she feels she was betrayed ... There is no real profit in gaining a new constitution if in the process you lose a nation ... If adopted, it will pose the dangerous, unnecessary, and unacceptable risk of precipitating Québec separation from Canada. It is a ticking constitutional time bomb with the potential to blow Confederation apart.[92]

THE NEW CONSTITUTION Act, proclaimed into law by Queen Elizabeth II on April 17, 1982, was not greeted with a day of national celebration, certainly not in Quebec. And it received no commemorations on its twentieth or thirtieth anniversaries either. If a constitution is intended to unify the country, then Trudeau's document failed to pass this test.

Trudeau proclaimed it a sign that Canada had come of age. In his view, the new constitution reinforced protection for French-speaking Canadians outside Quebec and English-speaking Canadians inside that province. Lévesque held a different view: "Sooner or later [federal Liberals] will have to answer to an entire people whose trust they have betrayed."

Turning to the opponents of the accord from Quebec, Trudeau suggested that they held a minority position, based on the results of the 1980 referendum. This argument confused Quebecers' desire to remain a part of Canada in 1980 with their judgement on whether the province received a fair deal in 1982.

Trudeau claimed that further constitutional change might yet meet the approval of Quebecers. "The process of constitutional reform has not come to an end. The two orders of government ... must try to work out a better division of powers among governments." In reality, Trudeau harboured little interest in giving any powers to the provinces. He believed in a strong central government. Trudeau's offer was as meaningful as the one he made when trying to win the referendum on sovereignty association, when he said he was not for the status quo. Indeed, Trudeau would later vehemently and decisively oppose the two unanimous constitutional accords reached after he left office.

The deal was done, and Trudeau was pleased. Canada had a new constitution, fully amendable by Canadians. In his memoirs he wrote:

> I certainly prefer to have a charter with a notwithstanding clause than no charter at all. I regretted the dropping of the referendum provision [for amendments], and I favoured the Victoria amending formula that would have given Québec a veto. But it would have been hard to insist on a Québec veto after the premier of Québec himself had given it away in his April 1981 agreement with the gang of eight. On the whole, the constitution act largely enshrined the values I had been advocating since I wrote my first article in *Cité Libre* in 1950. And most important, it meant that no longer would there be an easy way for provinces to blackmail the federal govern-ment by holding out for more new powers in exchange for allowing patriation.[93]

A great many Quebecers felt stunned by Trudeau's about-face. They voted for him in massive numbers in 1980, when he had said nothing about the constitution. They took his word during the referendum that he would reform the federation. At no time did they believe a vote for Trudeau was a vote to patriate the constitution over the express objections of the government of Quebec. At no time did they endorse constitutional reform that superseded Quebec's power over the language of its education system. At no time did they endorse recognizing multicultural communities across the nation, but not recognizing Quebec as a distinct society. Had Trudeau revealed his true plans during the heat of the referendum campaign, the outcome of that vote may have been entirely different.

Many federalists in Quebec, like Conservative Senator David Angus worried about what Trudeau had done.

The rest of the country may have thought Trudeau was doing good work by keeping Quebec in Canada, but he did no favour to those who were working on the ground in Quebec to extol the virtues of federalism to win the hearts and minds of the people. Trudeau's uncompromising gunslinger approach alienated many Quebec federalists who understood that a more cooperative approach to federalism was required. We were not cheering wildly when patriation came because we knew there would be a day of reckoning.[94]

In the end, what should have been a victory for all Canadians was a constitutional deal that few could feel good about. In his desperation to fulfil his lifelong political ambition, Trudeau presided over a process that alienated an already-isolated province. Had Trudeau failed in his quest for a new constitution, he still would still have been celebrated for keeping Quebec in Canada. He would have been the prime minister who stared down the separatists, defeated terrorists in the October Crisis, and won the 1980 referendum. He had also endeared himself to Quebecers with official bilingualism and profitable federalism. But rather than simply claiming victory for his side, Trudeau gave the separatists new ammunition with which to fight.

It remained to be seen what the Charter would mean to individual Canadians. That would be up to the Supreme Court of Canada to determine. The court would soon have the power to strike down federal and provincial legislation inconsistent with its interpretation of the Charter. It would soon rule on the great social and legal questions of the day, issuing a raft of new precedents that would define Canada for generations to come.

As to the incalculable consequences of patriating the constitution over the objections of one of Canada's founding partners, it would not take long for Canadians to appreciate their full impact — and the risk they represented to the nation.

CHAPTER 8

MEECH, CHARLOTTETOWN AND THE 1995 QUEBEC REFERENDUM

Alas, only one eventuality hadn't been foreseen: that one day the government of Canada might fall into the hands of a weakling. It has now happened.

I N 1982, TRUDEAU was unconcerned that Quebec's National Assembly had rejected the Constitution Act. To his thinking, he had given Canada a Charter of Rights and Freedoms and the power to amend its own constitution. He had bolstered minority language rights and triumphed over Quebec nationalists in the 1980 referendum. His work was done, and the show was over.

But many observers saw a sequel on the horizon. Unfinished business with Quebec posed a standing danger to national unity. And so, back to the storyboard: Trudeau's successor, Progressive Conservative Prime Minister Brian Mulroney, sought and obtained unanimity among first ministers on constitutional amendments at Meech Lake and Charlottetown.

Like a zombie who will not rest, Trudeau rose up to kill both deals with a few appearances, a scattering of op-eds, and behind-the-scenes work with the premier of Newfoundland. Never before has a former prime minister so actively and decisively thwarted the will of a sitting prime minister, not to mention the Canadian Parliament and the provincial legislatures representing over 95 percent of our citizens. The consequences of the failure to ratify the Meech Lake and Charlottetown Accords played themselves out in the 1995 Quebec referendum, a horror show for federalists that nearly destroyed the nation Trudeau purported to save with his patriation of the Constitution in 1982.

SHORTLY AFTER BEING sworn in as prime minister, with the largest number of seats in Canadian history, Mulroney asked Trudeau if he would give him the benefit of his views on a few matters, including the constitution. Trudeau agreed.

Mulroney had made his vision for constitutional reform clear when campaigning in the 1984 federal election. At a campaign stop in Sept Isles, Quebec, he observed that after the 1980 referendum, Trudeau had ostracized the province constitutionally. Mulroney committed himself to revising the constitution such that the Quebec National Assembly would give its consent with honour and enthusiasm.[1] This nation-building initiative was anchored in the premise that "If Québec is strong, then Canada is strong."

Perhaps Trudeau thought that with René Lévesque still premier of Quebec, Mulroney was just spouting political rhetoric. In his memoirs, Trudeau wrote that the constitution had been put to bed in 1982 and that Mulroney should have ignored complaints or aspirations coming from *la belle province*. This view contradicts Trudeau's statements during the 1980 Quebec referendum, and his long-standing pledge to provincial premiers that a "political round" of constitutional change on the division of powers would naturally follow his so-called "people's package" with a Charter of Rights and Freedoms.

But after Trudeau got what he wanted in 1982, he changed his tune. "For the first time since the first patriation attempt in 1927, Canadians had the luxury of giving themselves constitutional peace by closing – for years to come, if need be – this particular can of worms. Who could have foretold that a new government would be so unwise is to reopen it, a couple of years later?"[2]

But with the election of a federalist Liberal government in Quebec in May of 1985, and with the symbolic return of the Canadian flag to Quebec's National Assembly, Mulroney decided the time was right to fulfill his commitment and mandate.

For its part, the newly elected Quebec government of Robert Bourassa identified five conditions to be met before a constitutional package would be placed before Quebec's National Assembly for ratification. These were:

1. Veto over constitutional amendments
2. Role in the appointment of Supreme Court judges
3. Increased powers over immigration
4. Limitations on federal spending power in areas of provincial jurisdiction
5. Constitutional recognition of Quebec as a distinct society

According to Gordon Robertson, the most senior civil servant to have advised Pearson and Trudeau on constitutional matters, the five conditions were the most moderate proposals to emerge from any Quebec government since the Victoria constitutional conference of 1971.[3]

Motivated by the desire to heal the wound inflicted on Quebec by the 1982 patriation, the Government of Canada and all provinces reached an agreement at Meech Lake, Quebec on April 30, 1987. It was the first time the federal government and the provinces had unanimously agreed on a major constitutional arrangement since Confederation.

Under the amending formula established by Trudeau in 1982, each of the respective federal and provincial legislatures had three years to approve the deal. But with support from the opposition parties in the House of Commons, and with a unanimous agreement from the federal government and the provinces, Meech Lake looked like a *fait accompli*.

After the Meech Lake Accord was struck, representatives of both the federal and Quebec governments met personally with Trudeau to brief him on developments. Officials explained the fundamentals of the accord, pointing out that there was nothing in Meech Lake that Trudeau had not offered to the provinces over the previous 20 years. Trudeau told federal representative Norman Spector that he may not have done it that way, "But I don't want to pee on Mulroney's parade."[4] Initially Trudeau told a few Liberal MPs that he would not intervene in Meech Lake, but he changed his mind after criticisms about his constitutional legacy surfaced within Liberal ranks.

Trudeau had been stirred to anger. Then, a bombshell: Before the Meech Lake text was finalized, Trudeau penned an article that ran simultaneously in English and French in the *Toronto Star* and *La Presse* on May 27, 1987. He savaged both the Accord and its signatories.

Trudeau viewed Meech Lake not just as a bad deal, but the death of Canada. He predicted the end of a bilingual and multicultural country, replaced by two Canadas, each defined in terms of its language.

In his writings and speeches, Trudeau frequently recognized the social reality that Quebec was a "distinct society" within Canada. Yet he now warned that minority rights would be trampled if this reality received constitutional recognition. He called Meech Lake a plot to emasculate the Charter of Rights and Freedoms and lamented that those who believed in equality of citizenship founded on a set of commonly shared values "had nothing left but tears."

By allowing provinces to opt out of federal programs in areas of provincial jurisdiction and accept compensation instead, Trudeau predicted the balkanization of social services. By giving provinces a say in senate and judicial appointments, as well as a veto over constitutional amendments, Trudeau thought Canada was on the fast track to sovereignty association, with the federal government becoming a backwater for political and bureaucratic rejects.

Trudeau contended that he had ended a century-old constitutional debate in which provinces had withheld patriation unless and until they had been given more powers. Until the passage of the 1982 Constitution Act, Trudeau posited that provinces "had enrolled in the school of blackmail of which Québec was the founder and top-ranking graduate."

Trudeau admitted that the Quebec government was not pleased with the 1982 constitution, but that its provisions bound them nonetheless. He claimed to have made an effort at niceness in patriation, which ended up winning the support of nine provinces out of ten. Trudeau saw Meech Lake as a sop to Quebec nationalists, whom he called perpetual "sore losers."

> That bunch of snivelers should simply have been sent packing and been told to stop having tantrums like spoiled adolescents. But our current political leaders lack courage. By rushing to the rescue of the unhappy losers, they hope to gain votes in Québec; in reality, they are only flaunting their political stupidity and their ignorance of the demographic data regarding nationalism. It would be difficult to imagine a more total bungle.

Trudeau could not imagine why Mulroney would launch such an adventure when "he had inherited a winning hand." Since the provinces could no longer bargain for more powers as the price for patriation, Trudeau contended he had leveled the playing field. "Even a united front of the 10 provinces could not have forced the federal government to give ground." With the assurance of a creative equilibrium between the provinces and the central government, Trudeau claimed the federation was "set to last a thousand years!" (A disturbing reference, given that Hitler had predicted the same fate for his Third Reich).

Thinking back to his experience in 1971, Trudeau warned that Bourassa would reject Meech in the same way that he spurned the Victoria Accord, adding sarcastically that this "would inevitably clear the way for the real saviours: the separatists." On this point, Trudeau was correct: rejection of Meech Lake by any premier, modest as it was in the eyes of Quebec nationalists, would become a powerful tool in the arsenal of the Parti Québécois.

Trudeau then got personal with Mulroney:

> Alas, only one eventuality hadn't been foreseen: that one day the government of Canada might fall into the hands of a weakling. It has now happened. And the Right Honourable Brian Mulroney, PC, MP, with the complicity of 10 provincial premiers, has already entered into history as the author of a constitutional document which – if it is accepted by the people and their legislators – will render the Canadian state totally impotent. That would destine it, given the dynamics of power, to eventually be governed by eunuchs.

Trudeau did not temper his vitriol. Meech Lake was not just unwise, it was stupid; Mulroney was not just weak, he was a eunuch; "distinct society" did not recognize social reality, it emasculated the Charter of Rights and Freedoms; the unanimous agreement was not just irresponsible, it heralded the end of Canada.

The attack was vintage Trudeau. Even before running for Parliament in 1965, Trudeau was known to eviscerate rather than debate his opponents. One friendly biographer, George Radwanski, said Trudeau could be "ruthless in debate, abrupt in manner, and remote and indifferent in personal relations to the point of insult."[5] Another Trudeau friend, Ron Graham, wrote that whenever Trudeau felt he was under attack, his competitive instinct was to lash back with answers that may have been eminently quotable or made for electrifying moments on television, "but they weren't particularly informative or precisely true."[6] Bob Rae wrote that Trudeau needed an enemy to be at his best, which was when he was his most lucid, brilliant and acerbic, and could revel in the tricks and excesses of rhetorical argument.[7] Mark MacGuigan, Trudeau's foreign affairs minister in the early 1980s, wrote that Trudeau set out to destroy his opponents' self-respect. "He wanted to demean them, to rub their noses in their deficiencies."[8]

FRANCIS FOX, WHO had held a senior role in a Trudeau cabinet, was asked why his former boss was actively undermining Meech Lake. It was simple: "He couldn't stand to see Brian Mulroney succeed where he had failed."[9]

At the time, Trudeau sided with a small minority of detractors, but all he needed was to convince one provincial premier not to pass Meech Lake, and the deal died. The requirement for unanimity was a legacy from his 1982 constitutional pact. Despite the long odds, Trudeau laced up his boxing gloves. Citing ancient Greek battles, he issued this rallying cry to his friend Ramsay Cook: "So carry on the fight, like the little band at Thermopylae. But will we have our Salamis? Off to consult Thucydides again."[10]

Not only had every province supported Meech Lake, but so too had all parties in the House of Commons, including Trudeau's Liberal successor John Turner. In Turner's view, the Accord was not radically different from the Victoria Charter.[11] Turner noted that Trudeau had promised renewed federalism in the 1980 referendum debate and that promise had to be fulfilled.[12] Turner thought Trudeau's objections to Meech Lake were academic and legalistic and, in effect, not those worthy of a nation builder.[13]

With all-party support in the House of Commons, it was expected that Trudeau's objections would remain a footnote in Canada's constitutional history. Trudeau even acknowledged in his memoirs that he thought his interventions would likely be too little and too late. Still, he was not about to surrender to an agreement that he said would cause the breakup of confederation and drop Canada into the lap of the United States of America.

The three-year clock began ticking when the Quebec National Assembly ratified the Accord on June 23, 1987. The historic occasion finally answered the question: What did Quebec want? But in relatively short order, several of the premiers who had signed the accord found themselves out of office, or ended up facing greater opposition than at the time Meech Lake was signed.

A further complication arose after a 1989 Supreme Court of Canada ruling was handed down striking down certain provisions of Quebec's

Bill 101, a law that restricted the use of English on commercial signs. The court found the law violated Quebecers' Charter right to freedom of expression. In response, the Bourassa government invoked article 33 of the constitution, the Notwithstanding Clause, to override the ruling, as was his government's right.

Reaction was swift. The media reported claims that had the distinct-society clause been in force, the courts would not have disabled the law. For those who thought Charter rights should reign supreme, the distinct-society clause took on an unsettling new meaning.

Meanwhile, Trudeau continued his attack on Meech Lake by appearing before a joint committee of the House of Commons and Senate, and then before the Senate Submissions Group on the Meech Lake Accord in his capacity as an individual Canadian. Beyond warning parliamentarians in general, Trudeau confronted Jean Chrétien, who was by then running for the Liberal leadership to replace John Turner. In the spring of 1990, at the home of Senator Leo Kolber, Chrétien mused about the impact of the defeat of Meech on a future Quebec referendum. At the time, Chrétien privately supported Meech, provided the Charter of Rights and Freedoms would be supreme. Trudeau told Chrétien, "If you support Meech, I will personally campaign against you for the Liberal leadership.[14]

Knowing that his support of Meech Lake would put him in conflict with Trudeau, another Liberal leadership candidate, Paul Martin, had arranged a private lunch with Trudeau before the leadership race got underway. Inevitably the subject of Meech Lake came up. Martin said the clause describing Quebec as a distinct society simply reflected reality without an increase in powers. Trudeau told Martin he was wrong. "No, Mr. Trudeau, *you* are wrong," responded Martin, at which point Trudeau declared the Mount Royal Club luncheon over.[15]

WHILE THE DEBATE over Meech Lake was often more emotional than substantive, a key point of contention was whether Trudeau had, in fact, already offered to meet Quebec's five conditions during his 15 years of constitutional negotiations. If he had, Trudeau's opposition to Meech Lake would amount to little more than a vanity project.

Trudeau had long supported a veto for Quebec over constitutional amendments, including in the 1971 Victoria Charter. The difference with Meech Lake was that, rather than giving only Quebec and Ontario permanent vetoes, it treated all provinces equally. In 1976 Trudeau sent a letter to the premiers suggesting an amending formula that called for unanimity for all major constitutional amendments. As it was, the 1982 Constitution required unanimity over amendments to the monarchy, the use of English and French, the composition of the Supreme Court and the amending formula itself.

On the limitation of the federal spending power in areas of provincial jurisdiction, which Trudeau claimed would balkanize the nation, he himself had included a provision in the 1982 Constitution that enabled opting out on matters related to education and culture. Meech stipulated that compensation would only be paid to provinces implementing programs or initiatives compatible with national objectives. Trudeau quibbled over the meaning of the word "compatible" and who got to define "national objectives." Robertson thought Trudeau's position was absurd, arguing that it was only logical to provide offsetting compensation when the federal government unilaterally barged into areas of exclusive provincial jurisdiction.[16]

The idea of recognizing the particular societal needs of individual provinces was not new to Trudeau. He had agreed to the so-called Cullen-Couture agreement in 1978, which gave Quebec a role in selecting immigrants to the province based on ability to adapt and contribute to the province. This had allowed the Quebec government to make the capacity of immigrants to speak and work in French a key consideration.

On the composition of the Supreme Court, both the Victoria Charter and Meech Lake Accord included a role for the provinces in submitting nominations, while leaving it to the federal government to make the final selection. Trudeau worried that some deadlock might arise when the federal and provincial governments did not agree. The reality was that voters had been electing federal and provincial governments that disagreed in areas of shared jurisdiction since Confederation, but the business of the nation had always managed to continue.

On nominating senators from provincial lists, Trudeau had proposed that one-half of the senators be *directly appointed* by provincial governments in his Bill C-60, which never passed. Under Trudeau's proposal, the federal government would have had no say in these appointments. But in opposing Meech Lake, Trudeau claimed that senators chosen by the federal government from provincial lists would be loyal only to their province, creating a situation in which "no federal legislation could be passed." Yet Canada has regularly had Senate majorities appointed by a prime minister from one party who sit in judgment on the legislation put forward by a government of another party, and still, legislation is passed.

Trudeau was most agitated by the distinct-society clause. He did not deny the reality that Quebec *was* a distinct society, but thought that the clause was better placed in the preamble rather than as an interpretative clause in the body of the constitution. Trudeau detested the notion that any group, such as Quebec's French-speaking majority, would have rights and power that could work to the possible detriment of the rights of the individual and the minority. Of course, Trudeau's constitution also endorsed certain group rights: for Aboriginal peoples, women, multicultural communities and regions. But any provision that addressed the reality and distinctiveness of Quebec, and its role in protecting the French language, represented an affront. Trudeau absurdly wrote that future Quebec governments could use the distinct-society clause to "deport a couple of hundred thousand of non-French-Speaking Quebecers ... expel people, certainly to [force people to] shut their traps up if they think they can speak English in public."[17]

The reality, according to Brian Dickson, the late chief justice of the Supreme Court of Canada, was that that the courts already took into account Quebec's distinctive role in protecting and promoting its own francophone character.[18] Formally recognizing that fact, Dickson declared, would not have changed much. Constitutional scholar and University of Toronto Professor Emeritus Peter Russell believes that the distinct-society clause in Meech would have had little bearing on interpreting the Charter of Rights and Freedoms. "To those who say it would gut the Charter I say what evidence do they have for that? I don't think the evidence supports them. As to putting it into the preamble ... that's just splitting hairs, I have no respect for that distinction."[19]

Finally, Trudeau criticized the federal government for getting nothing of national value in return for Meech Lake, such as expanded powers to sustain the economic union. Trudeau failed to comprehend that Meech Lake was not intended to rebalance federal and provincial powers broadly, but to gain Quebec's political acceptance for Canada's constitution. Gordon Robertson described Meech Lake as a nation-building exercise that deserved to succeed, since it removed an injury that "could not be left untended." That's because Trudeau, unlike any prime minister before him, had enacted a constitutional change that directly affected the powers of a province without its consent. In short, Meech Lake's goal was to rectify Trudeau's flawed constitution.

AS NEW PREMIERS came on the scene, Trudeau recruited fresh allies to his cause. Frank McKenna replaced Richard Hatfield as premier of

New Brunswick on October 13, 1987. McKenna wanted changes to the Accord. The Manitoba NDP government of Howard Pawley in Manitoba was defeated in 1988, replaced with a minority Progressive Conservative government led by Gary Filmon. Like McKenna, Filmon wanted changes to Meech Lake. An even more vociferous opponent to Meech Lake in the Manitoba legislature was Liberal leader Sharon Carstairs. She didn't want to change the Accord: she wanted it dead.

Meech Lake's ultimate legislative foe was Newfoundland premier Clyde Wells. Despite having lost his own seat, Wells became premier on April 20, 1989. On April 21, 1990, the Newfoundland legislature rescinded his province's endorsement of Meech Lake. The original ratification had happened in July 1988, by a vote of 28 to 10.[20]

The federal government addressed the concerns of Manitoba and New Brunswick in a companion agreement to Meech Lake, which followed the work of a commission headed by Tory MPs Jean Charest and Jim Edwards. The Charest-Edwards committee tabled its report on May 17, but the "watering down" of the Accord caused Lucien Bouchard, a senior Mulroney cabinet minister, to lash out. "The government," claimed Bouchard "is making an alliance with those who want Québec to continue to be humiliated." Mulroney fired Bouchard from his post on May 22.

At that point, Meech Lake still showed signs of life, but the three-year deadline of June 23, 1990 was fast approaching. New Brunswick ratified the Accord on June 15. Premier Gary Filmon introduced it into the Manitoba legislature on June 20. But to consider the resolution on short notice, Filmon needed the unanimous support of the legislature to waive the rules. This support foundered on the opposition of a lone MPP, Elijah Harper, who said Meech Lake failed to address the concerns of Aboriginal peoples. (In this regard, the same could be said of Trudeau's 1982 constitution).

The situation in Manitoba was not considered fatal, however, since the federal government had a legal interpretation that would have given Manitoba's government more time to put the matter to a vote. Mulroney announced that Ottawa would apply to the Supreme Court to have the ratification deadline extended, but only if the province of Newfoundland ratified the Accord first.

And so it all came down to Newfoundland. Advising Premier Wells on constitutional policy was Deborah Coyne. She had briefly taught constitutional law at the University of Toronto and had once worked for Prime Minister John Turner. Wells hired Coyne because she was an outspoken critic of Meech Lake. But her involvement with Trudeau was more personal. Trudeau first spotted Coyne at a debate she co-hosted in 1979 as a fresh-faced law student. He later surprised her with an invitation to be his personal guest at a 1980 constitutional conference with the premiers.[21] The two had a romantic relationship, which produced a daughter, Sarah Elisabeth Coyne, born on May 5 1991.[22]

Mulroney pulled out all the stops to woo Newfoundland legislators and took the unprecedented step of addressing the province's legislature just before its scheduled vote on Meech Lake. In addition to articulating the nation-building elements of the Accord, Mulroney reflected on a future Quebec referendum and what might ensue should Meech Lake be defeated. After Wells gave his assurances that he would allow a free vote, Mulroney returned to Ottawa. Wells then reneged on his promise, and cancelled the vote.

The weekend that Meech Lake expired, the Liberal Party was holding its leadership convention to replace John Turner. Those in the Jean Chrétien camp were generally opposed to the Accord; most notable among them were Trudeau and Wells, who were seen laughing amiably together on the convention floor.[23] Some members of the Paul Martin leadership team had donned black armbands to signal the death of Meech Lake. "I was a supporter of Meech Lake," said Martin, "because I believed it strengthened Canada. It incorporated a fundamental recognition of Québec's place in our country and remedied a flaw in the 1981 patriation of the Constitution."

The editorial writers at *La Presse* concluded that Quebec could hold its head high. "After having said yes to Canada, it is English Canada which has said no to Québec."[24] Historian Desmond Morton assessed the blame this way: "The Meech Lake accord was made necessary by the promises of a renewed federalism made to Québec by Pierre Elliott Trudeau to win No votes in the 1980 referendum and by Trudeau's failure or reluctance to keep those promises in the Constitution Act of 1982. And no one played a bigger part in destroying Meech Lake than Trudeau."[25] Mulroney concurred, saying that Meech would have passed were it not for Trudeau.[26] For his part, Trudeau advised shelving any constitutional talks for a decade or more.

THE DEFEAT OF Meech Lake, along with the consequent split in Liberal ranks and the removal of Lucien Bouchard from Mulroney's cabinet, led to the creation of a new political party in the federal House of Commons: the Bloc Québécois. The Bloc, led by Lucien Bouchard, included seven other MPs, five from the Progressive Conservative

Party and two from the Liberal Party. Gilles Duceppe, who would go on to lead the party from 1997 to 2011, bolstered the Bloc caucus with a by-election win in 1990 in the riding of Laurier-Ste. Marie.

In making his case for the Bloc, Bouchard's target was not the Mulroney government or Clyde Wells, but Pierre Trudeau. Bouchard said that Trudeau went to Ottawa to "screw Québec ... with a persistence that bordered on provocation."[27] Bouchard stirred his troops by reminding them of Trudeau's role in the 1980 referendum and patriation of the constitution: "Remember the rape, the shameless rape, of the commitment he had contracted at the referendum ... There is no democracy in the world where a dictator would have dared to ram a constitution that they did not want down the throat of a founding people."[28] He called the demise of the Meech Lake Accord the last straw. "After having been humiliated, insulted and ostracized from the constitution, we decided to once again trust English Canada. We almost begged to be readmitted, and English Canada said NO!"

In the 1993 federal election, the Bloc took 54 of Quebec's 75 seats. Ironically, the Bloc, a political party intent on the separation of Quebec from Canada, became Her Majesty's Loyal Opposition. This new political force not only represented Quebec's interest in the House of Commons, but also worked from its beachhead in Ottawa to create the conditions for Quebec to become a sovereign state. The Bloc maintained a stranglehold over Quebec's presence in Parliament through six consecutive federal elections, faltering only in 2011. When Gilles Duceppe was asked to explain the longevity and electoral political success of the Bloc, he would point directly to Trudeau. Quebecers needed a nationalist voice in Ottawa, he said, to stop politicians like Trudeau from taking away its powers as he did in 1982.

The tumult caused by Trudeau over Meech Lake was not limited to the Mulroney government. The Liberal caucus split over Meech Lake with those loyal to Trudeau and his vision unwilling to accept the leadership and direction of John Turner on the matter. According to Turner, this was more than just a policy disagreement: "Trudeau intervened and caused great divisions in the party. He did not clear it with me first and he didn't talk to me. There was no courtesy at all."[29]

With the demise of Meech, Bourassa rose in Quebec's National Assembly to declare that, regardless of what English Canada determined, Quebec was a distinct society. Taking a stand familiar to nationalists, Bourassa said that Quebec remained free to control its destiny and development. The federalist premier stood open to all options, including a possible referendum on independence.

The Liberal government in Quebec set up two task forces to consider the province's future. Mulroney also set up two working groups to address the unity question and asked his Foreign Affairs minister, Joe Clark, to take ministerial responsibility for the constitutional file.

Rather than deal only with Quebec's five demands, the next round of constitutional negotiations brought more parties and issues to the table. These included:

1. The division of powers between federal and provincial jurisdictions
2. A social charter covering areas such as health care and the environment
3. The free flow of goods, services and labour across the nation
4. National characteristics of citizenship, including the recognition of Quebec as a distinct society within Canada
5. Principles for Aboriginal self-government
6. Supreme Court appointments
7. A more equal, and possibly elected, Senate

All recognized political parties in the House of Commons, all provincial governments, First Nations groups, and, in the early days, public opinion polls, endorsed the resulting accord reached in Charlottetown. But unlike Meech Lake, the people of Canada would determine the fate of the Charlottetown accord in a referendum on October 26, 1992.

Trudeau made his views regarding the Charlottetown accord known in an article published in *Maclean's* magazine, and at a speech delivered at a Chinese restaurant in Montreal on October 1.[30] He called himself a diehard federalist who would vote No because he wanted a strong federal government.

Gordon Robertson dismissed Trudeau's legalistic and intellectual interpretation of Charlottetown as a fraud, designed to frighten, not to inform.[31] Nonetheless, after Trudeau's single speech at an obscure restaurant, support for Charlottetown outside Quebec dropped 20 points.[32]

Not all Trudeau loyalists agreed with his interpretation, however. Trudeau faced important opposition from his key constitutional fixer, Jean Chrétien, who, as Liberal leader, had endorsed Charlottetown. Chrétien argued the matter with Trudeau at a meeting in 1992.

Trudeau said the phrase "distinct society" gave Quebec strong powers to discriminate against the English, while Chrétien countered that the significance was symbolic. "Jean, there are no words that mean nothing," Trudeau replied. Chrétien admitted that that he didn't know too many such words, but in this case Trudeau had it wrong.[33]

It is also noteworthy that very few of Trudeau's French cabinet ministers from Quebec joined him in his denunciations of either the Charlottetown or Meech Lake accords. Bob Rae, once the Ontario NDP premier, observed pithily that Trudeau made anti-French bigotry respectable.[34]

But Trudeau had some strange bedfellows. Reform Party leader Preston Manning opposed Charlottetown, not just over concessions to Quebec, but as a perceived obstacle to Senate reform. Then-Reform MP, later Prime Minister Stephen Harper also found himself on the same side as Trudeau. While a virulent opponent of most of Trudeau's policies, Harper said it didn't bother him to line up with Trudeau on this issue. "Even though we're not fans of Mr. Trudeau's record, there is a significant overlap of philosophy on constitutional matters... Mr. Trudeau and the Reform Party share very strongly the belief that Québec nationalism can only be victorious or defeated. It cannot be accommodated."[35]

In the ensuing national referendum, voters rejected the Charlottetown Accord nationally by a vote of 54 percent to 46 percent. The Accord passed in New Brunswick, Newfoundland, Ontario and PEI, and failed in all western provinces, in Nova Scotia and in Quebec. Ironically, 63 percent of Newfoundlanders supported Charlottetown, despite that being the same province that Clyde Wells had determined would not support Meech Lake.

THE CONSEQUENCE OF the defeats of Meech and Charlottetown became clear on October 30, 1995, the night Quebecers voted in a second referendum on sovereignty. Quebecers were asked that day if, after having made a formal offer to Canada for a new economic and political partnership, they should become sovereign.[36] In this referendum, Trudeau was told by the federalist campaign to disappear over fears that his presence on the No campaign would not only hurt their vote, but possibly cause a riot.

The forces supporting separation cited Meech's demise as proof that Canada did not respect Quebec's aspirations. Trudeau blamed Mulroney, arguing that the rejection of his Accord allowed Quebec nationalists to say they had been unfairly treated, even insulted and humiliated.

Indeed, on the eve of the referendum, with the vote too close to call, the speech Mulroney gave to the Newfoundland legislature in 1990 on the importance of passing Meech Lake proved prophetic. "If Mr. Parizeau gets a chance to have a referendum ... on referendum night ... one thought is going to go through your mind ... Do you mean to tell me that we could have avoided all this through Meech Lake? ... With the Meech Lake accord having been signed on behalf of a united Canada, I would look forward with confidence to entering a referendum in the province of Québec ..."

Initially the referendum campaign went well for federalist forces. But momentum shifted the instant that the Parti Québécois stopped arguing for a yes vote on the basis of its economic and social studies. Mulroney saw the change in momentum this way: "They made Lucien Bouchard the lead negotiator and spokesperson. His first decision was to throw the studies in the wastebasket. He said the only question was the treason and betrayal of Québec by Pierre Trudeau and Jean Chrétien. And the polls switched overnight."[37]

Trudeau told his friend Gerry Levitan, who stood with him watching a massive unity rally fill the streets of Montreal three days before the vote, that he regretted the timidity of the federalists. Levitan watched Trudeau as he looked out of his office window, surveying the pan-Canadian crowd amassed to support the federalist option. Trudeau was, he noted, deep in thought, and hurting.[38]

That day Trudeau predicted a close result. It was 50.6 percent to 49.4 percent in favour of the federalist side.

OVER THE COURSE of his career, both in public office and in private life, Trudeau had taken enormous risks with his country — first by patriating the constitution without Quebec's consent, and then by publicly attacking and undermining two constitutional accords that sought to address this failing. In 1981, René Lévesque had called the consequences of Trudeau's actions incalculable. On October 30, 1995, those calculations came down to a mere 54,288 votes, the margin of victory for federalist forces in a referendum that kept Canada intact.

In language that is uncharacteristically harsh for a former Clerk of the Privy Council, Gordon Robertson wrote in his memoirs that he was appalled by Trudeau's conduct:

> Nothing, I think, in Canadian history rivals the irresponsibility Trudeau, a former prime minister, displayed in coming out of retirement to destroy the only prospect of an agreement

that would bring Québec into willing acceptance of the constitution that he himself later admitted was the calculated result of a *coup de force*.[39]

Peter Russell has a similar perspective: "It was Trudeau's boldness and gamble that got us into the mess that Meech Lake was trying to pull us out of and here he was screwing it up."

Many lifelong federalists from Quebec who had fought the separatists on the ground were devastated. Senator David Angus offered this assessment: "We finally got Quebec on board on very reasonable terms with Meech Lake, the first time since Confederation that a unanimous agreement is reached, and Trudeau and his acolytes like Clyde Wells and Donald Johnston go berserk and torpedo an agreement that would have settled the sovereignist question for a very long time. It was heartbreaking."[40]

Stéphane Dion, a future leader of the Liberal Party, called the defeat of Meech Lake, "the worst constitutional error in the history of Canada."[41] Had Meech passed, Dion speculated, there never would have been a referendum on sovereignty in Quebec in 1995.

Had the 1995 Quebec referendum gone the other way, as surely it could have, Trudeau may well have been remembered as the most divisive and destructive prime minister in Canadian history. And for what? Scuttling a constitutional deal that he considered imperfect? Waging a personal vendetta against Quebec nationalists? Preventing his successor from succeeding where he had failed?

Since 1989, much of what was in the Meech Lake Accord has become reality through federal and provincial agreements. With respect to Quebec being a distinct society, Stephen Harper went one step further when he spearheaded the passage of an all-party parliamentary resolution in 2006 affirming that the Quebecois people were not just a distinct society but also a *nation* within a united Canada.

These steps were not, as Trudeau might have warned, a slow march to separation, but gestures of respect and tolerance. And the political results are there to see. Despite the election of a minority PQ government in 2012, support for Quebec separation in 2013 stands at historic lows, while the Bloc Québécois has been decimated, reduced to only four seats in the House of Commons in the 2011 election.

SECTION III

THE JUST SOCIETY

CHAPTER 9

THE TRUDEAU SOCIAL DOCTRINE

Heckler: Hey Trudeau, what happened to your Just Society?
Trudeau: Ask Jesus Christ. He promised it first.

PIERRE TRUDEAU CAME to power with three goals in mind. First, he wanted to crush Quebec nationalism by asserting the French Fact in Canada and by strengthening the federal government. Second, he wanted to patriate the Canadian constitution. Third, he wanted to achieve what he called a *just society*.

AS A CATCH phrase for the 1968 Liberal leadership campaign, the just society presented a view against whose nobility few could argue. Looking more like that of a philosopher than professional politician, Trudeau's posture fit well with an era in which protestors lined the streets demanding social change. The reality was that, as a political philosophy, it was difficult to distinguish Trudeau's vision for a just society from socialism. But the phrase sounded more eloquent — and was an easier sell.

In the early days of the 1968 election campaign, journalists asked Trudeau to elaborate on how he could know if a society were, in fact, just. He replied that, in a legal sense, it meant freedom: "It means freeing an individual so he will be rid of his shackles and permitted to fulfill himself in society in the way which he judges best without being bound up by standards of morality which have nothing to do with law and order but which have to do with prejudice and religious superstition."[1] This classically liberal reply aligned perfectly with the sorts of initiatives Trudeau undertook as a cabinet minister.

Shortly after being appointed to federal cabinet, Trudeau told journalist Peter C. Newman that it was his intention to use his position as justice minister to advance societal change. Rather than simply functioning as the government's legal advisor, Trudeau wanted to use his perch to plan for the society of tomorrow. Trudeau said he would apply the disciplines of sociology and economics to "provide a framework for our evolving way of life ... so there's no curtailment of intellectual or physical liberty."[2]

This approach was evident on December 21, 1967, when Trudeau declared, "The state has no place in the bedrooms of the nation." While Trudeau gets the credit for the quip (including in such notable books as *Speeches that changed the world*)[3] he cribbed the remark from a *Globe and Mail* editorial written by Martin O'Malley nine days previously ("Obviously the state's responsibility should be to legislate rules for a well-ordered society. It has no right or duty to creep into the bedrooms of the nation.")[4]

After landing the justice portfolio, Trudeau's officials advised him to gain some experience with the easy files. "No," he replied. "I prefer to start with the most difficult one." Removing homosexuality from the Criminal Code and making abortions more accessible might have been controversial, but not discordant with the liberalization of society happening across North America and in Europe at the time.

Trudeau clearly connected better with his times than did Robert Stanfield, the stiff and dour leader of the Progressive Conservative Party. It was hard to imagine Stanfield saying, as Trudeau did, "It is appropriate for an individual to ask forgiveness of sins from God, but not from the Minister of Justice." So began Trudeau's mission to make Canada a just society.

TRUDEAU'S VISION EXCEEDED the elimination of systemic barriers to individual liberty. He considered the capitalist economic system inherently oppressive, restricting the ability of the poor and weak to reach their full potential. Before he entered politics, Trudeau wrote about the protection of individual freedoms against "collective tyranny" and of "a just distribution of the national wealth."[5] Trudeau, of course, knew one side of this equation, having had the advantage of being born into privilege and wealth.

The support of an activist government, Trudeau argued, would enable individuals to succeed: "How can we call a society just unless it is organized in such a way as to give each his due, regardless of his state of birth, his means or his health?"[6] It troubled Trudeau that, in the Canada of the late 1960s, only the wealthy like himself had the opportunity to realize their full potential. He would later comment that liberty was actually oppressive if it only applied to the privileged:

> Who else right now can afford to be free except for the rich? But where does this leave others who are scrambling to survive? But equality of opportunity must be the essence of a just society. Because if liberty is not for everyone — an equality of liberty, if you like — then liberty too can become a tyranny.[7]

Beyond what freedom might mean to individuals, Trudeau wanted the government to ensure every region of the country was succeeding:

> Rather than develop [economic justice] in terms of social legislation and welfare benefits, which I do not reject or condemn, I feel that at this time it is more important to develop in terms of groups of people ... The just society means not giving them a bit more money or a bit more welfare. The just society for them means permitting the province or the region as a whole to have a developing economy. In other words, not to try to help merely the individuals, but to try to help the region itself to make all parts of Canada livable in an acceptable sense.[8]

Without offering particulars in 1968 about how he would deliver this just society, Trudeau dodged the likely critics who would have been keen to warn Canadians about the economic and social dangers of big and activist government. Trudeau focused only on the vision, and a new doctrine whereby our national government would intervene to address regional and individual inequality. While the federation had always provided for transfer payments to economically weaker provinces, Trudeau signaled his intent to use the power of the federal government much more aggressively.

Careful not to over-promise and threaten criticism regarding government excess, Trudeau said he would not open the spending floodgates, and that he was "no Santa Claus" with goodies to hand out. Canadians nodded affirmatively, and then willingly took the bait. A *Just Society* that wouldn't cost more was an easy proposition for Canadians to accept. It took fifteen-and-a-half years of incremental and radical change with Trudeau at the helm for Canadians to appreciate fully what he had in mind – and who would pay for it.

CHAPTER 10

THE RICH AND THE POOR

Beyond funding and protecting the Pearson government's legacy,
we also extended the welfare state.

LESTER PEARSON BEQUEATHED an ambitious social agenda to Trudeau, much of it cost-shared with provincial governments. Trudeau furthered that agenda, although he ended a prominent feature of our social programs – universality – to target income support better to those most in need.[1] While his programs offered improvements to low-income seniors, the basic distribution of income among Canadians remained largely unchanged after Trudeau's four terms as prime minister. If income equality across social classes was his goal, he came up well short of the mark. But in his attempts to remake the government's social contract with Canadians, he damaged the country by removing incentives to work and by diminishing the sense of self-reliance in many regions of the country.

TRUDEAU'S FIRST MAJOR foray in social policy came in 1971 with reforms to the Unemployment Insurance System (reviewed later in more detail in the economic section). Unemployment benefits increased by 65 percent. The qualification period was cut in half. The benefit period was extended by 40 percent. Persons who lost their jobs due to illness, maternity leave, and retirement became eligible to collect.

A more generous system gave a major income boost to regions experiencing chronically high unemployment, and to areas dominated by seasonal work. Those who worked the summer tourist trade could be employed for eight weeks, yet collect a year-'round income. Agricultural workers could make their hay when the sun was shining and collect the dole for the rest of the year. The fishing industry suddenly became dramatically more lucrative for those who followed predictable but short work schedule.

The changes also gave rise to a campaign led by the Canadian Federation of Independent Business, called "Wake up Canada: There is no free lunch."[2] The inevitable increase in unemployment insurance premiums was a drain on the resources of all employers and the large majority of workers who funded the system. It also created a dependency trap for those who came to rely on the UI system as a way of life.

Far from helping individuals reach their potential, as Trudeau had hoped, the reforms produced personal and regional stagnation. In his book *Fearful Symmetry*, Brian Lee Crowley chronicles how the number of people dependent on social programs in the 1970s rose regardless of whether the economy grew or not.[3] Workers no long migrated from areas with few jobs to areas of economic opportunity. This shift occurred, Crowley argues, because of unemployment insurance and regional development policies.

While Trudeau contended that people should not be required to move to find employment – allowing for habitual unemployment – Crowley believes the absence of work devastated those affected. "Work gives people a sense of power over their lives because they produce things that others value." His research documented that those not working had a 48 percent greater risk of having a major depression than those employed.

While those who collected unemployment insurance appreciated the financial support, Trudeau did them no favours by removing a need for substantive and enduring work. He also eradicated any sense of justice for workers and employers who paid into the system but rarely benefited from its provisions. Ultimately, even Trudeau had to backtrack on some of his reforms less than a decade after introducing them.

BEFORE TRUDEAU, UNIVERSAL accessibility meant that recipients of Canada's social programs were not stigmatized by class. Trudeau changed that policy, targeting benefits to those in greatest need. He started with Family Allowance, a foundational element of Canada's social support system since WWII. The "baby bonus," introduced in 1944, was a universal non-taxable benefit paid monthly to Canadian families, based on the number of dependent children per household. It was particularly popular in Quebec, which had the highest birth rate in the country.

Between 1945 and 1973, the benefit increased only once, which meant its value substantially eroded over time due to inflation. In 1972, Trudeau proposed to enhance the benefits paid to families in the bottom third of income earners, reduce benefits to those in the middle third, and cut off those in the upper third of the income stream. The legislation faced stiff resistance and never made it out of the House of Commons. However, the government ultimately advanced its agenda by making family allowance benefits taxable, and thereby relatively less valuable to high-income families. Looking back, we can say the decision to tax family allowance marked the beginning of the end of the universality of government social programs.

In 1979 Trudeau introduced a refundable Child Tax Benefit (CTB) of $200 per year for each child under 18. The benefit was income-tested so that those with incomes above $26,000 received nothing. To help pay for the CTB, Ottawa squeezed the Family Allowance benefit program by close to 30 percent. The CTB, which was integrated into the personal income tax system, proved simple to administer and targeted the benefits to those most in need.

Taking Trudeau's shift to its conclusion, the Mulroney government ended the family allowance system in 1992, replacing it with an enhanced Child Tax Benefit, tax-free and income-tested. But it was Trudeau who got this ball rolling by using the income tax system to deliver and target social benefits with refundable tax credits. In this way Trudeau served as the inspiration for the use of what we now call "tax expenditures" to achieve social policy objectives. All of his successors have followed this approach, especially Stephen Harper, who established a number of tax credits, including for fitness and culture activity for Canadian children.

At the other end of the age spectrum, Trudeau repeatedly increased payments to low-income seniors. The universally accessible Old Age Security (OAS), introduced in 1952, paid $76 per month when Trudeau came to power in 1968 and $272 per month when he left office in 1984. While the increase marginally exceeded the rate of inflation, had it kept pace with economic growth, the monthly OAS payment would have been $372. In other words, seniors receiving only OAS during the Trudeau era did *not* share fully in the growth of our national economy, effectively losing about $100 per month.

Rather than raise the stock of all seniors by enhancing the OAS program, Trudeau targeted the Guaranteed Income Supplement (GIS) for improvement. Introduced in 1967 and paid only to low-income seniors (over the age of 65), the GIS went from $30 per month in 1968 to $295 dollars per month in 1984. Factoring in economic growth, this doubled financial support to seniors in need. While low-income seniors fared better under Trudeau, those in the middle and upper income brackets received relatively less government support.

POVERTY LEVELS ALSO bear scrutiny when assessing Trudeau's legacy. They declined steadily from the end of the Second World War until the time Trudeau came to power. Between 1961 and 1969, the percentage of the population considered "poor" fell from 25 to 18.[4] Trudeau claims in his memoirs that he accelerated this trend by adopting policies that targeted support for low-income families with the Child Tax Benefit, helping low-income seniors with the GIS, and enriching and extending unemployment benefits.

While economists and social scientists perpetually debate the definition of poverty, by Trudeau's measure the percentage of Canadians in poverty dropped nearly 50 percent during his fifteen-and-a-half years in office.[5] Many of the books about Trudeau repeat this claim, but this is no authentication of its accuracy.

In his book *Towards a Just Society*, first published in 1990, Trudeau cited Statistics Canada data to make the claim that during his tenure, "the number of Canadians living in poverty was reduced by more than one-third: from 23.1 percent of Canadians in 1969 to 12.8 percent in 1984."[6] The associated footnote refers to two Statistics Canada publications, both entitled *Income Distribution by Size in Canada*. A review by the librarians at Statistics Canada and the research staff at the National Council on Welfare in 2012 revealed that data referenced from 1969 cannot be compared to data from 1984, since the methodology and sampling for poverty levels in Canada changed in 1976.[7] On a comparable basis, the numbers show an overall poverty rate based on a "low-income cut off" of 14.2 percent in 1975, and 12.9 percent in 1984.[8] According to the National Council on Welfare, an advisory group to the Minister of National Health and Welfare (as the portfolio was then known) established by Trudeau, the portion of Canadians living in poverty remained largely unaltered during Trudeau's final decade in power, with an exception for the elderly.[9]

Income distribution measures also reveal that Trudeau's policies made no dent in narrowing the gap between rich and poor.[10] Statistics Canada reported that for 1969 the share of household income for the lowest quintile of Canadian households was 4.3 percent. In 1984 the lowest quintile took in 4.5 percent of household income, a mere rounding error of a difference from when Trudeau came to power.[11] A seminal international study on worldwide poverty concluded that Canada's progress from 1970 to the mid-1980s was "less than moderate."[12]

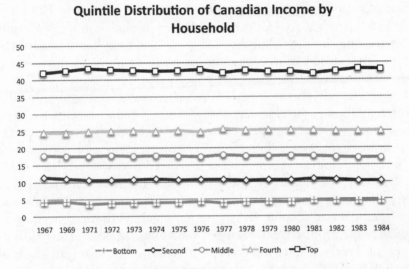

Quintile Distribution of Canadian Income by Household

Methodological issues aside, it's true, as Trudeau claims, that the percentage of impoverished families headed by a senior citizen fell from 41 in 1969 to 14 in 1980, and then to 9.5 percent in 1986, in large measure because of enhancements to the Guaranteed Income Supplement and the Canada Pension Plan.[13]

What Trudeau excluded from his analysis was that by the mid-1980s, 42.7 percent of seniors living on their own lived below the poverty line, as did 47.1 percent of all Canadian families headed by someone under the age of 25, as well as about one child in six.[14] Also missing from his analysis was the dramatic rise in poverty among households headed by women. Fully 42.5 percent of such families lived below the poverty line in 1984, compared with just 13.2 percent in 1961.[15] Families headed by a woman were four times as likely to be poor as those headed by a man.[16]

Women were not only disproportionately poor, but they worked in record numbers to sustain themselves and their families. In the mid-

1980s, one-income families were four times as likely to be poor as two-income families.[17] Interestingly, families headed by immigrants in 1986 had lower poverty rates than those with heads born in Canada (11.6 percent as opposed to 12.5 percent.)[18]

While the income gap between low- and high-income Canadians held remarkably steady during the Trudeau years, what did change was the regional distribution of income. In 1968, the GDP per capita in Atlantic Canada stood at 67 percent of the Canadian average. By 1984, Atlantic Canadian had income equal to 74 percent of the national average, a gain of seven percentage points. Ontario had a GDP per capita of 118 percent of the Canadian average in 1968, but by 1984 dropped to 110 percent of the national average.[19] Despite this regional leveling, families living in Newfoundland around the time Trudeau left office were almost twice as likely as those in the rest of Canada to live below the poverty line.[20]

It is difficult to say whether the narrowing of regional wealth differentials was the result of natural forces, enhancements to social programs, or the regional economic development programs that Trudeau championed. But by most measures, the gap between the "have" and "have not" provinces narrowed over the Trudeau era.

Crowley, president of the Macdonald-Laurier Institute and a former visiting economist at Finance Canada, contends that Trudeau presided over an income redistribution machine that did nothing to equalize the productive capacity of Canadian regions. "The evidence suggests Trudeau undermined the inherent incentive for Canadians at the low end of the income scale to improve their position. In countries without equalization mechanism the production gap narrowed more rapidly than in Canada."[21]

Crowley contends that Atlantic Canadians were cursed in living in a poor region in a rich country, since they became dependent on equalization rather than following market incentives to generate new wealth. He points to the evidence that indicates that the expansion of the welfare state goes hand-in-hand with the number of people living in poverty.

> Over time the dependency on government transfers becomes entrenched. It is not like an elevator where people get on and off, but an escalator without an end point. Once you are on, you stay there. When our economy returned to health, the number of people on social welfare continued to go up. It was only when entitlements were reduced in the 1990s that welfare

rates declined and were cut in half. You need to pull people into work and out of dependence on government support.[22]

While Trudeau touted regional economic development programs as a bridge to economic growth and sustainability, in reality they became hammocks, artificially sustaining regions with weak economies. They also constituted the ultimate cash-for-votes scheme. Trudeau acknowledged that caucus and party members from the Atlantic Provinces and Quebec were particularly appreciative of federal funds. As they say, when you are robbing Peter to pay Paul, you can always count on Paul's support.

Trudeau described regional development money as a practical response to bring jobs to people, rather than forcing people to go to the jobs.[23] More than that, he considered regional development intrinsic to being Canadian. Regardless of where one lived, or any individual's personal responsibility to make an economic contribution to the country, Trudeau's just society would give citizens "a fair share of the abundance of wealth in this country."[24] Such a program, argued Trudeau, was essential to national unity.[25] Nowhere was this more important than in Quebec, where profitable federalism had become a key argument in favour of keeping the country together.

Crowley does not oppose economic development programs *per se*, provided they find support in a rigorous cost-benefit analysis. But this was not, in his opinion, the Trudeau reality: "Our system was deeply infected with politics. It became a prop that promoted Liberal party fortunes." Indeed, Trudeau's key minister for Atlantic Canada, Allan MacEachen, was affectionately referred to by his constituents as "godfather". Trudeau's ministers were not the first or the last to use the public purse to gain political support, but MacEachen may rank as one of the most artful practitioners of the craft.

While Trudeau spread money around the country in the name of regional justice, he also compounded the national debt. It would take another Liberal prime minister, Jean Chrétien, to recognize that economic mismanagement had harmed the nation and its unity. Unlike Trudeau, he thought Quebecers would evince greater attachment to Canada if the country had a strong balance sheet.

But regional development policies left at least one lasting, if unintended, benefit. Dating back to 1897, the "Crow Rate" froze western grain freight rates for shipments going through West Coast ports and Thunder Bay. Following the provisions of the antiquated Crow Statute, revenues from the shipments did not cover variable costs, and railways had little incentive to make capital improvements. Money from the Western Economic Development Fund modernized the rail system to the point where farmers accepted market rates for transport, and the Crow Rate no longer applied.

Eliminating subsidies did not come naturally to Trudeau, and he did not mention the elimination of the Crow Rate in his memoirs, in part because he had resisted the change. He lamented market-oriented mechanisms and criticized his successor, Brian Mulroney, for "weakening the power of the state, limiting social security and forcing the burden of economic adjustment on individuals rather than society.[26]

TRUDEAU FOLLOWED A succession of prime ministers who substantially augmented the social welfare state after the Great Depression and the Second World War. But prior to Trudeau, governments linked growth in social programs to gains in incomes and productivity. Saskatchewan thus established Medicare without going into deficit and debt. In fact, social spending in Canada *rose* in the 1950s and 1960s at the same time as government debt levels *fell*.

Trudeau initially claimed he would fund spending on health care and poverty reduction by reducing military expenditures. This he certainly did, but those cuts did not fund his dramatic spending increases on their own. And the benefits were illusory. As Trudeau biographer Stephen Clarkson observed, the best you could say about Trudeau's social policies is that they did not let material inequality increase.[27] Social spending grew under Trudeau, but rather than raise new revenues to fund rising government largesse, he parked the tab on the country's credit card.

The burden of debt at the end of Trudeau's tenure as prime minister constituted the single biggest threat to the sustainability of long-established social programs. In 1968, government transfers to persons cost the treasury nearly twice what it paid in interest on the national debt. By 1984, these expenses were equal.

Trudeau reduced poverty levels for seniors and made incomes across the country more equal. People who simply didn't want to work, as well as people who had simply been laid off, had more options and more money. This was all paid for with borrowed money. Had Trudeau increased taxes to pay for his attempts to forge a just society, he would have faced the wrath of voters, something he carefully avoided. Instead, he opted for limited short-term gain and profound long-term pain.

CHAPTER 11

NATIVE LAND

The time is now to decide whether the Indians will be a race apart in Canada or whether it will be Canadians of full status.

IVEN THAT TRUDEAU held power for over 15 years, it is an admission of failure that all he could claim in his memoirs about native issues was that his work was "well advanced" when he left office.[1] But Trudeau was no different from other prime ministers who came into office thinking, or hoping, that the problems facing First Nations could be overcome. Compared with other prime ministers, Trudeau proved uncharacteristically brave and refreshingly bold in outlining his vision during his early days in office. But he quickly realized that on this file, he could not win and made an uncharacteristic retreat.

WHEN TRUDEAU CHALLENGED Aboriginal peoples, and the country, to embrace change, he had in mind fundamental reform of the government's aboriginal policy. With the release of a white paper on Indian policy in 1969, Trudeau declared that Canada stood at a crossroads:

Either we go on adding bricks of discrimination around the ghetto in which they live and at the same time perhaps helping them preserve certain cultural traits and certain ancestral rights. Or we can say – the time is now to decide whether the

Indians will be a race apart in Canada or whether it (sic) will be Canadians of full status. [2]

Trudeau's desire was for Natives to be "equal under the law."[3] But he recognized that this equality jeopardized their traditions and treaty rights. There was no question of denying these rights, but Trudeau thought the treaties shouldn't persist forever: "It's inconceivable, I think, that in a given society one section of the society have a treaty with the other section of the society. We must be all equal under the laws and we must not sign treaties among ourselves."

At the same time, Trudeau personally dismissed many Aboriginal land-rights claims because their foundational documents were too broad.[4] Many of these treaties, argued Trudeau, had little relevance in a modern society. A commitment by the federal government to supply twine and gun powder was neither realistic for nor pertinent to life in the 1970s. Trudeau encouraged Natives to achieve equality, personal responsibility, and self-sufficiency:

> They should become Canadians as all other Canadians and if they were prosperous and wealthy, they will be treated like prosperous and wealthy and they will be paying taxes for the other Canadians, who are not so prosperous and not so wealthy, whether they be Indians or English Canadians or French or Maritimers. (This) is the only basis on which I see our society can develop as equals.[5]

The White Paper was a bold document that called for:
- Repeal of the Indian Act
- Natives to be permitted to acquire title to their lands
- Provinces to take over social responsibility for Natives
- Interim funds for Native economic development
- The Department of Indian Affairs to be eliminated
- The appointment of a Commissioner to study and recommend procedures to adjudicate land claims[6]

Trudeau's proposition was courageous and entirely consistent with his philosophy of social justice through individual equality and personal freedom (albeit with a heavy dose of socialism). Despite his noble intent, he failed to appreciate at the time that Aboriginal peoples viewed their identity in the communal sense, as tribes and nations, and not as individuals. They did not individually own land on reserves; their territory was held in the collective.

Native leaders, whom Trudeau had invited to Ottawa to receive the white paper under his naïve assumption that they would welcome the shift in policy, were outraged. The white paper revealed Trudeau's ignorance of their hopes and dreams and demonstrated how not to engage Aboriginal leaders in dialogue. None of the ideas that Aboriginal people brought forward in the 19 formal consultations prior to the release of the white paper appeared in the government document. To his credit, Jean Chrétien, then Indians Affairs minister, began a more respectful dialogue — or, as he put it, he would speak first and then Native leaders would give him hell.

A frustrated Trudeau did not know which way to turn. He outraged Natives when he rejected their claims to Aboriginal rights with the provocative statement: "Society can't be built on historical 'might have beens.'"[7] He later added that he would not force Natives to do anything they did not want, condescendingly adding "We'll keep them in the ghetto as long as they want."[8] Trudeau sought to negotiate a deal with the provinces on Native issues without Native leaders being present other than as technical advisors.

The government withdrew the white paper in the spring of 1970, leaving it without an agenda on Aboriginal issues. Native leaders responded by issuing a "red paper" of their own in June 1970. In this way, the white paper ironically helped mobilize the Native community, leading to the creation of the Assembly of First Nations.

After a ruling by the Supreme Court in 1973, Trudeau had little choice but to begin bargaining on land claims. He ultimately opened an Office of Native Claims in 1974. Trudeau also ceded to the Quebec government a major portion of federal responsibilities for the education, health care, registration of beneficiaries and local government of the Aboriginal population of Northern Quebec.[9] It is curious that, in most instances, Trudeau sought to intervene in areas of provincial jurisdiction, but in the case of Native issues, he was inclined to decentralize.

When Trudeau was rewriting the constitution, he partially addressed the concerns of Natives, but only after much protest. Dealing with "queues of Indians" knocking on her door at 10 Downing Street was Margaret Thatcher's big concern about Trudeau's plan to patriate the constitution.[10] Thatcher's notes from a June 25, 1980 meeting with Trudeau in London reveal her reluctance to get caught up in a domestic

Canadian squabble. A delegation of Aboriginal chiefs and elders had been to London the previous year, saying they wanted a seat at the constitutional negotiating table, which Trudeau refused to provide. The meeting notes reveal that Trudeau did not expect unanimity in Canada over his approach, but was determined to proceed regardless, over the objections of Native leaders and reluctant provinces.

Trudeau did not worry about the government of Quebec opposing his plans, but he did fret about the impact of a sustained Native protest. In a last-minute compromise, he promised nothing new *per se*, but offered the assurance that nothing in the Charter of Rights and Freedoms could be construed to abrogate or derogate from any *existing* Aboriginal right or treaty. Native leaders would have preferred to see their rights recognized without the qualification.

It's worth noting that, in response to provincial demands, Trudeau had agreed to strip both women's and Native rights out of the constitutional agreement in their entirety. It was only after sustained lobbying by both groups in the weeks after the constitutional agreement was struck that the government restored some of the discarded language. Many Aboriginal leaders considered the inclusion of *existing* rights in the final document to be significant, since that would make it more difficult for a future Canadian government to abrogate or ignore a Native treaty unilaterally through simple legislation.[11]

A first ministers' conference, absent Quebec, was held in 1983 to help define what was meant by *existing* treaty rights. Trudeau tried to place limits on what those rights provided, while Native leaders advocated for a broader interpretation. The conference produced an accord providing an agenda to resolve the more contentious issues, and a resolution to amend the constitution.

Ultimately Trudeau never gave up on the belief that individual rather than group rights should guide Aboriginal Canadians.[12] In 1991 he clashed in an informal debate with Ovide Mercredi, the Grand Chief of the Assembly of First Nations. Mercredi wanted the collective rights of minorities enshrined in the Constitution, to which Trudeau replied, "If that ever happens then you (Native) people are finished."

Mercredi accused Trudeau of trying to assimilate Aboriginal peoples. Trudeau countered that he wanted to "integrate" them into the Canadian mainstream. "It is easy for you to say that individual rights should prevail," replied Mercredi, "because you belong to the dominant society. For us to deny the predominance of collective rights would be capitulating, and allowing us to be dominated by you on the assumption that we are all equal as individuals." He went on to call Trudeau's just society a "hoax" and to state that a charter of individual rights would mean misery for Aboriginal people. "On what basis should I tell you, 'Let's march together as individuals because your country has been so wonderful to us'?"

Mercredi wanted his people to have the same rights as the people of Quebec:

- A constitution to protect Native languages
- Civil laws Natives could establish and administer
- Governments of Native peoples
- Territorial control
- Institutional justice
- Agreements with the federal government over immigration

This request was a non-starter for Trudeau, resulting in irreconcilable differences with Canada's Native leaders.

Trudeau's accounts of his quest for a just society, published in his memoirs and in a 466-page book he co-wrote, barely mention the plight of Canada's Aboriginal peoples. Nonetheless, Aboriginal Canadian Elijah Harper did Trudeau a big favour in 1990, raising an eagle feather in the Manitoba legislature to oppose the introduction of a motion to approve the Meech Lake Accord, which Trudeau was desperate to kill. Natives resented that the document recognized Quebec as a distinct society while ignoring their own uniqueness. In this fight, Trudeau and Aboriginal peoples found themselves on the same side, although for completely different reasons.

Most prime ministers come to office with hope, inspiration and new ideas on Aboriginal issues. Sadly, few have made much progress. Trudeau falls into the same category as his predecessors and successors despite his promise of a just society for all of Canada.

CHAPTER 12

A LIBERAL SOCIETY

*No provision of the charter of rights is reasonably capable of an
interpretation that would either enshrine a right to abortion or a
right to life for the unborn or deny the ability of Parliament
to legislate on the matter.*

SOME POLITICAL OBSERVERS describe New Democratic Party supporters as "Liberals in a hurry." Pierre Trudeau, once an overt
enthusiast for Canada's socialist political party, embraced
many of their social causes while prime minister. He engorged his
preferred special interest groups with taxpayer dollars; established
a human rights industry to oversee the conduct of societal relations;
and supported Canadian cultural industries with regulatory protection and ever-growing government grants. And agree or disagree
with his position on abortion and capital punishment, we must credit
Trudeau for not ducking sensitive and controversial issues.

IF YOU HAD a complaint against society, the Trudeau government was
your friend. Jacques Hébert, who travelled with Trudeau to China in
1960 and whom Trudeau appointed to the Senate in 1983, boasted
that Trudeau empowered many categories of Canadians "who previously had little or no voice." Hébert recounted how feminist groups
got the wherewithal to influence public opinion and Aboriginal peoples received taxpayer dollars for the sole purpose of "telling the
government off."[1]

The Liberal Party of Canada reaped benefits by cutting cheques to groups that were largely of like mind. There would have been howls of protest had Stephen Harper's Conservative government approved grants to the *National Citizens' Coalition* and the *Fraser Institute*, two groups well-known for advocating limited government. But Trudeau saw nothing wrong in using the public purse to advance the causes of his political allies – and, thereby, his own electoral prospects. Indeed, Trudeau used taxpayer dollars to fund the sort of advocacy work normally undertaken by political parties. Groups such as the *National Action Committee on the Status of Women* went well beyond advocating an end to discrimination; they campaigned for a wide range of highly politicized social policy changes.

Trudeau institutionalized women's equality by appointing a minister responsible for the status of women in 1971, and then created the advisory council on the status of women in 1973. But Trudeau's egalitarian instincts had limits. Women represented only 14 percent of his Senate appointments (Trudeau's successor, Mulroney, achieved 22 percent). Trudeau elevated only one woman, Bertha Wilson, to the Supreme Court of Canada, out of eleven judicial appointments; to be fair, she was the first woman to receive the honour (women comprised two of Mulroney's ten appointments to the court). Trudeau also appointed Jeanne Sauvé as both Canada's first female Speaker of the House of Commons and first female Governor General.

One area in which the life of Canadian women changed dramatically during Trudeau's tenure was that of employment. In 1968, 33 percent of women over the age of 25 worked outside the home. By 1984, that number had hit 51 percent.[2] The higher participation rate helped explain the increase in real family incomes from $31,256 in 1971 to $37,300 in 1984 (in constant dollars). To some Canadians, this shift represented progress; to others it signaled the demise of traditional family values.

For seniors, Trudeau established a culture and recreation program called *New Horizons*. The political nature of the program was exposed when Canadians learned that Liberal MPs had the power to direct grants in their home ridings, a courtesy not extended to opposition MPs.[3]

For youth, Trudeau deployed tax dollars to fund pet projects, such as *Katimavik, Opportunities for Youth*, and *Canada World Youth*. (In 1986, the Mulroney government cut *Katimavik*, but the Chrétien government reinstated it in 1995. In the 2012 budget, the Harper Conservatives ended the program again, after revealing that it cost $21 million per year, some $28,000 per participant, and had a one-third dropout rate.)[4] While his supporters credit Trudeau with inspiring the youth of Canada, he did it on the public dime, with little accountability.

It turned out that many of the temporary job creation schemes Trudeau established became the subject of fraud, abuse and political interference. Independent evaluations found fraud and abuse, causing the responsible minister, Bud Cullen, to urge his cabinet colleagues to phase out the initiatives. They would have none of it.

Trudeau was always friendly to the union movement. Arrested during the 1949 Asbestos strike in Quebec, the miners nicknamed him St. Joseph, the patron saint of workers.[5] Before becoming a politician and professor, Trudeau served as a legal advisor and constitutional consultant to Quebec trade unions. When Trudeau sat in cabinet, the federal government gave public sector workers the right to strike. When he occupied 24 Sussex Drive, union membership in Canada nearly doubled.[6]

The Canadian Union of Public Employees (CUPE) became the largest union in the country. Public-sector workers were more than twice as likely to be unionized as their American counterparts.[7] These workers had an odd way of showing their gratitude, however. Work stoppages in the public sector hit record highs during Trudeau's time in office. During the 1981 postal workers strike Trudeau said there was not much point legislating them back to work since they would disobey the law if he did.[8]

PRIOR TO THE Charter, Trudeau pursued his interest in advancing individual human rights through legislative and institutional means. The passage of the Canadian Human Rights Act, along with the creation of the Canadian Human Rights Commission and the Canadian Human Rights Tribunal in 1977, created both a platform and industry for human rights in Canada.

The Act prohibited discriminatory practices in federally regulated areas based on sex, disability, or religion. In cases of discrimination, the Commission investigated and sought remediation, and exercised power under the Employment Equity Act to ensure federally regulated employers provided equal opportunities for women, aboriginal people, the disabled and visible minorities. The tribunal judged cases that the Commission could not resolve.

Eventually these human rights institutions overstepped their boundaries and, paradoxically, attacked liberties enshrined in another Trudeau document, the Charter of Rights and Freedoms, particularly freedom of speech. Conservative activist and Sun News media personality Ezra Levant faced the full force of the Canadian human rights industry after his libertarian-themed magazine, the *Western Standard,* republished cartoon images depicting the prophet Muhammad in 2006. Those same cartoons had caused an international furor when first published in the Danish newspaper *Jyllands-Posten* on September 30, 2005. Protests against the Danish publication were reported to have led to more than 100 deaths and the bombing of the Danish embassy in Pakistan.

Various Canadian Islamic and Muslim organizations complained about Levant to the Alberta Human Rights Commission (AHRC), which launched a lengthy investigation. On the day of the hearing in January 2008, Levant defiantly republished the cartoons on his website. Using Trudeau's Charter, Levant successfully defended himself and his right to free speech. The clash between the right to free speech and the right not to be subject to discrimination turned into a media frenzy. Levant stated afterwards that he spent $100,000 to defend his publication's right to free speech, a cost many publishers would have been unable to sustain. It cost taxpayers $500,000 to prosecute the case.

Trudeau may not have foreseen the battles that would play out between two enshrined rights — that to free speech and that to protection from hate — but it may not have bothered him even if he had. Trudeau was a great believer in counterweights as a means of balancing societal interests. Still, as a self-proclaimed champion of individual liberties, he largely tilted the playing field against free speech by imposing an expensive, bureaucratic, and at-times zealous Human Rights Commission and Human Rights Tribunal.

In 2012, critical media coverage of the Commission and Tribunal reached its zenith. When the press interviewed three officials from the Canadian Human Rights Commission (CHRC) in April 2008, they acknowledged they were under attack:

> The reality is we read the papers. We know about the current debate, we know the parameters, if you will. If you think that we're concerned, upset, from time to time discouraged with some of what we've been hearing and reading in the press, you're right, we are. Because to be quite clear about it, we do believe in what we do. We believe that in our society there should be limits on freedom of expression and freedom of speech, that there is a line, not one that we draw, but one

that must be drawn nevertheless. We are comfortable with what we do.[9]

The collection of rulings emanating from human rights tribunals is truly shocking from a common sense perspective. When the Platinum Athletic Club denied a customer's request to wear work boots inside the club, it was ordered to pay the aggrieved man $1,900, including $1,000 for loss of dignity.[10] When a McDonald's employee was fired after refusing to follow the company's hand-washing policy because of a skin condition, she launched a human rights case – despite the fact that McDonalds' had given her more than two years of disability leave to sort out her condition. The BC Human Rights Commission ordered McDonald's to compensate its former employee $23,000 for "lost income" plus $25,000 for the loss of dignity and self-respect.

Maclean's columnist Andrew Coyne described human rights commissions as operating as a parallel police and legal system, "without any of the procedural safeguards, rules of evidence, or simple professional expertise" to which more formal systems are subject.[11] He observed that those who launch complaints bear no costs or adverse consequences, while those implicated are put to considerable expense, and even invasions of privacy.

Trudeau's attempt to embed equality into Canadian society by way of human rights commissions and tribunals was well-intentioned. Other actors, including provincial governments, also joined him in this quest. But as the Levant-AHRC Commission incident demonstrates, the result can be the exact opposite of what was intended. Freedoms have become costly to defend, and have possibly been diminished, in post-Trudeau Canada.

WHILE TRUDEAU IS often credited with advancing the rights of gays and lesbians through the Charter and the Canadian Human Rights Commission, he did not champion their cause as true equals to heterosexuals – and neither did his government. When the bill to decriminalize homosexuality came before Parliament in 1968, Trudeau's minister of justice, John Turner, remarked:

> When acts are committed in private between two consenting adults, those acts, however indecent or repugnant or immoral, should remain a matter for their private consciences and not be a matter bringing into play the criminal code of Canada. The conduct contemplated in this clause — homosexual

acts between consenting adults in private — is repugnant (to) the great majority of the people of Canada.[12]

While removing homosexuality from the criminal code represented progress, labeling it as immoral and repugnant did not exactly hit the high-water mark for tolerance and respect. (It remained a crime for homosexuals to engage in group sex.) Trudeau could have ordered his minister to excise those gratuitous remarks – but he did not. In fact, Trudeau was sensitive about being called a homosexual by his critics. When confronted in 1968 about the matter, he furiously replied in private, "whoever said that about [me] should leave [me] alone in a room with his wife for a couple of hours and what transpired there would provide his rebuttal."[13]

A decade later, when drafting the Charter of Rights and Freedoms, Trudeau again stopped short of supporting true equality for gays and lesbians. In Section 15, which guaranteed equality rights, Trudeau prohibited discrimination on the basis of race, national or ethnic origin, colour, religion, sex, age or mental or physical disability. He did not include sexual orientation, despite a heavy lobbying campaign for him to do so.[14] His own chairman of the Canadian Human Rights Commission, Gordon Fairweather, told a joint Senate-Commons committee studying the constitution in 1978 that the proposed charter had serious holes and should be amended to include the outlawing of discrimination based on sexual orientation.[15] At the time, the RCMP was tracking activity in homosexual communities that went far beyond possible threats to national security.[16]

It was not Trudeau but the Supreme Court of Canada that declared discrimination on the basis of sexual orientation to be analogous to the other forms of discrimination in the constitution, and therefore "read in" a prohibition against sexual discrimination in 1995. Trudeau can be given credit for establishing a framework under which equality rights could be advanced. But to say he was a champion for gay equality rights is something of an overstatement.

TRUDEAU ALSO WADED into other sensitive social and legal issues, including divorce, abortion and capital punishment. Again, a review of the evidence reveals that he was not as "progressive" as his reputation would imply, nor were the changes he wrought the result of his work alone.

Prior to 1968, the provinces legislated divorces. In eight of ten provinces, adultery was the only ground parties could invoke. Quebec and Newfoundland required a private Act of Parliament to dissolve a marriage. In the year after Trudeau's reforms, when divorce could be granted on one of 15 grounds (including the catch-all "marital breakdown"), the divorce rate more than doubled. Immediately before the Trudeau reforms, it stood at 50 per 100,000 people. By the time Trudeau left office it had risen to 250 divorces per 100,000 people.[17] This is not to suggest Trudeau was the cause of divorce, or that making divorce easier to obtain was necessarily wrong. It is a simple observation that Trudeau was at the helm when these changes, which were largely in accord with societal views of the day, were enacted.

In 1969, Trudeau amended the Criminal Code to liberalize access to abortion. Abortion became legal if performed by a doctor in a hospital following the approval of a "therapeutic abortion committee" and a determination that a woman's life or health "would" be affected or "would be likely" to be affected by the continuation of the pregnancy. That same year, there were about three legal abortions per 100 live births; in 1975, 14.9; in 1978, 16.5.[18]

In 1998 the Supreme Court overturned the law, ruling that it violated Section 7 of the Charter, which guaranteed security of the person. This contradicted Trudeau's statement to Canadians in 1981 that no provision of the Charter could be interpreted to enshrine either a right to abortion or a right to life for the unborn, or deny the ability of Parliament to legislate on the matter.[19]

While Trudeau is recognized for officially ending capital punishment in Canada, for all intents and purposes Lester B. Pearson, as a matter of public policy, eliminated the practice by commuting death sentences that came to cabinet. The last hanging in Canada occurred in 1962. Parliament passed a law in 1967 imposing a five-year moratorium on the death penalty except in cases of the murder of police and corrections officers. Trudeau legislated a permanent ban in 1976, although the free vote in the House of Commons was tight, passing by a margin of 130 to 124. Capital murder thereafter carried a mandatory life sentence without eligibility for parole until 25 years of the sentence has been served. Trudeau said he did not oppose capital punishment on moral grounds and said he would have considered its reintroduction if evidence was offered that proved it to be a deterrent to murder.[20]

When it comes to marriage, abortion and capital punishment, the determination of what is "just" takes many forms. That Parliament has not decisively revisited these issues since Trudeau left office suggests that his positions, or the positions resulting from court rulings, reflected a broad and enduring societal consensus. To his credit, Trudeau did not duck many of society's most sensitive and difficult issues. Unlike his successors, he did not govern with a Charter of Rights on the books, the consequence of which was to give Supreme Court justices, and not the Parliament of the day, the final word on the great moral questions of the day.

WHILE TRUDEAU ENJOYED the company of John Lennon and Yoko Ono, he was mostly a lover of classical music. Arts and culture not only gave Trudeau personal pleasure, they embodied elements of nation-building he thought were worthy of taxpayer support and protectionism.

Surprisingly, the freedom-loving, self-declared anti-nationalist pursued a range of cultural policies that were decidedly pro-nationalist and anti-freedom. His government demanded that 60 percent of prime-time television had to be Canadian content. Cable signals from the United States were blocked. Canadian companies advertising on American television stations were denied a tax deduction. Radio stations were forced to play 25 percent Canadian content. Advertisers in Canadian editions of American magazines were also denied tax deductions.

Time Magazine responded by scrapping its Canadian edition. When radio stations started to play Canadian content during nocturnal hours only, the regulations were changed to ensure daytime coverage. The government relaxed its rules for classical music stations since filling the domestic quotient proved problematic in the absence of a Canadian Beethoven.

For those on the receiving end of cultural grants, the Trudeau era was golden. Over the two-year period between 1974 and 1976, funding for the Canada Council increased 64 percent, from $18.9 million to $31 million. Over his final decade in office, Trudeau increased support to the Canada Council by an average of 13.3 percent per year.

A love of the arts led Trudeau to commission two major museums in Ottawa: The National Gallery and the Canadian Museum of Civilization. Fearing that his successor would scuttle his plan, Trudeau instructed his officials during his final months in office to advance the project by digging the biggest hole they could possibly dig.[21] Given the size of the federal deficit and debt Trudeau had amassed, it was understandable that he might have thought his successor would second-guess his vision. But these museums were constructed and paid for after Trudeau left office; the National Gallery opened in 1988, the Canadian Museum of Civilization in 1989.

While taxpayer support for the arts was classic Trudeau, it is curious that an avowed liberty-loving anti-nationalist saw fit to limit Canadians' cultural freedoms. Trudeau lamented Quebec's insularity and repressive atmosphere under the policies of Maurice Duplessis. But as prime minister, Trudeau enacted policies that restricted even the most basic pleasures of everyday life: reading a magazine, watching television, or listening to the radio. Most of these policies, with some modification, remain in place in 2013.

THE FRAMERS OF our constitution made health a provincial responsibility. But as governments introduced provincial Medicare plans, Pearson's federal government offered financial support to help ensure more consistent standards across the country. Trudeau took a somewhat different approach: he *reduced* federal funding and demanded *increased* federal influence.

Pearson committed the federal government to fund roughly fifty percent of the cost of provincially run Medicare systems. With rising public expectations, and the provinces making all the decisions (but paying only half the tab), health spending ramped up dramatically in the early days of the Trudeau era. Provinces soon sought ways to contain costs and pursued alternatives to fund the system. One approach was to permit doctors to enhance their incomes by charging their patients for certain services, often referred to as "extra billing." Presumably this allowed provinces to dampen demands by doctors to increase their fee schedule while also serving as a check on front-end demand for health services.

Trudeau also sought ways to reduce the cost of Medicare to the federal government. By 1984, the federal portion of health spending had been cut in half, from 50 to about 24 percent of provincial budgets. Yet, even at this reduced level, the federal government sought to increase its sway over the system.

Trudeau was unhappy that some provinces introduced extra-billing; it violated his socialist sensibilities. Rather than reach an agreement with the provinces to ban the practice in exchange for federal cash, Monique Bégin, Trudeau's health minister, came forward with the idea that new "strings" should simply be attached to existing federal funds that would penalize any province that permitted extra-billing. Trudeau queried Bégin, "Who are the players, and where do they stand?" She said all provincial governments would oppose a penalty, and so would organized medicine and the "official elites." When told that the public opposed extra billing, Trudeau responded, "That's a sure win."[22]

The Canada Health Act was placed before Parliament in late 1983 and received Royal Assent on April 1, 1984. While the Act spoke to five broad principles – public administration, comprehensiveness, universality, portability, and accessibility – its real purpose was to deter provinces from allowing doctors and other health providers to charge user fees.

The Act stipulated that the federal government would withhold funds from provinces that failed to meet the five principles. In addition, funds could be denied if a province failed to provide the federal minister of health with certain information related to the provision of healthcare services. Provinces also had to recognize publicly the federal government's contribution (presumably to ensure Quebecers understood the federal role). While Trudeau had once opposed federal funding for education in the 1950s as a violation of the BNA Act, as prime minister he sought to exploit the power of the federal purse to ensure a robust central influence over health care.

On extra-billing, the federal government gave itself the power to withhold contributions, on a dollar-for-dollar basis, to any province that permitted user charges. Indeed, financial penalties totaling $246 million were withheld from provinces in the first two years the Act was in force. However, the Act cleverly provided for a return of these funds to provinces that eliminated the extra-billing practice within three years. All eventually complied to get back the cash.

The provisions of the Canada Health Act that prohibited extra billing were retained by Trudeau's successors. But this provision meant that Canadians who were prepared to pay out of their pockets for health services were denied freedom of choice. Many Canadians opted to seek treatment in the United States, including many politicians.[23] Private health clinics began appearing in Canada, operating outside of the Medicare system, especially in Quebec, where the provincial government saw benefit in allowing specialized services, like MRIs, to be delivered on an immediate basis without cost to or the involvement of the state.

In 2011, Prime Minister Stephen Harper surprised his provincial counterparts when he put forward a new funding mechanism for federal contributions to the health system with essentially no new strings attached.

AFTER TRUDEAU LEFT office, successive governments punted many of the nation's most sensitive social issues to the Supreme Court. It was jurists, rather than Parliament, who considered the parameters for abortion, euthanasia, homosexual rights and the rights of alleged criminals. Trudeau did not have that luxury, but one must give him credit for not shying away from potentially explosive issues, including capital punishment. And on most issues of social conscience, Trudeau was true to his classical liberal roots. But it is curious that someone who bravely faced the most difficult issues using liberal principles of freedom and equality would also see fit to restrict the way Canadians watched television or managed their health care. Under Trudeau, Canada became a more liberal and a more restricted society at the same time.

CHAPTER 13

MULTICULTURALISM AND IMMIGRATION

A policy of multiculturalism within a bilingual framework commends itself to the government as the most suitable means of assuring the cultural freedom of Canadians.

S INCE THE DAYS when John Cabot discovered Newfoundland and Samuel de Champlain fathered New France, Canada has grown and prospered through immigration. While Canada has been predominantly bicultural and bilingual for much of its history, late 20th and early 21st century immigration have transformed Canada into a multicultural state.[1]

Trudeau embraced multiculturalism as the antidote to nationalism and the dominance of Canada's "two solitudes." He adopted policies, devised programs and financed groups to enable minorities to maintain their own identity and resist social assimilation. Trudeau also entrenched multiculturalism into the Charter of Rights and Freedoms, which declared that our constitution "shall be interpreted in a manner consistent with the preservation and enhancement of the multicultural heritage of Canadians."

While immigration necessarily begat multiculturalism, it is a myth that Trudeau opened up the country to scores of new Canadians. Immigration levels actually *declined* during the Trudeau years. In addition, Trudeau weakened the link between immigration and economic development by favouring, for political purposes, the family-class component of immigration. Under Trudeau's watch, the usual countries of origin of immigrants to Canada also underwent a profound shift.

TRUDEAU USED MULTICULTURALISM in two ways: as a counterweight to English Canadians accusing him of leading a French takeover of the federal government, and as a force to resist Quebec nationalism.

On October 8, 1971 Trudeau announced that Canada would adopt policies embracing the country's multicultural dimension, a first on the world stage. Trudeau thought it "perfectly normal for people to want to associate with others with whom they feel certain cultural affinities, including language."[2] In the House of Commons, Trudeau opined:

> There cannot be one cultural policy for Canadians of British and French origin, another for the original peoples and yet a third for all others. For although there are two official languages, there is no official culture, nor does any ethnic group take precedence over any other. No citizen or group of citizens is other than Canadian, and all should be treated fairly ... A policy of multiculturalism within a bilingual framework commends itself to the government as the most suitable means of assuring the cultural freedom of Canadians. Such a policy should help to break down discriminatory attitudes and cultural jealousies. National unity, if it is to mean anything in the deeply personal sense, must be founded on confidence in one's own individual identity; out of this can grow respect for that of others and a willingness to share ideas, attitudes and assumptions. A vigorous policy of multiculturalism will help create this initial confidence.[3]

Since the policy implied an end to systemic racial and cultural discrimination, Trudeau faced no opposition. It was the sort of stance that former Tory Prime Minister John Diefenbaker could embrace, as he did when his government passed the Bill of Rights in 1960. Trudeau's multiculturalism policy thus received the unanimous support of Parliament in 1972. To implement his vision, he created a multiculturalism branch within the Secretary of State and appointed a minister of multiculturalism to cabinet.

While Canada had become officially bilingual, Trudeau did not want Canada's multicultural communities to feel left out. He thought it fair and just to support any group that wanted to preserve its mother tongue.[4] The state helped groups large and small retain their cherished language and values with taxpayer dollars — or more accurately, with public debt.[5] Contrary to Trudeau's lofty pronouncements about fairness, his government did not spend this money ending discrimination and inequality, but funding folk dances, festivals, language training and songfests. And Liberal party strategists quickly clued in that the recipients of all that cash might well return the favour at election time.

In addition to questioning multiculturalism spending, the editors at the *Toronto Star* saw danger in Trudeau's new direction: "No immigrant should be encouraged to think that Canada is essentially a chain of ethnic enclaves."[6] In contrast to the United States and its monolithic "melting pot" approach to cultural adaptation, Trudeau was prepared to sacrifice national cohesion to ensure that Canada became a beacon of multicultural wealth and diversity: "We were exposing the principle that a free and just society must accept pluralism and allow each citizen to make a personal choice of suitable lifestyle, customs, and culture, whether or not these flowed from his or her own ethnicity."[7] Not one to pronounce any culture superior to any other, Trudeau ignored the fact that certain cultures tolerated spousal abuse, honour killings, female genital mutilation and forced marriage. The government of Canada would eventually label such practices "barbaric" in its 2010 citizenship guide.

While most believe immigration has benefited Canada, policies that encourage the type of "ethnic enclaves" the *Star* cautioned against have increasingly come under attack, including from leaders of immigrant communities. Salim Mansur, associate professor of political science at Western University and board member of the Center for Islamic Pluralism in Washington, has argued that multiculturalism diminishes Canada's founding history. He concludes that because immigrant communities can retain their separate identities and traditions perpetually, they have failed to appreciate the values that built Canada as a model of civility.[8]

Not even the Québécois would be more distinct than any of the others. Mr. Trudeau cleverly proposed to abolish special status by offering special status to all." Mansur posits that multiculturalism has profoundly weakened the country by failing to ensure that new immigrants adopt Canadian values. "The historical legacy of multiculturalism leads many immi-

grants to no longer make the effort to become Canadian ...
The worm inside the doctrine of multiculturalism is the lie that
all cultures are worthy of equal respect and equally embracing
of individual freedom and democracy.[9]

Trudeau claimed that there was no official Canadian culture and
that no ethnic group should take precedence. But by 1984 taxpayers
were doling out $23 million annually in the name of multiculturalism,
$19 million of which went to 2,000 agencies and organizations across
the country, with $2 million going to advertising in the ethnic and
majority press.[10] The program pursued the somewhat contradictory
goals of enabling immigrant communities to retain their cultural
heritage while encouraging their integration into Canadian society.

And there were other agendas at play. Janine Brodie, Distinguished
University Professor and Canada Research Chair in Political
Economy and Social Governance at the University of Alberta,
assessed the policy in 1984 and concluded that Canada's federal
policy of multiculturalism was actually "a patronage vehicle." Angela
Kan, executive director of Vancouver's United Chinese Community
Enrichment Services Society, expressed her frustration with the use
of multiculturalism dollars, suggesting that employment should be
the priority. Language training should take precedence, she felt, over
paying immigrants to engage in song and dance.

Trudeau was not the only national leader of his day to promote
multiculturalism. Yet as the 9/11 attacks on the United States exposed
problems of radicalism, multiculturalism has fallen out of favour,
exposed as a practice with dangerous unintended consequences. "This
(multicultural) approach has failed, utterly failed," said German
leader Angela Merkel in 2010. She lamented that many immigrants
resisted learning the German language and did not integrate as easily
into society.

In a 2012 address, British Prime Minister David Cameron was
more blunt:

> Under the doctrine of state multiculturalism, we have encour-
> aged different cultures to live separate lives, apart from each
> other and the mainstream. We have failed to provide a vision
> of society to which they feel they want to belong. We have even
> tolerated these segregated communities behaving in ways that
> run counter to our values ... when unacceptable views or prac-
> tices have come from someone who isn't white, we've been too

cautious, frankly even fearful, to stand up to them … All this leaves some young Muslims feeling rootless. And the search for something to belong to and believe in can lead them to this extremist ideology. For sure, they don't turn into terrorists overnight. What we see is a process of radicalization.[11]

In contrast to many world leaders, Prime Minister Harper has stood up for multiculturalism, as he did in the English leaders' debate during the 2011 federal election. But his approach to multiculturalism has also supported integration:

What Canadians need to understand about multiculturalism is that people who make the hard decision to … come here, they first and foremost want to belong to this country … They also at the same time will change our country … And we show through multiculturalism our willingness to accommodate their differences, so they are more comfortable. That's why we're so successful integrating people as a country. I think we're probably the most successful country in the world in that regard … One can retain their culture and their cultural identity and still integrate into the mainstream language of the community, which is French in Québec, and English in most of the rest of the country … Canada is not creating ghettoes. [Ours] is the most successful integration policy in the world. It has helped Canadians retain their culture while being part of the broader community. That's what we are so proud of.

While some Canadians grumble about our approach to multicultural groups and the funding of foreign language training and ethnic festivals, all politicians since Trudeau have, to varying degrees, embraced the concept. That may be because it's almost impossible to divorce multiculturalism from politics. Trudeau biographer Richard Gwyn wrote that after losing his majority in 1972 Trudeau was prepared to use every tool in his arsenal, including the public purse, to restore his base of support and so, "up sprang a trebled multiculturalism program that functioned as a slush fund to buy votes."[12] The reality in Trudeau's day, as it is thirty years after he left office, is that ethnic politics is alive and well in Canada.

ASK MANY OLDER Canadians, particularly those not born in this country, why they think highly of Trudeau, and one answer stands out:

he opened Canada's doors to immigrants. This perception is perhaps one of the greatest myths about the Trudeau record.

The year Trudeau became prime minister, Canada welcomed 183,974 immigrants, equivalent to about one percent of its population. By 1984, the immigration rate was 0.3 percent of the population, a decline from 1968 of about two thirds.[13] These reductions did not reflect an anti-immigrant policy *per se,* but flowed out of choice made by the Trudeau government in response to a weaker economic climate and higher unemployment. Yet holding the line on immigration is exactly the opposite of what Trudeau is known for.

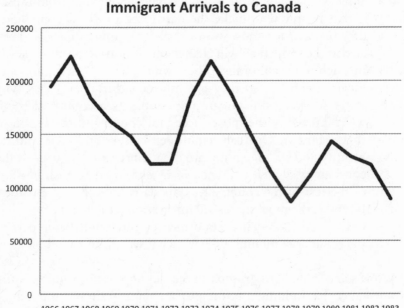

Immigrant Arrivals to Canada

In the mid-1970s, the government began setting quotas for immigration. The target for 1979 stood at 100,000, well below the 218,465 immigrants who entered Canada in 1974. Curiously, the government did not actively seek to attract people with job skills. The minister of immigration told Parliament that, in respect to the domestic labor market, "it is preferable, where possible, to employ or train Canadian citizens and permanent residents for Canadian jobs, rather than to admit workers from abroad."[14] To those who feared immigrants would take the jobs of Canadian residents, the government pointed out that, after factoring in expected emigration levels, the nation's population would not be significantly altered.

While the number of immigrants had begun to fall, their demographic composition changed dramatically. In the mid-1960s, 87 percent of immigrants were of European origin. By the mid-1970s, that number was 50 percent, falling to close to 30 percent by the time that Trudeau left office. While the Vietnam War produced a brief surge of American immigrants, consisting mostly of men seeking to avoid the draft and some of their supporters, the number of newcomers from south of the border declined dramatically after the conflict had ended, from 23,183 in 1970, to 12,237 in 1977, to 6,660 in 1984. Over the same period, immigrants from Great Britain and its colonies declined from 30,281 in 1970 to 10,167 in 1984. Italy dropped to 1,711 in 1984, less than 20 percent of the numbers from 15 years earlier.

Immigration quotas were filled mostly with citizens of Asian countries, excluding China. When pressed about the changing nature of immigration Trudeau's minister on the file, Lloyd Axworthy stated, "We are not trying to maintain the old stereotypes of what is a Canadian."[15] It was not the region or country of origin *per se* that was the main reason for the shift, rather it stemmed from increased migration from developing, rather than developed, countries.

In the pre-Trudeau era, immigrants to Canada were recruited based on labour shortages and the skill sets required to develop the economy. But under Trudeau, the portion of "family class" or sponsored relatives that were allowed into Canada expanded significantly. The system became increasingly skewed toward large extended families and against individuals. Changes to the Immigration Act proclaimed in 1978 allowed new Canadians to sponsor their parents *of any age*, which proved particularly enticing to those from less-developed nations, and less so to those from Europe.[16]

The political benefits of shifting to family-class immigrants proved enormous. Allan Gotlieb, who served the Trudeau government as deputy minister of immigration, recalled that one minister, Charles Caccia, was so persistent on behalf of his immigrant constituents that "[h]e almost drove me out of my mind."[17] Liberal MP Peter Stollery made the point in a 1976 memo to Minister of Immigration Bud Cullen:

> Immigration is a contributory factor to the winning of many constituencies ... I cannot understand why we have allowed such an important matter to be treated in such a bureaucratic fashion without political consideration ... I don't like to flay a dead horse, but our stupid decision not to admit any Portu-

guese-Angolans and to make it effectively impossible for most nominated [relatives] to come from the bastion Liberal area of Portugal has practically lost us the Portuguese community ... We allowed the Italian community to expand and guaranteed them as Liberal communities for many years. The Portuguese community is being thrown away ... You must realize that 66 percent of all our immigrants [are] coming from the Azores and they are practically 100 percent Liberal. The other 33 percent of immigrants coming from Portugal come mostly from Northern Portugal, which is the bastion of Conservative Portugal.[18]

To make political hay, during the short-lived government of Joe Clark, Trudeau castigated the Tories as anti-immigrant. "The policies that the Conservative Government seems to have been following in terms of cutting back support for the ethnic press, in terms of changing their immigration policies as we did so as to favor the reunification of families, their downgrading of multiculturalism by giving it to a minister who's apparently not very on top of the subject ... in all of these things we disassociate ourselves from Conservative Government policies."[19] Trudeau reminded voters that his government had given special attention to Canada's multicultural groups, including using money from Lotto Canada to support multiculturalism.[20]

Trudeau opposed any special deals with Quebec, particularly in areas within federal jurisdiction. But in 1978 he signed the Cullen-Couture Agreement, which gave Quebec the ability to influence the composition and size of its immigrant influx. Quebec was able to develop its own points system that took into account the likelihood of an immigrant integrating and prospering in the province. The agreement addressed Quebecers' fear that immigrants would not embrace the French language. Trudeau said he was open to a similar deal with other provinces, but only Alberta expressed an initial interest.

In Trudeau's final years in office, the government slashed immigration quotas by restricting newcomers who were not sponsored by families or were refugees. Independent skilled workers could only enter Canada if employers could prove they could not find a suitable Canadian worker.[21] Because of a weak economy and high unemployment, Trudeau also felt pressure from many quarters to reduce the numbers of refugees, which he did in 1983.[22]

It is therefore curious that there remains an impression that Trudeau opened up the immigrant floodgates, when immigration levels actually went in the other direction during his time as prime minister. One possible explanation for this perception, beyond clever political communication, is that, despite a decline in immigration, Trudeau held office during a period when large numbers of immigrants qualified to become Canadian citizens.

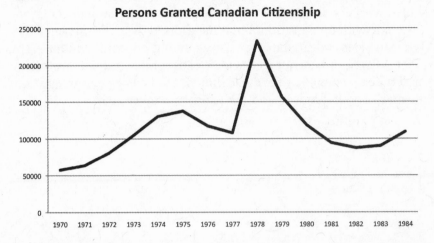

Ironically, immigration levels ramped up dramatically after Trudeau left office, almost tripling under the allegedly "anti-immigrant" Progressive Conservatives of the Mulroney era, from about 90,000 in 1984 to over 250,000 by 1993. And a record number of immigrants arrived in Canada in 2011 while Conservative Stephen Harper was in power.

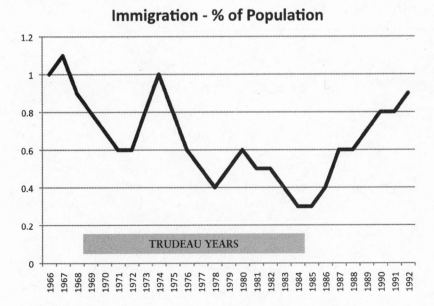

TRUDEAU TOOK OFFICE when immigration levels were high. He made his mark by reducing the number of immigrants and dramatically changing the composition of the immigrant pool, moving it away from developed to less-developed nations, from Europe and toward Asia. Tilting the system toward family reunification and away from skilled workers diminished the economic benefits that had traditionally come with immigration. But it maximized the political benefits to Trudeau. This endeared many existing immigrant communities to the Liberal Party and encouraged wide swaths of new Canadians to vote for Trudeau when the time came. But when it comes to immigration, the myth about Trudeau and the reality are miles apart.

CHAPTER 14

ENVIRONMENTAL TALK

The Mulroney government pulled the rug out from underneath our acid rain efforts.

A MONG THE MORE enduring images of Trudeau is one that depicts him shooting the rapids wearing his trademark buckskin jacket. Trudeau was an outdoorsman, an adventurer, and a canoeist. We know this because Trudeau often invited leading media personalities to join him on his treks to the far north. Many conflated Trudeau's love of the outdoors with a deep commitment to environmentalism. The record, however, reveals the opposite. Indeed, when notable Canadians chose Canada's Greenest Prime Minister in 2006, the jury awarded the honour to Brian Mulroney, not Pierre Trudeau. Some might say that Trudeau had a weak environmental record because he governed at a time when ecological awareness was in its infancy. But how to explain, then, that Canada fell behind other nations in terms of environmental stewardship during his tenure?

TO PUT TRUDEAU'S environmental record into context, Elizabeth May, environmental activist, leader of the Green Party, and its first member to be elected to the House of Commons, suggests we compare his accomplishments to those of Richard Nixon.[1] Nixon is known for many things, but not usually for his sensitivity to the environment.

May argues that Nixon's environmental policies put Trudeau's policies to shame.

During his term-and-a-half in office, Nixon signed the bill that established the Environmental Protection Agency. He also signed into law the Clean Air Act; Endangered Species Act; Safe Drinking Water Act; Coastal Zone Management Act; Ocean Dumping Act; Marine Mammal Protection Act; the Federal Insecticide, Fungicide, and Rodenticide Act; and the Toxic Substances Control Act. According to May, Trudeau accomplished much less in his fifteen-and-a-half years than Nixon did in his five-and-a-half years. Not surprisingly, Trudeau's biographers — and his own memoirs — make remarkably few references to environmental achievements.

Trudeau was not uninformed or uninterested. He included environmental issues in his first Throne Speech and engaged a senior Privy Council bureaucrat, Jim MacNeill, to advance the idea of putting environmental protection into the Canadian constitution. MacNeill's background paper made it into some constitutional working sessions, but not into any of Trudeau's constitutional blueprints. According to MacNeill, in the aftermath of the October Crisis, Trudeau focused on getting a constitutional deal and worried that throwing the environment into the mix would complicate or delay the process.[2] While disappointed, MacNeill thought Trudeau's inclinations to raise the environment in the constitutional setting were noble: "If the FLQ crisis had not happened, there is, in my view, a strong possibility the environment would be enshrined in the constitution today."[3]

In 1971 Trudeau gave green issues a seat at the cabinet table when he established the Department of the Environment, drawing together and rebranding the operations of the Meteorological Service of Canada and the Canadian Wildlife Service. The department also had responsibility for fisheries until 1979, when that became a separate ministry. While the merging of existing bureaucracies under the environmental banner made for good optics, it had little substantive effect. While McNeill considered Trudeau's change an accomplishment emulated in over 100 other countries, he concedes that the new ministry had no teeth: "[The ministry was given] only the very limited powers needed to clean up environmental pollution after-the-fact, largely through end-of-pipe measures and, unfortunately, it was given no power to influence the policies of ... finance, energy, industry, agriculture and other departments that resulted in pollution and environmentally destructive growth in the first place."

For example, health and agricultural policy remained divorced from environmental policy. The regulation and control of pesticides remained in the hands of Agriculture Canada, which carried a natural bias in favour of farmers. The military still had free reign on environmental matters. According to the Agent Orange Association of Canada, our military sprayed over one billion grams of Agent Orange, Agent Purple, and Agent White on CFB Gagetown and surrounding communities from 1956 to 1984.[4] The government confirmed usage only in 1966, although the defence minister added in 1981 that there was no confirmation that the chemical represented a health hazard.[5] In the United States, the EPA considered human health and the environment jointly. There, the human health aspects of toxins were considered alongside other environmental impacts.

Those who believe that environmental considerations receive undue weight in Canadian public policy may find Trudeau's lack of environmental steadfastness refreshing, even enlightened. But Trudeau's approach frustrated environmentalists.

When environmental lobbyists urged reductions in the use of fossil fuels, Trudeau subsidized the cost of fuel oil to consumers through the National Energy Program. He invested substantial tax dollars in energy exploration, subsidizing up to ninety percent of drilling costs for companies prospecting for oil and natural gas. His government also made a major federal investment to get the Alberta oil sands project off the ground. In his retirement, Trudeau sought no credit for helping to launch the oil sands, but he should be given his due, or blame depending on one's perspective.

When the United States lobbied for the construction of the Alaska Highway natural gas pipeline across Canadian territory to access the lower 48 states, Trudeau vigorously backed the project. He also said that if the project did not proceed as planned, he had other routes through the Mackenzie Valley in mind.[6] In 1974, in response to public pressure, the Trudeau government commissioned Justice Thomas Berger, a former leader of the British Columbia New Democratic Party, to lead the Mackenzie Valley Pipeline Inquiry. The $5.3 million inquiry, which reported in 1977, recommended a ten-year moratorium on the issue. In the end, the pipeline was never built despite Trudeau's initial urgings.

Trudeau unabashedly supported nuclear power, while expressing skepticism about alternative sources of energy. When pressed by a group advocating solar energy, Trudeau ridiculed their idea by giving them the proverbial finger while pointing to the sky on a cloudy day. When campaigning in British Columbia in 1979, Trudeau took offence at a protestor carrying a sign reading, "Trudeau = nuclear power. Dump both." In response Trudeau challenged his opponent, "What do you want to do, go back to the caves and live there? You'll still have to fight the dinosaurs."[7] In an address to Duke University graduates in 1974, Trudeau said, "To ensure nature's continued beauty, we are asked not to suffer, but we are asked to be reasonable.[8]

It was during the Trudeau era that we discovered that acid rain was killing lakes in Canada and the northern United States. Canadian officials were reluctant to call it acid rain, preferring the not-so-catchy phrase, "long range transport of acidic precipitation." Despite making some progress with Jimmy Carter in the White House, Trudeau lost Ronald Reagan's ear completely. The Reagan White House classified two National Film Board productions on Acid Rain as "political propaganda."

Despite his failure on acid rain, Trudeau can claim some credit for a number of environmental initiatives. He established the Canadian Environmental Advisory Council in 1970. In unison with the United States, Trudeau undertook the cleanup of the Great Lakes, which had become heavily polluted from industrial waste. Under his watch, Ottawa enacted the Clean Air Act (1970), the Canada Wildlife Act (1973), the Environmental Contaminants Act (1975), and the Ocean Dumping Control Act (1975). Successive budgets gave companies faster tax write-offs for pollution-control equipment. Trudeau asserted Canadian sovereignty over the Northwest Passage, largely on the grounds that Canada would protect it from pollution. New national parks were established. The federal cabinet established a policy of environmental assessment and review in 1973. But unlike the United States, which entrenched environmental reviews in legislation, the Canadian process was less formal, more malleable, and wide open to political manipulation.

Trudeau did not impress environmental groups. While Pollution Probe forged useful ties with members of the Toronto business community and built a constructive relationship with Ontario Progressive Conservative premier Bill Davis, it had less success with the Liberal prime minister of Canada. Dr. Ralph Brinkhurst, a former professor at the University of Toronto and early supporter of Pollution Probe, was no fan.

> We didn't get along with Trudeau ... He got away with being sort of arrogant and smart-assed at times. One perfect exam-

ple: he looked at the same young man [Tony Barrett] we'd been talking about, and he was wearing one of Pollution Probe's 'Do It' buttons. And there was this Trudeau, looked very archly at this young man, and sort of cocked an eyebrow and said, 'Oh, what does that mean?' with obvious innuendo. And the guy instantly reported 'It means think clean, sir.'[9]

There is little doubt that Trudeau had a personal, even romantic, connection to the far north, but according to May, he was less concerned about more mundane issues, such as poor people living in a toxic environment. In his book *Towards a Just Society*, it was acknowledged that Environment Canada "did not always succeed in impressing environmental values on the whole government."

Awarded the Order of Canada for his environmental leadership, Jim MacNeill believes that the Canadian political dynamic constrained Trudeau. "During the 70s and 80s, Canadians were generally speaking far more passive in the face of environmental destruction than their American cousins, who took to the streets in the millions demanding action."

This statement fully exposes Trudeau's half-hearted commitment to environmental management. Despite the suggestion, or the fact, that Trudeau was very much aware of environmental issues, he preferred to play the politics of the day than preserve the earth for future generations. Likewise, environmental consultant and author François Bregha saw Trudeau as someone who may have occasionally supported some conservation programs, but "protecting the environment was not his priority."[10]

On the environment, talk and action rarely aligned. In 1975 Trudeau defended the use a government helicopter on environmental grounds. He said using government aircraft to attend eight political events on the same day helped him to appreciate the lush southern Ontario countryside and the importance of preserving the environment. Trudeau added that he had a right to use government aircraft for both political and non-partisan events: "I really don't make a distinction. I [travel] in the most efficient way."[11]

On leaving office, Trudeau concluded that the department of the environment required stronger powers. But he was not prepared to allocate them while he was prime minister. In retirement, Trudeau's former environment minister admonished the Mulroney government for "pulling the rug out from underneath our acid rain efforts by abandoning our efforts to have the American government meet its agreed commitments under the 1980 memorandum of understanding, in favor of doing more research into acid rain."[12] Ironically, it was Mulroney who persuaded the Americans to act jointly and substantively on acid rain, a key reason why he, and not Trudeau, is considered to be Canada's Greenest Prime Minister.

CHAPTER 15

A BILINGUAL NATION

I was obviously determined to affirm the Québec fact, the French fact, within the central government.

WITHIN FOUR MONTHS of winning the 1968 election, Pierre Trudeau's government introduced the *Official Languages Act*. The law went well beyond the arrangements of Confederation to ensure Canadians would be able to address their federal government in either French or English, within reasonable limits. More important to Trudeau, the Act ended English dominance of the federal public service, taking away from Quebec separatists the argument that there was no place for French in their national government. While Trudeau often receives both credit and blame for official bilingualism, it was his predecessor, Lester B. Pearson, who did much of the initial heavy lifting.

Trudeau worried that his language policy could be rescinded just as easily as it was adopted, as it was initially an Act of Parliament. That's why, 14 years after its passage, Trudeau cemented language rights into the Constitution, placing them beyond the reach of mere legislators. As a further protection, Trudeau ensured that these constitutionally entrenched language rights could not, unlike most Charter rights, be overridden by the notwithstanding clause. This meant that, as long as there were a Canada, its federal government would be functionally bilingual, and English and French minority language rights would be protected across the land.

While achieving official bilingualism has been costly and divisive at times, the thrust of the Trudeau vision has not only endured but been expanded upon by his successors.

TRUDEAU UNDERSTOOD THAT in a federal country comprising two dominant linguistic groups, access to government services in French or English constitutes an issue of fundamental justice. Over Canada's first hundred years, French-speaking Canadians resented a lack of French-language services, their underrepresentation in the federal public service and the Canadian military, and the fact that unilingual anglophones ran the show in Ottawa. Taken together, these realities created a sense of unfairness, and contributed to rising nationalist sentiment in Quebec.

Graham Fraser, in his 2006 book *Sorry, I Don't Speak French: Confronting the Canadian Crisis That Won't Go Away*, reminds us that after England conquered France on the Plains of Abraham at Quebec City, the British treated the French not with condescension and disregard, but, at least initially, with benevolence and respect. When Sir Edward Thurlow outlined British policy during debate on the *Québec Act* of 1774, he made clear the altruistic intent of the legislation. "You ought to change those laws only which relate to the French sovereignty, and in their place substitute laws which should relate to the new sovereign. But with respect to all other laws, all other customs and institutions whatever, which are indifferent to the state of subjects and sovereign, justice and wisdom conspire equally to advise you to leave to the people just as they were."[1]

The BNA Act affirmed the use of English and French in the courts, in the federal legislature, and in their respective documents and journals. However, no provision compelled the federal government to treat English and French as the official working languages of the national government. From a citizen's perspective, section 133 of the BNA Act provided that English could be used in the courts and legislature of the province of Quebec, conferring a protection on the English-speaking minority. However, no corresponding section guaranteed a Franco-Ontarian or Manitoban the right to be heard at trial in French in a provincial court.

As Canada matured as an independent nation, it did not always offer an open hand of friendship to French-speaking Canadians. Whatever protections existed for the use of French in the public schools of

Ontario and Manitoba were effectively extinguished over time. James Mallory, in his book *The Structure of Canadian Government*, notes that the BNA Act was simply not an effective protector of language rights. As a consequence, "[t]he absence of constitutional protection for linguistic and cultural rights inevitably made the provincial rights of Quebec the only refuge in the constitution for the aspirations of French-Canadian nationalism."

Quebec politics has always been tinged with a streak of nationalism. Premier Maurice Duplessis, who held office for various periods from 1936 to 1959, challenged federal interventions into areas of provincial jurisdiction while standing up for an autonomous Quebec within the Canadian federation. But this had little impact on the use of French in and by the federal government.

It was not until 1958 that the Progressive Conservative government of John Diefenbaker introduced simultaneous translation into the House of Commons, fulfilling a campaign promise. Graham Fraser, Canada's sixth Official Languages Commissioner, dryly observed, "Members always had the right to speak in French in the House, but there was no right to be understood."[2] Of course, the same was true in reverse: unilingual French-speaking MPs could hear, but not understand, speeches delivered in English.

According to Fraser, it is a myth that Trudeau, a born-bilingual, highly educated, articulate academic and Montreal lawyer, imposed official bilingualism on the rest of the country.[3] Fraser contends that a unilingual diplomat from Ontario provided the vision and inspiration. Lester B. Pearson, Trudeau's predecessor, openly proclaimed that being a unilingual federal politician was a handicap, while correctly predicting that he would be the last unilingual prime minister.

While he was Leader of the Official Opposition, Pearson offered the country an inclusive view of the nation, stating on December 17, 1962: "To French-speaking Canadians, Confederation created a bilingual and bicultural nation. It protected their language and their culture throughout the whole of Canada. It meant partnership, not domination."[4]

Citing rising national disunity, Pearson sought to expand and enrich the partnership that had been established at Confederation. "French-speaking Canadians believed that this partnership meant equal opportunities for both founding races to share in all phases of Canadian development. English-speaking Canadians agree, of course, that the Confederation arrangements protected the rights of French Canadians in Québec, in Parliament, and in Federal courts; but most felt — and I think it is fair to say this — that it did not go beyond those limits, at least until recently."[5]

For Pearson there existed a direct link between bilingualism and national unity. But his vision for a united country ran much deeper. "I would like to repeat that we must agree on a cooperative federalism, i.e., a federative formula free of any unacceptable centralist thinking." He tended to side with the theory that Canada constituted a compact among the provinces, pledging that "[t]he government that I lead ... will do its utmost to reach equality between the two partners by starting to ensure an improved understanding, an easier exchange of views and opinions."

These were fine statements for an opposition leader. But soon after becoming prime minister, Pearson backed up his words with policy and action. "We want French to be able to be used just as easily as English in all the sectors of the federal administration. I know we will attain the desired result: a bilingual bureaucracy ... so that we can find permanent solutions to the problems which arise naturally in a bi-ethnic and bicultural country."[6]

In July of 1963 Pearson launched the Royal Commission on Bilingualism and Biculturalism (B&B), which gave rise to the recommendation that the federal government should become officially bilingual. Pearson announced his bilingualism policy on April 6, 1966 in the House of Commons, stating that within a reasonable period of time, it would be normal practice for oral or written communications within the public service to be made in either official language, and that communications with the public would be made in the language of the person being served.

Pearson's government paid a salary increment to those holding secretarial, stenographic, and typist positions in which working knowledge in both languages was required and used. His government launched a program, modest in scope, whereby twenty English-speaking civil servants and their families would spend a year in Quebec City, while ten French-speaking civil servants and their families would spend a year in Toronto. Going forward, the Pearson government indicated it would consider language proficiency, or the willingness to acquire it at public expense, a criterion in the selection and recruitment of university graduates for administrative trainee positions in government.

PIERRE TRUDEAU CONCURRED with the Pearson prescription of official bilingualism, but detested the notion that Canada was a creation of "founding partners." Countering the basic tenets of the B&B Commission, Trudeau did not accept Canada as a bicultural nation. He opposed nationalism in almost every form and advocated for a multicultural and pluralistic vision of society that embraced individual rights and protected minorities. It was not Canada's history, culture, institutions or even democracy itself that mattered most to Trudeau: it was a set of rights and freedoms to enable individuals in society to fulfill their potential and their destiny. Trudeau accepted only one element of Canada's history and culture as fundamental to nationhood: that we were a bilingual country. Even this he considered a concession on his part. To Trudeau, Canada could just as easily have had six or seven official languages, if society used them widely.

Graham Fraser observed that Trudeau's views often contradicted those of his ministers. "When the Bilingualism Act was being discussed Trudeau mused that 'maybe in the future there will be other official languages'. When he was asked why not make Chinese an official language he replied it was because, 'they were not threatening to break up the country.' The reality is that he saw the act in very pragmatic terms. This was legislatively necessary to keep Québec from separating."

Proficiency in multiple languages came easily to Trudeau. His mother was English and his father was French. With one sibling he conversed in French; with the other, English. With Fidel Castro, he spoke Spanish. In some ways, Trudeau lived beyond the limitations of language. When Margaret Trudeau asked her husband if he thought in English or French, he demurred. "I don't think in words, Margaret, I think in the abstract."[7] Trudeau switched to international French by abandoning his regional Québécois accent at the age of 14 or 15 years old. As he recalled in his memoirs, "Either I start reading something else, or I start speaking a bit more the way it's supposed to be done."

While Trudeau could weave effortlessly between English and French, his early loyalty and identity was to the French language and the Quebec nation. During one of his mandatory stints in military training during World War II, Trudeau ignored commands given to him in English. "I recall a run-in with an officer who was giving us orders in English. Since he was addressing French-speaking recruits, I wanted to know why he wasn't commanding us in our own language. But as you might expect, my request [spoken in French] had little effect."[8] Having made his point to the officer in charge, Trudeau replied in perfect English, "Good. Now I understand you. Remember that here in Canada, we are entitled to be commanded in two languages."[9] But he always wanted it known that his main language was French. While attending Harvard University, Trudeau wore a beret, which may have been a way to signal his heritage.

When back in Canada as a nomadic intellectual in the 1950s, Trudeau began to advocate for a bilingual federal public service. In 1954 he posited that federal civil servants who could pass a French-language proficiency test should receive bonuses. He also wanted federal buildings and embassies to be adorned with bilingual signage.

> Think about it. One year, an office would be opened in Ottawa offering, let's say, $100 to any federal civil servant who succeeded in proving his knowledge of French. The next year, the same could be done for Canadian military personnel in every city where there is a garrison. Yet another year, you and I could leave to nail bilingual plaques on all our embassies in the world.[10]

While advocating for his native language, during the 1950s and early 1960s Trudeau was often critical of French-speaking Quebecers for not developing themselves intellectually. He feared for the French language because he saw Quebec as a weak and decrepit society that was focused more on nationalism and separatism than on developing its culture and economy.

In a 1962 essay titled *New Treason of the Intellectuals*, Trudeau leveled a blistering attack on Quebec nationalists: "Now, except for a few stubborn eccentrics, there's probably not one French-Canadian intellectual who has not spent at least 4 hours a week over the last year discussing separatism. That makes how many thousand times two hundred hours spent flapping your arms."[11]

As a Quebecer, Trudeau boldly blamed his fellow citizens for their struggles, but he also criticized federal forces.

> It seems quite evident to me that the English-speaking majority has behaved as though French-Canadians were merely one of the country's ethnic minorities, with a few special privileges. The most striking example of this attitude occurs in the federal civil service, where English is, to all intents and purposes, the only working language ... The federal capital is an English capital. The Canadian Army is an English army in which French-Canadians have to overcome serious handicaps, especially from a linguistic point of view.[12]

For Trudeau, bilingualism was a key ingredient to achieving the just society he advanced during the 1968 Liberal leadership campaign. At the time when Trudeau came to power, francophones held only nine percent of jobs within the federal public service, while, collectively, they represented one-quarter of Canada's population.[13] Reflecting in his memoirs about this period, Trudeau wrote:

> The language of French-Canadians was not being accorded equal treatment, a situation that could not be tolerated for long in the just society of which I dreamed ... I talked about language rights across Canada, about equal opportunity, and the need for the government to protect the weak... I was obviously determined to affirm the Québec fact, the French fact, within the central government.[14]

FROM A CITIZEN'S perspective, especially in Quebec, being able to live and work in French, and communicate with one's government in French, was both fair-minded and just. But from an institutional point of view, implementing the mechanisms to achieve bilingualism was not for the faint of heart. According to Trudeau cabinet minister Jean-Luc Pépin, it took an insurrection to achieve these goals. "We ourselves were a very small group, Trudeau, Pelletier, Marchand, Lalonde, Chrétien, myself, and a few people in the civil service, say 50, all told... And we were bringing off a revolution. We held the key posts [in Ottawa]. We were making the civil service, kicking and screaming all the time, bilingual. We were a well-organized group of revolutionaries."[15]

While the policy of official bilingualism grounded itself in calls for social justice, it had a much more pragmatic side. Trudeau was acutely aware of how Quebec nationalists used the lack of respect for the French language in Ottawa as an argument to separate from Canada. "In effect, the language question had always been their best weapon for discrediting Canadian federalism."[16]

Within weeks of the 1968 federal election, Trudeau took charge of legislating Pearson's language policy, expecting it would "produce a veritable revolution within the federal public service in Ottawa."[17] Trudeau understood, however, that this battle would also produce something else: casualties.

The Official Languages Act affirmed that French and English were equal before the law, and established the principle that every Canadian citizen had the right to communicate with federal authorities in English or French. More controversially, Trudeau sought to make English and French the everyday working languages within the federal government and its agencies.

When the Official Languages Act was introduced in the House of Commons on October 17, 1968, Trudeau took dead aim at Quebec nationalists.

> Those who argue for separation, in whatever form, are prisoners of past injustice, blind to the possibilities of the future ... We have rejected this view of our country. We believe in two official languages and in a pluralist society not merely as a political necessity but as an enrichment. We want to live in a country in which French Canadians can choose to live among English Canadians and English Canadians can choose to live among French Canadians without abandoning their cultural heritage. French Canada can survive not by turning in on itself but by reaching out to claim its full share of every aspect of Canadian life. English Canada should not attempt to crush or expect to absorb French Canada. All Canadians should capitalize on the advantages of living in a country, which has learned to speak in two great world languages.

Trudeau then tried to calm the fears of unilingual public servants by announcing an extension of the language-training program for federal public servants begun in 1964. He acknowledged that implementing the government's objectives would take time and that their fulfillment would not prejudice the careers of unilingual civil servants.

Signaling even then that his policy work was incomplete, Trudeau cautioned that the language law had its limitations because it did not amend the constitution. "I have often stated my belief that such amendment is necessary to guarantee the fundamental language rights of our citizens. It does not affect provincial jurisdiction over the administration of justice or any other matter within provincial jurisdiction."

Trudeau bristled at criticism that he intended to make the citizens of Canada fully bilingual. As he told a friendly biographer, "The citizens can go on speaking one language or six languages or no languages if they so choose. Bilingualism is an imposition on the state and not on the citizens."[18] When people complained about French appearing on their Corn Flakes box, Trudeau told them to turn the box around.

John Turner, Trudeau's minister of justice, was responsible for introducing the Official Languages Act and obtaining the backing of provincial capitals. To gain support from British Columbia premier W.A.C. Bennett, Turner, with Trudeau's concurrence, agreed that the next justice appointment to the Supreme Court would come from British Columbia. The deal was sealed with a handshake, but Trudeau reneged, appointing Brian Dickson from Manitoba to fill the next vacancy.[19]

Despite support in the House of Commons from Progressive Conservative leader Robert Stanfield, Trudeau faced opposition on bilingualism from within his own ranks, including at the cabinet table from Manitoban James Richardson. "Canadians have been told by Prime Minister Trudeau and others for the past 15 years that the way to save Canada, the way to unite Canada, is to promote bilingualism throughout Canada," said Richardson. "The truth is that legislated and enforced bilingualism has never been a unifying force and it never can be."[20] Dissent within Liberal ranks, however, proved isolated and unsustained.

Pearson had no illusions about the difficulties involved in having anglophones learn French. But for Trudeau, languages formed so great a part of his upbringing that he did not empathize with those who struggled. Graham Fraser saw this as a flaw, at least insofar as it impacted on the implementation of official bilingualism.

> He was so academically brilliant that he underestimated and dismissed how difficult it was to learn another language, to the point of arrogance. There was an academic disdain in Trudeau stemming from his classical education and his belief that whatever you did not have you acquired with hard work and discipline until the goal was achieved.

What Trudeau had accomplished for himself in language proficiency he expected of others. When Joe Clark became prime minister in 1979, he introduced simultaneous translation for cabinet meetings. When Trudeau returned in 1980, he took the system out, on the grounds that ministers ought to be bilingual, which, of course, they often were not.[21]

TO COUNTER THE fear that French "was being shoved down the throats of English Canada," a well-used phrase of the time, the first two Official Languages Commissioners came from anglophone communities. The fluently bilingual Keith Spicer and Max Yalden faced the daunting challenge of gaining acceptance for the language law in English Canada.

And fears endured, especially among unilingual public servants whose working environment in Ottawa had been, to that point, exclusively English. In a bilingual environment, in which public servants could speak in the language of their choice, a unilingual anglophone would suffer the same fate as a unilingual francophone. While no one was being fired because of the new language law, becoming bilingual was essential to any federal public servant who wanted to rise to a position of influence.

In an attempt to calm the concerns of unilingual English-speaking public servants, Trudeau gave an adjustment period and free language courses to anyone whose job required knowledge of the other official language. Responding to criticism, Trudeau said, "It was never our intention, as some have maintained, to hand every fully bilingual employee in the public service a senior position on a silver platter." But to those who had invested many years in the public service, and who felt the rules had changed in the middle of the game, resentment became inevitable. Trudeau was unsympathetic. "I never thought that the opposition from the Anglophone community would be so shrill and so stubborn."[22]

The mechanisms to implement bilingualism were awkward, controversial and expensive. For civil servants, it was difficult to see the merits of the policy; after incurring the time and expense to pass their language proficiency tests, few spoke a word of French in their workplace. For many, the training regime involved one-on-one tutoring during the regular workday. Some public servants were able to take extended leave and travel to other parts of the country to learn a second official language.

Experience has revealed that there was a more effective and less expensive way to expand the use of French in the public service. "The model of sending large numbers of people across the river to learn French was triply expense," said Fraser. "We were educating older, and harder to train, staff. They were the ones making the highest salary. And it cost more to replace them."

Fraser also contends that public servants in the 1970s did not make an adequate personal commitment to the program. "There was a sense of entitlement. Many public servants believed it was the employer's responsibility to teach them how to speak French and that, well, 'it would take as long as it takes.' Without staff making a personal commitment to becoming bilingual the program was simply too expensive and not sustainable."

Once civil servants passed the oral and written language tests, the state rewarded them each year with an $800 bilingualism bonus. And since the bonus became part of the base pay for a public servant, it factored into pensions. In other words, it was a gift that kept on giving.

The best evidence of the bilingualism bonus's ineffectiveness? After being established by Trudeau in 1974, it was never increased. Fraser concludes, "Either it is essential for doing the job or it's not. The higher skilled jobs should have a higher pay scale." In 1977, Bilingualism Commissioner Max Yalden ridiculed the bonus in his annual report to Parliament. "However sympathetic one tries to be with respect to the much-discussed bilingualism bonus ... it is hard to avoid the judgment that it will prove to be enormously costly, harmful to morale and essentially out of line with the Government's own language policy."[23] In 1979 he added, "If there is one drawback bigger than its cost, it is that the bonus is virtually impossible to administer fairly."[24] In his final Annual Report in 1983, Yalden wrote: "Six years, and, let us say, almost a quarter of a billion dollars into the game, any question of the real contribution that the bilingualism bonus might be making to federal language programmes has pretty much been lost from view."[25] As with most government schemes, once in place, they become politically difficult to remove.

Notwithstanding the continued existence of the bonus, Fraser noted that by 2012, decisions about who received language training appeared more strategic, targeted at those expected to rise to supervisory position where bilingualism is considered essential.

While Trudeau acknowledged that it would take time to achieve a bilingual public service, he had limited patience and did not want to accomplish his objective simply by hiring new staff with strengths in both languages. While this would have restricted the public service hiring pool, under this approach taxpayers would not have paid to train unilingual staff in what for many positions was considered a mandatory skill.

BEYOND COST TO the taxpayer and frustration among unilingual public servants, Trudeau's language policies occasionally caused significant public anxiety. One such incident arose in 1976 when air traffic controllers in Quebec expressed their determination to operate in the French language. In what came to be known as the "Gens de l'Air controversy," many airline pilots were outraged that their safety, and that of their passengers, might be compromised because they would not be able to understand the instructions given to them in French from control towers.

While it was acknowledged that the international language of the skies was English, the French air traffic controllers wanted to be able to speak only French with those pilots who spoke French. It was their contention that in most instances this enhanced public safety.

The controversy, and a related strike by airline pilots in June of 1976, threatened to disrupt travel to the Montreal Olympics. Beyond the possible threat to this marquee event, Trudeau said the issue posed the biggest threat to national unity since conscription was introduced during the Second World War.[26] Trudeau set up a commission of inquiry headed by three judges to examine the issue, which led to a compromise agreement among pilots, air traffic controllers and the federal minister of transport. Jean Marchand, the federal cabinet minister who had been instrumental in bringing Trudeau into the Liberal party, thought the agreement was humiliating and criticized Trudeau's failure to defend the right to speak in French in Quebec. Marchand resigned from the cabinet.[27]

Trudeau was flummoxed by the Gens de l'Air controversy.

> The whole debate took us by surprise. The introduction of French was such a reasonable proposition that it is still difficult to comprehend how it grew into such a crisis ... Full-page ads were taken out in English-language newspapers denouncing bilingualism, and Québec newspapers responded with editorials saying Quebecers were being told to 'speak White.'[28]

According to Fraser, the resolution to the controversy had serious short- and long-term political implications. "Trudeau ultimately won, but by losing Jean Marchand and by compromising on language, he contributed to the conditions that led to the election of the Parti Québécois in 1976."[29]

Whenever Trudeau fell short of satisfying language advocates from Quebec, he would point to the "French power" being exercised in Ottawa. This included the appointment of francophones to senior government positions, including the commissioner of the RCMP, the speaker of the Senate, the Governor General, the chairman of the National Film Board, and the Chief of the Defence staff.

Trudeau did not deny that the Gens de l'Air controversy and the election of the PQ in Quebec were connected, but he blamed "English Canadian bigotry" for causing the problem in the first place.[30]

WHILE THE FEDERAL government headed one way on bilingualism, the government of Quebec went in the opposite direction. In 1974, the Liberal government of Robert Bourassa passed Bill 22 to make French the official language of Quebec. Trudeau resisted calls to disallow the bill, a federal power last used in the 1930s. But he did call the law "politically stupid" for insisting that there was only one official language in Quebec. Insulting the Liberal premier of Quebec did not advance the cause of federalism; however, Trudeau may have been right about Bourassa's political instincts at the time. Bill 22 inflamed Quebec anglophones, while not going far enough to appease Quebec nationalists. It was a no-win situation for the premier.

When the PQ defeated the Liberals in 1976, they made replacing Bill 22 with a charter of the French language their top priority. The intent of Bill 101, as the charter was known, was "to make French the language of Government and the Law, as well as the normal and everyday language of work, instruction, communication, commerce and business." Quebec's language law came with its own police force to root out even minor transgressions. Anglophones and allophones in Quebec objected to many provisions of the legislation, in particular the limitations that impeded the ability of parents to choose the language of instruction for their children.[31]

While Bill 101 went much farther than Bill 22 in limiting minority rights, Trudeau once again chose not to intervene. "I had no intention of using the constitution to disallow the legislation. The only way to change bad laws is to change the government, rather than using Ottawa to coerce a province." While Trudeau rarely backed down from a fight, he took a pass on defending the anglophone minority in Quebec.[32]

Among reflections by many public figures at the time of Trudeau's death, Stephen Harper said that he found the federal responses to Bill 22 and Bill 101 timid. In a less-than-flattering obituary, Harper wrote, "It was Mr. Trudeau who had remained largely silent and ineffectual as Quebec dismantled the very bilingualism he had proclaimed to be the great solution for Canada as a whole."[33]

But eventually Trudeau did respond to the anglophone minority in Quebec, and the francophone minority outside Quebec, by patriating the Canadian constitution with a Charter of Rights and Freedoms. The Charter was used by the courts to overrule parts of Bill 101 to give English-speaking Quebecers greater protection. (Minority-language constitutional protections will be discussed in detail in the chapter dealing with the Charter of Rights and Freedoms).

THE COST OF running a bilingual country has been a subject of much debate. Fraser offers no figures of his own, but he adds, "While no one knows the costs for sure, we also don't know what it would cost the nation if we were not officially bilingual."[34]

Detractors and supporters of official bilingualism suggest figures in the range of a few hundred million to around $2 billion per year to keep this policy alive. One substantive research study conducted by François Vaillancourt of the Department of Economics at the University of Montreal and lawyer Olivier Coche for the *Fraser Institute* estimated the incremental observable costs of federal language policy in 2006 at between $1.6 and $1.8 billion, about one tenth of one percent of the GDP.[35] Among the various elements of cost are:

- $216 million for communities to support the development of official-language programs
- Contributions to CBC and Radio Canada of between $186 million and $283 million
- $115 million to promote intercultural understanding
- Between $55 million and $86 million in language funding for Canadian films, television and publishing projects
- An estimated $281 million in direct departmental and agency spending to operate in both official languages
- Bilingualism bonuses at a cost of $51 million
- Maintaining an Office of the Official Languages Commissioner for $20 million
- Language training costs of $30 million

The Vaillancort/Coche estimate comes in somewhat lower than the calculation offered in the 1993 book on bilingualism by Scott Reid, *Lament for a Notion*. Reid, first elected to the House of Commons in 2000 under the banner of the Canadian Alliance (and re-elected as a Conservative in subsequent campaigns, including, most recently, 2011), estimated the costs at $1.7 billion in 1992, which, when adjusted for inflation to the same period as the Vaillancort/Coche study, works out to $2.3 billion. Reid's figures are somewhat higher, in part because he argues that equalization payments to Quebec would have been lower under more flexible language policies, and that the transfer of integration services for immigrants to Quebec caused an additional expense of $75 million.

Official bilingualism also imposes costs outside of government. Reid estimates that the cost of complying with consumer packaging and labeling for 1991/92 totalled $2 billion. Both Reid and Vaillancort/ Coche seem to agree that it is very difficult to differentiate compliance costs from marketing expenditures, which would have been incurred in any event to reach French-speaking consumers.[36]

Reid argues that official bilingualism represents a noble undertaking, but is misguided and unnecessarily expensive. He prefers "territorial bilingualism," the system he contends was proposed by the Royal Commission on Bilingualism and Biculturalism. A territorial model would apply bilingualism only in those areas featuring the strong presence of both languages, and would involve "the smallest amount of disruption to individuals."[37]

Costs are not the only factor giving rise to complaints about bilingualism. A bias in the allocation of funds also chafes. Some studies have shown that money for community support has disproportionately flowed towards francophone minorities. For example, out of $23 million handed out to 396 "official language communities," 18 were anglophone and 378 francophone (113 in Ontario).[38] Fraser believes in a "story behind the story," arguing that English-speaking Quebecers concentrated in the island of Montreal find themselves in a much stronger position to sustain their culture and language than the many francophone communities scattered across the country.[39] Trudeau gave a more crass political explanation for the disproportion: "Because it was the French who were talking about breaking up the country."

DESPITE THE OCCASIONAL protest or controversy, Trudeau's bilingualism policies have stood the test of time and maintain the support of the majority of the Canadian people.

The only major reform to the Official Languages Act came in 1988, when the Mulroney government brought the language law into conformity with the Canadian Charter of Rights and Freedoms. The 1988 reforms also gave new guarantees for federal public servants to work in either French or English, and committed federal institutions to assist in the development of minority language communities.

In 1991, Ottawa clarified regulations to define the circumstances under which federal institutions must offer their services in both official languages based on "significant demand," a criterion more stringently applied in circumstances involving public health and safety. In 2005, Parliament clarified that federal institutions were required to take positive measures to enhance the status of English and French linguistic minority communities throughout Canada. It also established legal measures to allow complainants access to courts to seek damages should the obligations in the Act be breached. At no point since its establishment has any government sought to weaken the Official Languages Act of 1969.

Over time, politicians enhanced language rights and programming because most Canadians support the essential elements of Canada's policies on bilingualism. In a poll conducted to coincide with the 40th anniversary of the Official Languages Act, 59 percent of those surveyed indicated that they believed bilingualism to be a success and a source of national pride.[40] Support was highest in central and Atlantic Canada, and among younger respondents and francophones. However, a majority of western Canadians disagreed with federal bilingualism policies.

The survey also revealed many misconceptions about the law. More than 60 percent of respondents believed that *all* federal public servants had to be bilingual, even though only five percent of federal jobs in western Canada were designated bilingual, and only 40 percent of federal positions overall require the ability to speak both languages. Almost 80 percent of those surveyed believed that all federal services must be offered in both languages, when the requirement exists only where there is significant demand.

While a majority of Canadians favour official bilingualism, only 40 percent of those surveyed agreed that bilingualism helps to keep the country united. But if the objective of official bilingualism was to keep Quebec in Canada, the data may have proven Trudeau correct. In the survey, 63 percent of francophones agreed that bilingualism kept the country united, while only 31 percent of anglophones thought this was the case.

A poll commissioned by Radio Canada in 2007 and conducted by the polling firm CROP found that 81 percent of those surveyed across the country supported the idea of Canada as a bilingual country.[41] More than 90 percent indicated that the prime minister should be bilingual, and 80 percent felt bilingualism would make them more employable. As Commissioner of Official Languages, Graham Fraser remarked, "[Canadians] are saying that if you want to participate in the national conversation, you ought to be able to do it in both languages. And we wouldn't have heard that 20 years ago."[42]

A poll of business leaders in 2003 conducted by Compass Inc. found that individuals in general benefit greatly from being able to speak a second language. This skill not only made individuals more employable, but higher-paid as well. Compass discovered that almost two in five businesses they polled offer language training or assistance to their staff.[43]

A survey conducted for Heritage Canada by Decima in 2006 showed that 72 percent of Canadians favoured bilingualism. The poll also showed that 70 percent of Canadians believe that the federal government has a significant role to play in promoting and protecting the status and use of French in Canadian society. Perhaps the most interesting statistic is that 80 percent of Canadians believe that senior public servants should be bilingual. This would have been reassuring to Lucienne Robillard, who, as president of the Treasury Board in 2003, announced that 200 of the most senior federal bureaucrats who failed to meet a deadline to become bilingual — about nine per cent of the total — would be transferred to other jobs or have their performance pay cut by up to 30 percent.[44]

Bilingualism has steadily progressed in the public service since the advent of Trudeau's policies.[45] In 1978, 25 percent of core federal public administration positions were classified as bilingual. By 2009, that ratio had increased to 40 percent. In 1978, 70 percent of the candidates in bilingual positions within the Canadian government met the requirement; by 2009, 92 percent did so. However, Trudeau minister and good friend Gerald Pelletier noted the reality that "[l]anguage courses lavished on English-speaking civil servants have often resulted in extremely theoretical certificates of bilingualism."[46]

Fraser believes we have reached the stage where most of the complaints about bilingualism in the public sector no longer concern policies, but sour grapes. "We receive relatively fewer complaints now about people not being served in the language of their choice. More complaints now come from staff about positions not being designated bilingual, but often from people who did not get hired [for these positions]."[47]

NOT ONLY HAS government embraced bilingualism but Canadians have increasingly sought to achieve it for themselves and their families. According to data from Statistics Canada, between 1951 and 2001 the number of bilingual Canadians tripled, jumping from 1.7 million to 5.2 million. This represents an increase from 12 percent of the population to 18 percent over the same period.[48]

The education system in Canada outside of Quebec has a lot to do with this rising bilingualism data. Statistics Canada reports that "[o]utside Québec, between 1981 and 2001, the number of elementary or secondary students enrolled in French immersion rose from 65,000 to 297,000, and the proportion rose from 2 percent to almost 8 percent of eligible school enrolment. Ontario accounted for close to three out of five students enrolled in French immersion, while New Brunswick had the highest proportion of their students in such programmes (26 percent)."[49/50]

In terms of the law, English immersion programmes for Francophones in Quebec at the primary and secondary schools level do not exist. Nonetheless, Quebec's population is more bilingual today than at any time in its history. Statistics Canada reports that in 2001, some 50 percent of Quebec's female labour force was bilingual, compared to 38 percent in 1971. In the male population, the percentage of bilingual people rose from 46 to 54 percent over the same period.

But this rosy data belies a darker reality. Part of Quebec's increase in bilingualism occurred because of a mass exodus of unilingual English-speaking Quebecers in the wake of the imposition of Bill 22 and Bill 101. Between 1971 and 1976, Canada saw a net migration of 52,200 Quebec anglophones to other provinces. That number increased to 106,300 between 1976 and 1981. The flow of anglophones out of Quebec has since slowed, but still averaged about 30,000 people every five years between 1986 and 2001. As a consequence, the percent of the population whose mother tongue is English in Quebec declined from 13.1 percent in 1971 to 8.2 percent in 2006.[51]

While the percent of the population of Quebec whose mother tongue is French has remained about the same over the past 30 years, the number of allophones (those whose mother tongue is neither French nor English) has increased significantly. Nonetheless, the percentage of Quebec households that use French most often at home grew from 80.8 percent in 1971 to 83.1 percent in 2001. Outside Quebec, the percent of the population using French at home declined from 4.3 percent of households in 1971 to 2.7 percent in 2001, owing largely to the number of French-speaking homes remaining steady when the population as a whole increased.[52]

So while the data suggests that we are becoming more bilingual across the nation, when it comes to first languages, Quebec has become more more French, and the rest of Canada more English.

RICHARD GWYN WROTE that "[b]ilingualism is to Trudeau as the CPR was to John A. Macdonald, his instrument for building a continent-wide country out of a huddled group of provinces."[53] That's why Trudeau would likely be pleased today with how Canada expanded bilingualism, how the federal government serves citizens in English and French, and how the federal public service theoretically functions in both official languages.

Building on the work of Lester B. Pearson, Trudeau brought forward legislation in the face of controversy and some opposition. In 1981, he enshrined bilingualism in the constitution, including minority-language education rights.

Official bilingualism might have been implemented more tactfully and diplomatically under Pearson; such was his character. But no one ever doubted that Trudeau's commitment or thought he would waver on the fundamentals, which may have been a factor in the success of his policies.

In 2001, Stephen Harper outlined his views on bilingualism in a column that appeared in the Calgary Sun.[54] He recalled that in his youth he accepted the view that a bilingual Canada would make us more united and more fair. His conclusion in 2001 was that it didn't work. While more people claim to be bilingual than in the 1960s, Harper suggested that if people have no deep economic, social or cultural reason to master and maintain the French language, the skill simply atrophies. "Why? It's extraordinarily difficult for someone to become bilingual in a country that is not."

Harper points out that real bilingualism in Canada remains geographically isolated to areas with significant numbers of both linguistic groups, regions narrowly concentrated near the New Brunswick-Quebec and Quebec-Ontario borders. He cautioned, "As Quebec becomes more French and the rest of Canada becomes more English, it really means the Québécois identify more with Quebec than with Canada." While he appears to accept Trudeau's point about the connection between bilingualism and national unity, Harper concludes that enforced official bilingualism did not bolster this connection. "As a religion, bilingualism is the god that failed. It has led to no fairness, produced no unity, and cost Canadian taxpayers untold millions."

As prime minister, Harper has been more hopeful and encouraging about the bilingual dimensions of Canada. He begins most of his speeches in French; that's the case whether he is speaking in Quebec City, Calgary or New York. His reasoning for beginning in French was that French was the first European language used in Canada.[55] In 2008, his government renewed the previous government's five-year $750 million Action Plan for Linguistic Duality, creating a five-year, $1.1 billion Roadmap for Canada's Linguistic Duality. And he has not loosened any provisions of the language law or policy. In this sense, Harper has not departed from the Trudeau vision in any meaningful respect.

Trudeau's policies and programs have not only been endorsed and expanded upon by his political successors of all stripes, but the public has increasingly come to support the notion of Canada as a bilingual nation. With some hesitancy in the West, and in the National Capital, where public servants are directly affected, these policies have strengthened the cause of Canadian unity and enhanced our citizenship.

CHAPTER 16

CHARTER OF RIGHTS
AND FREEDOMS

*The Constitution of Canada is the supreme law of Canada, and any
law that is inconsistent with the provisions of the Constitution is, to
the extent of the inconsistency, of no force or effect.*

SINCE 1980, THE role of the Supreme Court of Canada has evolved
dramatically. The advent of the Charter of Rights and Freedoms expanded both the number of litigants and the types of
suits coming before the court. Some cases pit Charter rights against
each other, demanding almost Solomonesque rulings. For example, if
a Christian college imposes a code of conduct banning homosexuality, which right should have primacy, the college's right to freedom
of religion, or the students' right to equality?

Rulings have ventured into areas beyond what the framers of the
Charter thought possible. Judgments have been as variable as the
quality and temperament of the judges themselves. Some rulings may
inspire while others seem to defy common sense. And while the Charter
was supposed to be used by individuals and minorities to protect
themselves against the power of the state, increasingly it has become
the instrument of choice for governments eager to rid themselves of
thorny political questions – by punting them to the courts.

Those with little faith in our politicians may see this last development as progress. But substituting judicial activism for government by elected officials creates its own set of problems. The Charter has arguably Americanized our legal system, giving our Supreme Court the same type of power enjoyed by the United States Supreme Court since 1791. This has created an antipathy, particularly among Canadian conservatives, towards the legal system and the Charter itself, and led to reforms, though timid, to the process by which Supreme Court judges are appointed.

After thirty years, Trudeau's baby is now all grown up – but the debate over its impact, both pro and con, rages on.

CRITICS OF THE Canadian Charter of Rights and Freedoms accuse it of allowing a liberal judiciary to run amok. Charter supporters contend that the courts have played a constructive and respectful role in safeguarding human rights and promoting justice. And while the courts have struck down relatively few pieces of legislation, they have not otherwise hesitated to use the power that Trudeau gave them in 1982.

While public opinion polls indicate that most Canadians don't believe the Charter affects their daily lives, it was a Charter ruling that opened up Sunday shopping when the Supreme Court ruled the Lord's Day Act, which since 1906 prevented stores from opening on Sunday, was unconstitutional.[1]

Two decades later, in another case involving religious freedom, the Court invalidated an order from a Quebec school prohibiting a Sikh child from wearing a kirpan (a ceremonial sword or dagger carried by baptized Sikhs) to school. In 2004, it threw out an agreement among owners of a Montreal condominium banning decorations on balconies, after a resident claimed it was used to prohibit the erection of a sukkah (a small temporary hut used by Jews each autumn during an annual religious festival).[2]

In 2007 the Court struck down a British Columbia law imposing a contract on B.C. hospital employees because it was judged to infringe upon a union members' freedom of association. The court interpreted this freedom to mean that collective bargaining was a constitutional right: a matter of "human dignity, liberty and autonomy."[3]

The court has also invalidated legislation in order to protect democratic freedoms. In 2003 the Supreme Court held that Parliament could not impose a law that restricted certain financial benefits from accruing to the Communist Party (or any party) because it ran fewer than 50 candidates in a general election.[4] In 2002 the court overturned the statute that restricted prisoners from voting.[5]

Even laws upholding so-called sacred cows, such as the public nature of Canada's health care system, have not proved immune to the Court's powers of disallowance. In 2005 the court ruled in *Chaouilli v. Quebec* that a provincial law prohibiting private medical insurance did not pass constitutional muster because it forced patients to accept overlong wait times for health care services.[6]

And in one of its earlier and most important rulings, the court struck down Canada's abortion law in the case of *R. v. Morgentaler* in 1988.[7] Thereafter a Bill introduced in the House of Commons in 1988 to ratify new legislation was defeated. Another much more restrictive Bill passed the House of Commons in 1989, but failed to become law on a tie vote in the Senate, the first time since 1941 that the upper body of the legislature thwarted the will of the House. No law has been enacted since, making Canada one of the few countries in the world not to regulate abortion.

This is just a small sample of cases in which the courts have ruled that legislators had overstepped their bounds. While parliamentarians do not oppose freedom and liberty or the provisions of the Charter itself, the Courts sometimes take a very different view of what those provisions mean than our elected officials.

WHILE TRUDEAU DID not hesitate to pass or amend laws in the Criminal Code dealing with questions of morality, such as gay rights and divorce, his successors faced quite a different landscape under the Charter.

The aforementioned case of *R. v. Morgentaler* made this new reality crystal clear. In the pre-Charter era, Dr. Henry Morgentaler had unsuccessfully challenged the law that abortions could be performed only at accredited hospitals and with certification of approval from the hospital's therapeutic abortion committee. Morgentaler served time in prison for conducting abortions. Trudeau, however, did not condemn the man, but instead praised him: "I've known Dr. Morgentaler for more than 20 years," offered Trudeau. "He's a real humanist."[8] Nonetheless, Trudeau was also of the view that abortion was morally wrong.[9]

It is noteworthy that when the Charter was publicly debated, Trudeau wrote this to Archbishop Joseph N. MacNeil on the matter of abortions: "The Government feels that the issue of abortion is not one which should be determined by the constitution ... therefore no provision of the Charter of Rights is reasonably capable of an interpretation that would either enshrine a right to abortion or a right to life for the unborn or deny the ability of Parliament to legislate on the matter." His justice minister, Jean Chrétien, elaborated that this view was based on legal advice the government had received, that the Charter of Rights was absolutely neutral in terms of the unborn. "Parliament and not the courts will continue to have supremacy over matters of conscience such as abortion."[10]

But post-Charter, by a vote of five to two, the Supreme Court ruled the abortion provision in the Criminal Code of Canada unconstitutional, because it was deemed to violate a woman's right to "security of the person." The reasons given to strike down the law varied, with only Justice Wilson, the sole woman on the High Court, proclaiming that the Charter absolutely protected a woman's a right to choice, at least for the early stages of pregnancy. Other justices voted with the majority on procedural grounds, noting delays in obtaining certificates or the unequal access to therapeutic abortion committees across the country. Two justices, in a minority opinion, ruled that the Charter did not give a woman the right to abort a fetus.

While Trudeau implied that such an outcome would not have been possible under the Charter, he was in no position to make good on such a promise when the time came, having given the courts the final power to rule on the matter.

That was not the only area where the Trudeau government was wrong about how the Charter would apply in practice. A concern was raised at the bureaucratic level about whether the Charter gave rights to illegal immigrants. Deputy Minister of Justice Roger Tassé, the man who drafted the Charter, assured other senior government officials that no such interpretation was possible. That was before the Supreme Court ruled in 1985 in the Singh case that the Charter applied to anyone present in Canada, regardless of status.[11] That made it possible for anyone in the world to come to Canada and apply for 'refugee status,' thereby gaining full access to social supports.

While the Court struck down the law on abortion, it upheld legislation on assisted suicide.[12] Sue Rodriguez, who faced certain death from amyotrophic lateral sclerosis (Lou Gehrig's disease), wanted the ability to direct her physician to end her life. She sought relief under the right to "life, liberty, and security of the person," as well as protection against "cruel and unusual punishment." The Court concluded that the prohibition against assisted suicide constituted a societal value and did represent a violation of fundamental justice.

Defining liberty based on societal values provides Supreme Court justices with a highly subjective field on which function.

Equality for gays and lesbians is another moral arena in which the Supreme Court has not feared to tread, despite the fact that such rights were not explicitly included in the Charter. Indeed, Trudeau had decided *not* to include sexual orientation in the list of conditions/ characteristics to be protected in section 15, despite the fact that gays and lesbians faced discrimination when he was prime minister.

Nonetheless, in 1995 the High Court declared in the case of *Egan v. Canada* that same-sex rights were "analogous" to other equality rights and deserved protection.[13] It went a step further in 1998 in the case of *Vriend v. Canada* when it "read in" the words "sexual orientation" into a section of the Alberta Individual Rights and Protection Act, which guaranteed the right to equality. The court held that the Act was intended to protect all individuals against discrimination, and that that included gays and lesbians even if they were not explicitly named. The court said the Act would be incompatible with the equality rights section of the Charter if it did not confer such protection, since the Charter's aim was to recognize and cherish the innate human dignity of every individual.[14]

Canadians may well hold strong opinions on abortion, assisted suicide and discrimination based on sexual orientation, but they also hold strong opinions on who should decide such issues. While Parliament was debating the same-sex marriage issue in the early 2000s after a spate of lower court decisions, an Ipsos-Reid poll found 71 percent of respondents agreeing with the statement that "it should be up to Parliament and provincial legislatures, not the courts, to make laws in Canada."[15] Of course the courts only have authority to uphold and reject laws, and not to write new laws. Nonetheless, fifty-four percent of respondents were of the view that "judges in Canada have too much power."

While it is easy to see inconsistencies on the Court's rulings related to matters of conscience, there is no clear public accountability for their decisions. Had politicians made these decisions, the voters would ultimately have had some say on the matter.

ONE AREA IN which the Charter makes news almost daily is criminal justice. While the courts have always used common law to adjudicate evidence, the Charter conferred on them the powers to reassess criminal statutes and the administration of justice itself, powers which were to have wide-ranging implications.

The 1986 case of *R. v. Oakes* provides a perfect example of this.[16] The decision set the standard for the evaluation of "reasonable limitations" on Charter rights not only in the criminal context, but in all civil Charter cases that came after it. The case involved federal tough-on-crime legislation that mandated that the possession of a certain quantity of drugs automatically elevated a charge of simple possession to one of drug trafficking. But when David Edwin Oakes was found guilty of trafficking because he had on his person 10 vials of hashish oil and $619.45 in cash, the Supreme Court overturned his conviction. The Court ruled that the violation of Oakes's rights was not reasonable, since abandoning the presumption of innocence in these circumstances could not be justified in a free and democratic society. While small-time drug traffickers may have cheered the ruling, Canadians living in neighbourhoods blighted by the drug trade probably did not.

When interpreting the meaning of "life, liberty and security of the person," the Court struck down a provision of the BC Motor Vehicle Act that created an automatic minimum prison term of seven days for driving a vehicle with a suspended license, whether the driver knew of the suspension or not. This counters the judgment of politicians and governments who believe that mandatory sentences can positively influence human behaviour. [17]

In 2008 the Supreme Court ruled that police couldn't make use of sniffer dogs in public spaces unless specifically authorized by legislation to do so.[18] This decision overturned a judgment against a student who had been convicted of narcotics possession after a sniffer-dog reacted to an unattended backpack in a school gymnasium. The police had been invited into the school by the principal, although that invitation was not based on what the Court considered to be a "reasonable suspicion."

A year later, however, the Court took a different direction when it ruled that police can sift through garbage for evidence without a warrant. In the case of *R. v. Patrick*[19] it concluded that an accused person effectively abandons privacy rights when he or she places material at the curbside and makes it accessible to passers-by. In this case, the accused, Russell Stephen Patrick, had been convicted of making the illegal drug ecstasy in his home.

Commenting on the practical application of the Charter to police work, former Ontario Provincial Police boss Julian Fantino lamented in his autobiography that the rights of criminals now supersede those of victims and of society in general. "I never believed the Charter was

designed to invent unreasonable and truly mind boggling schemes
to protect criminals, but to a large degree this is exactly what has
happened."[20]

The notion of the Charter being an instrument of process, rather
than one of pure justice, was echoed by Vern White, former Chief of
Ottawa Police Services and a former Assistant Commissioner of the
RCMP:

> The reality is that pre-Charter the focus in the courts, in my
> opinion, was on guilt or innocence. Post-Charter the emphasis
> is on the investigation. The conduct of police service and of-
> ficers became the focus and the guilt or innocence has taken a
> back seat. I understand the need for the Charter, but am chal-
> lenged at times when a case is thrown out due to police con-
> duct or tactics, because the victim is left out of the discussion.[21]

There is some irony that Margaret Trudeau, former wife of Pierre
Trudeau, invoked a Charter right in response to a charge of driving
under the influence of alcohol. Ontario Court Judge Lise Maisonneuve
concluded that Mrs. Trudeau's right to counsel of choice and
protections against unwarranted detention were violated when she
was arrested on May 30, 2004. This conclusion was based on the fact
that the police told Mrs. Trudeau that her attorney did not answer the
phone when called, rather than explaining that an answering machine
had picked up the call. She blew over the legal breathalyzer limit, but
her lawyer contended that she should have been permitted to confer
with counsel for up to two hours before taking the test. The acquittal
was overturned by a Superior Court and then reinstated by the Ontario
Court of Appeal. Her lawyer Michael Edelson did not feel that his client
received special treatment: "She's just one of thousands of Canadians
who found her rights were breached by police... It happens all the
time."[22] In 2008 a charge of possession of marijuana against Margaret
Trudeau was stayed because of a flaw in the search warrant.[23]

ON THE OCCASION of the Charter's 25th anniversary, Chief Justice
Beverley McLachlin mused about legislators passing "hot potato" issues over to the courts to manage. "While the evidence falls short, in
my view, of showing that in fact the Charter has caused politicians
to shunt difficult questions into the courts, the concern remains valid
and the possibility that this might occur must be guarded against."[24]
McLachlin was being circumspect.

In many cases, the prime minister refers questions directly to the Supreme Court even before Parliament has considered the matter. On the issue of same-sex marriage, the federal government sidestepped the pressing need to make a political decision by referring proposed legislation to the Supreme Court.[25] The court ruled that same-sex marriage fell within the purview of the federal Parliament and that same-sex unions are consistent with the Charter. It further concluded that religious freedom protects those who choose not to perform same-sex marriages. On the 30th anniversary of the Charter in 2012, Jean Chrétien admitted that he hadn't anticipated that the Charter would be used to legalize gay marriage. "It was something that did not exist, gay marriage, at that time. So I was very surprised when the court, using the Charter, said it was discrimination not to have gay marriage."[26]

Relying on the Supreme Court to do the heavy lifting is a convenient way for a prime minister to extricate him- or herself from a sticky political situation. And Chrétien was not above it himself. In 1996, following the razor-thin defeat of the separatists in the 1995 Quebec Referendum, Chrétien tasked the Supreme Court with one of the most consequential references in its history: Could Quebec secede from Canada unilaterally?

The Court concluded that Quebec does not have the right to separate on its own under Canadian or international law; however, if Quebecers expressed a clear will to secede, the federal government would be obliged to enter into negotiations. In response, the Chrétien government introduced the Clarity Act, which closely followed the Court's decision. Yet the Act itself remains ambiguous because it contains no precise definition of a "clear will by a clear majority."

In the secession reference, the high court established a framework of four principles to guide its decision-making: democracy, federalism, respect for minority rights, and constitutionalism (the rule of law). An Ontario court then applied these principles in 2000 to prohibit the provincial government from shuttering Ottawa's Montfort Hospital,[27] which largely serves the city's minority French-language community. The government defended the closure as a cost-saving measure, claiming it was not discriminatory, since it was based on the same criteria applied to other hospital closures across the province. The ruling held otherwise, leading to charges of judicial activism, imposing an obligation on an officially unilingual province to provide services in French. The result would have pleased Trudeau. He probably would have further approved of the fact that the federal Commissioner of Official Languages intervened in support of keeping the hospital open.

Another court reference stands out for its shockingly *self*-referential nature. It involved the pay of judges. The usual practice saw judicial wages and benefits established by an independent compensation commission. But the governments of Alberta, Manitoba and Prince Edward Island chose not to accept the recommendations of the commission, and established a different pay scale. In the *Provincial Judges Reference*,[28] it was determined that such "political manipulation" of judges' salaries violated the Charter provision for a fair and public hearing by an independent and impartial tribunal. Apparently, judges risked losing their impartiality if their pay rates were pegged to the general level of public service wages, rather than the special recommendations of an independent commission. Needless to say, the commission had recommended higher salaries than the province was proposing to pay. Constitutional expert Peter Russell called the ruling obnoxious and totally wrong.[29]

Finally, the Charter has also created situations in which governments do not even bother with a reference when they see the judicial writing on the wall. When Baltej Singh Dhillon was recruited to join the RCMP, he learned that he would not be able to wear a turban on duty. Nevertheless, after joining the force he pressed the point, and the issue hit the media. Canadians besieged the government with petitions not to change RCMP rules. Despite strong pressure in the Mulroney government caucus to maintain the Stetson as standard RCMP issue, the justice minister concluded that the courts would likely rule the ban on turbans a violation of Singh's religious and multicultural rights under the Charter. The government changed the regulations accordingly, allowing Charter provisions to trump popular will without the issue ever seeing the inside of a courtroom.

Trudeau may have not intended for the Charter to give politicians an excuse to duck responsibility for sensitive issues, but in many instances, that has been the reality.

OUR CONSTITUTION SHOULD protect citizens from the raw power of government when it oversteps its authority, and acts unfairly or unjustly. However, such a system also creates room for abuse, tempting advocacy groups and individuals with money, influence and a pet cause to use the Charter — and clever lawyers — to attempt to have the laws changed in their favour. Far from levelling the playing field, the Charter has merely tilted it in a different direction. Designed to protect minorities from the "tyranny of the majority," according to Tasha Kheiriddin and Adam Daifallah, leading conservative thinkers and authors of the book *Rescuing Canada's Right,* it instead imposed a new tyranny: that of interest groups on the legal system.[30]

Lorne Gunter of the *National Post* has argued that the problem is not so much the Charter itself but the enormous state apparatus of human rights commissions and government-subsidized special-interest groups that Trudeau created to leverage the document. He poses the question, "If Trudeau had genuinely seen the state as such a threat to individual liberty, why would he have subordinated individual rights to such giant institutional structures?"[31]

Gunter contends that Canadians have abandoned personal responsibility in favour of using the government to force others to give us what we want. He makes his point by referring to the case of Marise Myrand, a diabetic with heart and respiratory conditions. She sought a court order requiring her condominium association to give her a parking space near the building's door. With the assistance of a government-paid lawyer, Ms. Myrand persuaded the Quebec Human Rights Commission to give her the spot she wanted, and also to order her fellow condo owners to cough up $10,000 for the harm done. The Commission seemed unconcerned that its decision displaced the spot's owner, a woman in her 60s also suffering from health issues.

Many Charter critics harbour less concern about the words in the Constitution than about how the policies and programs of the federal government have financially supported rights litigants and interest groups. The main source of funding is the Court Challenges Program of Canada (CCP), which dates back to 1978. Created to provide financial assistance for important court cases that advance language and equality rights guaranteed under Canada's Constitution, it initially funded challenges to Quebec's Bill 101. But after the Charter was enacted, its mandate and scope grew dramatically. The Mulroney government expanded the program in 1985, before concluding it was no longer necessary in 1992, resulting in the CCP becoming an election issue the following year. The Liberal government under Jean Chrétien re-established the program in 1994. Stephen Harper's Conservatives terminated the $5.5 million in federal funding in 2006 before restoring limited funds for official languages cases.

This back-and-forth based on partisan perspective and electoral politics demonstrates how the pursuit of Charter rights can be influenced by the state's financial support. Over its lifetime, and especially in the Charter's early years, the CCP greatly impacted what kind of cases — and what litigants — came before the courts. Of twenty-four equality rights judgments rendered between 1984 and 1993, nine featured a party or intervener funded by the CCP.[32]

WHILE THE SPECTRUM of individual rights has evolved and expanded over the past thirty years in Canada, other countries without an equivalent to the Charter have experienced similar changes in that timeframe. The practical enjoyment of rights appears to be related less to the existence of codes or documents, and more to social and political trends. While the U.S. has had a Bill of Rights since 1791, African Americans had to wait until the middle of the last century for their Supreme Court to address systemic discrimination fairly. Gay marriage exists in the U.K. without a charter or even a written constitution.

Social pressure and political leadership often deliver the most dramatic change. The big difference wrought by the Charter is the extent to which those changes are decided by courts, rather than legislatures. As Trudeau hoped, the Charter provides a check on parliamentarians, which equates to a check on democratic will. Given the lack of success of two major attempts at constitutional and Charter amendment, it looks like Trudeau's legacy is here to stay, as-is.

Though conservatives often complain loudly that Charter-based jurisprudence is biased against them, court rulings have not been ideologically uniform. While social conservatives probably see their positions rejected most often, they do not lose every case. That's because courts incorporate prevailing public opinion when considering the limitations imposed on rights in a "free and democratic society." Issues are revisited, in different but related forms, depending on changing social norms. For example, while the Supreme Court rejected the assertion that the definition of "family status" in the Canadian Human Rights Act included gay families in 1993,[33] it affirmed the inclusion of same-sex partners in the definition of common law "spouse" in the Ontario Family Law Act six years later.[34] In other words, if social conservatives or social progressives want to influence the courts' interpretation of the Charter, they must first change the views of society.

These judicial checks and balances have had deleterious effects, however, on the public purse. The Charter has made Canada a more litigious society, slowed down the administration of justice, and made it more expensive. It has also changed the nature of criminal prosecution. By giving defence lawyers new grounds on which to challenge evidence, trials can be longer and more complex.

Overburdened court systems can even have the perverse effect of putting convicted criminals back on the street in the name of respect for their Charter rights. This was the case with Joseph William Hammer, a British Columbia man convicted of dealing cocaine in 2011. Because Hammer had to wait 42.5 months for his conviction (which was rendered in under 30 minutes), he was set free. The presiding judge explained his decision this way:

> The fact that an unrepentant drug dealer who ... while involved in the trial of this matter, has been charged with further like offences should now be able to be free of the consequences of this very serious offence because the judicial system could not accommodate his trial within a reasonable time should alarm and concern the community. However, all citizens, even drug dealers, are entitled to the full protection of their rights under the Charter.[35]

In the face of cases like these, many conservatives, like political activist Chris Froggatt, believe the Charter should get a second look. He wonders whom the Charter is protecting when, leaving issues of race aside, 85-year-old grandmothers receive the same treatment at airports as travelers presenting a higher-risk profile. And he wonders why those who enter Canada by illegal means enjoy the same protections, privileges, and support as citizens.[36]

Peter Russell evinces only modest appreciation for the Charter: "For most Canadians who do not have brushes with the police, it doesn't do much for them. On the whole the courts have not gone wild in interpreting the Charter, but they have done a particularly important job in improving criminal justice policy." Russell, who served as research director for a Royal Commission into the activities of the RCMP, does see merit in greater protection for individuals in their dealings with police, particularly for black and Aboriginal youth: "In this area the Charter was not an encroachment on the legislatures or on Parliamentary democracy since they have no particular purchase on how the police act on the streets in doing law enforcement."

Russell also believes the Charter moved the country forward in addressing systemic discrimination against gays and lesbians. Of course, as we have seen, Trudeau's Charter made no specific reference to protecting gays and lesbians, but the courts used the principles inherent in the Charter to broaden its terms.

Many complain about the Charter for the protections it does *not* provide. Conservatives would like to see property rights enshrined in the constitution. Socialists want the Charter to impose equality of outcome rather than just equality of opportunity. Neither is likely to get what they want, which underscores the fact that the Charter, like any legal instrument, is no path to utopia.

Nor has the Charter remade Canadian society, or unified it, along the lines that mattered most to Trudeau: language and cultural identity. The protections that Trudeau sought for minority language rights are modest in scope; they do not appear to agitate Quebec nationalists greatly or change how Canadians view bilingualism. The Charter facilitates minority-language education through the opening of new French-language schools across the country, reversing discriminatory actions that had been taken by governments to deny language rights. The grudge Quebec nationalists still hold against Trudeau has more to do with the constitution's patriation without their consent than with the contents of the Charter.

Most of what the Supreme Court has done with the Charter could have been accomplished legislatively. Instead, Trudeau gave the courts the ultimate power to rule on matters that had previously been within the primary, but not exclusive, domain of Parliament. The possible advantage of such a shift is that judges are unaffected by the political pressure exerted on elected officials. They are not affected by election cycles, can distil complex issues free from public pressure, and ruminate longer on expert advice and argument.

But judicial supremacy also spawns a host of negatives. Subscribing to the superiority of judicial decision-making implies that voters cannot trust their politicians, let alone themselves. It encourages political cowardice, and "passing the buck" on thorny issues. For this we cannot blame the courts, but our elected officials. This also entrenches an elitist view of how society functions best, through the judgments of unelected wise men and women. To give Trudeau credit, he gave politicians an escape hatch in the text of the notwithstanding clause. Ironically, he long considered this to be the Charter's greatest flaw.

The Supreme Court's decisions are also not wholly divorced from politics, because after all, judges are appointed by politicians. Court watchers have observed that, contrary to its early Charter judgments, the Supreme Court has taken a more conservative perspective on criminal matters in the new millennium.

Liberal prime ministers are more likely to appoint more liberal judges, while Conservatives would be more likely to favour more right-of-center choices. Compare Jean Chrétien and Paul Martin's picks with Stephen Harper's. On the bench in 2013 there remain three jurists named by the two Liberal prime ministers: Louis Lebel, Morris Fish, and Rosalie Abella. On many matters, notably civil liberties, the rights of the accused, and, in Abella's case, women's rights, this trio is considered progressive — Abella radically so in some quarters. Harper's five appointees — Marshall Rothstein, Thomas Cromwell, Michael Moldaver, Andromache Karakatsanis, and Richard Wagner — are anything but. As Fish and Lebel near retirement age, court watchers predict an even stronger "law and order bias" will permeate the court.[37]

Finally, while the Charter was arguably designed to confer voices to the previously voiceless, Canadians never had the chance to pronounce directly on it themselves, either in an election, as they did with the Free Trade deal in 1988, or in a referendum, as they did with the Charlottetown Accord in 1993. While former Supreme Court Justice Frank Iacobucci observed that "[o]ur Charter's introduction and consequential remedial role of the courts were choices of the Canadian people through their elected representatives as part of the redefinition of our democracy,"[38] this statement holds true only at the highest level. Yes, we did elect a government, and a prime minister, that created the Charter. Yes, a host of interest groups and individuals were invited to weigh in on what they thought should go into the document. But Canadians were never consulted on the basic question of whether they wanted a Charter or not. Had Trudeau done so, either at the ballot box or in a referendum, the Charter, had it passed such a test, might have made a real contribution to Canadian unity over the long term.

Instead, thirty years out, the Charter remains a divisive document. While it did achieve part of Trudeau's vision, enabling the federal government to exert influence in areas of provincial jurisdiction, and making provincial laws conform to Trudeau's vision of a bilingual and multicultural Canada, it also replaced parliamentary supremacy with constitutional supremacy. Trudeau's legacy is a system in which the courts have substantially more power and in which they, and not the voters, now tell our democratically elected politicians what they can and cannot do.

No parliamentarian opposes individual rights and freedoms, or favours an oppressive government. The critical question is who is best placed to balance competing rights. Before the Charter, Parliament made that call. Today, the judiciary has the final word. John Turner does not object to the Charter *per se* and concedes that the Supreme Court has issued many good decisions, but he thinks the Charter is a step backwards. "It all goes back to the Magna Carta," said the former prime minister, which is to say, we already had the foundation of what we needed to protect individual rights well before the Charter came along.

CHAPTER 17

NO APOLOGIES

You're sick if you're trying to take one wrong out of Canadian history and make great speeches about it and say that we're going to deal with this particular problem because there's a particular pressure group now.

OR A MAN preoccupied with a just society, Trudeau was surprisingly disinclined to acknowledge or address past injustices. This despite the evidence that dealing with unresolved conflicts can contribute to nation building. Be it our treatment of Canadians of Japanese descent during World War II, our unwillingness to detain and prosecute Nazi perpetrators of the Holocaust, the imprisonment without warrant of law abiding citizens during the October Crisis, or illegal activity by the RCMP revealed through a Royal Commission, Trudeau was not one to make apologies on behalf of the nation.

TO TRUDEAU THE Second World War was a distant reality. He claimed in his *Memoirs* that during the war he focused his attention on his studies, not current events. While it is difficult to categorize a six-year international conflagration as just a current event, Trudeau wrote that only at the "super informed environment" of Harvard University in the autumn of 1944 did he come to understand the true dimensions of the war. "I realized then that I had, as it were, missed one of the major events of the century in which I was living."[1] Curiously, he declared in his *Memoirs* that he had no regrets about his apparent disinterest in the conflict, calling regret a useless emotion. This aversion to regret seems to have endured for the balance of Trudeau's life.

It was not until the release of volume one of the Nemnis' biography in 2006 that we learned the true nature of Trudeau's wartime activities. During the Second World War, he was anything but idle. On November 25, 1942, a young Jean Drapeau, the future mayor of Montreal, was campaigning in a federal by-election in the riding of Outremont. He faced only one opponent, Major General Léo-Richer La Flèche, a war hero. The key campaign issue was conscription for overseas service, for which the Major General made the case to the people on behalf of the Liberal government.

Far from being uninvolved, Trudeau was one of six speakers to address the overflow crowd, where he called for a revolution: "Citizens of Québec, don't be satisfied with bellyaching. Long live the flag of liberty. We've had enough of band aids, the time has come for cataclysms."[2] Trudeau declared the war to be Imperial, imbecilic and disgusting. He argued that Canada was too eager to join Great Britain in battle; the country was not threatened with an invasion and, at the time, "Hitler had not yet won his staggering victories."[3] Of course, by the time Trudeau called for revolution, ships and lives had been lost in the Gulf of Saint Lawrence, some 300 kilometres from the capital of Quebec. Trudeau blamed Drapeau's by-election loss on the ethnic vote, citing the fact that two-thirds of the voters were Jewish and English.[4] (Ironically, Quebec Premier Jacques Parizeau would echo Trudeau's words fifty years later, when he blamed his 1995 referendum loss on "money and the ethnic vote.")

Trudeau's 1942 writings on conscription, though some were never published, provide further evidence of his strong and informed opinions about the war:

> The gourmets of Ottawa have prodded us, sniffed us, kneaded us and found us ripe ... We [French Canadians] are the first to forget those promises that we extorted from the government ... I am not only against conscription, but I'm also against mobilization, against participation, against rearming, against aid to the belligerent. I am against the war. Is that quite clear now[?][5]

More widely reported in the biographies was an incident during the war when Trudeau and a friend paraded around Northern Quebec in vintage German military uniforms and helmets, although the helmet may have been a French issue. It was a tasteless, disrespectful and frightening prank that Trudeau never adequately explained.

This brings us back to Trudeau as prime minister, when he was urged to confront the issue of suspected war criminals living in Canada. Despite mounting evidence of their presence, and calls from the Tories to act, Trudeau considered his options in 1981 and decided to do nothing. His justice minister, Jean Chrétien, told his parliamentary colleagues that he found enacting new legislation to bring alleged Nazis before a Canadian court repugnant. At a 1982 meeting of the Canadian Bar Association Chrétien added, "I don't think we should start in Canada today trials about crimes that have been committed in other nations. It's utterly unacceptable someone should be tried (here) for an alleged criminal offence that occurred more than 40 years ago."[6]

Trudeau later explained his thinking on war criminals at a 1987 international human rights conference, in remarks that were thought to be off-the-record.[7] He stated that he did not want to dredge up the past so that he could focus on the problems of the present.[8] But he felt reluctant to act not just because of the passage of time. Trudeau said that it was not easy to distinguish between crimes against humanity, such as the murder of 6 million Jews, and war crimes. He said that the Allied armies were involved in questionable activities, if not war crimes as well, citing the destruction of German cities and the use of nuclear bombs on Japanese cities.

In 1985 the Mulroney government established the Deschênes Commission to study the issue of suspected war criminals living in Canada. Its 600-page report, issued in December 1986, led to legislation that enabled the government to prosecute alleged war criminals for acts committed in other countries. Not included in the commission's final report was the research it sponsored by historian Alti Rodal. Rodal discovered that Trudeau actively and personally opposed the search and prosecution of war criminals in Canada. When the government ultimately released a heavily redacted copy of Rodal's report under the Freedom of Information Act, she said the missing sections dealt with Trudeau and his "political reasons" for not forging ahead with prosecutions.[9]

Trudeau concluded his remarks in 1987 by saying, "Everybody does things that are not nice in the war. It's necessary to try and forget that type of thing." This was not something he ever suggested to the Jewish constituents of his Mount Royal riding when he was seeking their votes.

IN THE EARLY days of the Second World War, the federal government required persons of Japanese descent living in Canada to register with the RCMP. Later it imposed a curfew, along with restrictions on possessing motor vehicles, cameras, radios, firearms, ammunition and explosives. Ultimately, it confiscated the assets of Japanese Canadians and interned some 22,000 in camps or forced them to work on sugar beet farms. More than 13,000 of those interned were Canadian-born. The entire operation was done legally under the powers of the War Measures Act (WMA).

In 1946 Diefenbaker urged the government to repeal the WMA, calling it an invitation to any government "to declare an emergency to the detriment of the rights of our people." At about the same time Diefenbaker made a fuss, so did Trudeau. In 1948, while studying at the London School of Economics, he wrote a letter concerning the treatment of Adrien Arcand by the Liberal government of Mackenzie King. Arcand, the leader of the anti-Semitic and fascist National Unity Party, was seeking compensation for being detained under the WMA. Trudeau described the law as tyrannical and complained that "the government ... found it much easier to intern those around whom hostile, or merely critical, opinion might crystallize."[10] Incredible as it seems, Trudeau chose to defend a Nazi sympathizer even after the horrors of the Holocaust had been revealed to the world — and, paradoxically, condemn the very legislation he would invoke twenty-two years later during the October Crisis.

While Ottawa did not repeal the WMA until 1988, remedying the harm done to Japanese Canadians constituted a pressing national issue while Trudeau was in office. In 1982 the National Association of Japanese-Canadians turned to Trudeau for help. Gordon Kadota, president of the association, said his people had been shamed: "We've been living with it for 40 years ... and something should be done to clear that."[11] Japanese Canadians launched a campaign in 1983 that sought an apology and a repeal of the War Measures Act. The case was not difficult to understand, as was demonstrated in a plea for justice from a victim of this oppression: "Born in Canada ... I had perceived myself to be as Canadian as the beaver. I hated rice. I had committed no crime. I was never charged, tried or convicted of anything. Yet I was fingerprinted and interned."[12] Trudeau declined the pleas for redress.

The matter came up again in the spring of 1984, just before Trudeau's resignation as Liberal leader came into effect. While Trudeau described the treatment as regrettable, he refused an apology or compensation. "I'm not sure where we stop in compensating." Trudeau cited other examples of injustice, including the deportation of the Acadians in the 1750s, and the Head Tax on the Chinese in the late 1800s. He said it was more important to be just in the present than to compensate people whose ancestors had been deprived. "(I am) not inclined to envisage questions of compensation about acts which have maybe discolored our history in the past."[13]

The Globe and Mail editorial board pointed to the clear flaw in Trudeau's reasoning: "The current calls for compensation have nothing to do with ancestors; they have to do with survivors. There are men and women younger than Mr. Trudeau who were victims of 'these terrible acts,' and who are very much alive in Canada in 1984 ... Whatever form the compensation takes, it should not be derailed by Mr. Trudeau's curious notion of where history ends and current affairs begin."[14] In his last days in office, Trudeau's minister of multiculturalism, David Collenette, said compensation was out of the question, since that would cast aspersions on decision-makers during the War. But that was precisely the point.

Members of the Japanese-Canadian community responded that Trudeau's statements made them feel like victims all over again.[15] Donald Anderson, general-secretary for the Canadian Council of Churches, called Trudeau's decision racist. Gordon Fairweather, chairman of the Canadian Human Rights Commission, said, "I am really sad and upset by the fact that Canada couldn't bring itself to apologize forthrightly for this very grave injustice... the policy was racist and wrong. Why not say so?"

The matter came to a head on June 29, 1984, Trudeau's last day in the House of Commons. Opposition leader Mulroney pressed the point: "On this, his final day, would the prime minister grasp the moment to right a historic wrong that has been inflicted on Canadians of Japanese origin? Will the prime minister, on this special day, take the time to convey, either on behalf of the government or on behalf of the Parliament of Canada, a formal apology to Canadian citizens whose rights were trampled upon in the war years?"[16] Trudeau chided Mulroney and asked if the Tories would compensate Franco-Manitobans for the loss of their right to educate their children in French, perhaps not realizing that it was a Liberal, Sir Wilfrid Laurier, who ultimately struck the fatal compromise on that question, something Mulroney eagerly pointed out.

Trudeau claimed that the only reason Mulroney was highlighting this historic wrong, and not the many others, was that he thought it would win votes. "You're sick," countered Trudeau, "if you're trying to take one wrong out of Canadian history and make great speeches about it and say that we're going to deal with this particular problem because there's a particular pressure group now."

While his cabinet remained divided on the issue, the media speculated that Trudeau would not consider an apology or compensation because he feared Quebecers imprisoned during the October Crisis under the WMA would come looking for money — or more.

On behalf of all Canadians, the Mulroney government issued a formal apology on September 22, 1988. It provided a compensation package of $21,000 to each surviving internee, and reinstated Canadian citizenship to all deportees.

WHILE TRUDEAU DID not believe in apologizing for indiscretions in his youth or past acts of Canadian governments, he also did not believe in expressing regret for his errors as prime minister. Following the October Crisis, Trudeau decided to use the full power of the federal government to infiltrate and undermine separatist voices in Quebec. This his government did by both legal and illegal means.

Trudeau asked his solicitor general to investigate the Parti Québécois, a political organization that repudiated violence and illegal activity and showed no evidence of law breaking. The RCMP broke into PQ party headquarters in 1973 and stole the party membership list.[17] After the PQ won power in 1976, members of their cabinet were subjected to covert surveillance.[18] (The RCMP had previously spied on the Liberal cabinet of Quebec premier Robert Bourassa). The RCMP anti-separatist squad also burned a barn near Montreal and stole dynamite. Trudeau responded by saying simply that, in some cases, the police are justified in breaking the law.[19]

To his credit, in 1977 Trudeau called a Royal Commission into the activities of the RCMP. The commission report, released in 1981, disclosed that the RCMP had informed Trudeau and his justice minister, John Turner, in December 1970 that the security service had been committing illegalities for some 20 years and had never been caught. Turner said in cabinet that he worried about the risk to the RCMP's reputation. A former Tory solicitor general told reporters that he knew of Trudeau's personal involvement in the planning of surreptitious security service operations.[20]

While the commission's findings led to changes in the structure and nature of policing and intelligence-gathering operations, no apology for the illegal acts ever ensued. Despite the commission's findings,

Trudeau and his ministers claimed that they knew nothing of law-breaking. But even if they didn't, it was of no great consequence, since the solicitor general said that the RCMP would continue to engage in illegal activities: "I don't think rules for police will ever be categorical. There'll always be a margin of judgment where the officer on the beat or the security service officer is going to have to make a judgment."

When Trudeau was asked to comment or apologize, he told reporters, "Are you serious? Is that all you can think of right now?"[21] A few days later, Trudeau said that there would always be grey areas and that it was up to the courts to determine what was legal and what was not, and not a Royal Commission. In other words, no apology.

WHEN OPPOSING THE Meech Lake and Charlottetown constitutional accords, Trudeau was not one to take a knife to a gunfight. When arguing against recognizing Quebec as a distinct society, Trudeau told a group of businessmen, "It will give the government of this society the power to say: 'Well, let's deport a couple of hundred thousand non-French-speaking Quebeckers' to maintain a French-speaking majority in the province.'"[22] Since Trudeau never spoke in hypotheticals, his audience — and Canadians — took the charge seriously.

Parti Québécois leader Jacques Parizeau responded that for many foreign-born Quebecers, deportation by totalitarian regimes like Nazi Germany held a precise meaning. "Mr. Trudeau, as a private citizen, has the right to say whatever he wants. But with that right, for someone like himself, comes duties. And one of those duties is not to try, for political reasons, to provoke or to float, not only falsehoods but accusations of great gravity."[23]

In condemning Trudeau, the separatist St. Jean Baptiste Society and the federalist Liberal Party of Canada found themselves, strangely, on the same page. The Quebec group called Trudeau's warnings repugnant. The deputy leader of the Liberal Party, Sheila Copps, stated that Trudeau's comments were an expression of his personal views rendered at a private meeting. "I'm not sure that it's part of a grand strategy that he has to torpedo the [Meech Lake Accord]."[24] Liberal leader Jean Chrétien said he disagreed with Trudeau, while the Liberal MP for Ottawa Vanier, Jean-Robert Gauthier offered that Trudeau "missed a good occasion to keep his mouth shut, once again." Willowdale MP Jim Peterson went further in countering Trudeau's opposition to the distinct society clause: "[Trudeau] didn't need a distinct society clause to put more than 400 francophones in jail. He just used the War Measures Act."[25]

While his deportation remark may have been flippant and inflammatory, Trudeau refused to issue a retraction. When confronted by the press, Trudeau only expressed anger that his off-the-record remarks had been made public. "Must have been some bum who reported that, breaking his word."[26]

AS TRUDEAU SAID, a prime minister should focus on the present and future, rather than dwell on the past. But when the past continues to haunt the present, a true nation-builder will not refuse justice to those who have been seriously harmed. When Stephen Harper rose in the House of Commons in June 2008 to offer an apology on behalf of the people of Canada to victims of the Aboriginal residential school system, the gesture represented a moment of nation-building and reconciliation. His voice cracked when he said, "We now recognize that, in separating children from their families, we undermined the ability of many to adequately parent their own children and sowed the seeds for generations to follow."

All Canadians benefited when the Canadian Parliament gave citizens of Japanese descent the dignity of an apology. And the positive response by Canadians after the government began to pursue Nazi war criminals shows it was the right thing to do. Jennifer Lind, faculty associate at Harvard University and author of *Sorry States: Apologies in International Politics*, argues that apologies for past abuses are essential to reconciliation, while denials of past abuses fuel distrust.

But when it came to expressing regret, Trudeau's playbook held a blank page. Even on small matters, like calling opposition MPs low-IQ nobodies when they stood 50 yards from Parliament Hill or mouthing "fuck off" on the floor of the House of Commons, Trudeau was not one to seek forgiveness. While he selectively used past persecutions of vulnerable minorities to justify the need for the Charter of Rights, he did not want other past acts, whether committed by him or anyone else, to be judged in hindsight.[27]

SECTION IV

THE ECONOMY

CHAPTER 18

THE SOCIALIST EXPERIMENT

We're going to build socialism here.
For country with such a small population there is no alternative.

WHILE TRUDEAU WOULD often shrug his shoulders at the "dismal science" and downplay his formal education in economics, he possessed more academic training and reflected more on the structure of the economy and society than any of his predecessors. Trudeau's disciples don't defend his economic record, and have claimed he was simply the product of his times and circumstances: no better, no worse. But Trudeau did not simply reflect the economic thinking of the notable experts of the day. He took office armed with a well-honed and coherent view of government as large, centralized, intrusive and indebted.

Trudeau recounted the development of this thinking about economic matters in his memoirs: "[While at university] we were witness on almost a daily basis to the spread of communism in Europe. Young people in particular were truly fascinated by the Soviet model."[1] Trudeau was not too far from the mainstream with his view that "savage capitalism of the prewar depression had shown itself in many respects to be a deplorable failure." But those who studied with Trudeau at the London School of Economics (LSE), a hotbed of socialist thinking, noted he went much further with his "flirtations with Marxism."[2] Trudeau's fascination with socialism also permeated his uncompleted doctoral thesis where he explored the interplay between Christianity and Marxism. [3]

Trudeau considered LSE professor Harold Laski his main teacher and influence. Laski was not only chairman of Britain's Labour Party, but also a proponent of Marxism and an executive member of the socialist Fabian Society over the years 1922–1936.[4] "Everything I have learned until then of law, economics, political science, and political philosophy," opined Trudeau, "came together for me [under Laski]."[5]

For Laski, Marxism and individual equality aligned as fundamental principles of justice. To these Trudeau, added Christianity. "I want a classless society because I believe that once freed from material cares, man will be more inclined to seek God."[6] He observed that communism and Christianity "are the only two [ideologies] that appeal directly to the masses and offer the prospect of an ideal life culminating in earthly and spiritual happiness."[7] To Trudeau, the world was evolving toward socialism and more: "The party of the people — socialism, communism — will eventually come out the winner."[8]

University students often see the world through idealistic and utopian eyes. But Trudeau asserted in his post-prime ministerial memoirs that when he left the London School of Economics, his personal and political choices had been made *for life*. His basic philosophy was fixed, and formed what he confirmed to be the foundation for all his political decisions and writings.[9]

While in office, Trudeau downplayed his knowledge of economic matters, falsely claiming that he understood little of economic theory. Yet he described his profession as "economist" after studying at Harvard. He is probably the only politician to have taken ten pages of notes after reading the book *The Art of Central Banking* by economist Ralph G. Hawthry.[10] John Kenneth Galbraith, a renowned leftist and political economist, observed, "Of all the politicians I have encountered over a lifetime (and there have been many), there have been few — if any — economically more perceptive and given to affirmative policy than Pierre Trudeau."[11] John Turner, who served as finance minister from 1972–75, described Trudeau as an academic economist.[12]

After touring the world as a graduate student to study the interplay of Marxism and Christianity, Trudeau returned to Canada to become a roving intellectual. He wrote of his belief in social democracy for Canada as a necessary antidote to the free enterprise system. He saw that for a country with such a small population as Canada, there was no alternative but socialism.

While writing about politics and the economy between 1951 and 1961, Trudeau held no full-time job and lived off the inheritance bequeathed by his father.[13] Yet capitalism was the system that produced wealth for his family, Trudeau posited that capitalism was fundamentally flawed because it did not produce an *equal* sharing of wealth among the population.

> We're forced — whether we like it or not — to turn to the State ... The most obvious solution would be to redistribute income equally among social classes, so that the poor have more to spend, and the rich have less to save ... As far as I go, it seems evident to me that the regime of free enterprise has shown itself incapable of adequately resolving problems posed in education, health, housing, full employment, etc. That's why I'm personally convinced that ... liberal democracy will not long be able to satisfy our growing demands for justice and liberty, and that it should evolve toward a form of social democracy.[14]

But unlike the teachings and practice of the eminent Canadian socialist Tommy Douglas, who led the government of Saskatchewan for 17 years without incurring deficits, Trudeau believed that massive state intervention can and should be accomplished on borrowed money:

> At the first sign of national economic weakness ... The State should distribute, extensively and resolutely, payments of all kinds: direct aid, unemployment insurance, agricultural assistance, various grants. At the same time, it should reduce taxes, to leave more money in the hands of the consumer (as well as the producer). Some might object that these methods were mutually opposed — how did one spend more while reducing taxes? The answer is quite simple: the State will have budgetary deficits and finance itself through loans ... in practice, that will be done through the intermediary of the Bank of Canada which will open a credit account in the name of the government in return for loan certificates. If the Bank doesn't have enough currency in circulation, it could always print some without any inconvenience when needed.[15]

Printing money "without any inconvenience" was a bold statement to make, even for a socialist. It also contradicts an observation Trudeau made after touring the world for his academic studies: "The first symptom of a sick society, a very sick one, lies in the country's financial condition."[16]

Just before joining the Liberal Party, Trudeau signed a manifesto, along with six other thinkers and academics, under the title "An Appeal for Realism in Politics." The declaration stated that in times of high unemployment, it was inconceivable that politicians should "pay homage to the sacred cow of a balanced budget."[17]

In the 1950s, Trudeau aligned himself with the CCF, because socialism, in his view, was a "powerful theoretical model, the most coherent, the most rational, perhaps also the most Christian ... of all systems ... Socialism is the only true form of democracy."[18]

As prime minister, Trudeau hesitated to admit his socialist beliefs. But in 1991, when chairing an international conference about economic transformations in Eastern Europe, Trudeau observed, "the failure of the socialist model should not be taken as a pretext to advance a 'theological' solution of pure capitalism as the only possible alternative."[19] When meeting Roy Romanow, the former NDP premier of Saskatchewan, in the summer of 1995, ironically in a private dining room at Montreal's posh Mount Royal Club, Trudeau greeted his guest by saying, "Well Roy, I guess we socialists have lost the fight."[20] Trudeau lamented the emerging influence of market forces, deregulation, and the pressures brought about from globalization.

What Trudeau said and believed is far less important than what he did. Curiously, his economic record gets scant attention from his biographers. They preferred to admire his work as a philosopher-king remaking society, rather than assess his impact on Canadians' standard of living.

When Trudeau came to power in 1968, he found the fundamentals of the Canadian economy in solid shape, at least relative to those of other developed nations. Our dollar was strong and stable, jobs were plentiful, the economy was growing, and interest rates were low. But during his second term as prime minister, virtually every economic indicator veered strongly in the wrong direction, and stayed on that path until Trudeau resigned from office. Never one to admit failure, Trudeau positively touted Canada's economic performance from 1968 to 1984 in his memoirs. But even a casual perusal of the economic data reveals the pain his administration inflicted on the country.

Some of Trudeau's economic decisions caused so much damage that he achieved the rare prime ministerial feat of both implementing and repudiating his own policies. Over a period of 18 budgets and fifteen-and-a-half years in office, his economic legacy constitutes a succession of failures.

CHAPTER 19

SPEND LIKE THERE IS NO TOMORROW

I was thus able to institute policies that I had been dreaming about for a long time, and the social Democratic faction of the opposition was forced to support them, or else deny their own social program.

I N THE 1968 federal election, Trudeau reassured Canadians that a Liberal government would not raise taxes or increase spending. The government, he deadpanned, was not a "Santa Claus." While this statement may have comforted voters worried about entrusting the nation's economy to a wealthy intellectual with little practical experience, Trudeau eagerly abandoned his pretense at the first opportunity. Eventually he imposed socialist economic policies that were experimental, extravagant, and ultimately destructive.

THERE WERE FEW social problems that Pierre Trudeau thought government could not fix. In the decade before he came to power, the ratio of federal spending to GDP dropped slightly from 15.1 percent to 14.3 percent; Trudeau reversed that trend, and then some.[1] As a share of Canada's economy, real federal spending under Trudeau increased from 17.1 percent of GDP to 24.3 percent. Put another way, the federal government increased its bite of the economic activity of the nation under Trudeau by some 42 percent.

Measuring spending relative to the size of the economy gives us a true measure of government growth, neutralized from the pressures of inflation and population growth. Had relative spending been maintained over the Trudeau years, federal expenditures would have been $76 billion in 1984, rather than the $109 billion that Trudeau racked up. That's $33 billion of real spending on the Trudeau account (in 1984 dollars).

Trudeau admitted that in his early days as prime minister, he worried that his leftist reputation would have an impact on his political longevity. This imposed on him, at least initially, what he called a certain reserve. Indeed, the day after he became prime minister, he declared at a press conference that he was not a radical or socialist, but a pragmatist.[2] At about the same time, he promised that his party did not stand for "giveaway programs," and that the Canadian voter was not interested in a party that wanted to levy its way into power with the citizen's taxes.

But there was a caveat. "We will not hesitate to spend the money that must be spent to bring opportunity to those regions of Canada, and to those groups of Canadians who have as yet little share in the affluent society."[3] It would prove hard to have it both ways.

The Trudeau government's first budget focused on trade liberalization and "severe restraint" on expenditure programs under the government's control. The government pledged to "maintain a virtual freeze on the size of the public service of Canada."[4]

In its second budget, the government boasted that it had "a firm grip upon the national finances."[5] Despite increasing spending on shared-cost programs for health, welfare, and education by a whopping 27 percent, it held the increase for other federal programs and services to less than four percent. "Despite all that has been said to the contrary," observed Finance Minister Edgar Benson, "I believe that this result provides clear evidence of the success of our efforts to limit expenditures and cut back wherever there has been scope to do so."

But the government could not simply ignore the rising expenses of shared-cost social programs negotiated by Trudeau's predecessor with the provinces, and expect federal finances to remain sound. Over Trudeau's first term in office, average annual spending grew by 13.7 percent, while transfers to the provinces rose by 20 percent.

When Trudeau lost his majority in Parliament in 1972, any clout that the finance minister had to restrain Trudeau's spending urges evaporated. In leading a minority government, Trudeau took advantage of the rebuke given by voters:

The minority government allowed me to put forward more advanced left-wing projects. I knew that the NDP, under David Lewis, would back me up — in fact, the NDP supported me when some of the more conservative members of my own party did not. I was thus able to institute policies that I had been dreaming about for a long time, and the social Democratic faction of the opposition was forced to support them, or else deny their own social program.[6]

Despite implementing double-digit spending increases, Trudeau lamented how rising costs from Pearson's deals with the provinces held back some of his pet projects. "Since we have been in power, we cut a number of things, for instance winter works, the causeway to Prince Edward Island, the telescope in British Columbia ... Despite all these cuts, you see that spending forecasts keep increasing because all the plans on which we have embarked for health, hospitals, education, the costs are climbing at a frightening pace."[7]

Trudeau had a point. Prime Minister Pearson had negotiated arrangements with provinces that obligated the federal government to pick up fifty percent of the costs for health and education, without limits. At the end of each year they submitted their bills to the federal government, which had little choice but to pay up. Provinces liked to get credit for spending 50-cent dollars.

Subsidies fashioned in this manner constitute bad public policy and become unsustainable for any government. At times the federal government urged the provinces, without success, to restrain the growth in shared-cost programs by seeking "maximum economy, and with a keen eye to what is really essential."[8] In 1978–79 the federal government abandoned efforts at voluntary restraint and sensibly capped the annual increase of its payments under the Medical Care Act at eight per cent.[9] Nonetheless, while federal transfers to the provinces and other governments represented 14 percent of federal spending in 1968, that level hit 17 percent by 1984. For many provinces, federalism had become "profitable," allowing them to ratchet up spending without bearing the political burden of increasing taxes.

Federalism proved more profitable for some provinces than others. The four Atlantic provinces, plus Quebec, Manitoba, and Saskatchewan reaped an additional $1.4 billion when Trudeau revamped the general equalization system in 1973–74. Among other things, Trudeau considered enhanced equalization a tool to give *la belle province* yet another reason to stay in Canada.[10]

Whereas Quebec premier Maurice Duplessis once rejected federal funds for education because he opposed Ottawa's intrusion into provincial jurisdiction, Trudeau's offerings to Quebec were happily accepted. Trudeau confided to a friend, the author Mordecai Richler, that if Canadians had any idea how much money his government was funneling to Quebec, "'they'd probably ride him out of Ottawa on a rail.'"[11] Because he believed in a powerful central government, Trudeau concluded that the federal government must retain and use its "strong and commanding position in the personal income tax field."[12]

Considering the steady double-digit spending increases over Trudeau's fifteen-and-a-half years in office, and his emphasis on creating a just society, one would think that citizens in need would have benefited disproportionately from this largesse. Yet transfers to individuals by the federal government increased only marginally under Trudeau, from 20.1 percent to 21.9 percent of total spending.

But within this envelope, one particular area rose dramatically: Unemployment Insurance (UI). In 1971 Trudeau launched a major policy shift that saw federal UI spending balloon from $459 million to $10 billion. In 1968 the accumulated deficit in the UI account for the year stood at $27 million. By 1984 this shortfall had skyrocketed *almost a hundredfold* to $2.4 billion.

Successive and massive deficits inevitably resulted in rising debt servicing costs, which became a dead weight on the Canadian economy. When Trudeau came to power, interest costs consumed 11.3 percent of the total budget. When he left office, interest swallowed 22.8 percent of federal spending. Trudeau stayed in office so long that even *his* hands were tied by interest payments on the debt he accumulated.

In 1968, the federal government spent more on Old Age Security, national defence, and transfers to other governments, separately, than it did on public debt. By 1984, interest costs were greater than Old Age Security, unemployment benefits, and family allowances — even when combined.

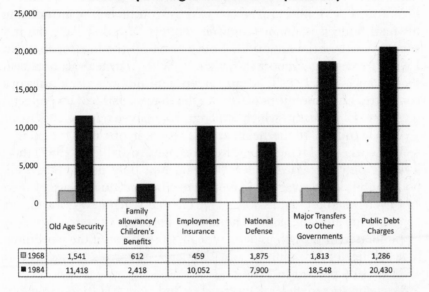

Federal Spending 1968 and 1984 (millions)

	Old Age Security	Family allowance/ Children's Benefits	Employment Insurance	National Defense	Major Transfers to Other Governments	Public Debt Charges
1968	1,541	612	459	1,875	1,813	1,286
1984	11,418	2,418	10,052	7,900	18,548	20,430

The only area in which Trudeau restrained spending was the Canadian military. Its budget accounted for 14.4 percent of federal spending in 1968, but Trudeau halved that to 7.2 percent by 1984. Relative to the size of the economy, military spending declined from 2.6 percent in 1968 to 1.8 percent in 1984. In 1968 we spent more on national defence than to service the debt. But by 1984, for every dollar we put into defence, three dollars went to debt service.

Over Trudeau's fifteen-and-a-half years in office he occasionally was pulled aside by someone who caught his ear to suggest that rampant spending increases and large deficits caused more harm than good. When West German Chancellor and Trudeau friend Helmut Schmidt suggested as much at the 1978 Bonn economic summit, Trudeau abruptly appeared on national television to announce $2.5 billion in spending cuts. In doing so, he had not bothered to consult or inform his finance minister, Jean Chrétien, who was then on holiday at his summer cottage. Trudeau said he did not want him disturbed.[13] More likely, Trudeau simply wanted to have his way without the bother, or as he said in his memoirs, "Sometimes you just have to move." Chrétien considered resigning over the indignity, but ultimately chose to stay. "I was made to look like a fool," he wrote in his autobiography.[14] Despite the pretense of $2.5 billion in cuts, federal spending in 1978 increased by eight percent.

From 1972 onwards, some voices inside the system saw a glaring need for spending restraint. Simon Riesman, the deputy minister of finance, resigned in 1974 to protest, in part, the government's lack of fiscal rectitude. John Turner expressed frustration before introducing his final budget as finance minister, noting, "I didn't have the full support of the prime minister. I put myself on the line for him but I wasn't receiving support in return."[15] When Turner vacationed in the summer of 1974, Trudeau set up a prime minister's advisory committee on economic policy under the chairmanship of his personal secretary, Jack Austin, which undercut his finance minister.[16]

With Trudeau at the helm, it was the best of times for public-sector workers. Having been given the right to strike in 1967, their leverage only increased under Trudeau. Not only did he massively boost public sector wages and employment, Trudeau also established 114 agencies and commissions.[17] He created seven new government departments and doubled the number of ministers of state.[18] Spurred by public-sector growth under Trudeau, the percent of the workforce that belonged to a union in Canada increased from 26.7 percent in 1971 to 30.6 percent in 1984.[19]

Trudeau spread federal money far and wide. He increased old age benefits and lowered the age of eligibility. The guaranteed income supplement grew on three occasions. Benefits on most government programs were indexed to inflation. Spending on short-term employment programs and regional development initiatives exploded. Crown corporations proliferated; many were simply thinly disguised regional development schemes. Canada Mortgage and Housing received a subsidy of close to $2 billion in 1984, compared to a negligible appropriation from the public treasury in 1968.[20] A 1979 study by the comptroller general counted 464 federal crown corporations, 213 subsidiaries and 126 associated corporations.[21]

During Trudeau's minority government (1972–1974), spending increased by 27.8 percent and 20 percent in consecutive years. During Trudeau's final term in power, spending increased by 22.5 percent in 1980, by 22.5 percent in 1981, then by 16.3 percent in 1982.

After the 1980 election government officials complained that spending controls were virtually non-existent. A Trudeau minister and future Governor General Romeo Leblanc told his officials that the Liberal government was defeated in 1979 because it had followed the advice of bureaucrats to restrain spending. Back in power Leblanc said things would be different: "[We] will act like politicians." But after 1980, the expenditure management system that had been in place was in shambles. Officials warned Trudeau that most new spending initiatives had ongoing costs that would lead to annual deficits in the range of forty billion dollars a year.

More evidence of Trudeau's spending addiction appeared in the 1983 budget. The day before its release, a group of photographers assembled in Finance Minister Marc Lalonde's office for a photo-op. Lalonde flipped the pages of the budget and some of the contents were inadvertently captured on film, enough to reveal some confidential elements. Rather than have the finance minister resign over the indiscretion, as was the precedent, the government determined that it would simply change the budget. The budget's "Special Recovery Program," set at $4.6 billion in the printed budget, grew to $4.8 billion in the new version. In other words, the government spent $200 million of taxpayers' money just to save the skin of its finance minister.

Lalonde turned this charade into a boast: "The events of the past 24 hours have led me to follow what my instincts have been urging me to do all along. If I err in this budget, I want to do it on the side of more jobs."[22] By that measure, it's a wonder that he changed his printed budget by only $200 million.

Before Trudeau came to power, the Canadian and American governments were of roughly equal relative size. In the 1970s, public sector employment declined in the United States, while in Canada the public sector expanded by nearly one-third.[23] Before Trudeau, public sector wages and benefits were roughly comparable to those in the private sector, but not long after he arrived, the public sector enjoyed a 20 percent advantage.[24]

The bottom line on federal spending? When Trudeau came to office, it totalled $12.3 billion annually; when he left, it was $106.5 billion. As a percent of our national economy, federal government spending consumed 7.2 percentage points more in 1984 than it did in 1968. Over the Trudeau era, spending increased about 15 percent *per year* on a compound basis.

As the federal government appropriated a much larger role in our economic affairs, it squeezed the private sector. This resulted in record deficits and created strong inflationary pressures. Regions of the country that had been self-reliant before Trudeau turned to Ottawa for easy money.

Trudeau's worst sin was not simply increasing spending, but putting the tab on the nation's credit card. And as everyone ought to know, today's deficits are tomorrow's taxes.

CHAPTER 20

OUR CHILDREN WILL PAY

Understand the country isn't ruined merely because
it has lent itself a lot of money.

RUDEAU TURNED ON the spending taps to pursue his vision of
a just society, but he lacked the political courage and moral
compass to fund his grand design. Instead of raising taxes —
and taking the ensuing political heat — Trudeau ratcheted up the national debt by a nominal factor of ten, leaving it to the next generation
to clean up his mess.

As long as he could sell bonds to keep his government afloat,
budget deficits were not matters of much concern. While he opposed
deficits when campaigning in 1968, no prime minister has come close
to his record deficit of 1984, equal to 8.3 percent of all goods and
services produced in the country. As a point of comparison, a deficit
of 8.3 percent of GDP in 2012 would have been $133 billion, or 23
percent of Ottawa's entire accumulated deficit.

WHEN TRUDEAU BECAME prime minister, the relative size of the federal
debt had declined during virtually every year since the Second World
War. Finance ministers in the 1950s and 1960s had insisted that government not only live within its means, but improve the country's
balance sheet by reducing its debt burden. Until 1975, Trudeau ad-
hered to that vision.

Despite rapidly increasing spending during Trudeau's first seven years in office, the federal government either recorded a surplus, or held the growth rate of the debt below that of the economy. It marked an impressive start for a man who, before becoming prime minister, seemed unconcerned by government debt. As a roving intellectual, he wrote, "If you want to smooth out economic cycles, you must distinguish between national accounting and that of the grocery store, and understand the country isn't ruined merely because it has lent itself a lot of money."[1]

Trudeau declared his policy goals were to "check the rise in prices and smooth the way toward more balanced and sustained economic growth."[2] When the deficit hit $450 million in 1969, Trudeau's finance minister, Edgar Benson, said that spending would have to be tightened, cautioning, "I have had to resist a good many well-intentioned temptations lest I run the risk of firing inflation."

When Trudeau went to the polls on October 30, 1972 the country boasted a relatively strong balance sheet. While government spending and revenues had grown, the federal debt, relative to the size of the economy, had declined in each of the preceding four years, and stood at the same level as that of most other leading industrial nations except for the United States.[3] American governments (federal and state) of the day had 2.4 times the debt level of Canadian governments (federal and provincial).

After the Liberals were reduced to a minority government in 1972, Trudeau mused that he was foolish not to have promised lower taxes and more public entitlements to keep his popularity high.

By 1975, a recession had hit the Canadian economy. For the first time since coming to office, Trudeau produced a stimulus budget.[4] He rejected fiscal restraint or a tightening of monetary policy, making the reduction of short-term unemployment his top priority. Despite his efforts, unemployment would remain stubbornly high for his remaining nine years in office.

Although inflation was rising, Trudeau determined that the economy needed continual stimulus. When deficits began piling up, Trudeau's finance minister, Jean Chrétien, admitted that the Liberal government had overspent during the boom economic times of the 1960s and early '70s. Inflation and unemployment, he lamented with surprising candour, were the consequences. "With the great advantage of hindsight, we can see that we did not always use our good fortune wisely."[5] When delivering his 1978 budget in the House of Commons, Chrétien confessed that the Liberal government had increased spending too quickly.

But with Chrétien in the finance portfolio, the general direction of the government's fiscal policy did not change. Even though the national debt rose at an alarming rate in 1978, Chrétien declared that spending cuts had produced some "fiscal room." He gave the economy an added nudge by temporarily reducing provincial sales taxes to the tune of $1.1 billion. The federal government compensated provinces by increasing transfer payments, on borrowed money.[6]

Stimulus also came from a reduction in the federal sales tax from 12 to 9 percent, costing the treasury $1 billion in revenues. The government doubled the employment expense deduction, indexed various features of the Tax Act to inflation, and cut Unemployment Insurance premiums. The temporary investment tax credit became permanent, with higher credits in underdeveloped regions, and a special Research and Development Tax Credit for small business was implemented. Trudeau declared these actions necessary to encourage investment and respond to the needs of sectors and regions. All the while, federal finances continued to deteriorate.

It is not unusual for government to incur deficits during an economic downturn. But when deficits persist, and rise faster than growth in the economy, they turn into a burdensome debt. Trudeau promised to restore balance when the economy improved. He told Canadians expenditure restraint was coming.[7]

ON DECEMBER 11, 1979 Progressive Conservative Finance Minister John Crosbie tabled the only Canadian budget not delivered by a Trudeau government between 1968 and 1984. The Tory government made Canada's deficit and rising debt its priority at a time when our debt level was the highest among developed nations. The budget proposed to increase the excise tax on gasoline by 18 cents per gallon.

Signaling this shift in policy, Crosbie declared, "As a country and as a government we must face the fact that we have to pay our bills and cannot continue by borrowing ever more at the expense of our future. A fundamental objective is to achieve a steady reduction in the federal deficit."[8] Crosbie's budget, and the Clark government, promptly fell to defeat in the House of Commons on a motion of no confidence.

With Trudeau back at the helm in 1980, whatever tough medicine the Conservatives had proposed was dismissed. With the federal debt approaching $150 billion, and another recession on its way,

Trudeau said it was no time to cut unemployment insurance or slash expenditures that provided steady income to Canadians.

In crafting his June 1982 budget, Finance Minister Allan J. MacEachen pondered the conflicting advice he was receiving. "Some say [the government] should print more money. Others say it should let the deficit rip ... The choice is ours."[9] Trudeau chose to let it rip. By his assessment, Canadian debt and deficit levels were not out of line relative to most other OECD countries. His government blithely implemented new programs to subsidize first-time homebuyers, reduce interest costs on small business loans that financed new investments, and further support research and development expenditures.

The Trudeau government made no apologies for its $32 billion deficit in 1983. Finance Minister Marc Lalonde said he was proud to be associated with a government that did not succumb to intense fiscal pressures.

Ignoring economics 101, Trudeau said he did not believe in bringing down the deficit because government borrowing was not "crowding out" the private sector or having a negative impact on interest rates. Veteran Canadian banker John Usborne believes government borrowing absorbed so much capital that the corporate bond market virtually disappeared. But as long as the financial markets would continue to buy government bonds, Trudeau felt no pressure to stabilize the government's deteriorating balance sheet. His finance minister, Marc Lalonde, would admit only that federal structural deficits "are not necessarily inappropriate."[10] To Trudeau, the response to Canada's economic problems, as it had been for the previous ten years, was to stimulate government on borrowed money.

In Trudeau's final year in office, the federal deficit hit $37 billion. The accumulated deficit totaled close to $200 billion, a tenfold increase over the nominal level when Trudeau came to power in 1968.

The data comes to life best when seen in graphical form. The deficit, which had been under control until 1975, skyrocketed to record levels.

Compared with our major international trading partners, Canada went from being in a comparable position in 1970 to the bottom of the pack in 1984.[11]

Deficit - % of GDP

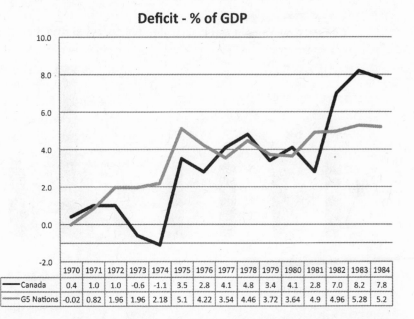

	1970	1971	1972	1973	1974	1975	1976	1977	1978	1979	1980	1981	1982	1983	1984
Canada	0.4	1.0	1.0	-0.6	-1.1	3.5	2.8	4.1	4.8	3.4	4.1	2.8	7.0	8.2	7.8
G5 Nations	-0.02	0.82	1.96	1.96	2.18	5.1	4.22	3.54	4.46	3.72	3.64	4.9	4.96	5.28	5.2

During Trudeau's tenure, the federal government's net debt mushroomed from $18 billion to $206 billion — from 24 percent of GDP to 43 percent. While the burden of the federal debt declined over Trudeau's first six years in power, it increased every year thereafter

Federal Debt as a % of GDP

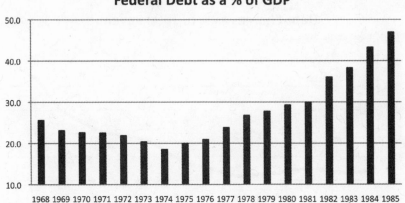

Other countries added debt in the 1970s and early 1980s, but with the exception of Japan, none added more than Canada. In 1970 Canada had one of the lowest debt loads and only about one-half the debt level of the G7 average (excluding Germany). By 1984, Canada had a debt load above the G7 average.

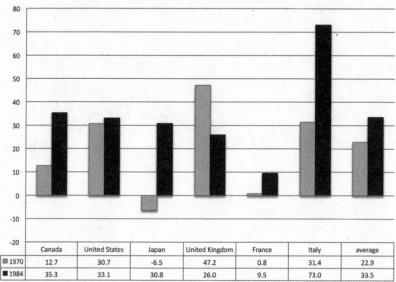

General Government Net Financial Liabilities - % of GDP

	Canada	United States	Japan	United Kingdom	France	Italy	average
1970	12.7	30.7	-6.5	47.2	0.8	31.4	22.9
1984	35.3	33.1	30.8	26.0	9.5	73.0	33.5

The consequence of a rising debt, particularly at a time of high interest rates, was that servicing costs consumed an increasing share of tax revenues. As the credit card bill grew, the interest on the balance consumed us.

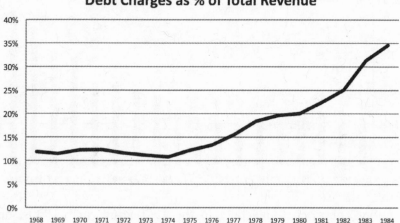

Debt Charges as % of Total Revenue

In 1968, public debt charges were $1.3 billion, representing 11.8 percent of all federal revenue. By 1984 debt charges had soared almost twentyfold to $24.9 billion, or about 35 percent of revenue.

The imbalance between government revenue and expenses became so great that for every year between 1976 and 1984, revenues did not even cover operating expenses. Even if there had been no debt, and no interest costs, the federal government would still have recorded annual operating deficits. For example, in 1984, government revenues came up $12.3 billion short of the operating costs of government. The federal government had not a nickel of income available to pay the $24.9 billion in interest costs.

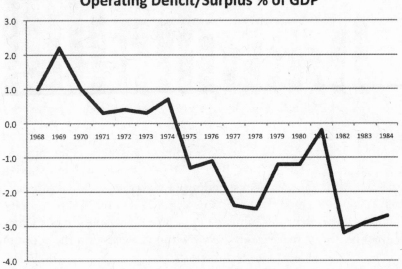

Operating Deficit/Surplus % of GDP

As total borrowing rose, Trudeau turned to international markets to keep his government solvent. When he came to office, non-residents held about four percent of the federal debt. By the time he left office, almost 12 percent of federal debt sat in foreign hands.

While Trudeau established policies, such as the NEP and the Foreign Investment Review Agency, to diminish foreign ownership of Canadians assets, he didn't seem to mind borrowing overseas to fund his spending plans. But this policy hurt Canadians. When foreigners convert interest payments into their home currency, it puts pressure on the Canadian dollar. In turn, a lower dollar makes it more expensive to buy imported goods, causing a decline in living standards.

% of Debt held by Non-Residents

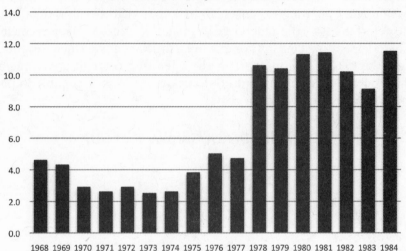

1968 1969 1970 1971 1972 1973 1974 1975 1976 1977 1978 1979 1980 1981 1982 1983 1984

Rising spending, more than declining revenue, caused the national debt to skyrocket. As a share of the economy, federal revenue comprised 15.7 percent of GDP in 1968. By 1984 this statistic had barely budged, to 15.9 percent. Government spending, however, increased dramatically over Trudeau's tenure, from 17.0 percent of GDP to 24.2 percent.

Future Liberal prime minister Paul Martin wrote in his memoirs that as the 1970s progressed, he grew out of sync with the economic policies of the Trudeau government.

> From my vantage point, it was clear that the global economy was changing fundamentally. The days of easy economic growth, abundant job creation, and low inflation were behind us. But like a lot of governments around the world, Canada was slow to recognize what was happening. Many people in power apparently still believed that Ottawa could spend its way out of economic difficulties, and all that borrowed money would be easily handled in the next upturn.[12]

By 1984 the burden of debt had emasculated the federal government's capacity to temper economic cycles. Columnist Andrew Coyne observed that this was one of the many ironies of the Trudeau years: "The federalist who believed in a strong central government left it cruelly weakened at the end. The nationalist who wished to preserve Canada's independence left it utterly dependent on foreign capital. The social democrat who wanted to expand the welfare state instead left social programs to be consumed by the debt."[13]

Our financial position did not deteriorate because of a shrinking economy. With more women participating in the workforce and growing international trade, Canada's real GDP per capita increased in every year but two during Trudeau's time in office, albeit at rates below those of many of our major trading partners. And federal government revenues grew every year during the Trudeau years. But bloated government spending and government debt dwarfed economic expansion. Our government lived in perpetual stimulus mode, artificially elevating Canadians' standard of living by borrowing from our children.

In the years before and after Trudeau, the government of Canada took in more revenue than it spent on programs. Once you factor out interest costs, Trudeau's record of successive operational deficits — ten out of his fifteen-and-a-half years in office — stands mercifully unmatched by any other prime minister.

After Trudeau left office, it took the efforts of two successive administrations and close to 20 years of hard work and sacrifice by the Canadian people to get a handle on his legacy of debt. But even after recording 13 consecutive reductions in Canada's debt-to-GDP ratio beginning in 1996, the government remained proportionally more indebted in 2012 than under Lester B. Pearson in 1968.

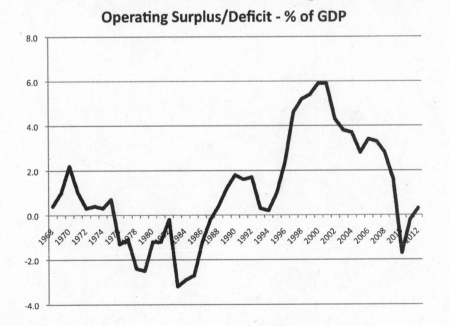

Operating Surplus/Deficit - % of GDP

In retirement, Trudeau defended himself by claiming his successors piled on more debt than he did. But from 1986 onwards, every Canadian government has paid its way by taking in more revenue than it spent on programs. Over his time in office, Trudeau spent $55 billion *more* on programs than he collected in revenues. On top of that, he had to pay $131.5 billion in interest costs. That's a $186.5 billion hole. For his part, Mulroney recorded cumulative operating *surpluses* of $41.5 billion. Jean Chrétien achieved operational surpluses of an astounding $455 billion. It was the interest costs on Trudeau's debt that handcuffed his successors, and the country.

From the year after Trudeau resigned up to the fiscal year-end of 2012, Canadian governments have recorded operational surpluses of $634 billion. But they also paid over $1 trillion in interest costs, all of which can be traced to Trudeau's debt.

CHAPTER 21

UNEMPLOYMENT ON THE RISE

The major transformation in unemployment insurance builds a firmer foundation of income support for virtually all Canadian wage and salary earners.

I N TRUDEAU'S JUST society, the landscape changed dramatically for those who could not find work — or who didn't want to. Being unemployed under Trudeau became much less of a hardship and substantially more generous. As a consequence, Unemployment Insurance (UI) became a financial drain on taxpayers and workers who contributed to the system, and a permanent crutch and thinly disguised welfare for seasonal workers and select regions of the country. For many Canadians, the financial gain derived from working as opposed to collecting UI became marginal. Affected provinces and companies preferred to exploit the new rules rather than develop their economies and industries with permanent jobs. In short, Trudeau's UI reforms damaged the Canadian economy.

IT TOOK A rare constitutional amendment for the federal government to implement a national unemployment insurance system. Previously, the British North America Act had placed this responsibility squarely within provincial jurisdiction, as affirmed by decisions of both the

Supreme Court and British Privy Council. But the legacy of the Great Depression and mobilization efforts of World War II smoothed the path of constitutional reform, and in 1940 the federal government introduced Canada's first compulsory national unemployment insurance program.[1]

The initial system featured much sensible exclusion. It restricted benefits for workers in agriculture, forestry, fishing, logging, hospital care, and education. It denied benefits to those who were on strike. It delayed benefits for persons fired with just cause, who quit, or who did not actively seek employment.

To be eligible, workers had to have contributed to the fund for at least the previous six months. Payments were calculated on the basis of one day's pay for every five days worked. That meant those with only six months of contributions would be cut off from benefits after seven weeks. Initially, UI was not meant to be a way of life.

Following the release of a white paper in 1970, Trudeau's 1971 Unemployment Insurance Act changed everything. The new Act paid benefits to those who had worked a mere eight weeks out of the previous 52, compared with 30 weeks out of the previous two years. Benefits increased dramatically, from 40 percent of earnings to 66 percent. Once on the dole, recipients could stay there for 51 weeks, compared with 36 weeks before the 1971 reforms. In addition, those who lost their jobs due to illness, retirement, or maternity became eligible for benefits.

The government boasted that the reforms would provide "a firmer foundation of income support for virtually all Canadian wage and salary earners.[2] Under the old system, benefits were modest and of limited duration, which gave the unemployed an incentive to find work. Under Trudeau's scheme, the unemployed could better afford to wait the better part of a year before feeling the financial squeeze that would impel them to return to the workforce.

While Trudeau said that the system would work like automobile and fire insurance, under the new rules workers could trigger their own claims simply by quitting.[3] The token penalty for self-termination was an additional waiting period of three weeks before the first UI cheque arrived. Compared with a potential run of 51 weeks of benefits, that was hardly a deterrent.

While the federal government remained on the hook for any financial shortfalls, the system, including administrative costs, was supposed to be funded entirely by contributions from employees and their employers. This left it to workers and businesses to pick up most of the tab for Trudeau's more lavish system.

The architect for the 1971 reform was Liberal warhorse Bryce Mackasey. He described it as a "beautiful system," totally self-financing provided that the unemployment rate stayed below the "historical average" of four percent.[4] However, at the time of the reforms, the unemployment rate hovered at almost six percent. And officials confirmed that there was no research within the government that substantiated the four percent estimate. In other words, Mackasey was either relying on wishful thinking or he deliberately deceived his colleagues that his plan would be self-financing to get it through cabinet. The government gave no regard to what would happen if unemployment rates went into double digits, as they did in the early 1980s.

A *Globe and Mail* editorial called the scheme another form of welfare and an incentive to the unemployed to sit at home. Rather than people looking for work in an "off season," the editorial predicted people would be content to work only one seasonal job.[5]

It did not take long for those so inclined to take advantage of the new system. At ski hills around the country, exuberant youth sported t-shirts pledging their affinity to the "UIC ski team." The Banff Springs Hotel reported that it could not retain staff because employees preferred to quit and ski rather than work. An investigation found that 29 of 32 claimants from Edmonton and Calgary were actually staying, rather than working, at the landmark hotel.[6]

Seasonal workers discovered that the loosening of the rules meant a bonanza for the taking. They didn't even have to work a full season to qualify for benefits. Take a job at a summer camp or work a short fishing season, and you could collect UI for the rest of the year. Line up another eight-week gig as your benefits expired, and the money would keep rolling in. When confronted at a call-in radio show about someone on UI vacationing in Hawaii, Trudeau could only say they would be going as a bum.[7]

Workers in seasonal industries were spared the burden of finding employment in the off-season, or at least a job in the legitimate economy. Those on benefits had an incentive to suppress their incomes, often by working for cash. In some regions, job sharing became the social norm so that as many workers as possible could get in their eight weeks and qualify for the dole.

Perhaps the scheme's biggest design flaw was its disincentive for certain regions to develop and diversify their economies. The evidence of economic disaster showed up almost immediately. Unemployment rates rose in regions with high rates of seasonal work.

In 1968, Canadians made 423,000 unemployment claims. That number declined in 1969. The year after Trudeau implemented his UI reforms, the number of claimants nearly doubled, to 804,000. The value of those claims, made all the more generous by Trudeau, increased by 427 percent between 1968 and 1972.[8]

While UI reforms increased unemployment numbers across the country, they hit some regions harder than others. The number of unemployed Newfoundlanders more than doubled from 10,000 in 1971 to 25,000 by 1975 — going from 8.4 percent of the workforce to 14.0 percent. When Trudeau left office, the unemployment rate in Newfoundland was over 20 percent. While a number of factors affected unemployment, none was as damaging or self-inflicted as the changes to UI, which created a lifestyle of dependency in parts of Atlantic Canada and Quebec.

The government had seriously underestimated both the claims and cost of the program, and this became a scandal in advance of the 1972 election. The projected deficit that year was $700 million, compared with an anticipated shortfall of $180 million, something Mackasey claimed was not something to worry about.[9]

Ultimately, even Trudeau recognized the flaws in his system. By 1976, he began to tighten, modestly, the rules he had relaxed in 1971. Claimants who quit their jobs had to wait six weeks rather than three before getting benefits. In 1977, those in high areas of unemployment required ten weeks of insurable earnings rather than eight to collect benefits (those in low unemployment areas needed 14 weeks). This discrepancy reinforced the concept of UI as a regional subsidy program, something that had become a de facto reality in 1971 when the qualifying periods were dramatically reduced to favour seasonal workers.

But Trudeau was loathe to reverse his flawed policy completely. The regional subsidy imbedded in the UI system carried serious political benefits. Not only did the more generous system do wonders for the Liberals in Atlantic Canada, but in Quebec, where they dominated their opponents. Studies have shown that while Quebecers represented about one-quarter of the Canadian population, their share of UI claims exceeded thirty percent in most years.[10] The Quebec government exacerbated the problem by designing short-term work programs to get people off provincially financed welfare — and make them eligible for federally financed UI.

The government raised UI premiums over the years to cover part of the program's rising cost, although lowered them in other years to stimulate hiring.[11] In 1979 the rules were changed to oblige high-income recipients to pay back benefits received. But the system still remained a growing and unjust financial burden on workers, employers and taxpayers.

BEYOND BEING A financial drain, Trudeau's folly, experts concluded, had caused unemployment rates in Canada to rise by between two percentage points nationally and up to four percentage points in Atlantic Canada.[12] This represented a contradictory, if not hypocritical, policy for a government that declared unemployment to be its number one priority.

Prior to the mid-1970s, Canadian and American unemployment rates were largely comparable. More often than not, Canada did better than its neighbour. But after UI reforms sank in, the United States began to outperform Canada significantly. In 1984, Trudeau's final year, the Canadian unemployment rate languished 3.7 percentage points above the American result.

Trudeau bequeathed his successors a broken and abused system in desperate need of reform. Initially, Mulroney extended the waiting period for those who quit without just cause or were dismissed for misconduct. Later in his mandate, Mulroney cut off benefits in their entirety to those not legitimately laid off.

Jean Chrétien implemented dramatic changes that tightened eligibility criteria and reduced the period for which benefits were paid, bravely risking his political popularity in the process. Mulroney and Chrétien saw the damage caused by a system that had institutionalized seasonal employment, encouraged workers not to relocate where jobs were more plentiful, and gave those with a poor work ethic a mechanism to sustain themselves with minimal effort. In May 2012 Stephen Harper announced a series of sweeping changes that would require serial claimants to accept jobs available within a one-hour commute, even those that paid only 70 percent of the wage level of a previous job.

If the 1971 UI reforms sought to create a more just society, they failed miserably. During the Trudeau years, the national unemployment level rose steadily, peaking at 11.8 percent in 1983. The rise in unemployment, which began in earnest in 1973, went largely unabated until the end of the Trudeau reign.

A former Clifford Clark Visiting Economist at Finance Canada, Brian Lee Crowley believes that Trudeau did no favours to Atlantic Canada with his UIC reforms, which he contends were an unintended attack on the character of Canadians. "Trudeau gave us a very stark choice between two styles of life. One of being responsible and making a contribution and the other where taxpayers funded unemployment for 8–9 months out of the year. This created a huge incentive for people to stop working, which was deeply damaging to the work ethic, something that has taken a generation or more to fix."[13]

Crowley, who also once served as the head of the Atlantic Institute for Market Studies, saw Trudeau's unemployment reforms as particularly damaging to that part of the country.[14] "Having lived in that region for twenty years, I saw the damage close up." The prevailing view was that once people had qualified for UI, the local term being "stamped up," they became disinclined to work. Those not "stamped up" would demand make-work projects to get them over the hump, provided the temporary work did not extend beyond the period required to get on the dole. Crowley, who also ran a small business in Halifax, recalls that job applicants would only agree to work if there was a promise to lay them off when they had accumulated the minimum number of weeks to get government cheques. Crowley concludes, "It was not a lack of work that sidelined these workers, but rather a settled habit of expecting to be paid not to work for part of the year."[15]

The longer Trudeau stayed in office, the more he realized his generosity with the unemployed may have been misguided. When confronted by a group of unemployed youth in Vancouver in the month before the 1979 election, he told them to "get off your ass, get up there and work a little bit ... Come on, there are people here who are working and are doing an honest day's work and not being paid just to carry a sign like you are."[16] To someone who shouted that he wanted a job, Trudeau replied, "You want a job? Well, stop drinking and you'll get a job." He called the protestors "credit-card revolutionaries."

Perhaps the most damning indictment of Trudeau's policies on unemployment — including UIC reform, job creation schemes, and regional economic development — was that despite the government intervention the unemployment rate continued to rise. It mattered little to the trend whether the economy was growing or in recession. Trudeau came to office when the unemployment rate was 4.5 percent, close to full employment by many definitions. When he left office fully 11.8 percent of Canadians who said they wanted to work could not find jobs. The unemployment rate only began to fall once Trudeau left office and the investment climate and regulatory climate had begun to change.

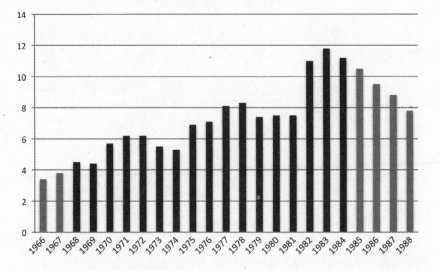

Unemployment rate - %

Trudeau's UI policies may have been a political winner for his party in some regions of the country. But Trudeau eventually learned for himself that his reforms damaged not only our economy, but the national character as well.

CHAPTER 22

FREE ENTERPRISE
UNDER ATTACK

We haven't been able to make it work, the free market system.

TRUDEAU WAS CAREFUL in his early days as prime minister not to expose his disdain for capitalism over fears that this would inflame both Bay Street and Main Street. But he had little faith in the free enterprise system, which he thought exploited workers to the detriment of society.[1]

In a 1975 conversation with Thomas Enders, the American ambassador to Canada, Trudeau commented that our economic system had failed. "Something is fundamentally wrong," he insisted. "The market system, intended to mediate greed for social benefit, is instead being dominated by it, with each group vying to out grab the others."[2]

Trudeau was even blunter later that year in his year-end interview with CTV journalists Bruce Phillips and Carole Taylor. When asked about the role of wage and price controls and the possibility of a new economic order, Trudeau talked about taking the economy in bold and novel directions. He did not see wage and price controls as a short-term measure to lessen inflation, but a blueprint for further government intervention. "Many people still see those controls as ... a bit of strong medicine we'll have to take in order to get inflation down, but it's really more than that. It's a massive intervention into the decision-making power of the economic groups and it's telling Canadians we haven't been able to make it work, the free market system."

In an echo of his exchange with journalist Tim Ralfe during the October Crisis, when Phillips and Taylor queried the prime minister about how far he would go, Trudeau did not back down:

> Some economists say all you've got to do is get back to the free market system and make this market system work. It won't, you know. We can't destroy the big unions and we can't destroy the multinationals ... But who can control them? The government. That means the government is going to take a larger role in running institutions, as we're doing now with our anti-inflation controls — and as we will presumably be doing even after the controls are ended because, I repeat, we don't want to go back to the same kind of society with high unemployment and high inflation. And this means that you're also going to have big governments. And it's not simply a matter of saying this government is spending too much and if they only cut down things would go better. Things don't necessarily go better because we spend less on health or on welfare and leave the private sector free to spend more on producing baubles or multi-colored gadgets. The state is important, the government is important. It means there's going to be not less authority in our lives but perhaps more.

Business leaders reacted with understandable alarm over what might come next. They responded by quickly forming a lobby group to educate Trudeau on the realities of private enterprise.[3] This group, comprising close to 150 CEOs from Canada's major corporations, became known as the Business Council on National Issues, later to be called the Canadian Council of Chief Executives, which, despite Trudeau's departure, has survived to this day.

For political reasons, Trudeau needed to backtrack on his remarks. He used his 1976 budget to declare that his government actually looked to the private sector "to deliver the right goods and services to the right place at the right time and the right price." Repudiating socialism, at least with words, Trudeau's finance minister, Donald Macdonald, added that "[p]roductivity growth results primarily from the actions of the private sector, not the policies of government ... government can expect the private sector to operate efficiently, competitively and with due regard to the interest of society."[4]

It was the sort of statement that a finance minister in a capitalist country doesn't normally need to make. These words were meant to calm markets, but there is nothing to suggest Trudeau actually altered his belief that the free enterprise system was fundamentally flawed.

TRUDEAU BELIEVED THAT Canadian business leaders were more than just greedy and oppressive; they were inherently indolent. "They have it so easy with the United States — where they already know the customers, the techniques, the language, and the geography." Trudeau seemed not to understand why companies would sell to willing, affluent customers who happen to live nearby. That's not slothfulness, but common sense and good business. Rather than winning customers in America, Trudeau preferred to seek markets in Asia or Africa or other parts of the world.[5]

Rather than secure and build on our trading relationship with the United States, Trudeau wanted Canada to pursue his so-called "third option" to reduce Canada's "vulnerability" to American influence and power. Trudeau offered no evidence or study to show that bypassing the wealth and proximity of the American market would benefit Canada. His proposal was about as realistic and effective as the plan put forward by Diefenbaker in the late 1950s to increase our proportion of trade with Great Britain, largely for sentimental reasons.

Trudeau did not oppose trade and did not come to office as an economic nationalist. While studying in the United States, he dubbed himself not a citizen of Canada but a citizen of the world. In 1957 Trudeau wrote that to increase domestic control of our economy, American capital could be excluded, but that such a policy "would be reactionary and result in a rapid decrease in our economic expansion and radically reduce our standard of living." But Trudeau offered another approach to deal with what he called "American domination." He urged labour unions to bargain in such a way that minimal profits would be left to foreigners.

When measures were introduced in the 1973 budget to reduce the tax burden of manufacturers, some economic nationalists argued that the lower rate of tax should apply only to Canadian-controlled companies. Trudeau insightfully shot back through his finance minister that "foreign controlled companies were a major source of employment and should not be shunned by some misguided policy intent on achieving greater control of our economy."[6]

Over time, Trudeau's disdain for capitalism in general, and American influence over Canada in particular, superseded his sensible free-trade views and opposition to economic nationalism. With a series of protectionist foreign investment policies Trudeau took Canada in a new direction, repudiating the relatively open attitudes toward investment that had helped us develop our economy.

Rather than welcome foreign capital, Trudeau repelled it with a new government body, the Foreign Investment Review Agency (FIRA). Trudeau established FIRA in 1973 to impose a bureaucratic and political roadblock to foreign acquisitions of Canadian businesses. FIRA constituted a hurdle for both foreign buyers and domestic sellers, and was a body they regarded as discriminatory, bureaucratic and arbitrary. While the test for approval of an acquisition was "net benefit to Canada," the regulations included assessments for such elements as compatibility with federal and provincial economic policies.

While fervent economic nationalists criticized FIRA whenever it approved foreign takeovers, the approval rate masked the chill FIRA instilled in foreign investors. As a consequence, potential employers abandoned many investment proposals in anticipation of rejection by FIRA, and those plans never came to light. The official rejection rate of seven percent does not include the applications that were withdrawn in expectation of disallowance.[7]

FIRA required that all acquisitions and new business by foreign-controlled entities be reviewed whenever they involved Canadian assets of at least $250 000, and gross revenues of at least $3 million.[8] For many transactions, the costs of preparing for a review by the applicant were significant, if not prohibitive, relative to the value of the assets being acquired.[9]

Whether because of his policies or not, Trudeau appears to have achieved his desired outcome: foreign direct investment in Canada plummeted during his time in power. Between 1970 and 1980, the ratio of foreign direct investment in Canada relative to GDP declined by one-third.[10] FIRA had its greatest impact on investors from the United States, whose portion of direct investment in Canada fell by about 10 percentage points between 1970 and 1984. This general downward trend was arrested only after Trudeau left office and his policies were reformed.

FIRA's greatest irony was that it stifled investment in Canada at the same time that Trudeau declared unemployment his government's number one economic priority. Had he really wanted to lower the unemployment rate, which had climbed to double digits in the early 1980s, Trudeau should have welcomed investors from around the world with open arms. Instead, he treated them with disdain, like vultures that needed to be repelled.

When discussing the protectionist legislation with his industry minister, Alastair Gillespie, Trudeau said, "You know I'm not a nationalist and this is a form of nationalism, which I find suspect."[11] He rationalized his conversion by claiming that FIRA could be used to strike better bargains for Canadian workers. But he would have helped workers much more had he followed his instincts and resisted the policies that the industry minister fancied.

After evidence mounted that FIRA scared away investment, Trudeau admitted his policy had been misguided, at least in its implementation. In his 1982 budget, he more than doubled the threshold for the review of new investments or direct acquisitions. For foreign-controlled Canadian companies acquired as part of their parent company's acquisition, the threshold tripled. Other streamlining allowed FIRA to pass on reviewing transactions that did not raise important policy issues.[12] But the bureaucratic FIRA was set in its ways. It failed to disregard insignificant cases and perpetuated administrative delays. Raising the thresholds did little to fix FIRA's inherent problems.[13]

When Mulroney came to office, he renamed FIRA "Investment Canada" and turned its mandate on its head by using it to *promote* and *facilitate* investment in Canada. The "net benefit to Canada" test remained, but investors believed Mulroney when he told 1,450 U.S. business leaders at the Economic Club in New York in December 1984 that "Canada was open for business, again." Standing in sharp contrast to Trudeau, Mulroney said his government was ready to assist, and not harass, those from the private sector who would create wealth and the jobs Canada needed to fulfill its potential.

In May 2012, Prime Minister Harper announced that foreign acquisitions of Canadian companies would not be subject to review if the value were less than $1 billion (although Harper's government had rejected the proposed foreign takeover of MacDonald, Dettwiler and Associates in 2008 and PotashCorp in 2009. In 2012, following approval of Chinese state-owned entity CNOOC's purchase of Calgary-based Nexen, Harper signalled that future acquisitions of Canadian energy companies by state-owned enterprises would not be approved).

NOT ALL OF TRUDEAU'S policies were anti-business. After a period of tough economic times, Trudeau allowed business losses to be applied against three years' worth of prior profits, rather than one, and carried forward for seven years instead of five.[14] Given the prevalence of business losses during the Trudeau years, it was the least he could do. In addition, Trudeau did not increase the portion of government revenues that came from corporate income tax over his tenure. Over his fifteen-and-a-half years as prime minister, corporate income tax represented 14.8 percent of federal revenues, down from 18 percent in the Pearson years.

The first three Trudeau budgets implemented few tax-policy changes, in part because the government was considering recommendations from a Royal Commission on Taxation commissioned by the Diefenbaker government in 1962. Known by the name of its chair, Kenneth Carter, the Carter Commission published its report in 1967, and the government tabled its response in a white paper in November of 1969.

The most important and memorable tax change emanating from the white paper was the taxation of one-half of capital gains, introduced in the 1971 budget. Previously, the government had not subjected capital gains to tax, although an estate tax generated revenue from appreciating assets. With the implementation of the capital gains tax, the estate tax was eliminated and income-averaging provisions were introduced to smooth out wide fluctuations in income owing to infrequent dispositions of capital assets.

Before the advent of the capital gains tax, a wealthy industrialist would presumably have preferred to make a productive business investment, rather than buy less-risky marketable bonds that generated taxable interest income. Trudeau's capital gains tax made such passive investments much more attractive. Carter had recommended that capital gains be fully taxable, offering the memorable quotation, "a buck is a buck is a buck." By going half-way, Trudeau's finance minister sought a compromise. "I believe that we have succeeded in striking a viable balance between equity and enterprise. This will enable us to get the savings and investment required for strong growth while ensuring that the less fortunate get a fair deal."[15] This new and complicated tax merely diminished the appetite for investment and job creation.

IN ONE RESPECT, Trudeau was correct when he said that the free enterprise system was not working. Under his leadership, Canada experienced a record number of bankruptcies. While Trudeau thought businesses exploited workers, in reality many companies were struggling just to survive.[16] It is worth noting that the dollar value of bankruptcies fell by almost half in just two years after Trudeau left office.

Estimated Liabilities of Bankruptcies/Insolvencies

Rather than supporting the private sector to create jobs, as Mulroney did by reducing taxes, eliminating red tape, signing free trade arrangements, and eliminating the job-killing manufacturers' sales tax, Trudeau thought government could do better than the private sector at making investments. Following recommendations from the Royal Commission on Canada's Economic Prospects, the Canada Development Corporation (CDC) was established in 1971. CDC was created to incubate and invest in businesses deemed to advance "Canadian interests." While the government was intended to be a minority shareholder in CDC, it did not achieve its mandate, and the Mulroney government privatized its assets in 1986.

Trudeau did little to create a positive climate for investors to create private sector jobs. Rather, to stimulate a sluggish economy, he pursued a succession of government-controlled and -financed job creation schemes. When the finance minister said in 1972, "No economy is working as well as it should if there are men and women seeking work," he meant the government would step up to offer those people jobs.[17]

Youth and depressed regions of the country proved the primary beneficiaries of government largesse. Pet programs such as Canada Works, Katimavik, Youth Internship, Summer Canada, Opportunities for Youth, and Young Canada Works received substantial funding and successive re-branding, with bureaucrats dreaming up new names to put a fresh face on comparable programs over successive budgets. All of these schemes were "make-work" programs, and their effects were economically dubious.

Each budget from 1975 through 1984 offered tax credits to spur employment. In 1983, a time of record deficits, the finance minister announced expenditures of $750 million to create jobs "quickly" in areas that had been hard-hit by the recession or by longer-run adjustment problems.[18] At a time when the economy needed lower interest rates and balanced budgets to bolster the efforts of business to create jobs, the Trudeau government went in the opposite directions on all counts.

TRUDEAU DID THE business community no favours when he decided to "go European" and adopt the metric system. Many social democratic and communist nations were metric, so why not Canada? Following the publication of a white paper in January 1970, it took ten years of planning, involving hundreds of sectorial committees and a billion dollars of investment, before the change was implemented.

It would have made sense to adopt the metric system if our dominant trading partner, the United State, had done so as well. The Americans had thought about making the switch, and Ottawa told Canadians that the Americans were guaranteed to do so. But thirty years after Canada went metric, America is no closer to converting. Trudeau believed the metric system would put Canada in sync with the world, calling those who refused to get on board dinosaurs. Apparently the United States continues to live in the Jurassic period. Derek Burney called it policy differentiation for the sake of differentiation: "Nutty, wasteful and madness."

Governments and business spent over a billion dollars to prepare for the conversion. Provinces and municipalities changed road signs, grocery stores replaced scales, automobiles had to be customized for Canadian standards, advertising had to be in metric measures only. Cultural and historical preservationists argued against abandoning both language and a centuries-old system ingrained in Canadian society.

Not everyone fell under the metric spell. A group of 31 Progressive Conservative MPs bought a gas station in 1983 on the outskirts of Ottawa and sold gas by the gallon, in defiance of federal law. Calling their venture "Freedom to Measure," they dared Trudeau to charge them with a crime. The government pursued a different test case, and lost. The courts held that forcing Canadians to use the metric system was unconstitutional. A number of public servants who publicly opposed metrification lost their jobs. And confusion about metric measurements was a key factor in an Air Canada plane running out of fuel at 41,000 feet on July 23, 1983. The plane became known as the Gimli glider after the pilot landed his Boeing 767 in an industrial park in Gimli Manitoba, fortunately without injury to those on board.

When Mulroney came into office he made the system more flexible, especially for small business. Ottawa relaxed many of the mandatory elements so that Canadians could conduct their lives using Imperial measures without facing the possibility of a criminal charge. Mulroney might well have abandoned the system altogether had the business community not already made significant investments to convert to metric. One conversion was enough.

The unwillingness of consumers to change their ways, shaped in part by the strong influence of our neighbour to the south, has kept the Imperial system alive and well in Canada. Some 30 years after Trudeau put mandatory metrification on the books, we may know the temperature in Celsius, but grocery stores in Canada still sell meat by the pound, babies are weighed in pounds and ounces, pants are measured in inches, golf holes are in yards, and Home Depot sells lumber by the foot.

EVERY NOW AND then Trudeau would create a new economic scheme to showcase his government taking action on the ailing economy. One such policy encouraged businesses to increase their spending on research and development. No one was against R&D spending *per se*, but in its rush to accelerate investment, Trudeau's government concocted a tax credit that invited abuse.

Existing programs allowed companies to claim an R&D tax credit that could be applied to reduce the taxes they owed from profits. The problem was that many R&D companies made no profits, and the tax credits simply accumulated. Trudeau's 1983 budget proposed that those who invested or lent money to companies to fund R&D expenditures could claim an immediate tax credit. The credit could even be claimed before qualifying expenditures were actually incurred.

Tax specialists pounced on the quick-flip possibilities and concocted plans for risk-free overnight profits. These deals were not all small-scale; one large petroleum company reduced its taxes by some $400 million. The decision makers ignored warnings from Revenue Canada that the plan primed the system for scams.

When it looked like a planned $200 million program would end up costing the treasury close to $2 billion, Trudeau's finance minister, Marc Lalonde, saw the take-up as evidence that the program had worked better than expected. In reality, accountants, lawyers, investors and some fraudsters made egregious profits under the scheme, but very little R&D was done. Parliamentarians dressed down Finance officials for the multi-billion dollar boondoggle by concluding that estimates had been generated the same way children pin a tail on a donkey.

In Trudeau's book *Towards a Just Society*, the badly flawed R&D tax credit was assessed by Joel Bell, a Trudeau advisor: "Abuses were committed ... Some of these credits, when combined with other tax provisions, proved too generous, blunting good investment judgment by providing a large enough tax saving to render investments profitable to the tax-paying investor regardless of their fundamental merits or results."[19] A month after Mulroney came to power the jig was up, and the scheme was killed.

THE BOTTOM LINE was that Trudeau had little faith in the free enterprise system and pursued a range of economic policies grounded in the belief that the system in place was fundamentally flawed. While he did not tax businesses to death, many of them foundered and perished under the weight of an interventionist government. While corporate Canada would have preferred benign neglect, Trudeau kicked it in the teeth by taxing capital gains, imposing a costly metric system, repelling foreign investment with FIRA, giving excessive wage increases to public-sector workers, cutting the legs out from under the energy industry with the National Energy Program, and offering up huge increases in unemployment benefits at the expense of employers. With Trudeau at the helm, Canada was not an attractive place to invest.

CHAPTER 23

INFLATION
TERGIVERSATION

Zap. You're frozen.

I N HIS EARLY years in power, Trudeau made low inflation his government's top economic priority. He cautioned that, if left unchecked, high inflation would impose misery on a vast segment of the population "who will be destroyed."[1] Edgar Benson, Trudeau's first finance minister, cautioned that unchecked inflation would precipitate the kind of economic disruption in which unemployment would surely increase, "and we would end up with more of these evils."[2]

During the Pearson years, inflation in Canada ran below three percent. Over the Trudeau years, the average increase in the Consumer Price Index was 7.6 percent, peaking at 12.1 percent in 1981. When the CPI was at its peak, Trudeau confessed that he did not understand how inflation had gotten out of control. Had he looked back at what he said about inflation when he became prime minister, the answer would have been evident.

TO ILLUSTRATE THE compounding effects of an extended period of inflation, consider that an item costing $1.00 in 1968 would set you back $3.22 in 1984 (and $6.66 in 2013).[3]

CPI % Change

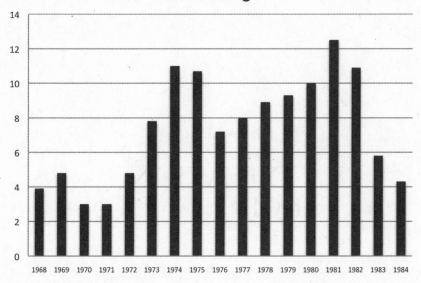

The 1969 budget speech reaffirmed that the government "really meant business" in its fight to keep inflation under control. "To accomplish that, we must not give way to the temptation of letting prices go on rising with all the injustice and destruction that will cause, and the hardships it will cause to the people who have the least opportunity in our country."[4] The government understood that while unemployment affected the few, inflation impacted every Canadian, including a wide swath of vulnerable people, especially senior citizens.

To ensure that the government did not contribute to the sort of excess demand that inspires inflation, the 1970 budget restrained its role in the economy, with a reduction in the net public debt for the first time since 1957.[5]

Trudeau's initial policy foray against inflation established the bureaucratic Price and Incomes Commission in 1969. Based on voluntary compliance, the Commission sought to obtain broad support among major economic groups for limits on increases in wages and prices. Ottawa disbanded the Commission in 1972, although its chairman, Dr. John Young, warned in his final address that Canada would have to resort to price and wage controls if inflation and high unemployment persisted.

To offset some of the damage that inflation caused to seniors, Trudeau fully indexed the Old Age Security and Veterans' Pension to the cost of living in the 1972 budget. If he could not control inflation, he would try to make people indifferent to it.[6] But the following year he boosted OAS not only by the inflation rate, but by an additional 15 percent, which in itself was inflationary.[7]

Despite acknowledging inflationary pressures, Trudeau claimed in 1974 that the nation was "thriving as seldom before in our history." But a spike in the price of oil imposed by OPEC nations in October 1973 had already started driving up inflation worldwide. The Canadian Consumer Price Index rose by 7.6 percent in 1973 and by 10.4 percent in 1974.

Meanwhile, the Trudeau government struggled with the decision of whether to impose mandatory wage and price controls. In the 1972 election, Tory leader Robert Stanfield said he was prepared to implement controls if they were necessary to control inflation, while Trudeau opposed their introduction.

In the 1974 budget, Trudeau's finance minister, John Turner, correctly surmised, "An indiscriminate or excessive increase in expenditures would exacerbate the pace of inflation." Then the government proceeded to go down that exact path. Ottawa proposed to stimulate the economy through a combination of higher government spending and tax reductions, while indexing the basic personal tax exemptions and income tax brackets. Inflation rose, just as the finance minister had predicted it would.

The government claimed it would take "a tough line" on its expenditures to ensure "outlays grow no faster than the economy as a whole."[8] In that year, government spending rose by 27.7 percent.

In the 1974 campaign, Trudeau said that wage and price controls failed everywhere they were attempted and that they were "a proven disaster waiting for a new place to happen."[9] Trudeau was not just spouting campaign rhetoric; by all accounts, he believed what he was saying. Trudeau made his point about the folly of price controls in 1974 by reminding Canadians that energy prices were going through the roof. "How are you going to freeze the price that is being set in the Middle East by the OPEC cartel? You can't just say 'zap — you're frozen,' and we're not going to pay more for your oil."[10] Indeed, Canada could not control the spot price for oil.

But Stanfield, who had given cautious support to controls in 1972, made them a major plank in his 1974 election platform. Having ridiculed Stanfield with his famous "zap — you're frozen" quip in 1974, for Trudeau to go back on his word after winning that election would equate to political suicide.

In the 1975 federal budget, Trudeau acknowledged his dilemma. His government was prepared to reconsider its policies on wage and price controls because, as he spun it, Canada faced escalating *domestic* costs in an underperforming economy. The government said it would introduce controls if they had widespread public support.[11] In other words, Trudeau would implement the policy he had previously ridiculed if he thought he could escape the political fallout.

Trudeau sent his finance minister, John Turner, to meet with labor and business leaders to plead for voluntary restraint.[12] But during the 1974 election, Turner had declared that wage and price controls would not work, stating, "The United States got itself into a depression with wage and price controls."[13]

Ronald Reagan, who had been contemplating a run for the Republican nomination for the 1976 election, argued that the key to taming inflation was a balanced budget. To achieve this goal, he posited that defending the public treasury demanded the same action as protecting one's virtue: just say no. But Trudeau was not prepared to scale back rapidly growing government spending.

Trudeau thought Turner would share responsibility for promising not to impose controls, but the finance minister abruptly resigned on September 10, 1975. According to Trudeau, Turner sought more recognition and influence, and Trudeau said that he was not prepared to get down on his knees to beg Turner to stay.[14] Turner only revealed the true reasons for his resignation decades after he left the government in 1975: "We campaigned in the 1974 election against wage and price controls and Trudeau brought them in over my objections. I told him the voters had been deceived and I won't be part of it."[15] Turner also believed that Trudeau did not give him the support that a finance minister required. [16] He cited the example of an advisory committee Trudeau set up on economic policy in 1974 while Turner was on vacation, a precursor to Trudeau changing economic policy when a subsequent finance minister, Jean Chrétien, was at his cottage.

Turner's resignation threw the Trudeau government into a crisis, creating the impression that the situation, by Trudeau's own assessment, was spinning out of control. According to Trudeau, "No economist anywhere in the world had any experience in dealing with (inflation and unemployment) at once, because the economic remedy for inflation is precisely the opposite of the economic remedy for unemployment." But the Americans under Richard Nixon had imposed controls in 1971 and abandoned them as ineffective by April of 1974. They concluded that a tight monetary policy, i.e., raising interest rates, combined with government spending restraint, would make a more effective policy response.

Turner's successor, Donald MacDonald, endorsed mandatory controls. Trudeau's economic advisor, Albert Breton, contends that Trudeau was reluctant, although it's not clear if he based his objections on political or economic considerations. According to Breton, "Of all the members of the cabinet, Trudeau was the last to agree to wage and price controls."[17]

After Turner resigned, but before the government adopted wage and price controls, the editorial writers of *The Globe and Mail* concluded that Trudeau had become indecisive and lethargic.[18] Liberal House Leader Mitchell Sharp thought it likely that the government would have imposed price controls in any event, but acknowledged "we had to make a decision at that time to offset the effect of [Turner's] resignation. His departure was a very serious matter."[19]

Trudeau announced the creation of the Anti-Inflation Board (AIB), along with mandatory wage and price controls, on Thanksgiving Day, 1975. A few months after launching the AIB, Trudeau gave a speech in Hamilton to say that he was only buying time. He went on to blame society for inflation because we were "too obsessed with material wealth (with) ... more for everybody, everywhere, all the time, a society which seemed to encourage groups and people to go every man for himself, and the biggest to take the biggest part."[20]

Rather than blame society, Trudeau should have looked in the mirror. While inflation was not limited to Canada, we suffered more of its affects not because of unrestrained personal consumption, but because of out-of-control government spending and generous wage settlements meted out to public-sector workers. Trudeau took no blame upon himself, but told Canadians that it was their personal greed that was the cause of the problem. But if ever a politician took an "every man for himself" stance, Trudeau did in 1974, when he ridiculed Stanfield for his position on wage and price controls. To Trudeau, it was just politics: "I kept up my attack on Mr. Stanfield's proposal, and I won the election."[21]

The AIB set a limit on wage increases of 10 percent for the federal government and large employers during the first year of the program, declining to eight percent and then six percent during the following two years. Settlements above this level could be rolled back by the AIB. But after a 42-day strike by postal workers, the Trudeau cabinet rejected a decision of the AIB and acquiesced to union demands for a 20 percent pay increase because Trudeau concluded it was in the greater public interest.[22]

By 1978 the complicated, costly and unpopular program gave no sign that it was working. Business and labour united and argued for its termination. Canada's first French Canadian finance minister, Jean Chrétien, removed controls effective April 14, 1978. Ironically, when announcing their end on October 20, 1977, Chrétien also proclaimed a personal income tax cut of up to $100 for low- and middle-income taxpayers, itself a stimulus measure that contributed to inflation.[23]

In the end, Trudeau reckoned that his flip-flop on controls and breaking his promise from the 1974 campaign cost him the 1979 election.[24] In reality, he lost for many reasons, but by reneging on his promise Trudeau came across as the proverbial politician who would say one thing to get elected and do another when in office.

Trudeau was far more effective on the inflation front when he replaced his state-imposed and bureaucratically monitored controls with his "Six and Five" program in 1982. "We're going to set an example for the country," declared Trudeau. "Rather than impose controls on everybody, we're going to impose them on ourselves.[25] Wage increases for public sector workers were legislated at six percent for 1982/3 and five percent for 1983/4. "Six & Five" also applied to Family Allowances and Old Age Security benefits, although the Guaranteed Income Supplement, paid to very low-income seniors, as well as Veteran's Pensions, continued to be fully indexed.[26] The idea for 6 and 5 came not from a minister or Finance official but political rainmaker Keith Davey.

The policy was meant not only to control government costs, but also set a benchmark for wage increases in the private sector. Donald Johnston, President of the Treasury Board, encapsulated the strategy with this ditty:

> What does it take to beat inflation?
> What does it take to make us thrive?
> How will we be a stronger nation?
> The answer, my friend, is "Six & Five."[27]

Ottawa phased out the program in 1984, but it was generally regarded as a success. The key ingredient was a government prepared to legislate, rather than negotiate, wage increases with its unions. Trudeau rarely risked his popularity with unions in general and public sector unions in particular, but on this occasion his conversion paid off for Canadians who had steadily lost purchasing power for over a decade.

When the legislated aspects of "Six and Five" ended, the government declared it would target a four percent increase in the year following: "We shall bargain responsibly. We shall bargain fairly. No catch-up payments will be allowed."[28] To demonstrate its seriousness, Trudeau's finance minister, Marc Lalonde, determined that public-sector wage increases would not exceed those of the private sector. To punctuate this goal, the government declared that arbitration awards in the public sector that violated the targets would be rolled back through legislation. Trudeau added that Ottawa would impose reasonable wage settlements rather than have the public suffer lengthy and disruptive strikes. It seems that Trudeau had become fed up with his union friends and determined that a change of course was in order.

INFLATION WAS A global phenomenon in the 1970s, but in Trudeau's first term as prime minister, Canada enjoyed a *lower* inflation rate than that of the United States. But in Trudeau's last term as prime minister, the reverse was the case. In 1981 the Canadian inflation rate was 2.2 percentage points *above* the American rate. In 1982 the spread grew to 4.7 points, before dropping back to 2.6 percentage points in 1983. While inflation ravaged most world economies in the late 1970s and early 1980s, because of Trudeau's economic policies, Canada experienced more of its ill effects than other countries.

While American policies on inflation influenced Canada's approach to the subject, we lagged in our responses. Ottawa provided far more government stimulus to our economy than Washington did to theirs, and Canadians suffered the consequences. We can give Trudeau credit for taking a tough stand with public sector unions in 1982, but at that point he did not have much choice. Canada was becoming an economic basket case, and at some point creditors would have refused to buy our bonds.

Trudeau abandoned fiscal rectitude in the 1970s and early 1980s, and he ultimately acquiesced to increase interest rates to control inflation. While the Bank of Canada had sufficient independence to bypass Trudeau's political wishes, the steady weakening of government finances gave the Governor of the Bank of Canada little choice but to act when he did. As the government ran out of borrowing capacity, interest rates skyrocketed. Businesses and consumers alike were caught in the crossfire. Homeowners saw higher interest rates jack up their monthly mortgage payments. Investors responded to higher rates by hoarding cash. Why bother putting money at risk creating jobs when you can clip high-yield bonds?

Oddly enough, inflation rose during the early 1970s when the evidence indicated that the economy was not overheating. In fact, growing unemployment over this period suggested there was some slack in the economy, which should have moderated wage demands. Trudeau and his advisors could not understand why Canada faced both high unemployment and high inflation, otherwise known as stagflation. At least until 1982, Trudeau seemed oblivious to or purposely ignored the fact that government spending and excessive wage settlements constituted a primary cause.

In the decade before Trudeau came to power, Canada's prime rate — the benchmark on which business loans and mortgages are based — hovered between four and five percent. During Trudeau's era, the prime rate averaged 10.4 percent, peaking at a whopping 19.3 percent in 1981. To entice investors to buy Canada Savings Bonds in 1982, the government offered a 19.5 percent return in the first year and 10.5 per cent for the remaining six years.[29]

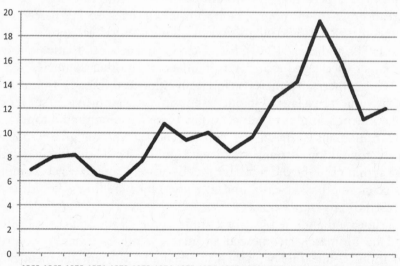

Prime Rate

High interest rates made purchasing a house difficult, particularly for first-time homebuyers. The government enhanced its new-housing savings vehicle, established in 1974, to permit anyone buying a newly-constructed home and associated furnishings to deduct from his or her taxable income the amounts needed to bring total RHOSP (Registered Home Ownership Savings Program) contributions up to the required $10,000 limit.[30] Rather than addressing the problem, Trudeau gave us a band aid and piled on another government program.

During the Trudeau era the Canadian prime rate was *higher* than its American equivalent by almost three-quarters of one percentage point. That might not sound like much, but on a $100,000 loan that difference meant a Canadian debtor would pay an additional $750 each and every year in interest costs. Translate this into a mortgage, and over the 15 years that Trudeau held power, the average Canadian homeowner shelled out over $7,000 in higher interest costs.

The unique combination of high unemployment and high interest rates led to the creation of a new measure to gauge economic strife. The *misery index* added the unemployment rate to the interest rate. In the pre-Trudeau era, the *misery index* hovered near 10. With Trudeau at the helm, the misery index rose steadily and approached 30 during his final term. By comparison, the misery index in early 2013 was 7.8.

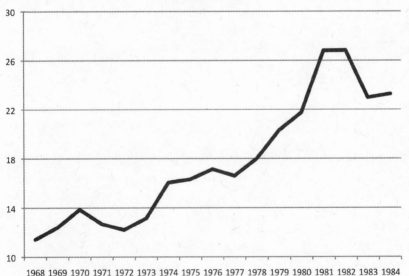

Misery Index

Trudeau's actions on inflation are maddening to follow. While he initially implemented the correct policy approach, he then changed course and spent foolishly and racked up debt. His decision to stimulate the economy with big increases in government spending while incurring substantial deficits compounded the misery caused by inflation. Canadians paid the price — not just those whose savings lost their purchasing power, or whose incomes did not keep pace, but everyone with a car loan, mortgage or other debt. They all saw their payments rise to levels that were unmanageable for many and unpredictable to all. Our most vulnerable suffered a decline in living standards, and there was a sharp rise in personal and corporate bankruptcies. While inflation was a worldwide phenomenon, Canada managed the file much worse than any of our major trading partners.

CHAPTER 24

NATIONAL ENERGY DISASTER

*The country did not have a system in place to
ensure that windfall gains from oil price increases
were shared equitably.*

A T THE TOP of the list of Trudeau's policy failures sits the much-detested National Energy Program. If Ottawa consciously wanted to design a policy to wreak havoc from an economic, environmental, and national unity perspective, the NEP was the ticket. More than thirty years after its introduction, its mere mention still sets Western Canadian blood boiling. And as Liberal leaders who followed Trudeau can attest, these bitter memories show no signs of fading anytime soon.

TRUDEAU HARBORED A longstanding discomfort with the Canadian petroleum industry. In April 1969, while attending a party fundraiser in Calgary with 1,100 guests, Trudeau refused to make even a passing reference to concerns preoccupying industry executives. Instead, Trudeau spoke about NATO and foreign policy. When asked about the omission, Trudeau replied, "Aren't Calgarians interested in foreign policy?" When told that industry executives were disappointed not to hear about recent discussions with the United States on energy policy, Trudeau remarked "I like to disappoint people sometimes."[1]

This marked the beginning of a mistrustful relationship that endured throughout Trudeau's time in office.

Furious that Israel was supplied with petroleum during the Yom Kippur War of 1973, the Arab members of the Organization of Petroleum Exporting Countries (OPEC) imposed an oil embargo against the United States and Western Europe. But as a net exporter of oil, Canada benefited from rising oil prices. Between 1971 and 1973 we imported $2.1 billion of crude petroleum, and exported $3.4 billion. The fact that the benefits of rising oil prices were not equally shared, however, violated Trudeau's vision of a just society. Canadians who saw their gas bills climb lived — and voted — in regions of the country where Trudeau was politically strong.

Trudeau responded to rising energy costs by trying to shield Canada from reality. Regardless of the world situation, Trudeau wanted a made-in-Canada price for oil. He did not set a made-in-Canada price for copper, oranges, cucumbers, or electricity — just oil and natural gas.

Ottawa had no precedent for such a discriminatory intervention. It did not subject gold producers to a special tax when the market for bullion quadrupled in the 1970s. But, as a consumable product, oil and gas were put into a different category by the government.

To finance a subsidy on the price of oil in Canada, Trudeau established an export tax on oil. It was a tax effectively borne by oil producers, since they sold at market prices inclusive of the tax. Trudeau had little sympathy for complaints from the oil patch since, as he saw it, they already made profits before the price rose and should not disproportionately benefit from events happening half-way around the world. It was not enough that the Canadian government, and as a consequence the Canadian people, already appropriated close to one-half of their profits through income tax. Trudeau wanted more of their "windfall gain".

Trudeau's intervention provoked stiff resistance and outright condemnation in Western Canada. Producers understood that they operated a risky business with cycles of rising and falling prices. But they did not expect that their national government would intervene to give consumers a break at their expense. Trudeau said a national price for energy strengthened Canadian unity. That may have rung true in Eastern Canada, which welcomed lower oil prices, but not in the West, whose oil assets were effectively being expropriated at below market prices. By imposing regionally discriminatory tax policies, Trudeau took western provinces for a ride.

The Export Tax, which Trudeau claimed was necessary to prevent Americans from draining our oil reserves, proved insufficient to pay for the subsidy.[2] So in 1974, Trudeau increased the rate of corporate tax applicable to the production profits from minerals, oil, and gas. In addition, corporations were denied an income tax deduction for royalties paid to provincial governments on petroleum production. The loss of the tax deduction made these royalty payments doubly expensive to operators. To spread the pain a little further, Trudeau imposed a special excise tax on high-energy consuming vehicles, paid for by consumers.[3]

Trudeau spelled out his appeal to Canadians in the House of Commons in the government's 1974 budget speech: "Surely all Canadians would agree that the Canadian people as a whole are entitled to a reasonable share of the profits earned by these industries." Eastern Canadians cheered their lucky break. Free enterprisers thought the government had gone mad. Oil producers felt like they had been robbed.

In 1973 the socialist New Democratic Party introduced a bill in the minority Parliament to create Petro Canada, a Crown corporation that would operate in the oil and gas development and retail sectors. In 1976 the Trudeau government gave the new venture $1.5 billion in start-up money, in what looked like a first step towards nationalizing the Canadian oil industry. It was not enough that the government could set tax rates, royalty rates, impose export conditions, and establish environmental regulations. Now it wanted to play the game, putting its own skin on the table. Westerners opposed to statist interference disdainfully dubbed Petro Canada's Calgary headquarters "Red Square."

Western provinces claimed that they were under attack by the federal government and its confiscatory tax policies. They argued that the BNA Act gave jurisdiction over natural resources to the provinces, and the feds should butt out. Trudeau went to the letter of the BNA Act to claim that the federal Parliament had unlimited taxing powers and could do what it wanted.[4]

The cost of subsidizing the price of oil approached $1 billion in 1975. On top of existing measures, the government imposed an excise tax of $0.10 per gallon of gasoline to help fund the program. While this supported a national price for oil, it negated the policy of shielding Canadians from the adverse economic effects of higher energy prices.[5] Subsidizing the East at the expense of the West amounted to a one-sided appeal to national unity.

Trudeau would sometimes argue that he had a precedent for regulating oil prices across the country. The Diefenbaker era saw the establishment of the so-called Borden Line, which divided Canada into two oil-marketing zones, east and west of the Ottawa River. Imported oil met the needs of consumers east of the line. But no imported oil could be refined or sold west of it. The policy, which held from 1961-73, ensured a market for western oil at 50 cents above the world price. But it also placed limits on Montreal-based refineries that could not market their products in Ontario.

The policy, which proved neither sustainable nor effective, was inevitably abandoned. But it allowed Trudeau to make the argument that Alberta's oil industry had long been subsidized by consumers in other provinces. Trudeau felt justified in saying that "(with) prices going sky-high, the shoe should be on the other foot and we would share in the opposite direction."[6]

THE SKIRMISHES OVER oil revenues and royalties in the early 1970s felt like small potatoes compared with the fallout after the launch of Trudeau's infamous National Energy Program (NEP) in the early 1980s.

After having won only three seats west of the Ontario border in the 1979 election, Trudeau said he was determined to reach out to western Canada more constructively in advance of the 1980 campaign. "In my decision to lead the Liberal party once more, I very much want Western Canadians not only to feel but to be fully involved in the continued nation building of Canada. I want to form a government with good people and good representation from western Canada."[7] It was not the first time that Trudeau would say one thing on the campaign trail, but act differently when in office.

After the election, Trudeau told his cabinet his three priorities were improving the economy, bolstering national unity, and strengthening the Liberal party in the western provinces. Some of his cabinet colleagues suggested regular cabinet meetings in the West, and for the prime minister to live in Vancouver or Calgary for a month each year. His new energy minister, Marc Lalonde, told his cabinet colleagues that he would not do anything that would alienate Western provinces. None of these intentions and sentiments would last for very long.[8]

With the price of oil doubling in 1979-80, Trudeau followed his precedent from the early 1970s of usurping "windfall profit" from producers. The familiar refrain came from Marc Lalonde, his energy minister: "The country did not have a system in place to ensure that windfall gains from oil price increases were shared equitably."[9]

But with 12 years in office under his belt, Trudeau's NEP cut much deeper than his policies did in the 1970s. As in 1974, he declared that the price for oil within Canada would "remain well below world prices." But beyond restraining prices, Trudeau wanted the government to become a major owner and player in virtually all oil and gas properties and developments. This included a "backing-in" provision by which oil and gas companies had to turn over 25 percent of their properties to the federal government, including established claims that had yet to be developed.

U.S. companies accused the Canadian government of attempted hijacking. Canada's Ambassador to the United States, Allan Gotlieb, reported to Trudeau that the NEP was deeply hated south of the border and considered confiscation.[10]

Governments usually subject such dramatic policy changes to study and consultation. But that was not the case with the NEP, claimed Gotlieb:

> I believe the energy program was poorly conceived, poorly put together, poorly rationalized, poorly explained. It was developed in secrecy by a handful of officials — Marshall Cohen, Michael Pitfield, Robert Rabinovitch, and Edmund Clark — without regard to the international impact and in total isolation from the government's foreign-policy advisers. As undersecretary, I was informed of the initiative only the night before it was announced and instructed to develop a plan to sell it in the United States after it was cast in concrete (that is, after it was unsalable).[11]

The Treasury Board was sidelined when the NEP came up for discussion. Under established rules it would have prepared a cost/benefit analysis for such a monumental policy shift. Had it been put to such a test the NEP would likely have been rejected out of hand. The President of the Treasury Board was not the only cabinet minister to learn of the NEP the day that it was announced.

Years later, Marc Lalonde wrote that the government came close to abandoning the provision to reserve a 25 percent Crown share on frontier lands, but ultimately held firm for fear of looking weak, of buckling under pressure to U.S. multinationals. Lalonde said the critics had overplayed their hand by exercising excessive pressure directly and through the American government.[12] Trudeau did not want it to look like he could be pushed around. In other words, the most important consideration was not the best policy for the Canadian economy, but the best image for the Trudeau government.

To pay for the various tentacles of the NEP, Trudeau introduced a new tax of eight percent on net revenue from the production of oil and gas in Canada. The new tax was called the Petroleum and Gas Revenue Tax and was expected to raise $11.7 billion over the following three years, a portion of which would finance major spending initiatives in energy and a new Western Development Fund. Once again, Trudeau had found an excuse to expand the influence of the federal government.

Trudeau worried about Alberta's growing wealth and the disparity that could result with other provinces. And he objected to the fact that the federal government received only a nine percent share of oil and gas revenues, while the producing provinces got 50.5 percent. Rising provincial wealth violated his belief in a strong central government and regional equality.

In an odd twist of logic, Trudeau thought that over time Alberta's wealth could undermine the system of equalization through which the federal government redistributed cash among "have" and "have not" provinces.[13] The only logic in this argument, hypothetical as it was, was that Alberta would eventually object to transferring wealth from its oil resources to fund social programs in other provinces, and would seek to end the system.

Trudeau's solution was to seize Alberta's wealth at the wellhead by dramatically upping Ottawa's share of production royalties. He proposed that the federal share of taxes from a provincially controlled resource increase from 10 percent to about 24 percent of the overall government take.

Trudeau's government introduced other measures to expand the use of natural gas in Canada, including extending the natural gas pipeline system to Quebec City and the Maritimes. Another pot of taxpayer money supported the conversion of Atlantic region oil-fired electrical plants to coal, presumably from Cape Breton reserves. Incentive payments were put in place to favour Canadian companies that explored on Canadian lands in the north and offshore.

Trudeau abandoned his aversion to nationalism and sought to increase Canadian ownership of both the oil patch and a slew of retail gas stations dramatically under the Petro Canada banner. He introduced a "Canadian ownership levy" to help finance the acquisition of the Canadian operations of one or more multinational oil companies.[14] When it came to oil, Trudeau was not just in for a buck, he was in for a barrel.

The NEP's unprecedented interference in the functioning of free enterprise violated many OECD investment guidelines governing foreign direct investment. The United States government, which had not been consulted on the NEP, was understandably furious. It even considered the drastic response of seeking the expulsion of Canada from the G7 group of nations.[15]

Just as soon as Trudeau launched the NEP, the price of oil began to fall. Trudeau had predicated his plan, which included massive investments in energy, on rising energy prices. Ironically, he got into the oil business just as the market peaked. Having paid top dollar, Ottawa suffered a major revenue shortfall when the price of oil plunged from over $100 per barrel in 1980 to about $60 by the time Trudeau left office.

ALBERTA PREMIER PETER Lougheed responded to the NEP by reducing oil shipments to the East by 180,000 barrels per day, forcing the federal government to import more expensive crude from elsewhere.[16] Producers halted development on several oil sands projects, which had been advanced in 1975 by a partnership of the federal, Alberta and Ontario governments. Trudeau offered a modest compromise of allowing "new oil" discovered after 1980 to be sold at the world price.

The Canadian and Alberta governments signed a truce on September 1, 1981. Trudeau and Lougheed famously celebrated the agreement by toasting with champagne, a gesture the Alberta premier would later regret.

At the time, Trudeau and Lougheed said their agreement produced neither winners nor losers. The deal took Canada to 75 percent of the world oil price over a five-year term. It eliminated the federal export tax on natural gas, although Trudeau did not concede Alberta's position that the tax was unconstitutional. *The Globe and Mail* editorialized that the long-simmering conflict exerted a paralyzing and debilitating influence on Canada: "The state of total confrontation between the West and the rest of Canada had begun to spread its paralyzing influence into a whole range of concerns and issues far beyond the limits of the energy industry itself ... Investors looked for friendlier, or more promising, climates elsewhere. Needed jobs were not created. Precious time and opportunities were lost."[17]

In his government's 1982 budget, Trudeau began to backtrack on the NEP. Trudeau compromised on royalty-sharing by scaling back the proposed federal increase to 26 percent, while Alberta's share and the industry's share each declined to 37 percent. His finance minister declared that there was "no need to accelerate the Canadianization of Energy ... because the government is running ahead in approaching the goal of 50 percent Canadian ownership by 1990.[18]

But Ottawa only met this objective because American and international oil companies fled Canada and the NEP. The desertion of foreign investors provided evidence that Trudeau had erred in terms of economic development. In the same way that homes became cheap in Quebec for the francophones who remained when English-speaking Quebecers left under the threat of separatism, Canadian ownership of Canada's industries climbed after Trudeau drove capital out of Canada. He saw it as a badge of honour that foreign interests in the Canadian economy had declined from 37 percent in 1971 to 23.6 percent in 1986, with American ownership falling from 28 percent to 17 percent.[19]

The NEP delivered limited benefits, but imposed dramatic costs. It contributed to deficits, inflation, high interest rates and unemployment. Businesses withdrew their investments in the oil patch, diplomatic relations with the United States were strained, and protectionist policies made Canada an outlier among trading nations. In terms of national unity, western sentiment was perhaps best expressed by the ubiquitous bumper sticker that read "Let the Eastern bastards freeze in the dark."

The pain of the NEP did not hurt only shareholders of oil companies and their executives. In some areas of Alberta home prices fell by one-third, wiping out the savings of many families. Alberta's share of the national income slumped, with personal income growth in 1983 at one-fifth of the national average. Alberta's unemployment rate soared from 3.8 percent in 1981 to 11.1 percent in 1984. Business capital expenditures declined by 30 percent.

While Trudeau garnered limited support in the West after the 1968 election, in the 1984 campaign his Liberals were wiped out in both Saskatchewan and Alberta. They took only one of 28 seats in British Columbia and one of 14 in Manitoba. The NEP has remained an albatross around the necks of every Liberal candidate trying to win a seat in the West, and in Alberta in particular, for a generation and counting.

Still, even with the benefit of hindsight, Trudeau boasted that he had no regrets about the NEP.

> It distressed me that Albertans were so vehement about the policy and that it quickly became a scapegoat for all the subsequent ills of the oil industry, so that Liberals in Calgary almost

became an endangered species for awhile. But I still hold that we were right to use Canada's energy self-sufficiency to our country's advantage, by setting our own prices rather than allowing the companies to have a windfall that was determined by the OPEC countries.[20]

The NEP inspired much subsequent political activity. Stephen Harper, who moved west from Ontario just in time to witness the effects of the NEP, recalls the economy going from boom to bust under Trudeau's watch. When Trudeau died, Harper reminded Canadians that the NEP was a radical, interventionist blueprint of economic nationalism that caused investment to flee Canada, businesses to close up shop, and the real estate market to crash. "The lives of honest, hard-working Albertans were upended and I came to know many of those who lost their jobs and their homes. In 1977, economics and finance didn't much matter to me. Beginning with the NEP, Mr. Trudeau would show me that they did matter." In other words, without Pierre Trudeau and the NEP, there may never have been a Prime Minister Stephen Harper.

The day after Trudeau died, Alberta Premier Ralph Klein remarked, "The legacy of the NEP was billions of dollars going into the federal coffers at the expense of Albertans. If there was any incident that brought about discord, especially in the West, it was that particular issue."[21] Gwyn Morgan, then of Alberta Energy Corp, called Trudeau world-class for the damage he caused: "Of all of the things that have happened in the last twenty or thirty years to the oil industry around the world, the NEP ranks up there as one of the worst."[22] Jim Gray, president of Canadian Hunter Exploration Ltd., said the NEP destroyed the oil patch: "People lost jobs and it affected families and there were social implications in terms of the tension and stresses. And it all focused on one man. It was Pierre Elliott Trudeau."

Mulroney put the NEP in the ash heap on March 27, 1985 with the signing of the Western Accord. The previous month, Mulroney had signed the Atlantic Accord, which entitled Atlantic provinces to collect petroleum revenues in the same way as Alberta. The Newfoundland premier, Brian Peckford, correctly proclaimed that there was no other agreement, including the 1949 agreement that brought Newfoundland into Confederation, that would achieve as much economic and social equality for his people.[23]

The NEP was bad for the environment, bad for the economy and divisive to the nation. It stands as one of the worst public policy decisions of any prime minister since Confederation.

CHAPTER 25

REPAIRING THE DAMAGE

Canada was as healthy when I left office as any of our major competitors and was probably ahead in many respects.

WHILE TRUDEAU HAD begun to redress some of his economic errors before he resigned, the fundamentals of the Canadian economy remained in rough shape in 1984. But Trudeau did not see it that way. In his 1993 memoirs he wrote, "Canada was as healthy when I left office as any of our major competitors and was probably ahead in many respects."[1]

Of the national debt, Trudeau compared the $180 billion he added over fifteen-and-a-half years to the $218 billion subsequently added by Mulroney in eight years.[2] Such a claim is intellectually dishonest. First, Trudeau increased the debt by a factor of ten, while the debt doubled under Mulroney. Second, and more importantly, every nickel of debt that Mulroney passed on to his successor can be traced to Trudeau.

The discrepancy between the economy Trudeau inherited from his predecessor and the mess he left to his successor could not be more dramatic. The unemployment rate increased from 4.5 percent in 1968 to 11.2 percent in 1984.[3] The accumulated deficit under Trudeau went from $19.4 billion to $194.4 billion, or from 25.5 percent of GDP to 43.2 percent. The annual budgetary deficit was 0.9 percent of GDP in 1968 and 8.3 percent in 1984. Total annual federal spending went from $12.9 billion to $109.2 billion, or from 17.0 percent of GDP to 24.2 percent.

Trudeau's rosy view of Canada's economic performance during his watch is particularly galling in light of the decline in the value of our dollar over the same period. If Canada were traded as a company on a stock exchange, the value of our dollar would be its ticker price. It represents an objective valuation absent political loyalty or emotional sentiment. But it is not merely an economic indicator. It affects our daily quality of life, determining the price of what we buy around the world, like fresh fruit and vegetables over the winter months.

When Trudeau became prime minister in 1968, it took $1.07 to purchase an American dollar. Near the end of Trudeau's first term, the Canadian dollar had strengthened and stood at par with the Yankee buck. Then began a slow and steady decline. When Trudeau left office, it took $1.30 Canadian to buy $1.00 American. (By inverse calculation, in 1984 the Canadian dollar was worth 77 American cents.) Over the Trudeau years, the purchasing power of our dollar fell over 17 percent relative to the American dollar; 47 percent against the Japanese yen; 68 percent against the German mark; and 120 percent against the Swiss franc. The Canadian dollar did gain against the British pound sterling and French franc.

The falling dollar made it more expensive for Canadians to buy imported goods and for Canadian companies to buy foreign machinery, and also made Canadian companies cheaper for foreign investors to acquire. Of course, it also lowered the relative price of our exports. But putting your goods and services "on sale" is no way to build a sustainable and vibrant economy.

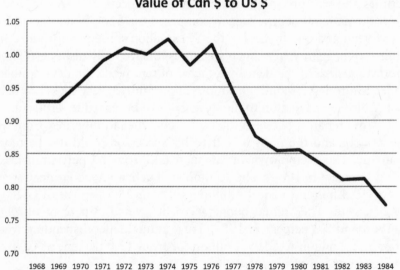

Value of Cdn $ to US $

The declining dollar reflected the fact that our economic growth under Trudeau did not match the gains of our major trading partners. Between 1968 and 1984, real GDP per capita increased by 42.4 percent in Canada and by 52.2 percent in the remaining G7 nations.[4] This discrepancy is even more disturbing when we consider that our economic activity was not restrained by a government paying down debt, but doing quite the opposite. Under Trudeau, the federal government rolled along in perpetual stimulus mode. Public-sector employment swelled and economic growth was increasingly related to an increase in the size of the workforce rather than to productivity gains. The modest reduction in the participation rate of men in the workforce, which decreased from 78.6 percent in 1968 to 76.6 percent in 1984, was more than offset by an increase in the participation rate of women, which went from 37.1 percent in 1968 to 53.6 percent in 1984. Women were stepping up to the plate to generate economic growth.

While GDP rose an average of 4.1 percent during the Trudeau era, constant dollar government spending went up by 7.3 percent. The proportion of our GDP attributable to government expenditures increased from 16.8 percent in 1968 to 20.0 percent in 1984.[5] In effect, Trudeau developed the economy on the backs of future taxpayers.

In 1982, after close to 15 years in office and with the economy suffering another decline, Trudeau was baffled as to what to do next. Bereft of ideas, he asked his former finance minister Donald Macdonald to chair a Royal Commission on Economic Union and Development. In part, Trudeau wanted the commission to help promote the notion of the free flow of goods and services within the Canadian economic union, a noble idea that provinces had sternly resisted. But according to Macdonald, the commission's mandate was broadened because the government sought solutions to problems it could not yet discern:

> In effect it was acknowledged that the government had exhausted its mandate and new policy directions required exploration. As a result, the government decided to constitute a commission with broad terms of reference, to be conducted by a group representative not only of the geographical interests of the country, but also different functional interests, including political parties.[6]

Having left the Trudeau cabinet in 1978, Macdonald reflected on the economic record in which he had taken part. After serving in the energy and finance portfolios, Macdonald knew well the National Oil Policy of 1973-4, the incorporation of Petro Canada, and mandatory wage and price controls. But as chair of the commission, Macdonald observed that these state-controlled programs had failed to achieve the rates of growth to which the nation aspired.

The Royal Commission on Economic Union and Development is best-known for recommending free trade with the United States. By extension, this makes the commission's creator, Pierre Trudeau — ironically one of our most anti-American prime ministers — father to the Canada-U.S. Free Trade Agreement later negotiated and implemented by Mulroney.

While the FTA is regarded as Mulroney's most significant legacy, Trudeau, in retirement, called it a monstrous swindle. He wrote in 1990 that with the FTA, Mulroney had ceded to the United States a large slice of the country's sovereignty in exchange for advantages that we already had, or that, he assumed, we were going to obtain in a few years anyway through the normal operation of the General Agreement on Tariffs and Trade.[7]

Trudeau also bequeathed to Mulroney the economically destructive Manufacturers' Sales Tax. During his entire term, advisors repeatedly urged Trudeau to repeal or reform the tax because it made our exports more expensive and favoured importers over domestic manufacturers. Mulroney famously scrapped the Manufacturers' Sales Tax and replaced it with the Goods and Services Tax, a shift most economists credit with improving the competitiveness of Canadian business and strengthening the federal balance sheet.

Cleaning up the fiscal mess left in 1984 was a painful exercise, and it took time. The federal government under Trudeau had been accustomed to growing at the rate of 15 percent per year. Mulroney tempered the growth in federal spending to below the level of inflation and population growth. After his first term as prime minister, Mulroney had cut the relative deficit in half, and had stabilized the debt-to-GDP ratio. Mulroney inherited a $12 billion operating *deficit* in 1984 and turned it into a $12 billion *surplus* by 1989. But the looming Trudeau debt, exacerbated by high interest rates to combat inflation, continued to compound. It took Mulroney's efforts and those of his successor Jean Chrétien to stabilize the government's financial position. They made the tough calls and imposed the fiscal discipline that Trudeau had rejected.

OTHER THAN TRUDEAU himself, few dared to defend his economic record. In the national debating series "History Wars," *Globe and Mail* columnist Lawrence Martin was tasked with offering the positive side of Trudeau's legacy. He conceded in debate that he was no fan of his economic record, an area "where he deserves much criticism."

Most of Trudeau's economic policies have been undone, and successive prime ministers have made the difficult decisions necessary to bring down the level of the national debt. The NEP was scrapped. Free trade was implemented. Crown corporations were privatized. Oppressive regulations were relaxed. FIRA was transformed into Investment Canada. Those who created jobs were applauded rather than criticized. A capital gains exemption was introduced to encourage investment and innovation. The reforms to the UI system that came during Trudeau's first term were undone. The Manufacturers' Sales Tax was replaced with the GST.

While Trudeau's economic data looks bleak, we should evaluate how his record compares with those of other Canadian prime ministers. It would hardly be fair to compare Trudeau's raw numbers with those of, say, R.B. Bennett, who became prime minister during the Great Depression. When judging prime ministers, it is more important to consider the progression or deterioration of an economy during their tenure rather than just the data in isolation.

McGill University associate professor of economics Tom Velk and historian Alvin Riggs undertook this type of "before and after" analysis. They examined the economic records of every post-World War II prime minister through a wide array of weighted economic data (inflation, unemployment, interest and exchange rates, taxes and deficits, income distribution, growth, productivity). Their analysis determined which prime minister had most improved upon or fallen behind on these economic indicators. The professors ranked Trudeau at the bottom of the pack for having the worst overall economic performance among his peers.[8]

Velk and Riggs did not give Trudeau poor marks because he'd failed to improve the Canadian economy, but because he'd inherited a strong hand and squandered it. According to Velk, Trudeau was the worst Canadian prime minister in statistical history because, unlike ordinary political failures, he was not idle, but activist. "The prime ministers who served before him endowed Trudeau with a healthy, balanced economy. He passed on to those who followed him a nation deeply indebted. He actively and aggressively provoked the U.S.A., our most important trading partner. He pushed up the spending and borrowing curve so irresponsibly that later governments of both parties took more than a generation to pull Canada back from what we today know as the Greek brink."[9]

Trudeau said he had nothing for which to apologize. Indeed, if we consider the views on economic management he expressed before he became prime minister, we should not be surprised by his assessment — or the results.

SECTION V

POLITICS AND GOVERNANCE

CHAPTER 26

DEMOCRACY, PARLIAMENT
AND THE PMO

*When they are 50 yards from Parliament Hill they are no longer
honourable members, they're just nobodies.*

RUDEAU CAME TO power with little experience in the backrooms
of the Liberal party. That makes it all the more remarkable
that he won the leadership without being saddled with campaign promises and political debts. "When I woke up after the convention I was very happy, because I won that convention without promising anything to anybody."[1] He was, as they say, his own man, starting
with a clean slate. That's not to say he lacked direction or ambition;
in addition to strengthening the federal government, defeating Quebec nationalism, and entrenching bilingualism, Trudeau talked about
modernizing democracy and our institutions of governance.

But his goals of participatory democracy and structural reform of
government were either abandoned or never fully realized. Despite
good intentions Trudeau ultimately became a politician who wanted
to win elections. To do so, he centralized power in the prime minister's
office and used patronage to keep the political wheels turning. He was,
in this sense, not much different from others who have attained high
political office.

FOR A MAN known to follow his own counsel, Trudeau's stated goal of participatory democracy ran counter to his inclinations. Before entering politics Trudeau shunned teamwork, preferring solo adventures without attachments or responsibilities. He felt most in his element when countering prevailing public opinion. He insouciantly wrote that if the Liberal Party did not agree with his opinions, then it could repudiate him; if his constituents did not like what he did, they could elect someone else. To ready-made or secondhand ideas, Trudeau said he always preferred his own.

But once in office, he saw an important distinction between *participation* and *decision-making*. He told his official biographer in 1970 that a person can engage without participating in the decisions. "In a society there's always some tool or instrument for somebody making a decision at some point. In our formal government, it is the cabinet. But what people want to know and be assured of, is that their point of view has been considered."[2] As Canadians soon discovered, consultation without consequence is not meaningful; it's arrogant.

Trudeau's plans for broad public consultation initially limited themselves to the Liberal Party of Canada, a process he equated to consulting all of Canada. Early in his first mandate, he brought the executives of provincial and federal Liberal riding associations together to attend seminars to review 62 discussion papers. They were to determine everything that was wrong with the country and decide how to fix it at a November 1970 "soul searching" Liberal Party conference in Ottawa. After calling for a guaranteed income policy and a loosening of marijuana laws, Trudeau recognized the difficulties associated with citizen-based engagement.

Participatory democracy supposedly included enhancing the role of parliamentarians. The first Throne Speech after the 1968 election lamented that Parliament was too far removed from the people it served; its operations too slow and ponderous; its decisions too few and much delayed.[3] But Trudeau's execution on parliamentary reform proved uneven at best.

In frustration over opposition members attacking his government, he famously remarked, "When they are 50 yards from Parliament Hill they are no longer honourable members, they're just nobody's [sic] ... I think we should encourage the opposition to leave. Every time they do, the IQ of the House rises considerably."[4]

He claimed to have innocently mouthed "fuddle-duddle" to an MP who was getting under his skin in the House of Commons, when it was evident that he really said "fuck off." When he stood accused of not having the guts to admit the truth of his remark, Trudeau said that he didn't run off to complain to his mama, unlike opposition members whining to the press. Earlier that month Trudeau had reportedly told a group of Montreal mail truck drivers, "mangez de la merde," so the public had every reason to question whether "fuddle-duddle" would be his English epithet of choice.

Ministerial accountability in the Trudeau era had its limits. He thought it a waste of time to have cabinet ministers divert their daily attention from their departments to address Parliament during Question Period. "It is complete nonsense to have 29 ministers hanging around for one and a half or two hours every day just in case some guy in the opposition thinks up a question."[5] He allowed his ministers to skip Question Period twice a week.

Trudeau gave Canadians a window into the business of Parliament by permitting the proceedings from the House of Commons to be broadcast, beginning October 17, 1977. Members of the media thought the move partially inspired by partisan advantage, although it gave the relatively unknown opposition leader, Joe Clark, an opportunity to gain public exposure. Looking back at how Question Period was run in 1977, in 2011 the CBC's national affairs editor, Chris Hall, noted that by modern standards it was quite subdued. Hall observed that, to his credit, Trudeau actually answered questions.[6]

While Trudeau talked about strengthening democracy, his commitment to the system varied. In 1977 he said that in certain countries and at certain times a one-party state would be preferable. "I wouldn't be prepared to think I would be successful in arguing that for Canada at the present time, but such times might come, who knows?"[7] Thankfully, some thirty years after his resignation, Canada is no closer to a one-party state that when Trudeau held office.

Trudeau also implemented changes that limited the amount of time a bill could be debated by the House of Commons, thus effectively ending the possibility of a filibuster by opposition parties. To gain acceptance for the "closure" gambit on debate proceedings, Trudeau awarded the opposition additional powers, such as the ability to set the parliamentary agenda for 25 sitting days. He also sensibly gave responsibility for clause-by-clause review to committees, providing MPs a useful opportunity to improve draft legislation. Political parties and parliamentarians received budget increases to conduct research. MPs likely had a mixed reaction to the reform that reduced the length of their speeches. Those who liked to pontificate were opposed; those forced to listen to pontificators were in favour. Most of Trudeau's parliamentary reforms remain in place today.

Perhaps the most significant amendment was the passage of the Access to Information Act in 1983, which limited the information the federal government could withhold from its citizens. This reform mirrored similar legislation already in force in France, Denmark, Finland, Sweden, the Netherlands, and the United States (U.S. legislation was passed in 1966). To complement the Access to Information Act, Trudeau introduced the Privacy Act that same year. Both laws served to secure the liberty of Canadian citizens and promote government transparency.

For these initiatives, Trudeau deserves kudos. They would be greater had Trudeau passed these acts when they might have had an impact on his tenure as prime minister. But openness had its limits. When the Auditor General requested cabinet documents in 1984, Trudeau told him to take a hike.[8] Trudeau's successors have strengthened privacy and access legislation, almost always on the side of citizens.

Another key accomplishment in citizen engagement was lowering the voting age to 18 in 1970. The electoral benefits to Trudeau and the Liberal party proved immediate and obvious, but this did not negate the positive impact of aligning the voting age with the capacity to commit to military service.

WHEN TRUDEAU FIRST sat in Pearson's cabinet, he thought it an amateur operation, poorly organized and inefficiently managed. As prime minister, he decided to introduce a measure of order and rationality to cabinet procedures, including a series of committees that ministers would need to meet before bringing legislation forward.[9] Trudeau astutely required that a formal memorandum be drawn up on the authority of the minister responsible before an issue could be discussed in cabinet.[10] John Turner thought the committee structure and formality ridiculous, saying it was impossible to govern the country "with 23 God-damned ministers of finance." It's true that a cabinet committee system diminished the authority and accountability of individual ministers, but it also provided a useful opportunity to test ideas with a wider section of opinion, albeit often a more political than functional review.

Issues that came before cabinet were rarely put to a formal vote, and Trudeau always had supremacy to interpret the consensus. To remind everyone at the table where power really lay, it was not unusual for Trudeau to say, "[I]t's 18 to 12, and the 12's have it."[11] Next to Trudeau, a clique of the second-most-powerful decision-makers worked in the Prime Minister's Office (PMO). This constituted a clear departure from his predecessors' habit of making cabinet their power chamber.

The PMO of R.B. Bennett had 12 staff. Mackenzie King initially ran the PMO with a similar number of staff, which he increased to 30 during the Second World War. Lester Pearson increased the PMO's complement to 40. Trudeau more than doubled its size to 92 employees.[12]

The PMO also featured four regional desks, a system that undermined cabinet ministers with regional responsibilities. Trudeau said that having a strong central government meant building up the executive and beefing up the PMO.[13] While his successors have largely retained this power structure, we can trace the initial shift to hand-picked staff and away from cabinet or Parliament to Trudeau.

Without a strong cabinet, few if any checks and balances exist on a majority prime minister. A prime minister in the Trudeau style of government, by contrast, is far more powerful than an American president, who has to deal with what Congress proposes.[14] Trudeau did not condone independent voices in cabinet and was ruthless when it came to protecting cabinet secrecy, warning his ministers that if the source of any leak of cabinet information were identified, "the action taken would have to be merciless."[15]

During the Trudeau era it was sometimes difficult to distinguish between the bureaucracy and the Liberal Party of Canada, and, more specifically, Trudeau allies within the Party. Political aides glided into top civil service positions, and retiring or defeated politicians readily became top-ranking bureaucrats. Take the case of Pierre Juneau. He had studied with Trudeau at the University of Paris and contributed to *Cité Libre*. In 1968, Juneau became the first chairman of the Canadian Radio and Television Commission (CRTC), where he led Trudeau's mission to increase Canadian content over the airwaves. So thankful was the music industry for Juneau's efforts that they named their annual "Juno" awards in his honour. Trudeau brought Juneau into his cabinet in 1975 as minister of communications *before* winning a seat in the House of Commons. Trudeau opened up a riding for Juneau by appointing the member from Hochelaga, Gerald Pelletier, to become Canada's ambassador to France. But Juneau lost what was considered a safe seat in the by-election and was forced to leave cabinet. Juneau then moved into the public service as undersecretary of state. In 1980, he became deputy minister of communications, and in 1982, the president of the CBC. It would be difficult to imagine a defeated Tory candidate, let alone one being a close friend of say Stephen Harper in 2013, being appointed a deputy minister and then president of the CBC.

Bryce Mackasey was another great Trudeau friend and workhorse. After serving in Liberal governments and cabinets, and resigning in 1976 to run unsuccessfully in a Quebec provincial election, he attempted a return to Parliament in 1978 in a by-election in Ottawa Centre. To open up the seat, the sitting Liberal member, Hugh Poulin, was appointed a judge of the Ontario Superior Court of Justice. Like Juneau, Mackasey lost the by-election, only to be appointed president of Air Canada. He returned to Parliament in the 1980 election. But just before Trudeau left office, he arranged for Mackasey to become Canada's ambassador to Portugal. Through a written agreement with Trudeau, John Turner made the appointment. The news caused Progressive Conservative leader Brian Mulroney to say of Mackasey, "There's no whore like an old whore." Upon becoming prime minister, Mulroney rescinded Mackasey's appointment and gave the diplomatic post to the former Liberal Speaker of the House of Commons, Lloyd Francis.

Don Jamieson's reward for faithful service to Trudeau was to serve as Canada's High Commissioner to Great Britain. His equivalent appointment from Great Britain to Canada, Lord Moran, disparaged the appointment in his final dispatch to his Foreign Office in 1984.

> No one would pretend for a moment that Mr. Don Jamieson is the most suitable man to represent Canada in London. He is there because he is an old Liberal war-horse who wanted one more job before he retired. Party appointees fill scores of federally appointed posts. Politics run on jobs for the boys.[16]

Moran concluded his dispatch by commenting that Canadian ministers were there to get cash for their ridings, citing the example of the deputy prime minister whose riding siphoned forty percent of grants slated for the entire province of Nova Scotia.

A key powerbroker in the Trudeau era was backroom boy Jim Coutts, who came into the PMO in 1975 to serve as Trudeau's principal secretary. But Coutts wanted a more public role. Coutts's sway with Trudeau was such was that he was given a shot at one of the safest Liberal ridings in the country. The member for the Toronto riding of Spadina, Peter Stollery, was enticed to vacate his seat with an appointment to the Senate, where he ultimately served for 29 years. But, as with Juneau and Mackasey, the voters rejected the ploy, and Coutts went down to defeat in the 1981 by-election. After 30 top Liberals were canvassed, it became clear that Trudeau had been the focus of voters' wrath. A loyal local Liberal observed, "there has been very clearly perceived a lack of concern by the Government to [sic] the issues that affect the people of Spadina. The defeat of Jim Coutts has been welcomed by most."[17]

This foreshadowed Trudeau's dwindling support across the country at a time when the economy had stagnated and Trudeau's fixation on the constitution hit overdrive. On the same evening, the Liberals lost a by-election in the Quebec riding of Joliette by a two-to-one margin. The Tory candidate, Roch Lasalle, had campaigned against Liberal economic and constitutional policies.[18]

Michael Kirby was another PMO insider well taken care of by Trudeau. Known as Trudeau's "son-of-a-bitch" on the constitutional file, Kirby served as the Secretary to the Canadian Cabinet for Federal-Provincial Relations and Deputy Clerk of the Privy Council. A month before Trudeau retired, he appointed Kirby, then 43, to the Senate. While in the Senate, Kirby maintained the vice-presidency of a Liberal-friendly polling firm and was often seen in the backrooms of the Liberal party. Nonetheless, he made useful contributions to Canadian public policy from the Senate on issues such as mental health.

The next rung down in Trudeau's power structure from the PMO was the Privy Council Office (PCO). The Clerk of the PCO, effectively the deputy minister to the PM, also serves as the country's top public servant. The Clerk is expected to be politically neutral, but Michael Pitfield, who first held the position from 1975-79, was exceptionally close to Trudeau.[19] He translated some of Trudeau's writings in the 1960s and was one of a small number of influential people Trudeau had consulted when deciding to run for the Liberal Party leadership.[20] He frequently vacationed with Trudeau, including on a trip to Spain and a three-week yachting trip in 1969 aboard a 100-ton vessel with a crew of four. The trip's financier went unreported, though the yacht, named *Adanac* (Canada spelled backwards), was owned by a Canadian resident of Monaco.[21]

Joe Clark dismissed Pitfield in 1979 because of his alliance with Trudeau, but Pitfield regained his position when Trudeau returned as prime minister in 1980. As if to thumb his nose at Clark's critique of their close relationship, Trudeau appointed Pitfield to the Senate on December 22, 1982. While nominally an independent senator, Pitfield was regarded as Trudeau's man.

Beyond the 81 Senate appointments made by Trudeau, the courts furnished another popular haven for Liberal ministers. While the Canadian Bar Association generally approved of Trudeau's appointments to the Supreme Court, they expressed concern about how he treated lower-court appointments. After Trudeau arranged for three federal court appointments on his retirement, the Bar Association wrote, "At present the [federal] court is perceived by many, rightly or wrongly, as a government-oriented court because so many former politicians and federal officials have been appointed to it ... As to appointments to the Federal Court of Canada, political favoritism has been a dominant, though not sole, consideration. Many appointees have been active supporters of the party in power." In his book *Spoils of Power*, Jeffrey Simpson observed that Trudeau had taken considerable care in making strong appointments early in his career, but by the end of his years in power, "he was practicing patronage as relentlessly as his predecessors."[22]

IN 1964, THE Pearson government appointed an Advisory Committee to Study the Curtailment of Election Expenses. Its 1966 report recommended that during an election writ period, only political parties or candidates should be allowed to advertise their support for political candidates. The recommendation was intended to prevent wealthy organizations, such as large corporations and labour unions, from influencing or corrupting the political process.

Trudeau did not respond with legislation until 1974. Even then, the Election Expenses Act only came into being because the NDP made it a condition to prop up a minority Liberal government. The legislation placed spending limits on political parties, but did not alter who could make political contributions or how much they could give. The Act was also generous to political parties by giving taxpayer-supported credits to help encourage individual donations, and it forced broadcasters to provide airtime for political party advertising. With a provision that this time be allocated based on a party's respective share of the vote in the previous election, the Liberals received the majority of the free publicity. Perhaps the most significant change was the requirement that parties disclose the source of any donation over $100. That meant it would be plain to see if a large bank, oil company, or union were bankrolling a political party.

While the democratic reforms appeared significant for their time, they fell far short of removing the influence of corporations and unions from the political process, something that subsequent governments have addressed. Nonetheless, Trudeau's claim that he made the electoral process much cleaner and fairer is justified.[23]

Despite the shift toward individuals in the financing of political parties, voter turnout declined during Trudeau's tenure, reaching a low point in the 1980 election, his last, before returning to more usual levels in 1984 and 1988.[24]

Voter Turnout - %

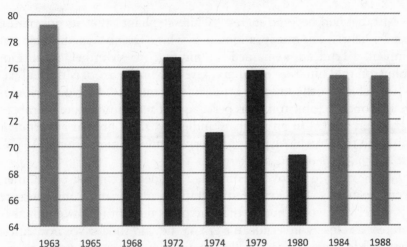

During the Trudeau era, 73.7 percent of eligible voters cast ballots. This compares with 77.0 percent in the two elections before Trudeau became Liberal leader, and 75.3 percent in the two elections after Trudeau resigned. If Trudeau made Canadians excited about their country, he didn't inspire them to show up at the ballot box.

TRUDEAU WAS NOTORIOUSLY cheap on matters big and small. He rarely left an appropriate tip at a restaurant, nor did he provide his ex-wife sufficient funds to help her land on her feet after their divorce. But sometimes his ministers used Trudeau's miserliness to their advantage.

After the opening of Mirabel Airport, 55 kilometers north of downtown Montreal, cabinet minister Don Johnston was deluged with complaints from travelers objecting to the lengthy trek, when Dorval Airport sat only 19 kilometers away. Trudeau's government had expropriated huge tracts of farmland for Mirabel, which at the time had the largest footprint of any airport in the world. Trudeau harboured little sympathy for farmers, whom he called a bunch of professional complainers: "'When there is too much sun, they complain. When there is too much rain, they complain. A farmer is a complainer.'"[25]

Originally pegged to cost $425 million, Mirabel's final bill came in close to $1.5 billion (about $6 billion in 2012 dollars). When the airport opened in October 1975, Trudeau boasted that it represented a harbinger of the year 2000,[26] then added that Mirabel would be so magnificent that "Torontonians will be down here on their knees."[27] Forget about Toronto: no one from Montreal wanted to use Mirabel, and the colossus of an airport racked up a $100 million deficit for 1978-1979.

Mirabel had become such a "white elephant" that its advertising department humorously adopted a white Dumbo as the airport's emblem. Trudeau remained committed to Mirabel until Don Johnston told him the return taxi fare to Mirabel from Montreal was $100. That got the miserly Trudeau's attention. "Are you serious?" he responded. Johnston then persuaded Trudeau to make Mirabel a cargo terminal.[28] In an ultimate indignity, the Chrétien government renamed the Dorval Airport the Pierre Trudeau International Airport after Trudeau's death.

While many controversies marked Trudeau's time in office, there were relatively few reported instances of personal malfeasance. However, it's worth noting that the press did not follow conflicts of interest as closely in Trudeau's era as they do today. We now know that Trudeau vacationed in Florida and the Caribbean with rich and powerful Canadians who had substantial dealings with the federal government. This included vacations at the Florida home of Paul Desmarais, the head of Power Corporation.[29]

In 1976, Trudeau spent Christmas vacation with his good friend, the architect Arthur Erickson. Trudeau personally intervened to award Erickson the commission to design the National Art Gallery after Erikson had initially failed to make the initial short list of bidders. Erickson returned the favour by allowing Trudeau final say on the choice of building design. Trudeau also overrode the architect selection process for architectural services for the new Canadian embassy in Washington D.C. to give the commission to Erikson after he, once again, had not made the short list of candidates.[30] Erickson would later design a cottage for Trudeau.[31]

Trudeau befriended developer Robert Campeau, whose company made a fortune erecting federal office buildings in the national capital region. The contract for one such building, Terrasses de la Chaudière, was awarded to Campeau for $160 million without a competitive bid. In 1988, Campeau, aware of Trudeau's love of popcorn, sent him a cubic metre of the confection from Bloomingdale's, a retail outlet he had acquired at the peak of his powers.[32]

Perhaps Trudeau's most interesting controversy involved the construction of an indoor swimming pool that he requested for 24 Sussex Drive, the home of the prime minister. The swimming pool, accessed from the residence through a 17-metre underground tunnel dug in pure Ottawa Valley granite, reportedly cost about $275,000 (about $1.1 million in 2012 dollars). Trudeau thought the taxpayers should pick up the tab, but his advisors, notably Jim Coutts and Michael Pitfield, said that would be political suicide. They dispatched Keith Davey, a perennial Liberal Party campaign chair, to talk Trudeau out of the idea. Trudeau understood the risks, but remained unmoved. "Keith, you have often told me that I'm the meal ticket for this party. Well, what would you say if I told you that your meal ticket considers the swimming pool a biological necessity?"[33] Davey agreed to try to find a way to meet Trudeau's request while limiting the negative political consequences.

The Liberal Party of Canada presented the obvious funding choice. Indeed, political parties commonly supplement the pay and reimburse the expenses of their leaders. But Davey dismissed the idea. "Clearly the Liberal party could not afford to build a swimming pool and any kind of nickel and dime scheme from kids' donations or some such just seemed unworkable." He advanced a plan to establish a "public fund," headed by a reputable doctor who would claim that the therapeutic value of a swimming pool for the prime minister would be in the public interest. Trudeau went along with the scheme and kicked in the first $10,000 (3.6 percent of the cost). No "big name" doctor would agree to head the fund, so Davey asked his personal physician to help out with the ruse. While Dr. Henry Fader of North York was a Liberal, he refused to solicit donations. That task fell to political master and Liberal bagman Keith Davey.

Minister of Public Works Judd Buchanan established an account within the Government of Canada so that donations would be fully tax-deductible to the donor. Davey recorded some 100 donations, with no single gift larger than $10,000. But this is where the mystery comes in. According to Davey, the full list of donors remains safely locked away.[34] In his memoirs, Davey made the remarkable claim that he could no longer recall the names of the donors. Of course, all he would have to do would be to open the vault in which the list of donors supposedly resides, but for reasons that have gone unexplained, he declined to do so. Davey contends that none of the contributors received any special favours from the government, although if that statement is true it certainly raises the question of why the list was kept under lock and key and never released. And of course by running the fund through the Government of Canada, taxpayers ended up paying a significant portion of the cost.

Having Davey head up the enterprise made it an overtly political operation. To suggest that contributors received absolutely nothing in return for their generosity is naïve. And despite claims that the pool was entirely funded by private donors, taxpayers directly kicked in $25,677 for design services.[35] As for Trudeau, there is little doubt that the opportunity to exercise and play with his kids in the pool was good for his mental and physical health. The pool, complete with a sauna and kitchen, was also a nice place to entertain his guests.[36] Trudeau defended himself by saying that private donors came up with the money to buy Stornoway, the official residence of the Leader of the Opposition, in the 1950s, and public money had been used to buy Harrington Lake, the prime minister's country retreat (although it was not initially purchased for that purpose). But the controversy centered not on the lifestyle benefit to future prime ministers but on the fact that Trudeau made the pool's financing a political operation while refusing to reveal to whom he might in turn be beholden. There is no such thing as a free lunch — or a free swim.

For those who revere Trudeau as the statesman who rose above the dark art of politics, the evidence indicates a myth is in play. He was certainly no stranger to cronyism, political skullduggery and self-interest. While he implemented some enduring and positive parliamentary reforms, he also undermined the notion of ministerial accountability and cabinet government. In this, he paved the way for his successors, who have maintained the Trudeau-style grip on power.

CHAPTER 27

THE POLITICIAN

If you can't do that when you are in a minority government, you shouldn't be in politics. If it's called manipulative, then so be it.

M OST CANADIANS THINK of Trudeau as a man of vision and purpose, not a traditional politician consumed with power and privilege. What politician would risk the wrath of farmers by asking the question, "Why should I sell your wheat?" When told his constitutional plans would break up the country, what prime minister would say that "if that was the result the country deserves to be torn apart"? After his campaign team booked a tour of a community centre for children with mental and physical handicaps, he felt so uncomfortable that he admonished an aide with the remark, "Don't ever do that to me again."[1] While many Canadians liked Trudeau for being so frank and unconventional, others thought him arrogant.

While these stories are oft-repeated, Trudeau was not unconcerned about public opinion. He was a consummate actor who carefully rehearsed most of his performances and stunts for maximum effect. We do not expect our politicians to do back flips off a diving board, but such moments formed part of the image that Trudeau wanted to portray. When his compatriots on a canoe trip in the far north wanted to cut short the trip for safety reasons, Trudeau dismissed the suggestion, fearing others might say he could not handle the challenge.[2]

Trudeau began to prepare himself for a life in politics in his teenage years, believing that one day he would pirouette for all to see on the world stage. His academic studies focussed on politics and economics in anticipation of a life in the public arena. He retained his letters and other documents, believing that one day a biographer would trace his life and career. He had a sense of destiny that his purpose in life would be to serve as a statesman. But he was, in the final analysis, more politician than statesman.

WHILE TRUDEAU THOUGHT about politics for most of his life, he was not always a Liberal. In 1949 he wrote in *Le Devoir* that a strong opposition was needed to counter Quebec premier Maurice Duplessis, and that it should come from *left* of the Liberal Party. Duplessis was an economic conservative and a Quebec nationalist, the first politician to use the phrase "maîtres chez nous" to describe Quebec's place within Canada, a slogan later picked up by the provincial Liberals in 1962.[3] Trudeau opposed Duplessis because of his stance on economics and Quebec nationalism, as well as his inclination to authoritarianism. But according to Jean-Louis Gagnon, a man who had abandoned the Communist Party to support the Liberals in Quebec, efforts to get Trudeau to join the Liberals were in vain. "He was quite a radical. He was fresh out of the London School of Economics and a Fabian socialist. I tried several times to get him into the Liberal Party but he wouldn't join."[4]

Over the 1950s, Trudeau attached himself politically to parties and causes on the left of the political spectrum. Socialist luminaries Eugene Forsey, Thérèse Casgrain, and Frank Scott welcomed him into the CCF, the precursor to today's NDP, with open arms.

While Trudeau coveted a political life, and considered running for elected office in Quebec in 1952 at the age of 33,[5] he did not follow an easy path, preferring instead to play David to a variety of Goliaths. He bravely confronted the Catholic Church in his writings, warning his fellow Quebecers, "We are conditioned to have the reflexes of slaves, bowing before established authority ... The divine right of prime ministers, or bishops, simply doesn't exist: they have authority over us only if we let them."[6]

Trudeau displayed his strategic sensibilities working to unite anti-Duplessis forces in a common front called Le Rassemblement. But when it was Trudeau's turn to head the group, he lost interest and it fell apart. Thérèse Casgrain was not surprised:

[Trudeau] was known as something of a dilettante, and although a prodigious intellectual, he lacked perseverance. He liked launching ideas and movements, and then lost interest and turned to something else ... During his tenure as president [of Rassemblement], he made a trip overseas and by the time he returned, the Rassemblement had ceased to exist.[7]

Trudeau wanted to join the federal Liberals in the early 1960s, but recoiled after Lester Pearson indicated his support for nuclear weapons on Canadian soil. Trudeau called Pearson the "defrocked prince of peace," a term he picked up from Pierre Vadeboncoeur, a fellow contributor to the *Cité Libre*. While plagiarized, the insult was nonetheless consistent with Trudeau's writings over the previous decades in which he once called Quebec Liberal MPs a bunch of "donkeys." During the 1963 federal election, Trudeau declared that he would vote NDP because of Pearson's "spiritual abdication."[8] But he hedged his bets and did not take out a membership in the NDP. "I don't have a card," he once told a friend. "I tell you the day I enter politics it will be with the Liberals. I don't want to be a missionary all my life. When I enter politics it will be to do something."[9]

To Trudeau, joining the Liberals was the sort of manoeuvre demanded of great leaders. "If our intellectuals had read a little Marx, Lenin and Mao Tse-tung, they would know that true revolutionaries are ready to accept a tactical compromise if necessary to allow a still-young left to come into the world."[10]

With Trudeau having no history or friends in the Liberal party, it was hard to imagine party brass rolling out the welcome mat when he contemplated running in 1965. "The philosophy of the Liberal party," Trudeau once said, "is very simple — say anything, think anything, or better still, do not think at all, but put us in power because it is we who can govern you best."[11] Ironically, it was René Lévesque, a future Trudeau foe, who suggested to Jean Marchand, the man Pearson wanted most from Quebec, that he take Trudeau with him to Ottawa for support.

Prime Minister Pearson told Jean Chrétien of his plans to recruit Marchand to run for the Liberals in the 1965 election, but said that this meant adding Trudeau and Gerald Pelletier into the mix, the so-called "three wise men" from Quebec. Chrétien responded that two wise men were enough. Regarding Trudeau, Chrétien remarked, "I'm not sure we will be able to get a guy like that elected."

Even with Pearson's support, Liberal party operatives had trouble finding a constituency for Trudeau. The MP from Trudeau's home riding refused to step aside. Chrétien observed that none of the riding associations in his area wanted to have anything to do with an "intellectual millionaire shipped in from Montréal." Trudeau wanted a French-speaking constituency, but Chrétien thought he was "too provocative."[12]

Fifteen days after the three wise men had been introduced to the press, there were no ridings prepared to embrace Trudeau or Pelletier. Claude Ryan observed in *Le Devoir*, "One finds the following paradox. Two men, after having declared they only wanted to become candidates through a democratic process, are reduced to depending on corridor conferences feverishly pursued in the vice-regal suite of the Windsor Hotel for their fates ... They are blessed from the top first, then they behave as if the mountain should come to them."[13]

The Liberals ultimately imposed Trudeau on a predominantly upscale English-speaking riding with a significant Jewish population. By any measure, Mount Royal was a safe Liberal seat that the Tories had last won in 1935. Since then it has stayed Liberal, including in the 2011 election when Liberals hit their all-time low. It has been said that the Liberals could nominate a mailbox in Mount Royal and still win an election because it is red. The Mount Royal Liberal machine gave Trudeau only lukewarm support, and he was contested for the nomination.[14] When he showed up for the nomination meeting in his Mercedes and wearing an open-collar shirt and sandals, he was sent home to change. The rebel complied.

Trudeau won in the general election in 1965, defeating his closest rival and friend Charles Taylor by a margin of two-to-one. While Trudeau garnered 55 percent of the vote, it represented a significant drop from the 70 percent of the vote earned by his Liberal predecessor in the 1963 election.

WHEN THE JOB of Liberal leader and prime minister came up in 1968, all eyes turned to Jean Marchand as the formidable Quebec-based candidate. When Marchand declined to run, he urged Trudeau to give it a shot, which at first Trudeau did not take seriously. Trudeau had been in Parliament for less than three years, and his loyalty to the Liberal party could easily be questioned. As pressure to run became more intense, Trudeau challenged his supporters to meet five conditions. First, there had to be enough party support that the campaign would not turn out to be an embarrassment or disaster. Second, his friends had to make a solemn commitment not to desert him. Third, there needed to be some indication that civil servants would work with him. Fourth, he wanted meaningful support from within the ranks of cabinet. And finally, he had to satisfy himself that he had the qualities to do the job.

Appearing to be reluctant proved a clever strategy. Trudeau not only drew out his supporters in public, but captured the imaginations of the press. When asked by a reporter how badly he wanted to become prime minister, he turned heads in the parliamentary press galley by saying, "Not very badly, but I can give you another quotation, from Plato — that men who want very badly to head the country shouldn't be trusted." The gallery members were unaccustomed to an aspirant to political leadership quoting Plato, let alone denying that the job meant that much to him. When asked if he would give up his Mercedes if he won the leadership, Trudeau inquired, "Are you talking of the car now, or the girl?," adding, "I won't give up either."[15]

Trudeau won the Liberal leadership on the fourth ballot with 50.9 percent of the vote. A significant contingent of Liberal Party members still believed Trudeau was a pretend Liberal. Jerry Grafstein, a backroom Liberal whom Trudeau ultimately appointed to the Senate, thought Trudeau's earlier broadsides at Pearson would be difficult to forgive. Trudeau exacerbated tensions with the Pearson gang by calling the 1968 election without having reconvened Parliament, thereby denying an opportunity for Pearson to receive tributes in the House of Commons. Grafstein wrote, "Mrs. Pearson was miffed at him, to say the least."[16]

TRUDEAU DISAPPEARED FROM public view after the April 6 convention to take an unannounced vacation, although the press eventually found him in Fort Lauderdale, Florida. Trudeau's cabinet was sworn in on April 20, just before he abruptly ended the parliamentary session. Tory leader Robert Stanfield expressed dismay. "No record, no policy, and no proof of his ability to govern the country."[17]

While no one questioned Trudeau's brilliance, he did not always live up to his billing as an overpowering debater and intellect. According to Ramsay Cook, a Trudeau friend and political advisor, Trudeau lost the leaders' debate to Stanfield in 1968. But rather than trying to repair the damage, which would have drawn attention to his poor performance, the Liberal strategists decided to carry on as if the debate never happened.

The 1972 re-election campaign went badly from the beginning. The party's English slogan, "The Land is Strong" failed to resonate. Trudeau put himself at the head of the campaign, treating it as a "conversation with Canadians" rather than a contest for power. Trudeau described his approach as cerebral, but in hindsight recognized that the voters wanted a leader to guide them, not a university lecturer.[18] This would be one of the few campaigns in which Trudeau defied the professionals in his party, who wanted their leader to act more like a retail politician.

Trudeau scraped through the 1972 election with a razor-thin victory. In the early days, he vowed that if his government were defeated in the House of Commons he would make all efforts to block the opposing Conservatives from forming a government. "If, for instance, there should be a clear vote of no confidence in the government, if the government should be defeated on fundamentals, on basic principles ... We shall go to the people."[19] In other words, he would oppose any move by the Governor General to allow the opposition Conservatives to form government, even though they had only two fewer seats than the Liberals. This was similar to the stance that Stephen Harper took when faced with the prospect of being replaced by a coalition of opposing parties after the 2008 election.

Following the 1972 election setback, Trudeau changed course, politically and ideologically. The cool-headed intellectuals were out and the political advisors were in. Financial prudence gave way to the big spenders. The political brain trust centered on Keith Davey, Jim Coutts and Tom Axworthy. Trudeau shed his professorial demeanor and resolved to become more gregarious and "to demonstrate the qualities of leadership that were expected of me."[20] In other words, he would become a politician like the others.

But Trudeau did not mourn his government's minority status because it allowed him to reconnect with his NDP roots, since that party held the balance of power. "I had nothing to be ashamed of regarding the balance sheet of those minority years. Quite the reverse."[21]

When the polls looked favourable to the Liberals in 1974, Trudeau wanted to trigger an election, but did not want to appear opportunistic. Rather than call a vote, as was by then his privilege, Trudeau engineered his government's defeat in the House of Commons, obliging the opposition, who trailed in the polls, to explain why an election was necessary. Trudeau recalled, "I had been ready to go to the people to solicit a new mandate on whatever day the opposition parties might commit the mistake of uniting against us. In fact, I had been asking myself whether it wouldn't be necessary to incite our opponents into making that fatal error."[22]

The 1974 budget was cleverly crafted to achieve Trudeau's political aims:

> We actually engineered our own defeat in the House of Commons ... We put things in Turner's budget that we knew the NDP couldn't support and others that we knew the Tories couldn't support. We made sure, in short, to produce a budget that would get both of them to vote against us. But we also put in the kinds of things that would let us go to the people and say: "see, these guys defeated us, they're just hungry for power, we were going to do this for you."[23]

To those who thought Trudeau calculating and cynical, he offered no apologies.

> Some people might say that this was being too political, that this kind of maneuvering breeds cynicism about politics. My answer is that if it does, it shouldn't any more than we should be cynical about Napoleon having won the battle of Austerlitz. What did he do? He divided the enemy. If you can't do that when you are in a minority government, you shouldn't be in politics. If it's called manipulative, then so be it.[24]

Trudeau told a biographer that it didn't take him long to learn that politics was about winning. "You know, if I wanted to be right rather than prime minister, I'd have stayed in university."[25] And he was not above old-style political games. When the polls tightened, Trudeau turned out the goodies, promising a leisure park for Shawinigan and a harbourfront project for Toronto.

Despite a majority win in 1974, Trudeau's standing within his own party had begun to slip. At a Liberal Party of Canada convention in 1975, one in five delegates voted in favour of a leadership review. That was double the percentage that had voted for review after the 1972 election. While Liberals liked winning, they saw faults in Trudeau, including his decision to reverse himself on wage and price controls.

An August 1976 Gallup poll pegged the Conservatives under Joe Clark at 47 percent support, compared with only 29 percent for Trudeau. Of the 15 by-elections held in six provinces on October 16, 1978, Trudeau's Liberals lost all but two. Political columnist Jeffrey Simpson observed that in riding after riding, organizers and candidates conceded that antipathy to Trudeau overrode every other issue in the campaign. Liberals, it was suggested, should start looking for someone to tell Trudeau that for the good of the party he must go.[26]

When reporters asked Trudeau if he was worried about dissension within Liberal ranks over his leadership, he replied, "If I found in my own ranks that a certain number of guys wanted to cut my throat I'd make sure I cut their throats first."[27]

Trudeau delayed calling the next election as long as he could. It had been four years, seven months and 26 days since Canadians had last gone to the polls in 1974, well beyond the traditional four-year election cycle. More than a tired administration, the government, a senior cabinet minister told journalist Craig Oliver, had become "an essentially corrupt operation."[28]

Sensing his time in office was nearing an end, Trudeau took one last desperate shot at fulfilling his constitutional obsession by making it the centerpiece of his 1979 platform. In doing so, he ran counter to the advice of Liberal Party professionals. The Tories came within six seats of winning a majority. On November 21, 1979 Trudeau resigned, twisting an old Richard Nixon quotation from when Nixon lost the race to become Governor of California to tell reporters, "I'm kinda sorry I won't have you to kick around anymore." Trudeau claims he resigned in November because he thought the Clark government would be defeated in Parliament the following year, and he wanted the Liberal party to have sufficient time to hold a leadership convention before that took place.[29]

Yet Trudeau did not discourage the defeat of the Clark government after he had resigned and his party was leaderless. At the time, the Clark government had fumbled a number of issues, giving the Liberals a 19-point lead in the public opinion polls. At the same time, the Parti Québécois announced the date of a referendum that would ask Quebecers for a mandate to negotiate sovereignty-association with the rest of Canada. On top of that, Trudeau had to deal with what the press were saying about him. *Globe and Mail* columnist Jeffrey Simpson was a case in point: "[Trudeau] had read the press notices after his resignation and had not liked what he had seen: the general impression was of a man and a prime minister who had failed to fulfill the promise expected of him when he took office in 1968."[30]

Still, Trudeau was surprised that Clark was so inept as to allow his government to lose a vote on the 1979 budget.

I always wondered why Clark didn't either postpone the vote or make some small modifications to his budget to win the support of the Creditistes, which would have enabled him to win the vote and remain prime minister. Perhaps he didn't think we — now officially a leaderless party, since I had announced my intention to resign — would have the nerve to defeat him and risk being wiped out in an election, or perhaps he was sure that if he lost in the House he would win the popular vote with ease ... Some people believe that I somehow manipulated this whole series of events and that my resignation three weeks earlier was a ploy to induce false confidence in Joe Clark. Had I had that kind of cunning, I would probably still be in politics today! But it certainly wasn't a ploy. As soon as Clark was defeated, many supporters asked me to return. I conjured up the true tale of a former prime minister of Yunan province in China who had been asked by the Emperor to come back to be prime minister again but replied, "I've had enough of it: I will come back only if the Emperor asks me three times on bended knees." [31]

Defeating the government was not without risk. Jeffrey Simpson told Keith Davey, "You guys have just made the biggest mistake of your life."[32] But that's not to say Trudeau was not ready or even surprised to return to the fray after he had resigned as Liberal leader. While hosting his canoeing companion and CTV journalist Craig Oliver for dinner in 1979 at Stornoway, Trudeau told his guest he had kept his monogrammed matchboxes from 24 Sussex Drive so they would not have to be reprinted when he returned.[33]

After his supporters in caucus had orchestrated Trudeau's resurrection, he was placed in the hands of his political professionals, who advised him to become invisible for the 1980 campaign. Joe Clark said Trudeau ran a "peek-a-boo" campaign. As if to confirm his absence, Trudeau said that if elected he wouldn't stay around for too long, suggesting he would depart in 1981.[34]

In the 1980 election, Trudeau called Clark a ditherer who could not make and hold decisions. He belittled Clark as the "headwaiter" for the provinces. But Trudeau also cowered, declining to confront Clark directly in debate because, as he lamely spun, "it was run by journalists rather than the voters."[35] The reality was that the journalists were either his friends or admirers. Craig Oliver, who covered the Joe Clark campaign plane for CTV, observed that Trudeau's return to politics was warmly welcomed by an adoring press gallery, who gave him a comparatively free ride, adding, "It didn't hurt that some of Trudeau's key aides were literally in bed with principal reporters."[36] If journalists didn't love or admire Trudeau, they certainly had cause to fear him. When one reporter asked him a question in the early '70s that Trudeau found lacking in substance, he turned and asked, "Excuse me. Are you a journalist? I ask because, maybe I'm mistaken, I don't know, I thought journalists were supposed to, how can I put it? Be educated. Knowledgeable."

Trudeau's stealth campaign won him a majority government in 1980, largely on the basis of picking up 74 of 75 seats in Quebec. But he won only two seats west of the Manitoba-Ontario border. By winning in 1980, Trudeau joined rare company: Sir John A. Macdonald and William Lyon Mackenzie King, the only prime ministers to have been defeated and then reelected in a subsequent campaign.

After helping federal forces win the 1980 Quebec referendum, Trudeau only had one final goal: patriating the constitution with a charter of rights and freedoms. It would be a challenge, since his government could not be called national in scope, and he had no mandate on the issue. Soon after the election, Trudeau met with NDP leader Ed Broadbent to invite his party into an alliance or coalition government. Cabinet positions were offered to Broadbent and some of his colleagues:

> I felt that the unity effort would be strengthened if we could consolidate our forces. There have been talks with the NDP along these lines on and off since Pearson's day, of varying degrees and seriousness. This offer was very serious. But Broadbent declined my offer, because he feared that his party would lose its power and credibility. As it turned out, the NDP did generally support us on the Constitution anyway.[37]

Once Queen Elizabeth II signed the Constitution in 1982, Trudeau looked for a grand exit. He had little regard for what was best for the Liberal Party, preferring to find ways to enhance his legacy. His choice was a world "peace" tour. This left his successor insufficient time in office to form a government, propose a budget and make a mark before going to the polls.

When Trudeau came to power, the Liberal Party held four provincial governments. By 1984, provincial Liberals had been shut out of office across the land. The Ontario Liberal leader, David Peterson, had held his post for over two years by then, and had never had a one-on-one meeting with Trudeau. "He had other things on his mind, and so did I," said Peterson. In January 1984, when Trudeau mused about his retirement, Conservative support in the polls had soared to 47 percent, while the Liberals languished at 22 percent.[38]

THE FOURTH ANNIVERSARY of the 1980 election was February 18, 1984. The day before, Trudeau came under attack after PMO officials were discovered to be digging through land registry records on Mr. Mulroney's personal residence.[39] On February 28, Liberal Party president Iona Campagnola told Trudeau that for the good of the party he should resign.[40] Trudeau announced his resignation the next day, auspiciously on February 29. Undaunted by the polls or his party's own lack of support, Trudeau quipped at his resignation press conference, "I was my best successor, but I decided not to succeed myself." He cast no vote of confidence for the pool of candidates lining up for Canada's top job.

While his potential successors crisscrossed the country, Trudeau commanded that they return to Ottawa on April 12 so he could inform them of his plans to make a number of patronage appointments. The 17 MPs he wanted to reward would erode the Liberal majority in the House of Commons, making the party vulnerable to defeat. Trudeau offered to delay the appointments, provided he had an agreement that his successor would follow through before the next election was called. John Turner, the front-runner, agreed, although when he saw the list he turned to an aide and said, "Turn away when I tell you this because you're going to vomit."[41] The agreement was not a gentlemanly affair: Trudeau demanded that Turner put his commitment in writing.

When Turner made the controversial appointments, opposition leader Brian Mulroney remarked that it was "something right out of an Edward G. Robinson movie. You know, the boys cutting up the cash." Three MPs were appointed to the Senate, one member became consul general in Bordeaux, France, and two members went to the bench. *The Toronto Sun* editorial noted, "No outgoing prime minister ever so offensively and publicly hamstrung his successor. It was a parting kick at the man Trudeau least wanted in the job."[42]

Turner inevitably tried to distance himself from the Trudeau regime. "I have felt for some time that the cabinet, the cabinet committee system, and indeed the entire decision-making process were too elaborate, too complex, too slow, and too expensive. Because of the system, the responsibility of the ministers and other departments has become defused, eroded and blurred. Decisions are difficult to arrive at in an efficient and timely fashion."[43] To amplify his differences with Trudeau, Turner told the media, "Leadership is less a Cartesian master plan than a human procedure. My skills are people skills, and those of the skills required to put a human face on technology and government."[44]

Trudeau took the distinction Turner was trying to make not as winning political strategy but as a personal insult. Trudeau was not about to let the matter go unchallenged, and he took his revenge. When Turner said he resigned from cabinet claiming Trudeau had repudiated his promise over wage and price controls, Trudeau threatened to reveal a letter he sent to Turner in 1975 that stated there had been "no policy differences" between them. Turner never responded to Trudeau's letter, and therefore never confirmed Trudeau's characterization of the absence of policy differences. Nonetheless, Trudeau issued a press release in 1984 claiming that Turner had misrepresented the facts and had apologized to him for doing so.[45] Mulroney ended up winning 211 seats to 40 for the Liberals. Trudeau told a friendly CTV reporter that had he still been leader, the Liberals would have won the election.[46]

A prolific chronicler of the Liberal Party, Stephen Clarkson, argues that Trudeau was indifferent to Liberal fortunes before and after they had served his purpose: "The Grits were an agglomeration of the ambitious, dependent on one man who cared very little about the party's past and even less about its future. The Liberal party has become the Trudeau party, and when he retired, it fell apart."[47] Donald Brittain, the documentary filmmaker who followed the intersecting career of Trudeau and Lévesque, observed that Trudeau had "left his party in ruins." Beyond Turner, both Jean Chrétien and Paul Martin would occasionally suffer from Trudeau's political interventions.

Trudeau was a politician but he never was a party man. He reminded Liberals of that fact in 1984 when he cancelled his planned attendance at a British Columbia Liberal policy conference on account of illness, but was then photographed dancing at a New York discotheque in great health and vigour. Indeed, when Trudeau's personal interests and views collided with those of his party, the personal trumped the political every time.

John Turner, who worked with Trudeau and cabinet and then succeeded him as leader concluded that Trudeau's loyalty was to his ideas and that he had little regard for the interests of the Liberal party.[48] The Liberal Party was merely a vehicle through which he could implement his vision for the nation, which, as a measure of conviction, is something to be admired.

CHAPTER 28

ELECTION MASTER?

Welcome to the 1980s.

PIERRE TRUDEAU'S THREE majorities and one minority government make him Canada's third-longest-serving prime minister. He tasted defeat only once, and stayed out of power a mere 273 days. Electorally speaking, Trudeau ranks among the most successful Canadian politicians since Confederation. But without overwhelming support from Quebec, Trudeau would have been a one-term prime minister.

Over his five campaigns, Trudeau's Liberals won 42.2 percent of the popular vote, compared to the Progressive Conservatives' 34 percent.[1] More importantly, the Liberals won 49.2 percent of the seats, while the Tories only took 37.7 percent. Even the graph illustrating Trudeau's popular vote over five elections resembles a "W" for winner.

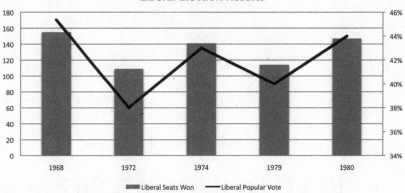

Liberal Election Results

Trudeau added to the hegemony that Liberals had enjoyed since the days of Sir John A. Macdonald.

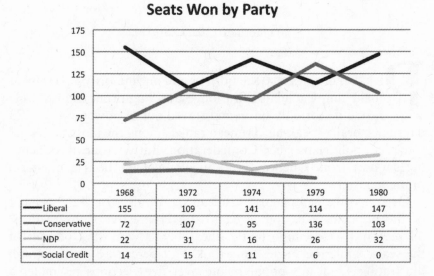

Seats Won by Party

	1968	1972	1974	1979	1980
Liberal	155	109	141	114	147
Conservative	72	107	95	136	103
NDP	22	31	16	26	32
Social Credit	14	15	11	6	0

Trudeau's greatest electoral triumph came in 1968, when he won 45 percent of the popular vote and 58 percent of the seats, taking 73 percent of the seats in Ontario, 76 percent in Quebec, and 70 percent in British Columbia. While Canadians may remember 1968 as the greatest electoral landslide of all time, in terms of popular vote it fell short of eleven twentieth-century victories: Mulroney in 1984, Diefenbaker in 1958, St. Laurent in 1953 and 1949, King in 1940, Bennett in 1930, Borden in 1911 and 1917, and Laurier in 1900, 1904 and 1908. Not included is Meighen, who earned more than

45 percent of the vote in 1925 and 1926 but did not form the post-election government. "Trudeaumania," as it was called in 1968, leaves the impression that it was a crushing political force, but it captured fewer Canadians than previous elections.

The most distinguishing fact about Trudeau's 1968 mandate was its national scope. In no future election could Trudeau make that claim again. But the one constant throughout his five victories proved to be strong support in his home province of Quebec.

% of seats won in Quebec

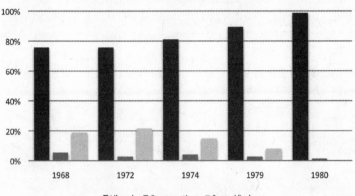

WHILE TRUDEAU WON 84 percent of all Quebec seats over his five election campaigns, the only election that gave him majority support outside Quebec was 1968. Over his final four elections, he won only 32 percent of the seats in the rest of Canada, compared with 54 percent for the Tories.

% of seats won outside Quebec

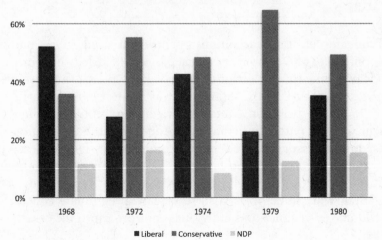

After the 1968 campaign, Trudeau's results in western Canada turned particularly abysmal. In British Columbia he took only 14 percent of the available seats. After 1968 he won zero seats in Alberta, eight percent of the seats in Saskatchewan, and 15 percent of what was up for grabs in Manitoba. In the 1979 election, Trudeau captured a scant three seats west of the Ontario border. In 1980 he won just two seats — out of 77.

While Trudeau's vote steadily declined in the West, his fortunes rose consistently in Atlantic Canada, especially in Newfoundland and in the bilingual province of New Brunswick. It makes sense that Trudeau gained the most from provinces that benefited from regional economic development and bilingualism, causes he championed.

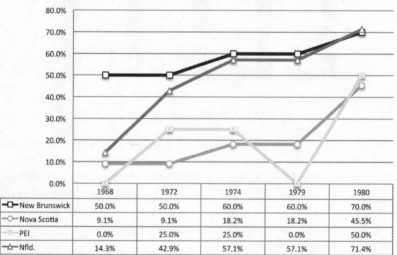

% of Seats Won by Trudeau in Atlantic Canada

	1968	1972	1974	1979	1980
New Brunswick	50.0%	50.0%	60.0%	60.0%	70.0%
Nova Scotia	9.1%	9.1%	18.2%	18.2%	45.5%
PEI	0.0%	25.0%	25.0%	0.0%	50.0%
Nfld.	14.3%	42.9%	57.1%	57.1%	71.4%

Trudeau's electoral accomplishments also need to be put into the context of the opponents he faced. Stanfield led the Tories for Trudeau's first three elections. Widely known as "the best prime minister we never had," Stanfield was honest and forthright to a fault. But he was not a retail politician and could not unite his caucus and his party. In his farewell address at the convention that chose his successor, Stanfield bluntly told Progressive Conservatives that they needed to look no farther than the mirror to explain their electoral failure: "Some Progressive Conservatives would rather fight than win. Some of us wish to elevate a legitimate concern for individual self-reliance and individual enterprise into the central and dominating dogma and theme of our party. Why do we spoil a good case by exaggeration? Why do we try to polarize a society that is already taut with tension and confrontation?"[2]

Joe Clark stands out as the only politician to defeat Trudeau, which he did in 1979. But despite winning only a minority government, Clark made the fatal decision to act as if he had a majority. In what many consider the biggest blunder in Canadian political history, Clark lost his well-intentioned but incompetent government on a confidence vote after only nine months in office. As *Montreal Gazette* columnist L. Ian MacDonald observed, "Joe Clark never misses a chance to miss a chance."[3]

WHILE TRUDEAU ENJOYED overwhelming support in the province of Quebec, after patriating the constitution without the consent of the Quebec government, he never again faced voters. Trudeau earned 57 percent of the vote in Quebec over five elections, but his successors over nine subsequent elections received only 30 percent. While Trudeau won 84 percent of Quebec's seats, his successors managed to capture only 24 percent, largely in anglophone-heavy ridings on the island of Montreal. This was despite the fact that in seven of these nine elections, the Liberals' leader hailed from Quebec.

Liberals performed poorly in the West under Trudeau, but so did his successors. The average Liberal popular vote under Trudeau in the four Western provinces over five elections was 28 percent. Up to and including the 2011 election, his successors garnered only 23 percent of the vote. As every Liberal leader after Trudeau has come to realize, the National Energy Program remains an albatross around the party's neck.

While Trudeau's policies scorched Liberal fortunes in the West and Quebec, they did not similarly offend voters in other parts of Canada. Had it just been Trudeau's personality that grated, rather than his programs, the animosity he inspired would probably not be so regionalized or sustained.

In the Atlantic Provinces, Trudeau carried 43 percent of the vote and his successors 42 percent. In Ontario, the electorate gave Trudeau 42 percent of the votes, and 41 percent to Liberals who followed him. And these figures include the 2011 election, in which Liberals were reduced to the third party in the House of Commons.

While Trudeau is considered an "election master," the reality is that he won only one national mandate and held onto power only because of overwhelming support from his home province of Quebec.

And why wouldn't *la belle province* support him? He was not only a native son, but a helpful one. He showered money on Quebec businesses through regional development programs. He augmented social programs that helped the province's unemployed. He brought French into the corridors of power in Ottawa by implementing official bilingualism. And while voters knew that Trudeau believed in a strong central government — which was to Quebec's financial benefit — they could also count on PQ leader René Lévesque to keep him in check.

Trudeau never tested his popularity after his one major offense to Quebecers, patriating the constitution over Lévesque's objections in 1981. He left that hangover to his successors. The first to face the voters, John Turner, was clobbered by Brian Mulroney. Trudeau's medium-term successor, Jean Chrétien, won three majority governments, but due in large part to a divided conservative opposition. Chrétien made no inroads in the west and won only a fraction of the seats in Quebec that Trudeau had secured over his five campaigns. Almost immediately after the Progressive Conservative and Canadian Alliance parties united as the new Conservative Party of Canada, Liberal fortunes plummeted. In 2011, for the first time since Confederation, the Liberals fell to third-party status in the House of Commons.

If the Liberal Party of Canada wants to understand why many pundits predict the permanent demise of this once great and dominant political institution, its members need look no farther back than the Trudeau years. Mulroney points to data to make this point: "[I]f what Trudeau did was so great then what has happened to the Liberal party since he left?"[818] Indeed, Trudeau's legacy is one of the main reasons why the electorate has tilted away from the Liberals, and toward other parties, including the NDP in Quebec and the Conservatives in Ontario and the West.

SECTION VI

CONCLUSION

CHAPTER 29

CANADA'S MOST OVERRATED PRIME MINISTER?

*He is an odd fish and his own worst enemy, and on the whole I think
his influence on Canada in the past sixteen years has been detrimental
— British High Commissioner to Canada, Lord Moran.*

C ANADA'S THIRD-LONGEST-SERVING prime minister had no regrets when he left office.[1] Indeed, Trudeau enjoyed the self-
satisfaction of checking off most of the items on his prime
ministerial to-do list:
- The federal government and Canadian military were officially
  bilingual
- Vis-à-vis the provinces, the federal government had a much
  stronger role in the social and economic life of the nation
- Federally-funded regional development programs had grown
  significantly in size
- The social safety net had been expanded
- The FLQ was no more
- The country had a made-in-Canada constitution with a Charter
  of Rights and Freedoms
- A referendum on sovereignty-association in Quebec had been
  defeated.

Trudeau, without question, achieved most of his goals. But what consequences, intended or otherwise, did these accomplishments have for Canada?

On the economic front, Trudeau proudly boasted in his memoirs, "Canada was as healthy when I left office as any of our major competitors and was probably ahead in many respects."[2] But investors saw it differently. Before Trudeau's resignation, tendered at 12:45 PM on February 29, 1984, the Toronto Stock exchange was flat. In the 30 minutes after his announcement, it soared a whopping 3.34 percent, which led to the largest daily gain in seven months.[3] "I understand there are parties all over town. There is a feeling of celebration," said Andrew Kniewasser, president of the Investment Dealers' Association of Canada.[4] Even the Canadian dollar climbed on the news of the resignation, up 15 basis points from the previous day.[5]

Ironically, Trudeau may well have taken this reaction as a badge of honour. In his speech at the Liberal convention that chose his successor, he chastised his opponents and critics as small-minded whiners:

> I have found that in any of the reforms, the difficult reforms that we have tried to bring in my years, whenever the going was tough and we were opposed by the multinationals or by the provincial premiers or by the superpowers, I realized that if our cause was right, all we had to do to win was to talk over the heads of the premiers, over the heads of the multi-nationals, over the heads of the superpowers to the people of this country.

It's true that Trudeau had electoral success, albeit based largely on near-total dominance of his home province, and not on a broadly expressed national will. But it's not true that he took his most controversial policies to the people. The patriation of the constitution and the National Energy Program were final-term initiatives. Having left it to his successor to defend these policies, Trudeau helped hand the Liberal Party its worst drubbing in the party's history in 1984, eclipsed only by its distant third-place result in the 2011 election. And in in the 1974 election, Trudeau fought *against* wage and price controls, and then promptly brought them in after winning a majority. He lost the next election he fought.

In considering the immediate aftermath of Trudeau's second resignation, it is perhaps best left to an outsider to deliver an assessment of his political legacy. The British High Commissioner,

John Wilson, Lord Moran, offered this view of Trudeau to his superiors at the Foreign Office in 1984:

> He is an odd fish and his own worst enemy, and on the whole I think his influence on Canada in the past sixteen years has been detrimental ... He treated provincial premiers with contempt and provincial governments as if they were town councils. But I think few Canadians share his extreme centralizing stance. Most believe that Canada's diversity and geographical spread need a federal system and a division of powers, with each level treating the other, as seldom happened in Mr. Trudeau's time, with courtesy, respect and understanding.[6]

This lack of respect for others flowed from a key Trudeau character trait, that of the lone wolf. Trudeau described his temperament in the style of Cyrano de Bergerac, he did not engage in team sports or activities, and even his friends described him as a dilettante, a spoiled brat and an intellectual snob.[7] His philosophy was *personalism*. He did not lead through cooperation and teamwork, which ultimately made him poorly suited to running a federation.

One cannot dispute Trudeau's prowess as an intellect, a warrior, and a visionary. In these dimensions, Conrad Black, who has made the acquaintance of many world leaders, describes Trudeau as a tantalizing figure, a strong, natural leader who possessed a mental agility in a Cartesian rhetorical fashion. "Personally, he was a most engaging and interesting man to have lunch or dinner with."[8] Leading conservative thinker David Frum acknowledged many Trudeau virtues: "He was afraid of nobody, not even the media. He was charismatic, he was brilliant, he was determined, he was principled."[9]

When Trudeau died in 2000, Prime Minister Chrétien described his mentor as a man of brilliance, action, grace, style, wit, complexity and courage, and someone who inspired young Canadians to engage in acts of citizenship. Stephen Harper, then president of the National Citizen's Coalition, had a different take on Trudeau.[10] In an op-ed that appeared in the *National Post* the week after Trudeau's death Harper recalled the time when Trudeau asked the question, "Why should I sell your wheat?" While the sentiment may have represented a play for free markets, to Harper it incarnated a distant leader who neither understood, nor cared to understand, a group of people upon whom his actions would have immense impact. Having relocated from Ontario to the West, Harper saw firsthand how an

economy collapsed from historic boom to deep recession in a matter
of months, solely because of a radical, interventionist blueprint of
economic nationalism.

> Flailing from one pet policy objective to another, he expanded
> the welfare state, created scores of bureaucratic agencies, offices
> and ministries and encouraged the regulation and government
> control of major industrial sectors. Under his stewardship,
> the country created huge deficits, a mammoth national debt,
> high taxes, bloated bureaucracy, rising unemployment, record
> inflation, curtailed trade and declining competitiveness. From
> these consequences we have still not fully recovered, and they
> continue to have an impact on my pay cheque, and my family's
> opportunities, every single month.

While Harper found himself cheering for Trudeau in the 1980
Quebec referendum, he recalled that Trudeau had remained silent
when Quebec dismantled the very bilingualism he wanted for Canada
as a whole. Harper challenged the notion that Trudeau continued to
define the Canadian psyche.

> Only a bastardized version of his unity vision remains and
> his other policies have been rejected and repealed by even his
> own Liberal party. His definition of Canadian nationalism —
> centralism, socialism, bilingualism — is the polar opposite of
> the trends in Canadian history that are now triumphing — re-
> gionalism, globalization, Québec particularism — in no small
> measure a reaction to the policies Mr. Trudeau practiced.

Harper considered it crucial to remind Canadians that when the
world struggled against evil, the man who championed the "just
society" stood on the wrong side of history. As a member of the
"greatest generation," the one that defeated the Nazis in war and
resolutely stared down the Soviets in the decades that followed,
Harper noted that Trudeau took a pass on both battles. Reflecting
on Trudeau, Harper may have been thinking about what Winston
Churchill said in the Canadian House of Commons in 1941: "There
is no room now for the dilettante, for the weakling, for the shirker
or the sluggard."[11]

The *New York Times* obituary of Trudeau reflected the image he
projected around the world. The piece dwelled not on Trudeau's

policy record but his flamboyance, which it regarded as counter-cultural to Canada's traditionally staid and fusty image.[12]

In his heyday, Pierre Trudeau ran his country with a pa-nache that was aggressively and un-Canadianly immodest. He drove sports cars, flaunted his wit, dated celebrities like Barbra Streisand, toured the discos, married a former flower child much younger than himself and once, in an act of ap-parent insouciance, was photographed as he pirouetted alone in Buckingham Palace while other guests walked off to meet Queen Elizabeth.

Trudeau received a state funeral, although his immediate family had concerns about making it a formal affair. Ottawa Funeral director Brian McGarry was told that the family worried about the country's reaction since "he was not as popular as he once had been."[13] But public outpouring was overwhelming. People stood in line until 3:30 a.m. to pay their respects as the casket lay in state on Parliament Hill. More than 60,000 mourners passed by in two days.

TRUDEAU-MANIA ENJOYED a revival in the mid-90s, almost to the point of idolatry. The late prime minister's memoirs hit bookstores in 1993, and the CBC released a friendly documentary in 1994. The following 15 years would see a succession of flattering biographies, including books that won the Shaughnessy Cohen prize for political writing in 2006 and 2009. Even in 2012, two of five nominees for the honour had penned tomes about Trudeau, though the award that year went to Richard Gwyn for his second volume on the life of John A. Macdonald.

In the weeks after Trudeau died, Chrétien sought to immortalize his former leader, and considered renaming Mount Logan, Canada's highest peak, in his honour. After growing opposition to this plan, Chrétien rechristened Montreal's Dorval Airport for Trudeau, and a mountain in British Columbia's Premier Range became Mount Pierre Elliott Trudeau.

But that was not enough. In 2002 Chrétien handed over $125 million of taxpayer money to the Pierre Elliot Trudeau Foundation, a charity established in 2001 by Trudeau's family, friends, and colleagues as a living memorial to the former prime minister. The foundation pays people to contemplate major political, social and economic issues in line with Trudeau's philosophy. It's hard to imagine a better way to keep a prime ministerial legacy alive at the taxpayers' expense, a luxury not available to any other former prime minister.

Yet, despite this blinding adulation, a few critics dared to offer a less-sunny view. While Trudeau was launching an English version of his journal *Cité Libre* in 1998, the editor-in-chief of *The Globe and Mail*, William Thorsell, took the occasion to observe that almost everything Trudeau did after 1980 was "decisive, dramatic, and disastrous." Noting Quebec's rejection of the Constitution Act, and Trudeau's aggressive attacks on later efforts to remedy this breach, Thorsell concluded, "Lucien Bouchard is Pierre Trudeau's child, and the Bloc Québécois his most enduring political legacy outside the Charter of Rights."[14]

In an attempt to objectively assess the record of all Canadian prime ministers, *Maclean's* magazine asked a panel of historians, political scientists, economists, and other "experts" in 1997, and again in 2011, to rank Canada's best prime ministers.[15] In both surveys, Trudeau took fifth place.[16] In the 2011 survey he ranked behind Mackenzie King, John A. Macdonald, Wilfrid Laurier and Lester B. Pearson. While respondents praised Trudeau for enacting the Charter and facing up to Quebec nationalists, they damned him for alienating the West, patriating the constitution without Quebec's participation, and mismanaging the economy. While he was Canada's third-longest-serving prime minister, Trudeau's fifth place ranking put him in the middle of the pack among the nine former leaders who won more than a single election. Fifth place out of nine is hardly the lofty standing one might expect for a person who ranked third in the CBC's populist project to name the greatest Canadian *of all time.*

To situate Trudeau's true place in history, his defenders and critics exchanged blows in a series of popular debates that took place in 2011, more than ten years after Trudeau's passing.[17] There are not many, if any, other prime ministers who could capture such interest thirty years out of office. The provocative resolution for the "History Wars" debate was: "Resolved: Pierre Trudeau: Canada's most disastrous prime minister." Arguing against the motion in separate events were Trudeau biographer John English and *Globe and Mail* columnist Lawrence Martin. Arguing for the motion in both debates was conservative thinker and columnist David Frum.

To John English, Trudeau's key legacy was keeping Quebec in Canada. "Trudeau will not be judged in history by his economic policies or his foreign policy but rather by how he responded to what the Royal Commission on Bilingualism and Biculturalism rightly called, in February, 1965, 'the greatest crisis in our history' — the challenge of Québec nationalism and separatism." Parti Québécois leader René Lévesque needed a worthy foe and Trudeau was up to the task as "an irreplaceable leader for his times," concluded English.

Lawrence Martin delivered a more balanced defence of Trudeau. While critical of his economic policies and coziness with communist dictators, Martin judged Trudeau on non-traditional measures. He considered Trudeau's greatest accomplishment his impact on the conscience and character of the country. "I was a young undergraduate when he crashed through the stained glass windows. You had to be there to understand his force, to witness how he lifted the spirits of a generation. He allowed us to think independently of the Americans ... Intellectuals tend to be scorned in today's political climate. But we loved Trudeau's braininess." Beyond Martin's youthful impressions, he offered no evidence that Trudeau had actually mobilized the entire nation to a higher calling. On English's claim that Trudeau kept Quebec in Canada, Martin put the issue in the form of a question: "Could any other prime minister have stood up to separatism the way Trudeau did?" Consequently, Martin thought we should not much care if Trudeau was overly "arrogant, surly, stubborn, and insensitive."

Martin, among many other journalists, suggested that Trudeau incarnated a Canadian version of John F. Kennedy.[18] Even Lucien Bouchard, an arch Trudeau detractor, conceded that people admired Trudeau as a man of style, of grace under pressure: "He was some kind of a Kennedy for us."[19] Certainly the two leaders shared charisma, sex appeal, a young family, wealth, and certain ideas. Kennedy championed the Peace Corps; Trudeau, Katimavik. But their style differences were noteworthy as well. Trudeau was as arrogant as Kennedy was charming. Trudeau played the intellectual while Kennedy enjoyed a more common touch. Kennedy was decorated for his service during the Second World War, while Trudeau either sat on his hands or protested. But in matters of nation-building, their substantive differences were more profound and had greater impact. Kennedy believed in a strong military, confronting the communists directly as well as through NATO. Trudeau supported unilateral disarmament, withdrawal from NATO and making friends with the communists. Unlike Trudeau, the Kennedy game plan included no measures to repel foreign investment or rack up massive government debt. The most we could say is that, in their day, the two men incarnated the zeitgeist of their eras. They also gave voice to those who believe in the power of the state to solve society's problems. But by 1979, even Lawrence Martin had conceded that the magic was gone: "The confidence they inspired in the institution of government, liberal government, has vanished."[20]

In response to Martin and English in the debates, David Frum called Trudeau "world-class" for the damage he inflicted on Canada. "Pierre Trudeau inherited a strong, growing and diversified Canadian economy. When Trudeau at last left office for good in 1984, Canadians were still feeling the effects of Canada's worst recession since the Great Depression." While Canadians thought Trudeau represented Canada well on the world stage, Frum concluded otherwise: "Trudeau had little taste for the alliances and relationships he inherited in 1968... Trudeau repudiated that inheritance ... showing remarkable indifference to the struggle against totalitarianism that defined the geopolitics of the 20th century."

Economic incompetence and international ineptness aside, Frum thought Trudeau's greatest disaster was his lasting impact on the unity of Canada. "Trudeau ascertained what each of Canada's regions most dearly wanted — and then he offered them the exact opposite. Unsurprisingly, Trudeau's flip-them-the-finger approach to national unity did not yield positive results. In fact, he nearly blew apart the country — and his own party." Evincing mild appreciation for the Charter, Frum poses this question: "Would it really have been impossible to combine the adoption of the Charter with a less-destructive economic policy, a less destructive foreign policy, a less destructive national unity policy?"

Frum's point about national unity, and more particularly the division between Quebec and the rest of Canada, was borne out in a Leger Marketing survey that marked the 30th anniversary of the patriation of the constitution.[21] In Quebec, 71.4 percent of respondents opposed patriation, compared with only 16.2 percent in the rest of Canada.[22] The majority of Quebecers surveyed indicated they would lean toward independence if the constitution passed by Trudeau were not ultimately reformed. Three-quarters of Quebecers thought society's ability to protect the French language and culture should supersede protection of individual rights. Commenting on the poll, University of Ottawa political scientist François Rocher concluded, "Patriation has left a deep scar that is not yet ready to be healed."[23]

But many Trudeau admirers, like John Geddes of Maclean's Magazine, scoff at the critique. "Although I've long since come to recognize his serious shortcomings, it's like the hockey player you idolized as a 10-year-old — you never entirely get over it."[24] Beyond the adolescent emotion, Geddes stuck by Trudeau for the sole reason that he stood up to the separatists and won the referendum in 1980. Geddes admits that Trudeau failed in just about every other important dimension, but "I won't be tearing up my signed Trudeau rookie card on that basis."

Geddes hangs his hat on this key question: What would have been the fate of federalism had it been left to Bob Stanfield or Joe Clark? No one can definitively answer that hypothetical question, but there is no reason to assume Canada would have fared worse than under Trudeau. It might have even done better. We can easily imagine that Clark or Stanfield, not to mention Mulroney, would have approached the unity issue with a cooperative style of federalism, much in the same way Lester B. Pearson did. We may have ended up with a constitution much like that proposed at Meech Lake, or we might have had no deal — and no crisis — at all. But Quebec would not have been isolated or have a sense of betrayal.

In the early 1980s, Canadians were not clamouring for a new constitution or a Charter. They were struggling to cope with high inflation, double-digit unemployment, and rising interest rates. Patriating the constitution was Trudeau's obsession, which he imposed without popular mandate. What would have happened if, instead of pouring all his energies into constitutional reform, Trudeau had focused on economic matters instead? What if he had never convened the premiers to a constitutional conference, and the infamous night of the long knives had never happened? It may well be the case that these alternative scenarios may have served long-term national unity better than Trudeau's *coup de force*.

NO UNIVERSAL REPORT card exists for prime ministers. In broad terms, however, we consider our leaders successful if they keep the country unified, enhance our prosperity, and ensure we stay safe from harm. In each of these dimensions, the evidence reveals that Trudeau not only fell well short of the mark, but below that of all other two-term prime ministers.

Macdonald, Laurier, King, Diefenbaker, and Mulroney all made unity and cooperative federalism a priority. They avoided needlessly antagonizing regions of the country, helped expand our economy, and effectively represented Canadian interests abroad. Other than Trudeau, the only two-term prime minister who enacted profoundly divisive policies was Robert Borden, who brought in conscription during the First World War. But unlike Trudeau, Borden's foreign interventions produced results, and he did not pursue policies that undermined economic growth. Only Trudeau accomplished the trifecta of damaging national security, eroding federal finances and rupturing national unity with his self described "putsch."[25]

Trudeau's most fervent supporters say little about his contribution to world affairs or his management of the economy. On international relations, Trudeau's judgment has been proved wrong far more often than right. While the Cold War intensified and the nuclear arms race escalated, Trudeau weakened Canada's relations with our democratic allies. He sought to place Canada as a neutral third party between the Soviets and the Americans, as if these two super powers were morally equivalent. Trudeau profoundly weakened our defences, which not only diminished our military capacity but also reduced our clout in world affairs. To countries that mattered — economically and strategically — Canada became an annoyance. Our proud legacy of punching above our weight in two world wars was abandoned. While many Canadians may have admired Trudeau for taking the moral high ground on peace, the net result of his efforts made us the subject of indifference or ridicule among world leaders. If results matter more than style, then Trudeau failed us on the world stage.

Conrad Black called Trudeau's foreign policies an unmitigated disaster:

> His truckling to Castro and facilitation of the Cuban military presence in Angola was outrageous. He was no friend of NATO and his Third Option and Third Way, like his quest for non-US foreign trade were all complete failures. He had absolutely nothing to do with the end of the Cold War and his disarmament proposals near the end of his term, like his enthusiasm for North-South matters, was just faddish nonsense. He purported to believe that Yalta had legitimized Soviet control of Eastern Europe, which was rubbish, and preferred the Russians to the Americans, which was inappropriate to a country so wholly dependent on the United States. Nixon and Reagan had no use at all for Trudeau. Trudeau's opposition to Reagan's SDI was insane.[26]

The Soviets and the Chinese admired Trudeau. So did Fidel Castro. But our real friends, the Brits and the Americans, thought of him in disparaging terms. Our military leaders despised Trudeau for gutting the capacity and spirit of our fighting forces. He seemed stubbornly oblivious to Canadians interests, not something we should expect from our prime minister, but perhaps not surprising from a man who considered himself a "citizen of the world."

No prime minister devoted more time to studying the economy, or had a clearer vision of how he wanted to reform society, than Trudeau. Yet no prime minister did more economic damage. Trudeau embarked on his string of deficits when the federal debt level equaled less than 20 percent of GDP, and interest costs were relatively low. His 1983 deficit remains unmatched outside of times of war: the equivalent of a $132 billion deficit in the 2012 economy. Every year after 1974, Trudeau ran an annual operating deficit, meaning not a nickel of government revenues was available to pay interest on the debt. In fact, over his fifteen-and-a-half years in office, Trudeau spent $54.4 billion more on programs than he collected in revenue. This, together with $133 billion in interest costs, piled on to our national debt for the next generation to handle. After crunching all the numbers, Trudeau increased the federal debt in nominal terms tenfold. Trudeau's compounding debt made balancing the books a Sisyphean task for his successors.

On Trudeau's watch the value of our dollar declined and we ran up one of the worst inflation records among developed nations. Nothing contributed more to exacerbating inflation than out-of-control government spending, which increased at an average of 15 percent every year Trudeau was in office. But Trudeau did more than just weaken our financial position. He repelled investment and jobs with the Foreign Investment Review Agency, devastated the West with the National Energy Program, and undermined the Canadian work ethic with his Unemployment Insurance reforms.

Mulroney, who was first in line to mop up Trudeau's financial mess, found it ironic that the proponent of a strong central government left it in such a decrepit state. "No one weakened the federal government more than he did. He weakened the capacity of the federal government to act."[27]

Pierre Trudeau inherited a strong federal balance sheet and a vibrant economy. But after his first term in office, he unleashed his socialist impulses and drove our nation's finances to the brink. It's no wonder that even his fiercest defenders stay silent when the matter of the economy comes up for discussion.

AS ONE SENIOR Trudeau loyalist privately observed, "Forget about the economy, the just society and his hare-brained forays around the world. All that can be excused because Quebec remains in Canada."

This points to the key unresolved question about Trudeau's success as a prime minister. Did he inflame the tensions regarding Quebec's place in Canada and leave the matter so profoundly unresolved that it will yet be the undoing of the nation as we know it? Or will his actions be judged as decisive in keeping the country together.

We can give Trudeau credit for implementing bilingualism. No longer can Quebec nationalists claim that there is no place for them in Ottawa, at least for those who are bilingual. The federal government provides services to citizens in English and French where numbers warrant. Because of Trudeau, and more particularly Lester Pearson, along with the backing of Conservative leader Robert Stanfield, we now have some measure of language equity in Canada. Had Trudeau stopped there, he would have made a great contribution to keeping Quebec in Canada.

We can also say that had Trudeau succeeded in passing the Victoria constitutional accord in 1971, we would have been spared much wrangling over the last 40 years. It was a sensible agreement, but Trudeau was unable to bring the Quebec government onside, in part because he had spent much of the previous decade insulting Quebec politicians and opinion leaders. When the editor of *Le Devoir* came out against the Victoria accord, Trudeau had no reservoir of goodwill left within the province with which to fight. Not only did the separatists and soft nationalists oppose him, but so did many federalists.

When Trudeau became prime minister, some leading Quebec separatists were overjoyed. Pierre Bourgault, one of Quebec's independence-movement founders, called Trudeau "the best candidate we could hope for."[28] Of the confrontation that was to come, Bourgault said that Trudeau purposely aggravated the rift between Quebec and the federal government. "He exists only on the strength of his adversaries. If [separatism] didn't exist he wouldn't be in power."[29]

Indeed, it was only while Trudeau was in Ottawa defending the federation that Quebecers felt comfortable sending a pro-sovereignty majority government to Quebec City. Trudeau said he welcomed the Parti Québécois's 1976 victory because it gave him the opportunity to take on separatists in open combat. But Trudeau's stated goal of keeping Quebec in Canada would have been far better served had the voters not felt it necessary to put René Lévesque in office in the first place.

Trudeau's key speech during the 1980 Quebec referendum was indisputably important. But what if Joe Clark had been prime minister, and uttered a similar speech (minus the Elliott reference) promising constitutional change? Was the messenger really more important than the message? This last question cannot be answered, yet Trudeau loyalists, without any clear evidence, take it as an act of faith that federal forces would have lost the referendum had Trudeau not been there to save the day.[30]

Canadians cannot fault Trudeau for wanting a charter of rights and freedoms or a constitution that was wholly amendable by Canadians. But we can fault him for the damage he caused in fulfilling his objectives. The fatal mistake committed by Trudeau and the nine provincial premiers was proceeding with constitutional reform while a sovereignist government held power in Quebec.

In 1981, it was well within Trudeau's grasp to secure a simple patriation that took Great Britain out of the equation, as every province, including Quebec, agreed to that outcome. But while René Lévesque remained premier, Trudeau had no prospect of gaining Quebec's support for an agreement permitting the federal government to intervene in areas of provincial jurisdiction, or to water down Quebec's language law. *He could not have done so even with a federalist premier of Quebec at the table.* The result was that the prime minister of Canada and nine provincial premiers broke precedent, and broke faith with Quebec. Trudeau in particular betrayed the promises of constitutional reform he made to Quebecers in the 1980 referendum, the consequences of which reverberate 30 years after the fact.

Even some Trudeau loyalists and federalists from Quebec acknowledged that patriation without Quebec would be unforgivable. As the Queen was signing the constitution on the front lawn of Parliament Hill, the Liberal Speaker of the House of Commons, Jeanne Sauvé, turned to her husband and said, "My God, what have we done?" When Trudeau was about to affix his signature to the document, Liberal senator Jean Marchand, a mentor to Trudeau in the 1960s, whispered "*traitre*" into the ear of Maureen McTeer. Even Trudeau's justice minister and constitutional fixer, Jean Chrétien, wrote that it was one of the saddest moments in his career to see Quebec so isolated.[31]

Former Tory leader Robert Stanfield remarked, "No premier of Québec within living memory would have agreed to the Constitution of 1982 ... I believed and I still believe that the exercise of 1982 endangers Canada as a country. We gave the separatists a stick to beat us with ... Ottawa had betrayed French-speaking Quebeckers who had voted for constitutional renewal in the referendum."[32]

Trudeau never faced the voters of Quebec after the patriation of the constitution. But his Liberal successors felt their wrath. In the pre-Charter 1980 election, Trudeau won 68% of the vote in Quebec. In 1984, the Liberal vote fell by nearly half. By 1993, the separatist Bloc Québécois secured 54 of Quebec's 75 seats, and formed Her Majesty's Loyal Opposition.

While Trudeau helped federalist forces to win the 1980 referendum decisively, he did not have to mislead Quebecers about constitutional reforms to achieve this goal. His patriation gamble risked leading to disunion. Trudeau alienated separatists and Quebec federalists alike. A key reason why the 1995 referendum came within a whisker of passing, as opposed to the clear victory for federalism in the 1980 referendum, were Trudeau's actions both during and after his time in office. Many Quebecers felt betrayed by Trudeau and the nine provinces when they abandoned the bargain made at Confederation. They felt betrayed once again when the Meech Lake Accord fell to defeat, largely at the hands of Trudeau.

Trudeau's decision to force patriation on a resistant Quebec was not worth the risk. It remains a lingering wound and a breach of trust in a federal country that depends on trust. Trudeau's obsession with patriation and a charter of rights blinded him to what might yet prove to become the worst prime ministerial gamble in Canadian history.

While Trudeau caused serious and perhaps irreparable damage to national unity from a Quebec perspective, he also had an impact in both the East and the West. In Atlantic Canada, citizens found themselves advantaged by Trudeau's policies of enhanced regional development and easy unemployment benefits, which neatly converted seasonal work into year-'round income. Far from promoting the region's economic prosperity, Trudeau promoted its economic dependence on Ottawa. This did not benefit Atlantic Canadians in the long run, but certainly helped the Liberal Party, Trudeau, and his successors at the ballot box.

The West was an entirely different matter. It favoured Trudeau with just two seats west of the Ontario border in 1980 — and he returned the favour. In response to rising oil prices, Trudeau forced the West to its knees, sacrificing its interests in the name of economic nationalism and political gain elsewhere in the country. Trudeau remained willfully blind to the damage his policies caused the oil patch, savaging home values and bloating unemployment lines. When westerners started displaying the bumper sticker, "Let the Eastern bastards freeze in the dark," they meant the epithet for Trudeau.

Citizens of Atlantic Canada and even Ontario may not have minded Trudeau's vision of a strong central government, but many in

Quebec and the West preferred the agreement struck at Confederation of co-operative federalism. Every prime minister before Trudeau understood and valued this concept. But to get his way, Trudeau saw the provinces as vulnerable to a "putsch" and a "coup de force." That's not the best way to keep a country united.

One the economy and government finance, Trudeau's record is revealed to be something close to disastrous. On national security, he weakened us. And on national unity he helped to solve a crisis in his time, but with an approach that may have won the battle but weakened us in the war.

LEARNED HISTORIANS ARE mixed in their assessments of Trudeau. Desmond Morton, the Hiram Mills chair at McGill University, called Trudeau "the disappointment of the century and a man who left Canada dramatically more divided and drastically poorer than he found it."[33] René Durocher of the University of Montreal wrote that Trudeau was a resounding failure, on the grounds of both public finance and national unity.[34] University of Toronto historian Michael Bliss titled the chapter on Trudeau in his book on Canadian prime ministers, "The Politics of Confrontation." He credits Trudeau's enduring popularity to him having captured the spirit of his age.[35] He also endorses the view that had Trudeau been a separatist, Quebec would no longer be part of Canada.

Trudeau biographer Stephen Clarkson observed that when Jean Chrétien became prime minister, he did not look to his old mentor for guidance and inspiration. "Chretien for me represents a continuation of what Mulroney started, rather than a return to Trudeau-ite thinking."[36] Indeed, as the Liberal Party contemplates its survival in the wake of the 2011 election, some partisans believe that it must repudiate the Trudeau vision and record. Zach Paikin, Liberal Party executive member of Trudeau's home riding of Mount Royal, offered this view: "Pierre Trudeau's vision of federalism — a strong central government with ten subservient provinces and no recognition of the distinctness of any of them — is a thing of the past."[37]

Despite all that went wrong under his watch, Trudeau still has great popular appeal. But it is the man, rather than the record, that holds our attention. Trudeau was the gunslinger who showed no fear in the face of terrorism. He was the maverick who bucked protocol, whether pirouetting behind the Queen's back or sliding down a banister. He was the anti-American and our man of the world. He was our intellectual and philosopher king, the millionaire socialist with glamourous women on his arm. He was our radical prime minister. He was fascinating, eccentric, and entertaining. We admired him for never backing down from a fight, or ducking for cover when under attack.

For a leader whose motto was "reason over passion," it is paradoxical, observed Chris Vivone, a former policy advisor to Liberal Finance minister Ralph Goodale, that Trudeau's enduring popularity is best explained in emotional terms:

> People will not remember what a powerful figure said or did, but they'll always remember how he made them feel. I think those who supported Trudeau and continue to admire him today loved the way he made them feel, regardless of misguided policies or wrongheaded decision-making. He gave Canadians confidence and a sense of independence. You can't measure this like you can GDP, unemployment or foreign aid. But that doesn't mean they're not important.[38]

When Trudeau's reign was over, it took successive leaders many decades to clean up the disorder. Fixing our finances demanded years of budgetary restraint and economic reform. Unifying the nation required continued constitutional negotiation — which Trudeau actively undermined — and a spate of bi-lateral federal-provincial agreements. Restoring our international alliances required quiet personal diplomacy in the backrooms, a renewed investment in our military, and bold public commitment in the arenas of war. In short, Canada had to be remade in many respects, both by its politicians and its people, to survive and prosper in the twenty-first century. It was not all destructive, but much of the Trudeau legacy has been undone by his Liberal and Conservative successors alike. Yet there is an image of Trudeau, nurtured by his friends and supporters, that has endured.

The truth about Trudeau is not what Canadians have been led to believe. Far from being one of our best prime ministers, he was one of the worst. Despite the fact that he boldly confronted Quebec separatists, Trudeau left deep divisions and scars that remain to be healed. Any progress Canada made on bilingualism, the protection of individual rights, and the promotion of a multicultural society was dwarfed by a legacy of economic destruction, regional alienation, military emasculation, and international isolation. Trudeau may have brought Canada moments of glamour, but in the end his pirouettes were not worth the price.

ENDNOTES

CHAPTER ONE: THE TRUDEAU DOCTRINE

1. Ramsay Cook, *The Teeth of Time: Remembering Pierre Elliott Trudeau* (Montreal and Kingston: McGill-Queen's University Press, 2006), 63.
2. Derek Burney, discussion with the author, September 29, 2011. All quotations from Burney in this book are from this interview unless otherwise noted.
3. John English, *Just Watch Me: The Life of Pierre Elliot Trudeau: 1968-2000* (Toronto: Alfred A. Knopf Canada, 2009), 70.
4. David Somerville, *Trudeau Revealed by His Actions and Words* (Richmond Hill, ON: BMG Publishing), 1978, 203.
5. Ibid., 83.
6. Edith Iglauer, "Prime Minister/Premier Ministre," *The New Yorker*, July 5, 1969. 36–60.
7. George Radwanski, *Trudeau* (Scarborough, ON: Macmillan, 1978), 165.
8. English, *Just Watch Me*, 464.

CHAPTER TWO: LOSING AMERICAN FAVOUR

1. Taken from the Foreign Affairs and International Trade website, accessed October 7, 2011, http://www.international.gc.ca/history-histoire/world-monde/1968-1984.aspx?lang=eng&view=d. This page has since been removed from the site.
2. J.L. Granatstein and Robert Bothwell, *Pirouette: Pierre Trudeau and Canadian Foreign Policy* (Toronto: University of Toronto Press. 1990), 50.
3. Pierre Trudeau and Ivan Head, *The Canadian Way: Shaping Canadian Foreign Policy, 1968-1984* (Toronto: McClelland & Stewart, 1995), 41.
4. Ibid., 46.
5. Ibid., 55.
6. Trudeau and Head, *The Canadian Way*, 165.
7. MacGuigan, Mark, *An Inside Look at External Affairs During the Trudeau Years: The Memoirs of Mark MacGuigan*. Edited Whitney Lackenbauer (Calgary: University of Calgary Press, 2001), 10.0.
8. Taken from the Foreign Affairs and International Trade website, accessed November 1, 2011, http://www.international.gc.ca/history-histoire/world-monde/1968-1984.aspx?lang=eng&view=d. This page has since been removed from the site.

9. Taken from the Foreign Affairs and International Trade website, accessed October 7, 2011, http://www.international.gc.ca/history-histoire/world-monde/1968-1984.aspx?lang=eng&view=d. This page has since been removed from the site.
10. Trudeau and Head, *The Canadian Way*, 187.
11. Richard Nixon, "Address to a Joint Meeting of the Canadian Parliament, April 14, 1972," The American Presidency Project, accessed March 24, 2013, http://www.presidency.ucsb.edu/ws/?pid=3377.
12. *CBC News,* "Prime Ministers and Presidents," last modified July 7, 2006, http://www.cbc.ca/news/background/canada_us/pms-presidents.html.
13. Robert Russo, "Nixon Tapes Reveal Loathing for Trudeau," *New Brunswick Telegraph Journal*, March 18, 2002, n.p.
14. English, *Just Watch Me*, 166.
15. Russo, "Nixon Tapes," n.p.
16. English, *Just Watch Me*, 166. 251.
17. Trudeau and Head, *The Canadian Way*, 184.
18. English, *Just Watch Me*, 171.
19. *The Globe and Mail*, "Trudeau, Ford Leave Bodyguards for Ski Lift," December 31, 1977, 14.
20. Geoffrey Stevens, "Trudeau Once on Blacklist," *The Globe and Mail*, February 17, 1968, 10.
21. James Rusk, "Liberal Knew about Hidden Americans: Trudeau's Questions on Iran Surprised Clark," *The Globe and Mail*, January 31, 1980, 9.
22. Trudeau and Head, *The Canadian Way*, 212.
23. Conrad Black, email exchange with author, November 28, 2010.
24. Rick Perlstein, *Nixonland: The Rise of a President and the Fracturing of America* (New York: Simon and Shuster, 2008), 184.
25. Trudeau and Head, *The Canadian Way*, 213.
26. Allan Gotlieb, *Washington Diaries: 1981-89* (Toronto: McClelland & Stewart, 2006), 81.
27. Ibid., 113.
28. Ibid., 66.
29. Ibid., 70.
30. Ibid., 72.
31. Craig Oliver, *Oliver's Twist: The Life and Times of an Unapologetic Newshound* (Toronto: Viking Canada, 2011), 141.
32. *Canada NewsWire,* "Former German Chancellor Helmut Schmidt Praises 'a Beloved Friend' in Unique International Tribute to Pierre Elliott Trudeau in This Week's *TIME Canada*," October 2, 2000, n.p..
33. Gotlieb, *Washington Diaries*, 100.
34. Ibid., 103.
35. Ibid., 179.
36. Brian Mulroney, *Memoirs* (Toronto: McClelland & Stewart, 2007), 498.
37. Rt. Hon. Brian Mulroney, discussion with the author, January 20, 2011.
38. Trudeau and Head, *The Canadian Way*, 267.
39. Ibid., 271.
40. Ibid., 272.
41. Trudeau and Head, *The Canadian Way*, 273.

42. Canada. Statistics Canada, *Canada Year Book*. [Ottawa], *1988*, Table 21.5, section 21, 5.
43. Trudeau and Head, *The Canadian Way*, 275.
44. Ibid., 271.
45. bid., 291.
46. *Canadian Press*, "Former Trudeau Secretary Says French Secret Service Had Agents in Canada," July 28, 2005, n.p.
47. Jim Bronskill, "Old Documents Paint Chaos of FLQ crisis: Trudeau and Cabinet Feared Civil War," *Calgary Herald*, April 24, 2001, A5.
48. *The Globe and Mail*, "CBC Says Trudeau Approved Spying on French Envoys," August 28, 1981, 10.
49. Trudeau and Head, *The Canadian Way*, 291.
50. Gotlieb, *Washington Diaries*, 240.

CHAPTER THREE: A FRIEND TO COMMUNISTS

1. Somerville, *Trudeau Revealed*, 53.
2. Elizabeth Thompson, "Trudeau lacked sense: US told," *Montreal Gazette*, May 21, 2003, A12.
3. Ibid.
4. Max Nemni and Monique Nemni, *Trudeau Transformed: The Shaping of a Statesman, 1944-1965*, trans. George Tombs (Toronto: McClelland & Stewart, 2011), 264, 268.
5. John English, *Citizen of the World: The Life of Pierre Elliot Trudeau: 1919-1968* (Toronto: Alfred A. Knopf Canada, 2007), 267-8.
6. Nemni and Nemni, *Trudeau Transformed*, 270.
7. Somerville, *Trudeau Revealed*, 59.
8. Ibid., 61.
9. Nemni and Nemni, *Trudeau Transformed*, 271.
10. Ibid., 279.
11. Trudeau also visited China in 1949.
12. Pierre Trudeau and Jacques Hébert, *Innocents in Red China*, 1961 (Reprint: Vancouver: Douglas and McIntyre, 2007), 41.
13. Nemni and Nemni, *Trudeau Transformed*, 400; Somerville, *Trudeau Revealed*, 139.
14. Somerville, *Trudeau Revealed*, 169.
15. Granatstein and Bothwell, *Pirouette*, 195.
16. *The Globe and Mail*, "Bukovsky Upset by Trudeau Views," May 7, 1977, 12.
17. Somerville, *Trudeau Revealed*, 208.
18. Granatstein and Bothwell, *Pirouette*, 196.
19. Allan Levine, "The Night Gorbachev Came to Dinner," *National Post*, March 18, 2013, A3.
20. English, *Just Watch Me*, 469.
21. Ibid., 580.
22. David Frum, "History Wars," debate sponsored by the MacDonald Laurier Institute, Ottawa, September 27, 2011.
23. *The Globe and Mail*, "Reagan Issues Warning on TV," February 1, 1982, 1.

24. *Ottawa Citizen*, "Trudeau Ignored our Appeal for Aid — Sakharov's children," December 11, 1984, 12.
25. English, *Just Watch Me*, 581.
26. John Gray, "Shouting at Soviets No Answer to Crisis, PM tells Mulroney," *The Globe and Mail*, October 5, 1983, 1.
27. Pierre Trudeau, *Memoirs* (Toronto: McClelland & Stewart, 1993), 336.
28. *The Windsor Star*, "Trudeau No P.E.T. of Iron Lady," October 19, 1993, A15.
29. George Jonas, "The Evil Men Do Lives after Him," *National Post*, October 16, 2000, 14.
30. Brian Mulroney, discussion with the author, January 20, 2011.
31. Leo Kolber with L. Ian MacDonald, *Leo: A Life* (Montreal and Kingston: McGill-Queen's University Press, 2006), 134.
32. P. Trudeau, *Memoirs*, 351.
33. Nemni and Nemni, *Trudeau Transformed*, 415.
34. English, *Just Watch Me*, 229.
35. *The Globe and Mail*, "Trudeau Expresses Optimism about Acupuncture Techniques," November 3, 1973, 33.
36. Mulroney, discussion with the author, January 20, 2011.
37. English, *Just Watch Me*, 618.
38. John M. Kirk, *Canada-Cuba Relations: The Other Good Neighbor Policy* (Gainsville, FL: University Press of Florida, 1997), 190.
39. Link Byfield, "Why the West Has No Love for Trudeau," *The Globe and Mail*, September 30, 2000, A14.
40. *The Globe and Mail*, "Crumbs from Cuba," June 22, 1981, 6.
41. Robert Stephens, "Cuba Seized Millions: Pays Back $850,000 to Canadian Claimants," *Globe and Mail*, 19 June 1981, 1.
42. Robert Wright, *Three Nights in Havana: Pierre Trudeau, Fidel Castro, and the Cold War World* (Toronto: HarperCollins, 2007), 2.

CHAPTER FOUR: AT WAR WITH THE CANADIAN MILITARY

1. P. Trudeau, *Memoirs*, 7.
2. Ibid., 2.
3. English, *Just Watch Me*, 59.
4. Somerville, *Trudeau Revealed*, 206.
5. *The Globe and Mail*, November 8, 1968, from the Reuters News Agency and the New York Times, 1.
6. Pierre Trudeau and Thomas S. Axworthy, eds., *Towards a Just Society* (Toronto: Penguin Books, 1990), 63.
7. Rt. Hon. John Turner, discussion with the author, March 16, 2013.
8. Sheldon Alberts, "Trudeau Considered Pulling out of NATO," *National Post*, February 10, 2000, A6.
9. John Dafoe, "Canada to Reduce NATO Force," *The Globe and Mail*, April 4, 1969, 1.
10. Cook, *The Teeth of Time*, 62.
11. English, *Just Watch Me*, 63.
12. Trudeau and Head, *The Canadian Way*, 75.

13. English, *Just Watch Me*, 558.
14. Trudeau and Head, *The Canadian Way*, 79.
15. "Yoko Ono and John Lennon Visit Parliament Hill," CBC Digital Archives, accessed November 11, 2011, http://www.cbc.ca/archives/categories/politics/ prime-ministers/trudeaumania-a-swinger-for-prime-minister/peace-on-parliament-hill.html.
16. P. Trudeau, *Memoirs*, 3.
17. Somerville, *Trudeau Revealed*, 206.
18. Peter C. Newman, *True North Not Strong and Free* (Toronto: McClelland & Stewart, 1983), 133.
19. "Inflation Canada 1969," Inflation EU, accessed December 9, 2011, http:// www.inflation.eu/inflation-rates/canada/historic-inflation/cpi-inflation-canada-1969.aspx.
20. Statistics Canada. *The Canada Year Book, 1988*. [Ottawa], Table 21.16, section 21, 16.
21. Newman, *True North Not Strong and Free*, 45.
22. Ibid., 53.
23. Ibid., 49.
24. Ibid., 59.
25. Ibid., 59.
26. Ibid.
27. Ibid., 26.
28. Ibid., 25.
29. Ibid., 21.
30. Ibid., 27.
31. J.L. Granatstein, *Who Killed the Canadian Military?* (Toronto: Harper Collins, 2005), 124.

CHAPTER FIVE: A NEW WORLD ORDER

1. *The Windsor Star*, "Trudeau no P.E.T. of Iron Lady," A15.
2. P. Trudeau, *Memoirs*, 224.
3. English, *Just Watch Me*, 378.
4. Trudeau and Head, *The Canadian Way*, 164.
5. P. Trudeau, *Memoirs*, 329.
6. Ibid., 332.
7. English, *Just Watch Me*, 591.
8. Ibid., 597
9. P. Trudeau, *Memoirs*, 338.
10. Nancy Southam, ed., *Pierre* (Toronto: McClelland & Stewart, 2005), 216.
11. Ronald Reagan, *An American Life* (New York: Simon & Schuster, 1990), 353.
12. Mulroney, discussion with the author, January 20, 2011.
13. Gotlieb, *Washington Diaries*, 160.
14. English, *Just Watch Me*, 592.
15. Margaret Trudeau, *Beyond Reason* (New York: Simon and Schuster, 1979), 129.
16. English, *Just Watch Me*, 587.
17. Ibid., 589.

18. Keith Davey, *The Rainmaker: A Passion for Politics* (Toronto: Stoddart, 1986), 298.
19. P. Trudeau, *Memoirs*, 334.
20. Martin Zeilig, letter to the editor, *The Globe and Mail*, May 18, 1983, 7.
21. *Toronto Star*, "Axworthy Says He Almost Quit Trudeau Cabinet," December 10, 1986, A4.
22. English, *Just Watch Me*, 600.
23. Ibid.
24. "Trudeau's Push for Cold War Peace," CBC Digital Archives, accessed April 20, 2012, http://www.cbc.ca/archives/categories/war-conflict/peacekeeping/peacekeepers-and-peacemakers-canadas-diplomatic-contribution/trudeaus-push-for-cold-war-peace.html.
25. Conrad Black, email exchange with the author, January 8, 2011.
26. Ibid.
27. Paul Litt, *Elusive Destiny: The Political Vocation of John Napier Turner* (Vancouver: UBC Press, 2011), 165.
28. Turner, discussion with the author, March 16, 2013.
29. Andrew Cohen and J.L Granatstein, eds., *Trudeau's Shadow: The Life and Legacy of Pierre Elliot Trudeau* (Toronto: Random House of Canada, 1998), 204.
30. Granatstein and Bothwell, *Pirouette*, 378.
31. Gotlieb, *Washington Diaries*, 208.

CHAPTER SIX: OCTOBER CRISIS

1. P. Trudeau, *Memoirs*, 7.
2. Nemni and Nemni, *Trudeau Transformed*, 31.
3. Ibid., 129.
4. Ibid., 34.
5. Radwanski, *Trudeau*, 66.
6. P. Trudeau, *Memoirs*, 134.
7. Nino Ricci, *Extraordinary Canadians: Pierre Trudeau* (Toronto: Penguin Canada, 2009), 126.
8. P. Trudeau, *Memoirs*, 131.
9. Ibid.
10. For its part, the RCMP Security Service had already recruited a source from within the separatist movement, future PQ cabinet minister Claude Morin. Morin admitted that he worked for the RCMP beginning in the early 1950s to address possible infiltration of the Quebec government by foreign powers, notably France (Radio-Canada website, accessed January 2, 2013, http://archives.radio-canada.ca/guerres_conflits/securite_nationale/clips/10095/). After the Parti Québécois won the 1976 Quebec election, Trudeau continued to press the RCMP and the solicitor general to investigate the separatist political party. In his book *Spying 101: The RCMP's Secret Activities at Canadian Universities, 1917-1997* (Toronto: University of Toronto Press, 2002), Steve Hewitt revealed that Trudeau instructed government agents to spy on the Parti Québécois. It was also revealed that the RCMP anti-separatist squad burned a barn near Montreal. Trudeau responded to reporters by saying

that in some cases police are justified in breaking the law. ("Trudeau's Era Was Full of Surprises," *The Globe and Mail*, March 1, 1984, T5).

11. Max Nemni and Monique Nemni, *Young Trudeau: 1919-1944: Son of Quebec, Father of Canada*, trans. William Johnson (Toronto: McClelland & Stewart, 2006), 58.
12. Nemni and Nemni, *Young Trudeau*, 215..
13. M. Trudeau, *Beyond Reason*, 57.
14. P. Trudeau, *Memoirs*, 135.
15. Ibid., 135
16. Michel Vastel, *The Outsider: The Life of Pierre Elliot Trudeau* (Toronto: Macmillan of Canada, 1990), 135.
17. Tim Ralfe went on to work for CTV News. He was recruited by Senator Lowell Murray to work for the Progressive Conservative Party in 1979.
18. The following section draws all quotations from Trudeau and Ralfe's full exchange, available on the Youtube channel of the CBC TV Archives, uploaded December 3, 2008, http://www.youtube.com/watch?v=XfUq9b1XTa0.
19. Guy Bouthillier and Édouard Cloutier, *Trudeau's Darkest Hour: War Measures in Time of Peace, October 1970* (Montreal: Baraka Books, 2010), 62.
20. Ibid.
21. It is worth noting that when the premier of Newfoundland made a request under the National Defence Act to deploy federal troops in response to a 1959 strike of the International Woodworkers of America in Grand Falls (now Grand Falls-Windsor), Prime Minister John Diefenbaker refused.
22. Radwanski, *Trudeau*, 300.
23. P. Trudeau, *Memoirs*, 141.
24. Bouthillier and Cloutier, *Trudeau's Darkest Hour*, 62.
25. Ibid.
26. Hubert Bauch, "Extraordinary Measures," *Montreal Gazette*, October 2, 2010, B3.
27. Eric Kierans, "Why I Quit the Trudeau Government," *Ottawa Citizen*, March 18, 2001, A12.
28. Litt, *Elusive Destiny*, 131.
29. Turner, discussion with the author, March 15, 2013.
30. English, *Just Watch Me*, 86.
31. Trudeau, *Memoirs*, 143.
32. Mulroney, discussion with the author, January 20, 2011.
33. In a similar refrain, federal Liberal cabinet minister Jean Marchand later said it was "like using a canon to kill a fly." English, *Just Watch Me*, 90.
34. Four members of the NDP voted with the government.
35. P. Trudeau, *Memoirs*, 151.
36. Jeff Sallot, "Ministers Vetted List of October Crisis Detainees, PM Revealed," *The Globe and Mail*, August 27, 1981, P11.
37. William Tetley, *The October Crisis, 1970: An Insider's View* (Montreal and Kingston: McGill-Queen's University Press, 2007), xxxv.
38. Bouthillier and Cloutier, *Trudeau's Darkest Hour*, 113.

39. Guy Bouthillier, "Forty Years After Canada's War Measures Act: Trudeau's Darkest Hour," Counterpunch, accessed January 12, 2013, http://www. counterpunch.org/2010/10/06/trudeau-s-darkest-hour/.

40. Pierre Vallières, *The Assassination of Pierre Laporte,* trans. Ralph Wells (Toronto: Lorimer, 1977), 186.

41. M. Trudeau, *Beyond Reason,* 58.

42. English, *Just Watch Me,* 89.

43. Litt, *Elusive Destiny,* 128.

44. English, *Just Watch Me,* 91.

45. Litt, *Elusive Destiny,* 131.

46. Turner, discussion with the author, March 15, 2013.

47. Gordon Robertson, *Memoirs of a Very Civil Servant: Mackenzie King to Pierre Trudeau* (Toronto: University of Toronto Press, 2000), 264.

48. Reg Whitaker, "Apprehended Insurrection? RCMP Intelligence and the October Crisis," *Queen's Quarterly* 2 (1993): 383-406.

49. Bouthillier, "Forty Years After."

50. Bouthillier and Cloutier, *Trudeau's Darkest Hour,* 64.

51. Robertson, *Memoirs of a Very Civil Servant,* 258.

52. Cook, *Teeth of Time,* 113.

53. Gordon Donaldson, *The Prime Ministers of Canada* (Toronto: Doubleday, 1994), 261.

54. Bauch, "Extraordinary Measures," B3.

55. Bouthillier and Cloutier, *Trudeau's Darkest Hour,* 102.

56. Ibid., 195.

57. "Shock and Awe" is frequently referenced as the code name for the U.S. military invasion of Iraq in 2003. It refers to the use of overwhelming force to destroy an opponent.

58. Dominique Clément, "The October Crisis of 1970: Human Rights Abuses under the War Measures Act," *Journal of Canadian Studies* 42, no. 2 (Spring 2008): 160-186.

59. Tetley, *The October Crisis,* 149.

CHAPTER SEVEN: A CONSTITUTIONAL OBSESSION

1. Nemni and Nemni, *Young Trudeau,* 62-3.

2. Ibid., 215.

3. Ibid., 219.

4. Ibid., 220.

5. Ibid., 222.

6. Ibid., 295.

7. Nemni and Nemni, *Trudeau Transformed,* 203.

8. Nemni and Nemni, *Young Trudeau,* 309.

9. P. Trudeau, *Memoirs,* 25.

10. Nemni and Nemni, *Trudeau Transformed,* 88.

11. Nemni and Nemni, *Young Trudeau,* 187.

12. Ibid., 192.

13. Trudeau and Axworthy, *Towards a Just Society,* 404.

14. Pierre Trudeau, *Federalism and the French Canadians* (Toronto: Macmillan, 1968), 124-151.
15. Nemni and Nemni, *Trudeau Transformed*, 205.
16. Ibid., 426.
17. Trudeau and Axworthy, *Towards a Just Society*, 6.
18. Frank Scott and Michael Oliver, eds., *Quebec States Her Case* (Toronto: Macmillan, 1964), 52.
19. Pierre Trudeau, "Some Obstacles to Democracy in Quebec," *Canadian Journal of Economics and Political Science,* August 1958, reprinted in Pierre Trudeau, *Federalism*, 103-123.
20. P. Trudeau, *Federalism*, 103-123.
21. Vastel, *The Outsider*, 43.
22. Radwanski, *Trudeau*, 117.
23. P. Trudeau, *Memoirs*, 73.
24. Ibid., 74.
25. Nemni and Nemni, *Trudeau Transformed*, 410.
26. Ibid., 412.
27. Radwanski, *Trudeau*, 285.
28. Tom Kent, *A Public Purpose: An Experience of Liberal Opposition and Canadian Government* (Montreal and Kingston: McGill-Queen's University Press, 1988), 269.
29. Vastel, *The Outsider*, 132.
30. P. Trudeau, *Federalism*, xxiv.
31. *London Spectator*, Editorial, June 1968.
32. Litt, *Elusive Destiny*, 91.
33. P. Trudeau, *Memoirs*, 231.
34. Robertson, *Memoirs*, 277.
35. Ibid., 279.
36. Nemni and Nemni, *Trudeau Transformed*, 83.
37. Jonathan Manthorpe, "Trudeau Not Greatly Concerned by Refusal to Endorse Package," *The Globe and Mail*, June 24, 1971, 8.
38. P. Trudeau, *Memoirs*, 234.
39. P. Trudeau, *Memoirs*, 245.
40. *The Globe and Mail*, "Quebec Separatism Dead, Trudeau Says," May 11, 1976, 2.
41. P. Trudeau, *Memoirs*, 240.
42. Ibid.
43. Robertson, *Memoirs*, 291.
44. P. Trudeau, *Memoirs*, 247.
45. Vastel, *The Outsider*, 1.
46. P. Trudeau, *Memoirs*, 50.
47. Nemni and Nemni, *Trudeau Transformed*, 4.
48. P. Trudeau, *Memoirs*, 235.
49. Davey, *The Rainmaker*, 239.
50. English, *Just Watch Me*, 388.
51. Davey, *The Rainmaker*, 258.
52. Stephen Clarkson and Christina McCall, *Trudeau and Our Times, Volume One: The Magnificent Obsession* (Toronto: McClelland & Stewart, 1990), 179.

53. William Johnson, "Leaders Hold Tongues on Constitution Ideas,"
    The Globe and Mail, February 13, 1980, 8.
54. The premier was Ross Thatcher of Saskatchewan; John Gray, "Trudeau:
    Lone Man in a Team Game," *The Globe and Mail*, April 15, 1982, 3.
55. P. Trudeau, *Memoirs*, 270.
56. Ibid., 281.
57. Pierre Trudeau, "Speech at the Paul Sauvé Arena, Montreal, Quebec,
    May 14, 1980," Library and Archives Canada, accessed March 10, 2013,
    http://www.collectionscanada.gc.ca/primeministers/h4-4083-e.html
58. Ibid.
59. Marina Strauss, "Trudeau's Pledge on Constitution 'Strongest Yet',"
    The Globe and Mail, 16 May 1980, 10.
60. *The Globe and Mail*, "Trudeau tries to heal wounds of division,"
    21 May 1980, P11.
61. Ibid.
62. P. Trudeau, *Memoirs*, 272.
63. Clarkson and McCall, *Trudeau and Our Times*, 278.
64. P. Trudeau, *Memoirs*, 300.
65. Ibid., 302.
66. Clarkson and McCall, *Trudeau and Our Times*, 281.
67. Ibid., 283.
68. Clarkson and McCall, *Trudeau and Our Times*, 290.
69. P. Trudeau, *Memoirs*, 105.
70. Southam, *Pierre*, 111.
71. P. Trudeau, *Memoirs*, 19.
72. Clarkson and McCall, *Trudeau and Our Times*, 322.
73. Ibid., 291.
74. Ibid., 336.
75. P. Trudeau, *Memoirs*, 303.
76. Ibid., 306.
77. Trudeau and Axworthy, *Towards a Just Society*, 421.
78. P. Trudeau, *Memoirs*, 308.
79. Ibid., 309.
80. P. Trudeau, *Memoirs*, 310.
81. Clarkson and McCall, *Trudeau and Our Times*, 340.
82. The justices appointed by Trudeau at the time the reference was made
    were: Bora Laskin, March 19, 1970 – March 17, 1984; Brian Dickson,
    March 26, 1973 – June 30, 1990; as Chief Justice, April 18, 1984; Jean Betz,
    January 1, 1974 – November 10, 1988; William Estey, September 29,
    1977 – April 22, 1988; William McIntyre, January 1, 1979 – February 15,
    1989; Antonio Lamer, March 28, 1980 – January 6, 2000.
83. *The Globe and Mail*, "Trudeau's Era Was Full of Surprises," T5.
84. Philip Slayton, *Mighty Judgment: How the Supreme Court Runs Your Life*
    (Toronto: Penguin Group, 2011), 21.
85. P. Trudeau, *Memoirs*, 316.
86. Clarkson and McCall, *Trudeau and our Times*, 376.
87. Ibid.
88. Jean Chrétien, *Straight from the Heart* (Toronto: Key Porter Books,
    1985), 188.

89. Ibid.
90. Section 59 of the Constitution Act (1982).
91. P. Trudeau, *Memoirs*, 327.
92. B. Mulroney, *Memoirs*, 511.
93. P. Trudeau, *Memoirs*, 328.
94. Senator W. David Angus, discussion with the author, March 11, 2013.

CHAPTER EIGHT: MEECH, CHARLOTTETOWN AND
THE 1995 QUEBEC REFERENDUM

1. Mulroney, *Memoirs*, 515.
2. P. Trudeau, *Memoirs*, 329.
3. Robertson, *Memoirs*, 337.
4. Derek Burney, *Getting It Done: A Memoir* (Montreal: McGill-Queens University Press, 2005), 93.
5. Radwanski, *Trudeau*, 25.
6. Southam, *Pierre*, 17.
7. Ibid., 286.
8. MacGuigan, *An Inside Look,* 19.
9. Mulroney, *Memoirs*, 526.
10. Cook, *The Teeth of Time*, 160.
11. Litt, *Elusive Destiny*, 329.
12. Ibid., 337.
13. Turner, discussion with the author, March 15, 2013.
14. Mulroney, discussion with the author, January 20, 2011.
15. Paul Martin, *Hell or High Water: My Life in and out of Politics* (Toronto: McClelland & Stewart Limited, 2008), 88.
16. Robertson, *Memoirs*, 357.
17. Mulroney, *Memoirs*, 537.
18. Cited in Mulroney, *Memoirs*, 543.
19. Peter Russell, discussion with the author, April 14, 2011.
20. *Montreal Gazette*, "Newfoundland Votes to Ratify Meech Accord," July 8, 1988, B1.
21. Deborah Coyne, *Unscripted: A Life Devoted to Building a Better Canada*, ebook, 2013, www.deborahcoyne.ca, 14.
22. When Sarah was born, Deborah Coyne was 36 and Trudeau was 71.
23. *The Windsor Star*, "Liberal Convention 1990: Despite Criticism, Wells Surprised by Warm Reception," June 25, 1990, 9.
24. John Yorston, "Editors Hand Out Blame for Meech Failure," *Montreal Gazette*, June 27, 1990, B3.
25. Desmond Morton, "In the Wake of Meech Lake We're All to Blame for a Nasty Mess," *Toronto Star*, June 26, 1990, A17.
26. Mulroney, discussion with the author, Jan. 20, 2011.
27. Lawrence Martin, "Trudeau Had the Last Laugh," *Victoria Times Colonist*, Oct. 3, 2000, A12.
28. Bernard St-Laurent, "Drive for Quebec Sovereignty Can't Be Fuelled by Anger Alone," *Montreal Gazette*, July 16, 1990, A2.
29. Turner, discussion with the author, March 15, 2013.

30. The speech is often referred to as the "eggroll speech," since it was delivered at the restaurant La Maison du Egg Roll.
31. Robertson, *Memoirs*, 358.
32. Stephen Clarkson, "Charisma and Contradiction: The Legacy of Pierre Elliott Trudeau," *Queen's Quarterly*, 107, no. 4 (Winter 2000): 590-607.
33. Jean Chrétien, *My Years as Prime Minister* (Toronto: Random House Canada, 2007), 122.
34. Mulroney, *Memoirs*, 537.
35. George Oake, "Pied Piper Manning Lures the Voters Away from Getty," *Toronto Star*, Oct. 5, 1992, A10.
36. The referendum question was: "Do you agree that Québec should become sovereign after having made a formal offer to Canada for a new economic and political partnership within the scope of the bill respecting the future of Québec and of the agreement signed on June 12, 1995?"
37. Mulroney, discussion with the author, Jan. 20, 2011.
38. Southam, *Pierre*, 344.
39. Robertson, *Memoirs*, 339.
40. Angus, discussion with the author, March 11, 2013.
41. L. Ian MacDonald, "The tragedy of Meech Lake's death," *National Post*, April 11, 2008, A16.

CHAPTER NINE: THE TRUDEAU SOCIAL DOCTRINE

1. English, *Just Watch Me*, 20.
2. Peter C. Newman, *Ottawa Journal*, April 26, 1967, n.p., as noted in Radwanski, *Trudeau*, 83.
3. *Speeches That Changed The World* (London: Bounty Books, 2005), 38.
4. *The Globe and Mail*, "Unlocking the Locked Step of Law and Morality," December 12, 1967, 6.
5. Quotation from Trudeau taken from the CBC show *The Greatest Canadian*. The final episode of the show was broadcast on CBC on November 29, 2004.
6. Trudeau and Axworthy, *Towards a Just Society*, 402.
7. Southam, *Pierre*, 347.
8. English, *Just Watch Me*, 20.

CHAPTER TEN: THE RICH AND THE POOR

1. P. Trudeau, *Memoirs*, 191; also, Vastel, *The Outsider*, 101. It should be noted that Trudeau was not entirely pleased with Pearson's management of social spending. His decision to allow Quebec to implement its own pension plan, in place of the Canada Pension Plan, with a tax-point transfer in compensation, was criticized by Trudeau, who called it "a bonus for separation."
2. John Bulloch, "Hail and Farewell: Old Sparring Partner John Bulloch Remembers Pierre Elliott Trudeau," *Profit Magazine* 19.7 (November 1, 2000), 11.
3. Brian Crowley, *Fearful Symmetry: The Rise and Fall of Canada's Founding Values* (Toronto: Key Porter, 2009), 26.

4. G.C. Ruggeri, *The Canadian Economy: Problems and Policies* (Toronto: Gage Publishing, 1981).

5. P. Trudeau, *Memoirs*, 357.

6. Trudeau and Axworthy, *Towards a Just Society*, 174.

7. Cathy Oikiwa, senior researcher, National Council on Welfare Secretariat, Human Resources and Skills Development Canada, discussion with the author, June 22, 2012.

8. Canada. Statistics Canada. *Income Distribution by Size in Canada, 1986.* [Ottawa], November 1988. Table 72, 110.

9. National Council of Welfare. *Poverty Profile, 1988.* [Ottawa], April 1988, 1.

10. Lars Osberg, "A Quarter Century of Economic Inequality in Canada: 1981-2006" (working paper 2007-09, Department of Economics, Dalhousie University, October 2007).

11. Canada. Statistics Canada. *Income Distributions by Size.* [Ottawa], cat. 13-207.

12. Michael Förster and Marco Mira d'Ercole, "Income Distribution And Poverty In OECD Countries In The Second Half Of The 1990s" (OECD Social, Employment And Migration Working Papers No. 22, Feb. 18, 2005).

13. Trudeau and Axworthy, *Towards a Just Society*, 174.

14. National Council of Welfare, 1, 34.

15. Ibid., 19.

16. Ibid., 114.

17. Ibid., 116.

18. Ibid., 116.

19. Canada. Finance Canada. *Economic Reference Tables.* [Ottawa], August 1992, 31.

20. National Council of Welfare, 12.

21. Brian Lee Crowley, discussion with the author, May 19, 2012.

22. Ibid.

23. Trudeau and Axworthy, *Towards a Just Society*, 287.

24. Ibid., 334.

25. Ibid., 404.

26. Trudeau and Axworthy, *Towards a Just Society*, 31.

27. Clarkson, "Charisma and Contradiction," 590-607.

CHAPTER ELEVEN: NATIVE LAND

1. Trudeau and Axworthy, *Towards a Just Society*, 27.

2. Robert Head, "Trudeau's Words about Aboriginals Resonate," *Calgary Herald*, January 3, 2012, 9. Article based on an address of August 8, 1969, given by Prime Minister Pierre Trudeau at the Aboriginal and Treaty Rights meeting in Vancouver.

3. For the sake of clarity and convenience, the terms "Native" and "Aboriginal" are taken throughout this work to mean, equally, First Nations, Inuit, and Métis people.

4. "1951-1981: Aboriginal Rights Movement," Canadiana, accessed January 7, 2013, http://www.canadiana.ca/citm/themes/aboriginals/aboriginals12_e.html#whiteandred.

5. Robert Head, "Trudeau's Words about Aboriginals Resonate," *Calgary Herald*, January 3, 2012, 9.
6. Canada. Aboriginal Affairs and Northern Development Canada. *Statement of the Government of Canada on Indian policy (The White Paper, 1969)*. [Ottawa], accessed January 11, 2013, http://www.aadnc-aandc.gc.ca/eng/1100100010189/1100100010191.
7. Pauline Cameau and Aldo Santin, *The First Canadians: A Profile of Canada's Native People Today* (Toronto: James Lorimer & Company, 1995), 15.
8. Ibid., 10
9. Trudeau and Axworthy, *Towards a Just Society*, 180.
10. Jim Bronskill, "Thatcher was keen to avoid interference," *Calgary Herald*, August 3, 2012, A6.
11. Doug Cuthand, "Trudeau Helped Natives – Unintentionally," *Saskatoon Star-Phoenix*, October 22, 1999, A15.
12. Benoit Aubin, "A Rights Discussion; Mercredi and Trudeau Cross Swords over Constitutional Guarantees for Minorities," *Montreal Gazette*, December 14, 1991, B3.

CHAPTER TWELVE: A LIBERAL SOCIETY

1. Trudeau and Axworthy, *Towards a Just Society*, 176.
2. Canada. Finance Canada. *Economic Reference Tables, August 1992*. [Ottawa], Table 27, p. 51.
3. Geoffrey Stevens, "Not Even Embarrassed," *The Globe and Mail*, July 3, 1980, 6.
4. CBC News, "Katimavik Killed for 'Ideological' Reasons, Trudeau Says," accessed April 10, 2012, http://www.cbc.ca/news/canada/nova-scotia/story/2012/04/05/pol-trudeau-katimavik-budget-cuts.html.
5. Nemni and Nemni, *Trudeau Transformed*, 172.
6. Canada. Statistics Canada. *Canada Year Book, 1988*. [Ottawa], Table 5.9, pp. 5-24.
7. Crowley, *Fearful Symmetry*, 125.
8. Brauch, letter to the editor, 6.
9. Joseph Brean, "Rights Group Defends Itself," *National Post*, April 5, 2008, 10.
10. Jake Edmiston, "Gym Violated Man's 'Dignity' with Boot Ban, Tribunal Says," *National Post*, May 24, 2012, 1.
11. Andrew Coyne, "Human Rights Racket — Ezra Levant's Case Against a Tribunal System that Flattens Civil Liberties in Canada," *Maclean's*, April 2, 2009, accessed March 16, 2013, http://www2.macleans.ca/2009/04/02/human-rights-racket/.
12. Litt, *Elusive Destiny*, 103.
13. John Fraser, "For the Benefit of Dr. Foth: Personal Invective is the Price of Friendship I Still Gladly Pay," *National Post*, October 25, 2000, B5.
14. Robert Sheppard, "Analysis: PM's Proposed Charter of Rights Could Have Far-Reaching Effects," *The Globe and Mail*, February 14, 1981, 13.
15. *The Globe and Mail*, "Human Rights Chairman Finds Holes in Ottawa's Proposals on Freedoms," September 8, 1978, 9.

16. *The Globe and Mail*, "McDonald Highlights," August 26, 1981, 1.
17. Canada. Statistics Canada. Vital Statistics, accessed April 1, 2013, http://www23.statcan.gc.ca/imdb/p2SV.pl?Function=getSurvey&SDDS=3235 &lang=en&db=imdb&adm=8&dis=2.
18. English, *Just Watch Me*, 249.
19. *The Globe and Mail*, "Minister Jean Chretien Told the Commons Yesterday the Government Has No Intention of Changing Its Proposed Charter of Rights Because of a Controversy Over Abortion," June 6, 1981, 20.
20. *The Globe and Mail*, "Would Reconsider Stand Against Hanging if Deterrence Were Proved, Trudeau says," September 15, 1978, 1.
21. English, *Just Watch Me*, 578.
22. Southam, *Pierre*, 54.
23. For example, In 2010, Newfoundland Premier Danny Williams made headlines when it became public news that he went south of the border for heart surgery. See http://www.theglobeandmail.com/news/politics/danny-williams-travels-to-us-for-heart-surgery/article1452524. Accessed April 10, 2012.

CHAPTER THIRTEEN: MULTICULTURALISM AND IMMIGRATION

1. Hugh Maclennan's 1945 novel *Two Solitudes* (the title of which was taken from a letter of German poet Rainer Maria Rilke's) has led Canada to be known as a nation of "two solitudes," or sometimes "three solitudes," including the English, French, and Aboriginal cultures. Interestingly, Aboriginal peoples are grouped as one "solitude" even though they are themselves a collective of many cultures.
2. Nemni and Nemni, *Trudeau Transformed*, 73.
3. English, *Just Watch Me*, 146.
4. Trudeau and Axworthy, *Towards a Just Society*, 183.
5. Ibid.
6. English, *Just Watch Me*, 146.
7. Trudeau and Axworthy, *Towards a Just Society*, 182.
8. *Ottawa Sun*, Multiculturalism fails Canada, May 1, 2010, accessed March 16, 2013, http://www.torontosun.com/comment/columnists/salim_mansur/2010/04/30/13777901.html.
9. Robert Sibley, "9/11 Series: The Failure of Multiculturalism," *Ottawa Citizen*, September 5, 2011, 6.
10. Caitlin Kelly, "Multicultural Policy: Patronage or Paragon?" *The Globe and Mail*, June 30, 1984, 20.
11. David Cameron, "Radicalisation and Islamic Extremism," speech delivered in Munich, February 5, 2011, accessed December 8, 2012, www.newstatesman.com/blogs/the-staggers/2011/02/terrorism-islam-ideology.
12. Daniel Stoffman, *Who Gets In: What's Wrong with Canada's Immigration Program – and How to Fix It* (Toronto: Macfarlane, Walter & Ross, 2002), 128.
13. Canada. Statistics Canada. *Canada Year Book, 1988*. [Ottawa], Table 2.34.
14. *The Globe and Mail*, "Ottawa Sets Immigration Target of 100,000," October 25, 1978,10.

15. Kenneth McDonald, *His Pride, Our Fall: Recovering from the Trudeau Revolution* (Toronto: Key Porter Books, 1995), 80. (From House of Commons debates, May 24, 1980).
16. Stoffman, *Who Gets In*, 82.
17. Gotlieb, *Washington Diaries, 173.*
18. Stoffman, *Who Gets In*, 78.
19. *The Globe and Mail*, "PCs the Enemy, Trudeau Tells Ethnic Press," January 12, 1980, 13.
20. Christ Kostov, "Canada-Québec Immigration Agreements (1971-1991) and Their Impact on Federalism," *The American Review of Canadian Studies* (Spring 2008): 91-103.
21. Thomas Walkom, "Rules to Ease Jobless Rate Will Curb Immigration: Axworthy," *The Globe and Mail*, November 2, 1982, 8.
22. *The Globe and Mail*, "PM Matches Wits with Thailand's Best Minds," January 6, 1983, 16.

CHAPTER FOURTEEN: ENVIRONMENTAL TALK

1. Elizabeth May, M.P., discussion with the author, March 22, 2011. All May quotations in this chapter are from this discussion.
2. Jim MacNeill, discussion with the author, May 24, 2012.
3. Ibid.
4. Agent Orange Association of Canada, accessed December 8, 2012, www.agentorangecanada.com.
5. Yves Lavigne, "Knew Last September Agent Orange Tested in N.B," *The Globe and Mail*, January 27, 1981, 8.
6. Jeff Carruthers, "Canada to Push Hard for Alaska Line Project," *The Globe and Mail*, August 9, 1977, B1.
7. John King, "Street Rally in Vancouver's Chinatown: Get Out and Work, Trudeau Answers Hecklers," *The Globe and Mail*, April 9, 1979, 9.
8. Pierre Trudeau, speech to graduates, Duke University, Durham, North Carolina, May 12, 1974.
9. "Trudeau Meets Pollution Probe," The Great Green North, accessed March 20, 2013, http://www.thegreatgreennorth.com/2011/07/pierre-trudeau-meets-pollution-probe.html.
10. François Bregha, discussion with the author, January 16, 2013
11. *The Globe and Mail*, "Trudeau Meets 3,500 Liberals at Picnic after Defending His Political Use of Helicopters," June 9, 1975, 1.
12. Trudeau and Axworthy, *Towards a Just Society*, 219.

CHAPTER FIFTEEN: A BILINGUAL NATION

1. William Henry Moore, *The Clash: A Study in Nationalities* (London-Toronto: J. M. Dent and Sons, 1918), 16-17.
2. Graham Fraser, discussion with the author, March 21, 2011.
3. Graham Fraser was appointed Official Languages Commissioner by Prime Minister Stephen Harper in September 2006.

4. Walter Gordon, *Walter Gordon: A Political Memoir* (Halifax: Formac Publishing Company Limited, 1983), 111.

5. Davey, *The Rainmaker*, 64.

6. Lester Pearson, speech to the Congress of the Association des hebdomadaires de langue française du Canada, Ottawa, August 17, 1963. Accessed April 1, 2013, http://www.collectionscanada.gc.ca/primeministers/h4-4030-e.html.

7. M. Trudeau, *Beyond Reason*, 52.

8. P. Trudeau, *Memoirs*, 117.

9. Clarkson and McCall, *Trudeau and Our Times*, 41.

10. Somerville, *Trudeau Revealed*, 87.

11. Radwanski, *Trudeau*, 73.

12. P. Trudeau, *Federalism*, 5.

13. Canada. Office of the Commissioner of Official Languages. *Report of the Official Languages Commissioner, 1969*.

14. P. Trudeau, *Memoirs*, 104, 120.

15. Richard Gwyn, *The Northern Magus: Pierre Trudeau and Canadians* (Toronto: McClelland & Stewart, 1980), 135.

16. P. Trudeau, *Memoirs*, 128.

17. Ibid., 125.

18. Radwanski, *Trudeau*, 287.

19. Litt, *Elusive Destiny*, 138.

20. Russell Doern, *The Battle over Bilingualism* (Winnipeg: Cambridge publishers, 1985), 187.

21. Fraser, discussion with the author, March 21, 2011.

22. P. Trudeau, *Memoirs*, 125.

23. Canada. Office of the Commissioner of Official Languages. *Annual Report of the Official Languages Commissioner, 1977*, 16-17.

24. Canada. Office of the Commissioner of Official Languages. *Annual Report of the Official Languages Commissioner, 1979*, 17.

25. Canada. Office of the Commissioner of Official Languages. *Annual Report of the Official Languages Commissioner, 1983*, 15.

26. *The Globe and Mail*, "Bilingual Air Control Presents No Danger, Federal Tests Show," January 5, 1979, 1.

27. For a review of the Gens de l'Air controversy, see Sandford F. Borins, *The Language of the Skies: The Bilingual Air Traffic Control Conflict in Canada* (Montreal and Kingston: McGill-Queen's University Press, 1983).

28. P. Trudeau *Memoirs*, 237.

29. Fraser, discussion with the author, March 21, 2011.

30. P. Trudeau, *Memoirs*, 235.

31. In Quebec (and Canada in general), an allophone is someone whose primary language at home is neither French or English.

32. P. Trudeau, *Memoirs*, 235.

33. Stephen Harper, "Looking Back at Trudeau," *National Post*, October 5, 2000, 18.

34. Fraser, discussion with the author, March 21, 2011.

35. Fraser Institute. *Official Language Policies at the Federal Level in Canada: Costs and Benefits in 2006*.

36. Some English-rights advocates have used figures as high as a trillion dollars as the cost to Canada for bilingualism. This includes not only the cost to governments, but costs throughout Canadian society. See http:// officialbilingualism.blogspot.com/2010/04/official-languages-act-40-years-later.html

37. Scott Reid, *Lament for a Notion* (Vancouver: Arsenal Pulp Press, 1993), 27, 33-35.

38. Kenneth McDonald, *His Pride, Our Fall: Recovering from the Trudeau Revolution* (Toronto: Key Porter Books, 1995), 56.

39. Fraser, discussion with the author, March 21, 2011.

40. The poll was conducted by Leger Marketing for the Association for Canadian Studies. The poll was based on a web-based survey of 1,366 respondents, and considered accurate to within 3.1 percentage points, 19 times out of 20.

41. CROP questioned 2,000 Canadians between Oct. 23 and Nov. 19, 2007. The poll has a margin of error of three per cent, 19 times out of 20.

42. Fraser, discussion with the author, March 21, 2011.

43. The survey included a panel of surveys of 133 respondents, deemed accurate to within approximately 8.5 percentage points, 19 times out of 20.

44. CTV News, "Poll Reveals Canadians Favour Bilingualism," April 6, 2003.

45. Data in this paragraph is drawn from *Treasury Board's 2008-2009 Annual Report on Official Languages* (Table 2, statistical appendix).

46. Trudeau and Axworthy, *Towards a Just Society*, 262.

47. Fraser, discussion with the author, March 21, 2011.

48. Canada. Heritage Canada website, accessed May 11, 2011, http://www.pch. gc.ca/pc-ch/conslttn/lo-ol_2007/101-eng.cfm.

49. Canada. Statistics Canada. *Languages in Canada — Census Year 2001*, catalogue no. 96-326-XIE.

50. In 1977, 237 schools had 37,835 students enrolled in French-language immersion programmes; by 1988, this figure had increased sevenfold, to 1512 schools and 241,140 students (Trudeau and Axworthy, *Towards a Just Society*, 248).

51. Canada. Statistics Canada. *Portrait of Official-Language Minorities*, catalogue no. 89-642x, 2010.

52. Canada. Statistics Canada. *Languages in Canada*, 1994, 150.

53. Gwyn, *The Northern Magus*, 220.

54. Stephen Harper, "Canada's not a bilingual country," *Calgary Sun*, April 6, 2001, accessed April 1, 2013, http://www.torontosun. com/2011/07/15/canadas-not-a-bilingual-country.

55. Scott Reid, M.P., discussion with the author, January 21, 2013.

CHAPTER SIXTEEN: CHARTER OF RIGHT AND FREEDOMS

1. R. v. Big M. Drug Mart Ltd., [1985] 1 S.C.R. 295 (Can.).

2. Slayton, *Mighty Judgment*, 72.

3. Health Services and Support – Facilities Subsector Bargaining Assn. v. British Columbia, [2007] 2 S.C.R. 391 (Can.).

4. Figueroa v. Canada (Attorney General), [2003] 1 S.C.R. 912 (Can.).

5. Sauvé v. Canada (Attorney General), [2002] 3 S.C.R. 519 (Can.).

6. Chaoulli v. Québec (Attorney General), [2005] 1 S.C.R. 791 (Can.).

7. R. Morgentaler, [1988] 1 S.C.R. 30 (Can.).

8. William Johnson, "PM calls Morgentaler a fine humanitarian, but says he must pay for breaking the law," *The Globe and Mail*, May 23, 1975, 8.

9. *The Globe and Mail*, "Just what was said 'When people hit out at me, I just hit back' Feb. 24, 1982, 7.

10. *The Globe and Mail*, "Minister Jean Chretien Told the Commons Yesterday the Government Has No Intention of Changing Its Proposed Charter of Rights Because of a Controversy over Abortion," June 6, 1981, 20.

11. Singh v. Minister of Employment and Immigration, [1985] 1 S.C.R. 177 (Can.).

12. Rodriguez v. British Columbia (Attorney General), [1993] 3 S.C.R. 519 (Can.).

13. Egan v. Canada, [1995] 2 S.C.R. 513 (Can.).

14. Vriend v. Alberta, [1998] 1 S.C.R. 493 (Can.), at paragraphs 101 and 104.

15. Jeff Sallott, "Public Against Judges Making Laws: Poll," *The Globe and Mail*, August 11, 2003. The poll was based on a random sample of 1,060 Canadian adults. The results are considered accurate to within 3.1 percentage points 19 times out of 20.

16. R. v. Oakes, [1986] 1 S.C.R. 103 (Can.).

17. Reference re Section 94(2) of the Motor Vehicle Act (1985), 2 S.C.R. 486.

18. R. v. Kang Brown, [2008] 1 S.C.R. 456 (Can.); R. v. A.M., [2008] 1 S.C.R. 569 (Can.).

19. R. v. Patrick, [2009] 1 S.C.R. 579 (Can.).

20. Julian Fantino, *Duty: The Life of a Cop* (Toronto: Key Porter, 2007), 181.

21. Vernon White, discussion with the author, April 3, 2013.

22. Jake Rupert, "Trudeau's Charter Rescues Ex-Wife," *Ottawa Citizen*, November 23, 2005, C1.

23. *Toronto Star*, "Maggie's Pot Charge Stayed as Legal Flaw Found with Warrant," April 20, 1988, A3.

24. Right Honourable Beverley McLachlin, "The Charter 25 Years Later: The Good, the Bad and the Beverley Challenges," *Osgoode Hall Law Journal*, 45, no. 2 (2007): 365.

25. Reference re Same-Sex Marriage, [2004] 3 S.C.R. 698 (Can.), [2004] S.C.C. 79.

26. *Canadian Press*, "Chrétien: Patriation, Charter Benefited Québec," April 17, 2012.

27. Lalonde v. Ontario (Commission de restructuration des services de santé), [2001] 56 O.R. (3d) 577 (C.A.).

28. Provincial Judges' Reference, [1997] 3 S.C.R. 3 (Can.).

29. Russell, discussion with the author, April 14, 2011.

30. Tasha Kheiriddin and Adam Daifallah, *Rescuing Canada's Right: Blueprint for a Conservative Revolution* (Mississauga, ON: John Wiley and Sons, 2005), 99-100.

31. Lorne Gunter, "Trudeau's Weapon Against Personal Responsibility Was the Charter," *National Post*, January 28, 2011, 15.

32. Ian Brodie, "Interest Group Litigation and the Embedded State," *Canadian Journal of Political Science*, 34, no.2 (June 2001): 375.

33. Mossop v. Canada (Attorney General), [1993] 1 S.C.R. 554 (Can.).

34. M. v. H., [1999] 2 S.C.R. 3 (Can.).

35. *Canadian Press,* "Cocaine Dealer Freed Due to Trial Delay: Judge Blasts Government after Prince George Case Dismissed Due to 3.5-Year Delay," September 15, 2001, n.p.
36. Chris Froggatt, "Charter Must Be Periodically Debated And, If Necessary, Updated," iPolitics, November 29, 2010, accessed April 1, 2013, http://www.ipolitics.ca/2010/11/29/charter-needs-to-be-debated-and-updated/.
37. Philip Slayton, "Expect a Strong and Growing Law and Order Bias," *Canadian Lawyer,* November 2011, accessed March 18, 2013, http://www.canadianlawyermag.com/3934/expect-a-strong-and-growing-law-and-order-bias.html.
38. Slayton, *Mighty Judgment,* 61.

CHAPTER SEVENTEEN: NO APOLOGIES

1. P. Trudeau, *Memoirs,* 37.
2. Nemni and Nemni, *Young Trudeau,* 123.
3. Ibid., 122.
4. English, *Citizen,* 97.
5. Nemni and Nemni, *Young Trudeau,* 171.
6. David Vienneau, "Cabinet Ruled Out Action on Nazi Suspects; Liberals under Trudeau Decided in '81 Nothing Could Be Done," *Toronto Star,* July 10, 1985, A02.
7. "Nuremberg 40 Years Later: The Struggle Against Injustice in Our Time," conference held at McGill University, November, 1987.
8. David Vienneau, "Trudeau Tells Why He Ignored Nazi Issue," *Toronto Star,* November 5, 1987, A1.
9. Peggy Curran, "Ask Kaplan, Replies Trudeau to Charges He Vetoed Nazi Trials," *Montreal Gazette,* August 13, 1987, B7.
10. Bouthillier and Cloutier, *Trudeau's Darkest Hour,* 45.
11. *The Globe and Mail,* "Making Amends," August 23, 1982, 6.
12. Ken Adachi, "Internment scars run deep," *Toronto Star,* September 24, 1988, 2.
13. Ibid.
14. *The Globe and Mail,* "This Side of History," April 4, 1984, 6.
15. Ann Silversides, "Japanese Canadians Disturbed Over Refusal to Apologize," *The Globe and Mail,* June 29, 1984, M4.
16. Mulroney, *Memoirs,* 134.
17. Mary Trueman, "RCMP Broke into PQ Office Without Warrant, Fox Says," *The Globe and Mail,* October 29, 1977, 1.
18. Dean Beeby, " Trudeau Pressed Mounties to Spy on Newly Elected Parti Québécois: Book," *Canadian Press,* October 20, 2002.
19. *The Globe and Mail,* "Trudeau's Era Was Full of Surprises.
20. Robert Sheppard and Jeff Sallott, "Trudeau Ignored Illegal Acts by RCMP, Inquiry Concludes," *The Globe and Mail,* August 26, 1981, 1.
21. Jeff Sallot, "Ministers Vetted List of October Crisis Detainees," *The Globe and Mail,* August 27, 1981, 11.
22. David Johnston, "Distinct-Society Clause: PQ Chief Blasts Trudeau over 'Deportation' Remark," *Ottawa Citizen,* October 7, 1991, 3.
23. Ibid.

24. Edison Stewart and William Walker, "PM's lieutenant slams Trudeau," *Toronto Star*, Oct. 8, 1991, A9.
25. Ibid.
26. Peggy Curran, "Trudeau is Dead Wrong, Clark Insists," *Montreal Gazette*, October 8, 1991, B1.
27. John Gray, "Past Persecution Cited as Showing Need for Charter," *The Globe and Mail*, October 9, 1980,1.

CHAPTER EIGHTEEN: THE SOCIALIST EXPERIMENT

1. P.Trudeau, *Memoirs*, 44.
2. Somerville, *Trudeau Revealed*, 28.
3. P. Trudeau, *Memoirs*, 47.
4. Ibid., 46.
5. Ricci, *Pierre Trudeau*, 2009, 84.
6. Nemni and Nemni, *Trudeau Transformed*, 128.
7. Ibid., 158.
8. Ibid., 154.
9. P. Trudeau, *Memoirs*, 47.
10. Nemni and Nemni, *Trudeau Transformed*, 20.
11. Southam, *Pierre*, 209.
12. Turner, discussion with the author, March 16, 2013.
13. Nemni and Nemni, *Trudeau Transformed*, 288.
14. Somerville, *Trudeau Revealed*, 80.
15. Ibid., 81.
16. Nemni and Nemni, *Trudeau Transformed*, 150.
17. Somerville, *Trudeau Revealed*, 170.
18. Nemni and Nemni, *Trudeau Transformed*, 292.
19. "Economies in Transformation: Limitations and Potential of Transition Process," conference held in London, UK, chaired by Pierre Elliott Trudeau, April 6-7, 1991.
20. Southam, *Pierre*, 340.

CHAPTER NINETEEN: SPEND LIKE THERE IS NO TOMORROW

1. Budget speech, October 22, 1968 (net of transfers to provinces), delivered by Edgar Benson, accessed April 1, 2013, http://www.parl.gc.ca/parlinfo/Documents/Budgets/English/1968-10-22.pdf.
2. English, *Just Watch Me*, 4.
3. Anthony Westell, "Trudeau Blueprints a Three Point Thrust against Regional Poverty," *The Globe and Mail*, June 1, 1968, 10.
4. Budget speech, October 22, 1968 delivered by Edgar Benson, accessed April 1, 2013, http://www.parl.gc.ca/parlinfo/Documents/Budgets/English/1968-10-22.pdf.
5. Budget speech, June 3, 1969, delivered by Edgar Benson, accessed April 1, 2013, http://www.parl.gc.ca/parlinfo/Documents/Budgets/English/1969-06-03.pdf.

6. P. Trudeau, *Memoirs*, 165.
7. Radwanski, *Trudeau*, 215.
8. Budget speech, October 22, 1968, delivered by Edgar Benson, accessed April 1, 2013, http://www.parl.gc.ca/parlinfo/Documents/Budgets/English/1968-10-22.pdf.
9. Budget speech, June 23, 1975, delivered by John Turner, accessed April 1, 2013, http://www.parl.gc.ca/parlinfo/Documents/Budgets/English/1975-06-23.pdf.
10. Brian McKenna, dir., *Pierre Elliot Trudeau: Memoirs* (Richmond Hill, ON: BFS Video, 2009), DVD.
11. Southam, *Pierre*, 237.
12. Budget speech, Feb. 19, 1973, by John Turner, accessed April 1, 2013, http://www.parl.gc.ca/parlinfo/Documents/Budgets/English/1973-02-19.pdf.
13. P. Trudeau, *Memoirs*, 199.
14. Chrétien, *Straight from the Heart*, 177.
15. Litt, *Elusive Destiny*, 174.
16. Ibid., 186.
17. Cohen and Granatstein, *Trudeau's Shadow*, 231.
18. Ibid., 231.
19. *Canada Year Book, 1988*, Table 5.9, section 5, 24, accessible at http://www66.statcan.gc.ca/acyb_000-eng.htm.
20. Cohen and Granatstein, *Trudeau's Shadow*, 235.
21. Crowley, *Fearful Symmetry*, 126.
22. Budget speech, April 19, 1983, delivered by Marc Lalonde, accessed April 1, 2013, http://www.parl.gc.ca/parlinfo/Documents/Budgets/English/1983-04-19.pdf.
23. Cohen and Granatstein, *Trudeau's Shadow*, 125.
24. Ibid.

CHAPTER TWENTY: OUR CHILDREN WILL PAY

1. Somerville, *Trudeau Revealed*, 1978.
2. Budget speech, June 3, 1969, delivered by Edgar Benson, accessed April 1, 2013, http://www.parl.gc.ca/parlinfo/Documents/Budgets/English/1969-06-03.pdf.
3. For international comparisons, "general government" data is used, which includes all levels of government. Budget speech, May 8, 1972, accessed April 1, 2013, http://www.parl.gc.ca/parlinfo/Documents/Budgets/English/1972-05-08.pdf.
4. Budget speech, June 23, 1975, delivered by John Turner, accessed April 1, 2013, http://www.parl.gc.ca/parlinfo/Documents/Budgets/English/1975-06-23.pdf.
5. Budget speech, April 10, 1978, delivered by Jean Chrétien, accessed April 1, 2013, http://www.parl.gc.ca/parlinfo/Documents/Budgets/English/1978-04-10.pdf.
6. Ibid.

7. Budget speech, November 16, 1978, delivered by Jean Chrétien, accessed April 1, 2013, http://www.parl.gc.ca/parlinfo/Documents/Budgets/English/1978-11-16.pdf.

8. Budget speech, December 11, 1979, delivered by John Crosbie, accessed April 1, 2013, http://www.parl.gc.ca/parlinfo/Documents/Budgets/English/1979-12-11.pdf.

9. Budget speech, June 28, 1982, delivered by Allan J. MacEachen, accessed April 1, 2013, http://www.parl.gc.ca/parlinfo/Documents/Budgets/English/1982-06-28.pdf.

10. Budget speech, April 19, 1983, delivered by Marc Lalonde, accessed April 1, 2013, http://www.parl.gc.ca/parlinfo/Documents/Budgets/English/1983-04-19.pdf.

11. When making international comparisons, it is necessary to combine the results of the federal and provincial governments, with some alteration of the basis of presentation. But in terms of deficit financing by governments at the time, the federal results dominate. In this chart, the G5 includes the United States, Japan, the United Kingdom, France, and Italy.

12. P. Trudeau, *Memoirs*, 72.

13. Cohen and Granatstein, *Trudeau's Shadow*, 242.

CHAPTER TWENTY-ONE: UNEMPLOYMENT PAYS OFF

1. D. A. Smith, "Employment Insurance," *The Canadian Encyclopedia*. Accessed March 23, 2013, http://www.thecanadianencyclopedia.com/articles/employment-insurance.

2. Budget speech, June 18, 1971, by Edgar Benson, accessed April 1, 2013, http://www.parl.gc.ca/parlinfo/Documents/Budgets/English/1971-06-18.pdf.

3. Hugh Windsor, "Trudeau Defends UIC: Increased Payments No Concern," *The Globe and Mail*, October 7, 1972, 11.

4. Radwanski, *Trudeau*, 226.

5. *The Globe and Mail*, "Let's Call It Welfare," February 10, 1971, 6.

6. *The Globe and Mail*, "Roster of Banff 'UIC ski team' Is Reduced but Jobs Go Unfilled," March 15, 1973, 2.

7. John Slinger, "Odd Incidents Stalk Trudeau," *The Globe and Mail*, September 25, 1972, 8.

8. Canada. Statistics Canada. *Canada Year Book, 1975,* accessible at *http://www66.statcan.gc.ca/acyb_000-eng.htm*.

9. John Rolfe, "Mackasey 'Not Excited' If UIC $700 Million in Red," *The Globe and Mail*, August 23, 1972, 1.

10. Crowley, *Fearful Symmetry*, 192.

11. Budget speech, June 23, 1975, delivered by John Turner, accessed April 1, 2013, http://www.parl.gc.ca/parlinfo/Documents/Budgets/English/1975-06-23.pdf.

12. Crowley, *Fearful Symmetry*, 212.

13. Crowley, discussion with the author, May 18, 2012.

14. Brian Lee Crowley, "EI Has Caused Shameful Damage Down East," *Ottawa Citizen*, May 19, 2012, B7.

15. Crowley, discussion with the author, May 18, 2012.

16. *Canadian Press*, "Do honest day's work: Trudeau tells hecklers," April 9, 1979, n.p.

CHAPTER TWENTY-TWO: FREE ENTERPRISE UNDER ATTACK

1. P. Trudeau, *Memoirs*, 189.
2. English, *Just Watch Me*, 298.
3. P. Trudeau, *Memoirs*, 198.
4. Budget speech, May 25, 1976, delivered by Donald Macdonald, accessed April 1, 2013, http://www.parl.gc.ca/parlinfo/Documents/Budgets/English/1976-05-25.pdf.
5. P. Trudeau, *Memoirs*, 206.
6. Budget speech, February 19, 1973, delivered by John Turner, accessed April 1, 2013, http://www.parl.gc.ca/parlinfo/Documents/Budgets/English/1973-02-19.pdf.
7. A.E. Safarian, *Multinational Enterprise and Public Policy: A Study of the Industrial Countries* (Northampton, MA: Edward Elgar Publishing, 1993), 130.
8. The limits were raised in 1982.
9. Canada. Industry Canada. "Canadian Government Policies Toward Inward Foreign Direct Investment" (working paper 24, September 1998), 19.
10. Canada. Industry Canada, "Canadian Government Policies Toward Inward Foreign Direct Investment" (working paper 24, September 1998), 16.
11. English, *Just Watch Me*, 218.
12. Budget speech, June 28, 1982, delivered by Allan J. MacEachen, accessed April 1, 2013, http://www.parl.gc.ca/parlinfo/Documents/Budgets/English/1982-06-28.pdf.
13. Trudeau and Axworthy, *Towards a Just Society*, 139.
14. Budget speech, April 19, 1983, delivered by Marc Lalonde, accessed April 1, 2013, http://www.parl.gc.ca/parlinfo/Documents/Budgets/English/1983-04-19.pdf.
15. Budget speech, June 18, 1971, delivered by Edgar Benson, accessed April 1, 2013, http://www.parl.gc.ca/parlinfo/Documents/Budgets/English/1971-06-18.pdf.
16. Canada. Statistics Canada. *Canada Year Book* (various years). Note that the liabilities were estimated by debtors, and Statistics Canada suggests that these numbers are to be accepted only with reservations, accessible at http://www66.statcan.gc.ca/acyb_000-eng.htm.
17. Budget speech, May 8, 1972, delivered by John Turner, accessed April 1, 2013, http://www.parl.gc.ca/parlinfo/Documents/Budgets/English/1972-05-08.pdf.
18. Budget speech, April 19, 1983, delivered by Marc Lalonde, accessed April 1, 2013, http://www.parl.gc.ca/parlinfo/Documents/Budgets/English/1983-04-19.pdf.
19. Trudeau and Axworthy, *Towards a Just Society*, 131.

CHAPTER TWENTY-THREE: INFLATION TERGIVERSATION

1. Radwanski, *Trudeau,* 224.
2. Budget speech, October 22, 1968, delivered by Edgar Benson, accessed April 1, 2013, http://www.parl.gc.ca/parlinfo/Documents/Budgets/English/1968-10-22.pdf.
3. Bank of Canada Inflation Calculator, accessible at http://www.bankofcanada.ca/rates/related/inflation-calculator/
4. Budget Speech, June 3, 1969, delivered by Edgar Benson, accessed April 1, 2013, http://www.parl.gc.ca/parlinfo/Documents/Budgets/English/1969-06-03.pdf.
5. Budget Speech, March 12, 1970, delivered by Edgar Benson, accessed April 1, 2013, http://www.parl.gc.ca/parlinfo/Documents/Budgets/English/1970-03-12.pdf.
6. Budget Speech, May 8, 1972, delivered by John Turner, accessed April 1, 2013, http://www.parl.gc.ca/parlinfo/Documents/Budgets/English/1972-05-08.pdf.
7. Budget speech, Feb. 19, 1973, delivered by John Turner, accessed April 1, 2013, http://www.parl.gc.ca/parlinfo/Documents/Budgets/English/1973-02-19.pdf.
8. Budget speech, November 18, 1974, delivered by John Turner, accessed April 1, 2013, http://www.parl.gc.ca/parlinfo/Documents/Budgets/English/1974-11-18.pdf.
9. Radwanski, *Trudeau,* 267.
10. P. Trudeau, *Memoirs,* 182.
11. Ibid., 53.
12. Ibid., 192.
13. Litt, *Elusive Destiny,* 191.
14. P. Trudeau, *Memoirs,* 194.
15. Turner, discussion with the author, March 16, 2013.
16. John Turner, interview by Peter Mansbridge, *One on One,* CBC Television, October 29, 2011, accessed November 1, 2011, http://www.cbc.ca/video/#/News/TV_Shows/Mansbridge_One_on_One/1455754065/ID=2163028634.
17. Southam, *Pierre,* 37.
18. *The Globe and Mail,* "Editorial," September 12, 1975, 6.
19. Radwanski, *Trudeau,* 272.
20. Ibid, 274.
21. P. Trudeau, *Memoirs,* 182.
22. *The Globe and Mail,* "Trudeau's Era Was Full of Surprises," March 1, 1984, T5.
23. Economic statement, October 20, 1977, delivered by Jean Chrétien, accessed April 1, 2013, http://www.parl.gc.ca/parlinfo/Documents/Budgets/English/1977-10-20.pdf.
24. Southam, *Pierre,* 37.
25. P. Trudeau, *Memoirs,* 298.
26. Budget speech, June 28, 1982, delivered by Allan J. MacEachen, accessed April 1, 2013, http://www.parl.gc.ca/parlinfo/Documents/Budgets/English/1982-06-28.pdf.
27. Clarkson and McCall, *Trudeau and Our Times,* 257.

28. Budget speech, February 15, 1984, delivered by Marc Lalonde, accessed April 1, 2013, http://www.parl.gc.ca/parlinfo/Documents/Budgets/English/1984-02-15.pdf.

29. *CBC News,* "An Old Standby Faces New Challenges," accessed April 1, 2013, http://www.cbc.ca/news/background/canada-savings-bonds/.

30. Budget speech, May 6, 1974, delivered by John Turner, accessed April 1, 2013, http://www.parl.gc.ca/parlinfo/Documents/Budgets/English/1974-05-06.pdf and Budget speech, April 19, 1983, by Marc Lalonde, accessed April 1, 2013, http://www.parl.gc.ca/parlinfo/Documents/Budgets/English/1983-04-19.pdf.

CHAPTER TWENTY-FOUR: NATIONAL ENERGY DISASTER

1. *The Globe and Mail,* "Trudeau Dodges Oil Industry in Calgary," April 14, 1969, 1.

2. P. Trudeau, *Memoirs,* 287.

3. Budget speech, May 6, 1974, delivered by John Turner, accessed April 1, 2013, http://www.parl.gc.ca/parlinfo/Documents/Budgets/English/1974-05-06.pdf.

4. Budget speech, November 18, 1974, delivered by John Turner, accessed April 1, 2013, http://www.parl.gc.ca/parlinfo/Documents/Budgets/English/1974-11-18.pdf.

5. Budget speech, June 23, 1975, delivered by John Turner, accessed April 1, 2013, http://www.parl.gc.ca/parlinfo/Documents/Budgets/English/1975-06-23.pdf.

6. P. Trudeau, *Memoirs,* 293.

7. Remarks made at a press conference, December 18, 1979, accessed December 13, 2012, http://www.cbc.ca/archives/categories/politics/prime-ministers/pierre-elliott-trudeau-philosopher-and-prime-minister/hes-back.html.

8. *Saskatoon Star–Phoenix,* "Go West, Liberals Suggested to Trudeau," May 23, 2000, A8.

9. Trudeau and Axworthy, *Towards a Just Society,* 99.

10. Gotlieb, *Washington Diaries,* 16.

11. Ibid., 29.

12. Trudeau and Axworthy, *Towards a Just Society,* 110.

13. P. Trudeau, *Memoirs,* 287.

14. Budget speech, October 28, 1980, delivered by Allen J. MacEachen, accessed April 1, 2013, http://www.parl.gc.ca/parlinfo/Documents/Budgets/English/1980-10-28.pdf.

15. English, *Just Watch Me,* 577.

16. P. Trudeau, *Memoirs,* 292.

17. *The Globe and Mail,* "Two Wasted Years Later," September 2, 1981, 6.

18. Budget speech, June 28, 1982, delivered by Allan J. MacEachen, accessed April 1, 2013, http://www.parl.gc.ca/parlinfo/Documents/Budgets/English/1982-06-28.pdf.

19. P. Trudeau, *Memoirs,* 205.

20. Ibid., 295.

21. *Canadian Press,* "Pierre Trudeau's national energy program still a bitter legacy in Alberta," October 1, 2000, n.p.

22. CBC Television, "Western Canada's Feelings Toward Pierre Trudeau," *The National*, September 29, 2000.
23. *Montreal Gazette*, "Peckford OKs Offshore Pact with Ottawa," February 11, 1985, A6.

CHAPTER TWENTY-FIVE: REPAIRING THE DAMAGE

1. P. Trudeau, *Memoirs*, 355.
2. Ibid., 356.
3. Canada. Finance Canada. *Economic Reference Tables*, August 1992, Table 27, page 51.
4. U.S. Department of Labor. Division of International Labor Comparisons. *International Comparisons of GDP per Capita and per Employed Person*, July 28, 2009, accessed April 1, 2013, http://www.bls.gov/fls/flsgdp.pdf.
5. Canada. Finance Canada. *Economic Reference Tables*, 1992, table 4.1, and table 5.0, 8-9.
6. David E.W. Laidler and William B.P. Robson, "Prospects for Canada: Progress and Challenges Twenty Years after the Macdonald Commission," C.D. How Institute Policy Study 41, 6. Accessed September 26, 2011, http://www.cdhowe.org/pdf/policystudy_41.pdf.
7. Trudeau and Axworthy, *Towards a Just Society*, 429.
8. Tom Velk and Alvin R. Riggs, "Brian Mulroney and the Economy: Still the Man to Beat," McGill University, North American Studies Program, accessed December 9, 2012, http://people.mcgill.ca/files/thomas.velk/still_the_Man.pdf.
9. Tom Velk, discussion with the author, December 19, 2012.

CHAPTER TWENTY-SIX: DEMOCRACY, PARLIAMENT AND THE PMO

1. Radwanski, *Trudeau*, 102.
2. Ibid., 113.
3. Donaldson, *The Prime Ministers of Canada*, 250.
4. Somerville, *Trudeau Revealed*, 205.
5. Ibid., 204.
6. CBC Television, "CBC Turns 75: A Look Back at the First Televised Question Period," *The House*, Aug 27, 2011.
7. Somerville, *Trudeau Revealed*, 199.
8. *Toronto Star*, "The Country's Most Powerful Accountant 'Just a Bean Counter'," October 29, 1990, C1.
9. Trudeau, *Memoirs*, 108.
10. Ibid., 110.
11. Radwanski, *Trudeau*, 169.
12. Donaldson, *The Prime Ministers of Canada*, 252.
13. Radwanski, *Trudeau*, 131.
14. Gordon Donaldson, *Sixteen Men* (Toronto: Doubleday Canada, 1980), 253.
15. English, *Just Watch Me*, 41.
16. Lord Moran, "Last Impressions of Canada," BBC Radio 4, accessed May 2, 2012, http://downloads.bbc.co.uk/radio4/transcripts/Lord-Moran.pdf.

17. Paul Palango, "The Liberal Debate: Did Coutts Master Own Defeat?" *The Globe and Mail,* August 22, 1981, 4.
18. Robert Sheppard, "Results Give Liberal Universe a Jolt," *The Globe and Mail,* August 18, 1981, 1.
19. English, *Citizen of the World,* 24.
20. Ibid., 462.
21. *The Globe and Mail,* "Trudeau on Yacht Vacation," August 20, 1969, 1.
22. Frederick Lee Morton, *Law, Politics and the Judicial Process in Canada,* 3rd ed. (Calgary: University of Calgary Press), 134.
23. Trudeau and Axworthy, *Towards a Just Society,* 304.
24. Elections Canada, accessed March 22, 2013, http://www.elections.ca/content.aspx?section=ele&dir=turn&document=index&lang=e.
25. *The Globe and Mail,* "Trudeau's Era was Full of Surprises," March 1, 1984, T5.
26. Victor Malarek, "White Elephant Called Mirabel Seems Stuck in the Red," *The Globe and Mail,* August 10, 1981, 10.
27. Richard Cleroux, "Trudeau says Mirabel Airport Will Have Torontonians on Their Knees," *The Globe and Mail,* October 6, 1971, A1.
28. English, *Just Watch Me,* 468.
29. Clarkson and McCall, *Trudeau and Our Times,* 160.
30. Burney, discussion with the author, September 29, 2011.
31. Coyne, *Unscripted,* 32.
32. Ibid., 32.
33. Davey, *The Rainmaker,* 194.
34. Ibid., 194.
35. *The Globe and Mail,* "PM's Pool Cost Taxpayers $25,677, Papers Show," August 10, 1983, 1.
36. New Brunswick singer and actress Catherine McKinnon wrote that Trudeau invited her for a late-night swim at 24 Sussex Drive after an event at which they had first met. See Southam, *Pierre,* 136.

CHAPTER TWENTY-SEVEN: THE POLITICIAN

1. Oliver, *Oliver's Twist,* 88.
2. Ibid., 126.
3. Nemni and Nemni, *Trudeau Transformed,* 165.
4. Somerville, *Trudeau Revealed,* 39.
5. Nemni and Nemni, *Trudeau Transformed,* 262.
6. Ibid., 235.
7. Nemni and Nemni, *Trudeau Transformed,* 382.
8. Nemni and Nemni, *Trudeau Transformed,* 452; Somerville, *Trudeau Revealed,* 164.
9. Somerville, *Trudeau Revealed,* 40.
10. Ibid., 158.
11. Radwanski, *Trudeau,* 113.
12. Southam, *Pierre,* 195.
13. Somerville, *Trudeau Revealed,* 177.

14. His opponent was Victor Goldbloom. See Jean Chrétien, *My Years as Prime Minister* (Toronto: Random House Canada Ltd., 2007), 281. Goldbloom ultimately became a Quebec cabinet minister and Canada's Commissioner of Official Languages.
15. Terrance Wills, "Famous Words," *Montreal Gazette*, September 29, 2000, A18.
16. Southam, *Pierre*, 70.
17. English, *Just Watch Me*, 15.
18. P. Trudeau, *Memoirs*, 158.
19. Radwanski, *Trudeau*, 247.
20. P. Trudeau, *Memoirs*, 161.
21. Ibid., 172.
22. P. Trudeau, *Memoirs*, 172.
23. Ibid., 176.
24. Ibid., 177.
25. Radwanski, *Trudeau*, 254.
26. Jeffrey Simpson, "Analysis: Liberals Trace Their Defeat to Trudeau," *The Globe and Mail*, October 18, 1978, 1.
27. Robert Lewis, "The Turner Campaign," *Maclean's*, March 21 , 1977, n.p.
28. Oliver, *Oliver's Twist*, 94.
29. P. Trudeau, *Memoirs*, 262.
30. English, *Just Watch Me*, 437.
31. P. Trudeau, *Memoirs*, 158, 264.
32. Davey, *The Rainmaker*, 262.
33. Oliver, *Oliver's Twist*, 95.
34. *The Globe and Mail*, "Trudeau's Era Was Full of Surprises" March 1, 1984, T5.
35. P. Trudeau, *Memoirs*, 269.
36. Oliver, *Oliver's Twist*, 101.
37. P. Trudeau, *Memoirs*, 273.
38. Litt, *Elusive Destiny*, 227.
39. Jeff Sallot, "PM Says Title Search Was Not Snooping," *The Globe and Mail*, February 17, 1984, 1.
40. Oliver, *Oliver's Twist*, 182.
41. Litt, *Elusive Destiny*, 256.
42. Ibid., 257.
43. Ibid., 260.
44. Ibid., 237.
45. Litt, *Elusive Destiny*, 243-4.
46. Ibid., 289.
47. Clarkson and McCall, *Trudeau and Our Times*, 11.
48. Turner, discussion with the author, March 16, 2013.

CHAPTER TWENTY-EIGHT: ELECTION MASTER?

1. Election data in this chapter comes from the Elections Canada website, http://www.elections.ca/home.aspx.

2.   Bob Plamondon, *Blue Thunder: The Truth about Conservatives from Macdonald to Harper* (Toronto: Key Porter, 2009), 291.
3.   L. Ian MacDonald, "True to Form, Clark Goes Out a Loser," *Montreal Gazette*, December 10, 2003, A27.

CHAPTER TWENTY-NINE: CONCLUSION

1.   Trudeau, *Memoirs*, 342.
2.   Ibid., 355.
3.   George Linton, "Resignation Sparks Rise in Oil Stocks," *The Globe and Mail*, March 1, 1984, B1.
4.   Jennifer Hunter, "The Trudeau Years: TSE Buoyed by Resignation," *The Globe and Mail*, March 1, 1984, 1.
5.   *The Globe and Mail*, "Resignation by Trudeau Spurs Dollar," March 1, 1984, B2.
6.   Moran, "Last Impressions of Canada."
7.   Somerville, *Trudeau Revealed*, 7.
8.   Black, email exchange with the author, November 28, 2010.
9.   David Frum, "He Was Great: His Legacy Bad," *National Post*, October 5, 2000, A18.
10. Stephen Harper, "On second thought," *National Post*, October 5, 2000, A18.
11. Winston Churchill, "Address to the Canadian Parliament in the House of Commons," December 30, 1941, accessed March 23, 2013, http://www.winstonchurchill.org/learn/speeches/speeches-of-winston-churchill/106-preparation-liberation-assault.
12. Michael T. Kaufman, "Pierre Trudeau Is Dead at 80; Dashing Fighter for Canada," *New York Times*, September 29, 2000, accessed March 23, 2013, http://www.nytimes.com/learning/general/onthisday/bday/1018.html.
13. Brian McGarry, *From Paupers to Prime Ministers* (Renfrew, ON: General Store Publishing House, 2012), 89.
14. William Thorsell, "Pierre Trudeau and the Dance of the Acolytes," *The Globe and Mail*, January 24, 1998, D.6.
15. Norman Hilmer and Stephen Azzi, "Canada's Best Prime Ministers," *Maclean's*, accessed May 2, 2011, http://www2.macleans.ca/2011/06/10/canadas-best-prime-ministers/.
16. Turner, in discussion with the author on March 16, 2013, said the 5th place ranking was fair.
17. The opening remarks for the debates can be found in the *National Post*: David Frum, "The Disastrous Legacy of Pierre Elliott Trudeau," March 24, 2011, A.21, and John English, "The Man Who Saved Canada," March 25, 2011, A.17; and in the *Ottawa Citizen*, Lawrence Martin, "Was Trudeau a Disaster?," September 29, 2011, A.13.
18. Allan Fotheringham, "Like Kennedy, Trudeau Won't Go Away," *Financial Post*, November 23, 1993, 15.
19. *Montreal Gazette*, "On Trudeau," September 30, 2000, A1.
20. Lawrence Martin, "Republican Dream Nearer to Reality," *The Globe and Mail*, June 9, 1979, 9.

21. Andy Blatchford, "Sovereignty Far from a Dead Issue in Québec, Poll Finds," *Canadian Press*, March 26, 2012, The poll, commissioned by the *Association internationale des études Québécoises*, surveyed more than 2,039 people across Canada in March 2012, 1,002 of whom lived in Quebec. The survey has a margin of error of plus or minus 2.2 percentage points, 19 times out of 20.
22. Ibid. (These percentages exclude survey respondents who were undecided).
23. Ibid.
24. John Geddes, "The Case against Trudeau: That's It?," *Maclean's*, accessed January 7, 2013, http://www2.macleans.ca/2011/09/28/the-case-against-trudeau-thats-it/.
25. Clarkson and McCall, *Trudeau and Our Times*, 281.
26. Black, email exchange with the author, November 28, 2010.
27. Mulroney, discussion with the author, January 20, 2011.
28. Somerville, *Trudeau Revealed*, 192.
29. Ibid., 216.
30. This was the conclusion of noted historian Michael Bliss in *Right Honourable Men: The Descent of Canadian Politics from Macdonald to Mulroney* (Toronto: Harper Collins, 1994), 266.
31. Chrétien, *Straight from the Heart*, 188.
32. Plamondon, *Blue Thunder*, 336.
33. Cohen, *Trudeau's Shadow*, 310.
34. Worst Canadian Prime Ministers," *Maclean's*, Apr 21, 1997, 34-39.
35. Bliss, *Right Honourable Men*, 274.
36. Tonda McCharles, "Another Milestone for 'P'tit Gars'," *Toronto Star*, April 7, 2003, A03.
37. Zach Paikin, "How the Federal Liberals Can Rise again in Québec," iPolitics, May 18, 2012, accessed March 23, 2013, http://www.ipolitics.ca/2012/05/18/zach-paikin-how-the-federal-liberals-can-rise-again-in-Québec/.
38. Chris Vivone, discussion with author, April 16, 2013.

BIBLIOGRAPHY

Major Works Authored and Co-Authored by Pierre Elliott Trudeau

1956   *La grève de l'amiante. Une étape de la révolution industrielle au Québec.* Montréal: Éditions Cité Libre.

1968   *Federalism and the French Canadians.* Toronto: Macmillan of Canada.

1970   *Approaches to Politics.* Translated by I.M. Owen. Introduction by Ramsay Cook. Toronto: Oxford University Press.

1972   *Conversation with Canadians.* Toronto: University of Toronto Press.

1977   With Alain Stanké and G.-V. Robillard. *Pierre Elliott Trudeau: Portrait intime.* Éditions Stanké: Montreal.

1988   *With a Bang, Not a Whimper: Pierre Trudeau Speaks Out.* Edited by Donald Johnston. Toronto: Stoddart Publishing Co.

1990   With Thomas Axworthy. *Towards a Just Society: The Trudeau Years.* Markham, Ont.: Viking.

1991   *Fatal Tilt: Speaking Out About Sovereignty.* Toronto: HarperCollins.

1991   *Energy for a Habitable World: A Call for Action.* Taylor and Francis.

1992   *A Mess That Deserves a Big No: Pierre Elliot Trudeau's Historic Speech at the Eleventh Cité Libre Dinner.* Montreal: Robert Davis.

1993   *Memoirs.* Toronto: McClelland and Stewart.

1995   With Ivan Head. *The Canadian Way: Shaping Canada's Foreign Policy, 1968–1984.* Toronto: McClelland and Stewart.

1996   *Against the Current: Selected Writings 1939–1996.* Toronto: McClelland and Stewart.

1998   *The Essential Trudeau.* Edited by Ron Graham. Toronto: McClelland & Stewart.

1999   With C. David Crenna. *Lifting the Shadow of War.* Toronto: McLelland & Stewart.

2007   With Jacques Hébert. *Two Innocents in Red China.* Vancouver: Douglas and McIntyre. First published 1961.

2010   *Approaches to Politics.* Foreward by Ramsay Cook. Toronto: Oxford University Press.

Other Works

Alliston, Karen, Rick Archbold, Jennifer Glossop, Alison Maclean, and Ivon Owen, eds. *Trudeau Albums*. Toronto: Penguin, 2000.

Axworthy, Thomas S. *Passionate Rationalist: Pierre Trudeau and the Transformation of Canada*. Toronto: Penguin Books Canada, 2004.

Azzi, Stephen. *Walter Gordon and the Rise of Canadian Nationalism*. Montreal and Kingston: McGill-Queen's University Press, 1999.

Banting, Keith and Richard Simeon, eds. *And No One Cheered: Federalism, Democracy, and the Constitution Act*. Toronto: Methuen, 1983.

Bastien, Frédéric. *La Bataille de Londres: Dessous, secrets et coulisses du rapatriement constitutionnel*. Montreal, Boréal, 2013

Bliss, Michael. *Right Honourable Men: The Descent of Canadian Politics from Macdonald to Mulroney*. Toronto: Harper Perennial, 1995.

Borins, Sandford. *The Language of the Skies: The Bilingual Air Traffic Control Conflict in Canada*. Montreal and Kingston: McGill-Queen's University Press, 1983.

Bothwell, Robert. *Alliance and Illusion: Canada and the World, 1945–1984*. Vancouver: UBC Press, 2007.

Bouthillier Guy, and Édouard Cloutier. *Trudeau's Darkest Hour: War Measures in Time of Peace*. Montreal: Baraka Books, 2010.

Brinkley, Douglas, ed. *The Reagan Diaries*. New York: HarperCollins, 2007.

Burelle, André. *Pierre Elliott Trudeau: L'Intellectuel et le Politique*. Montreal: Fides, 2005.

Burney, Derek. *Getting it Done: A Memoir*. McGill-Queens University Press, 2005.

Butler, Rick, and Jean-Guy Carrier. *The Trudeau Decade*. Toronto: Doubleday Canada. 1979.

Cahill, Jack. *John Turner: the Long Run*. Toronto: McClelland and Stewart, 1984.

Cameau, Pauline, and Aldo Santin. *The First Canadians: A Profile of Canada's Native People Today*. Toronto: James Lorimer & Company, 1995.

Carney, Anne. "Trudeau Unveiled: Growing Up Private with Mama, the Jesuits, and the Conscience of the Rich." *Maclean's*, February 1972.

Carter, Jimmy. *Keeping Faith: Memoirs of a President*. New York: Bantam, 1981.

Chrétien, Jean. *My Years as Prime Minister*. Toronto: Vintage Canada, 2008.

—. *Straight from the Heart*. Toronto: Key Porter Books, 2007.

Clarkson, Stephen. *The Big Red Machine: How the Liberal Party Dominates Canadian Politics.* Vancouver: UBC Press, 2005.

—. "Charisma and Contradiction: The Legacy of Pierre Elliott Trudeau." *Queen's Quarterly* 107. 4 (Winter 2000): 590-607.

Clarkson, Stephen and Christina McCall. *The Magnificent Obsession.* Vol. 1 of *Trudeau and Our Times.* Toronto: McClelland and Stewart, 1990.

—. *The Heroic Delusion.* Vol. 2 of *Trudeau and Our Times.* Toronto: McClelland and Stewart, 1994.

Claude Couture. *Paddling with the Current: Pierre Elliott Trudeau, Étienne Parent, Liberalism, and Nationalism in Canada.* Edmonton: University of Alberta. 1998.

Cohen, Andrew. *A Deal Undone: The Making and Breaking of the Meech Lake Accord.* Vancouver: Douglas and McIntyre, 1990.

Cohen, Andrew, and J.L.Granatstein, eds. *Trudeau's Shadow: The Life and Legacy of Pierre Elliott Trudeau.* Toronto: Random House, 1998.

Coleman, Ronald. *Just Watch Me: Trudeau's Tragic Legacy.* Bloomington, IN: Trafford Publishing, 2003.

Cook, Ramsay. *The Teeth of Time: Remembering Pierre Elliott Trudeau.* Montreal and Kingston: McGill-Queen's University Press, 2006.

Coyne, Deborah. *Unscripted: A Life Devoted to Building a Better Canada.* EBook, www.deborahcoyne.ca, 2013.

Crowley, Brian. *Fearful Symmetry: The Rise and Fall of Canada's Founding Values.* Toronto: Key Porter, 2009.

Danson, Barney, with Curtis Fahey. *Not Bad for a Sergeant: The Memoirs of Barney Danson.* Toronto: Dundurn, 2002.

Davey, Keith. *The Rainmaker: A Passion for Politics.* Toronto: Stoddart, 1986.

Dobell, Peter. *Canada's Search for New Roles: Foreign Policy in the Trudeau Era.* Toronto: Oxford University Press, 1972.

Doern, G. Bruce, and Glen Toner. *The Politics of Energy: The Development and Implementation of the NEP.* Toronto: Methuen, 1985.

Donaldson, Gordon. *The Prime Ministers of Canada.* Toronto: Doubleday, 1994.

Duchaîne, Jean-François. *Rapport sur les événements d'octobre 1970.* Quebec: Ministry of Justice, 1981.

Duffy, John. *Fights of Our Lives: Elections, Leadership, and the Making of Canada.* Toronto: HarperCollins, 2002.

English, John. *Citizen of the World: The Life of Pierre Elliott Trudeau*. Toronto: Alfred A. Knopf Canada, 2006.

—. *Just Watch Me: The Life of Pierre Elliot Trudeau, 1968-2000*. Toronto: Alfred A. Knopf Canada, 2009.

English, John, Richard Gwyn, and P. Whitney Lackenbauer, eds. *The Hidden Pierre Elliott Trudeau: The Faith Behind The Politics*. Ottawa: Novalis, 2004.

Fraser, Graham. *Sorry, I Don't Speak French: Confronting the Canadian Crisis that Won't Go Away*. Toronto: McClelland and Stewart, 2006.

Freeman, Linda. *The Ambiguous Champion: Canada and South Africa in the Trudeau and Mulroney Years*. Toronto: University of Toronto Press, 1997.

Gossage, Patrick. *Close to Charisma: My Years Between the Press and Pierre Elliott Trudeau*. Halifax, NS: Formac Publishing Co., 1987.

Gotlieb, Allan. *The Washington Diaries*. Toronto: McClelland and Stewart, 2006.

Graham, Ron. *One-Eyed Kings: Promise and Illusion in Canadian Politics*. Toronto: Collins, 1986.

Granatstein, J. L., and Robert Bothwell. *Pirouette: Pierre Trudeau and Canadian Foreign Policy*. Toronto: University of Toronto Press. 1990.

Gwyn, Richard. *Northern Magus: Pierre Trudeau and Canadians*. Toronto: McClelland and Stewart, 1980.

Gwyn, Sandra. "The Politics of Peace." *Saturday Night,* May 1984.

—. "Where Are You, Mike Pearson, Now That We Need You? Decline and Fall of Canada's Foreign Policy." *Saturday Night,* April 1978.

Haddow, Rodney. *Poverty Reform in Canada, 1958–1978*. Montreal and Kingston: McGill-Queen's University Press, 1978.

Hustak, Allan. *Peter Lougheed: A Biography*. Toronto: McClelland and Stewart, 1979.

Iglauer, Edith. "Prime Minister/Premier Ministre." *The New Yorker,* July 5, 1969.

Jackman, Martha. "Canadian Charter Equality at 20: Reflections of a Card-Carrying Member of the Court Party." *Policy Options,* Dec. 2005–Jan. 2006.

Kissinger, Henry. *White House Years*. Boston and Toronto: Little, Brown, 1979.

Kolber, Leo, with L. Ian MacDonald. *Leo: A Life*. Montreal and Kingston: McGill-Queen's University Press, 2006.

Laforest, Guy. *Trudeau and the End of a Canadian Dream*. Translated by Michelle Weinroth and Paul Leduc Browne. Montreal and Kingston: McGill-Queen's University Press, 1995.

Laxer, James, and Robert Laxer. *The Liberal Idea of Canada: Pierre Trudeau and the Question of Canada's Survival*. Toronto: Lorimer. 1977.

Lévesque, René. *Memoirs*. Translated by Philip Stratford. Toronto: McClelland and Stewart, 1986.

Lind, Jennifer. *Sorry States: Apologies in International Politics*. Ithaca, NY: Cornell University Press, 2010.

Litt, Paul. *Elusive Destiny: The Political Vocation of John Napier Turner*. Vancouver: UBC Press, 2011

—. "Trudeaumania: Participatory Democracy in the Mass-Mediated Nation." *The Canadian Historical Review* 89, March 2008.

MacDonald, L. Ian. *From Bourassa to Bourassa: Wilderness to Restoration*. 2nd ed. Montréal and Kingston: McGill-Queen's University Press, 2002.

MacGuigan, Mark. *An Inside Look at External Affairs During the Trudeau Years: The Memoirs of Mark MacGuigan*. Edited by Whitney Lackenbauer. Calgary: University of Calgary Press, 2001.

MacLennan, Christopher. *Towards the Charter: Canadians and the Demand for a National Bill of Rights, 1929–1960*. Montreal and Kingston: McGill-Queen's University Press, 2003.

Martin, Paul. *Hell or High Water: My Life In and Out of Politics*. Toronto: McClelland & Stewart Limited, 2008.

McCall-Newman, Christina. *Grits: An Intimate Portrait of the Liberal Party*. Toronto: Macmillan, 1982.

McWhinney, Edward. *Canada and the Constitution, 1979–1982: Patriation and the Charter of Rights*. Toronto: University of Toronto Press, 1982.

Muggeridge, John. "Why Trudeau, in 1973, Became a Monarchist." *Saturday Night*, January 1974.

Mulroney, Brian. *Memoirs, 1939–1993*. Toronto: McClelland and Stewart, 2007.

—. *Where I Stand*. Toronto: McClelland and Stewart, 1983.

Nemni, Max, and Monique Nemni. *Trudeau Transformed: The Shaping of a Statesman, 1944-1965*. Translated by George Tombs. Toronto: McClelland & Stewart, 2011.

—. *Young Trudeau, Son of Québec, Father of Canada, 1919-1944*. Translated by William Johnson. Toronto: McClelland & Stewart, 2006.

Newman, Peter C. *The Distemper of Our Times: Canadian Politics in Transition, 1963–1968.* Toronto: McClelland and Stewart, 1990.

—. *Here Be Dragons: Telling Tales of People, Passion, and Power.* Toronto: McClelland and Stewart, 2004.

—. *A Nation Divided: Canada and the Coming of Pierre Trudeau.* New York: Alfred A. Knopf, 1969.

—. *True North Not Strong and Free.* Toronto: McClelland & Stewart, 1983.

Oliver, Craig. *Oliver's Twist: The Life and Times of an Unapologetic Newshound.* Toronto: Viking Canada, 2011.

Pelletier, Gérard. *The October Crisis.* Translated by Joyce Marshall. Toronto: McClelland and Stewart, 1971.

Pickersgill, J.W. *Seeing Canada Whole: A Memoir.* Markham, ON: Fitzhenry and Whiteside, 1994.

Plamondon, Bob. *Blue Thunder: The Truth about Conservatives from Macdonald to Harper.* Toronto: Key Porter, 2009.

Potvin, André, Michel Letourneux, and Robert Smith. *L'Anti-Trudeau: Choix de textes.* Montreal: Éditions Parti-pris, 1972.

Powe, B.W. *Mystic Trudeau: The Fire and the Rose.* Toronto: Thomas Allen, 2007.

Radwanski, George. *Trudeau.* Toronto: Macmillan, 1978.

Rae, Bob. *From Protest to Power: Personal Reflections on a Life in Politics.* Toronto: Penguin, 1997.

Reagan, Ronald. *An American Life.* New York: Simon & Schuster, 1990.

Ricci, Nino. *Extraordinary Canadians: Pierre Elliot Trudeau.* Toronto: Penguin Canada, 2009.

Robertson, Gordon. *Memoirs of a Very Civil Servant: Mackenzie King to Pierre Trudeau.* Toronto: University of Toronto Press, 2000.

Romanow, Roy. *Canada Notwithstanding: The Making of the Constitution 1978–1982.* Toronto: Carswell/Methuen, 1984.

Scott, Frank, and Michael Oliver, eds. *Québec States her Case.* Toronto: Macmillan of Canada, 1966.

Sharp, Mitchell. *Which Reminds Me — A Memoir.* Toronto: University of Toronto Press, 1994.

Sheppard, Robert, and Michael Valpy. *The National Deal: The Fight for a Canadian Constitution.* Toronto: Fleet, 1982.

Simpson, Jeffrey. *Discipline of Power: The Conservative Interlude and the Liberal Restoration*. Toronto: University of Toronto Press, 1996.

Slayton, Philip. *Mighty Judgment: How the Supreme Court Runs Your Life*. Toronto: Penguin Group, 2011.

Somerville, David. *Trudeau Revealed by His Actions and Words*. Richmond Hill, ON: BMG Publishing Limited, 1978.

Southam, Nancy, ed. *Pierre: Colleagues and Friends Talk About the Trudeau they Knew*. Toronto: McClelland and Stewart, 2005.

Steed, Judy. *Ed Broadbent: The Pursuit of Power*. Markham, ON: Penguin, 1989.

Stevens, Geoffrey. *Stanfield*. Toronto: McClelland and Stewart, 1973.

Stewart, Walter. *Shrug: Trudeau in Power*. Toronto: New Press, 1971.

Sullivan, Martin. *Mandate '68*. Toronto: Doubleday, 1968.

Tetley, William. *The October Crisis: An Insider's View*. Montreal and Kingston: McGill-Queen's University Press, 2006.

Thordarson, Bruce. *Trudeau and Foreign Policy: A Study in Decision-Making*. Toronto: Oxford University Press, 1972.

Toner, Glen. *The Politics of Energy: The Development and Implementation of the ˙NEP*. Toronto: Methuen, 1985.

Trudeau, Margaret. *Beyond Reason*. New York and London: Paddington Press, 1979.

Vastel, Michel. *The Outsider: The Life of Pierre Elliott Trudeau*. Toronto: Macmillan of Canada, 1990.

Westell, Anthony. *Paradox: Trudeau as Prime Minister*. Scarborough, ON: Prentice-Hall, 1972.

Whelan, Eugene, with Rick Archbold. *Whelan: The Man in the Green Stetson*. Toronto: Irwin, 1986.

Wright, Robert. *Three Nights in Havana: Pierre Trudeau, Fidel Castro, and the Cold War World*. Toronto: HarperCollins, 2007.

Zinc, Lubor. "The Unpenetrated Problem of Pierre Trudeau." *National Review*, June 25, 1982.

ACKNOWLEDGEMENTS

THIS BOOK WAS born at the *Politics and the Pen* dinner in 2009, just after John English, a member of the Pierre Elliot Trudeau Foundation, was given the Shaughnessy Cohen Award for the best political book of the year for the second volume of his Trudeau biography. Lawrence Martin cornered me that night and said that enough was enough and that the record was just as important as the man. What makes his encouragement all the more significant is that Lawrence Martin is a defender and admirer of Trudeau.

My journey began with the numerous Trudeau biographies and many books that Trudeau authored. Despite the spate of published material, there was much about the Trudeau record that was absent from the copious collection. It's not that important material was inaccessible to those prepared to do the digging. I concluded that the inclinations of the legions of literary lions who reveled in the Trudeau persona had largely failed to dissect his record fully and fairly.

Beyond the fresh insights obtained through interviews, I was amazed at the extent to which a substantial portion of the journalistic account of Trudeau's tenure was ignored by his biographers. It may well be that I am the only person to have read and scrutinized every federal budget document produced from 1968 to 1984. I certainly had the advantage of coming to my subject after Internet search possibilities advanced to the point where a subject matter query produced a wide array of content. In this regard, I am grateful to the digital services of the Ottawa Public Library, ably supported by the remarkable Craig Ginther.

Three solid years of research, analysis and interviewing have produced a surprising number of revelations and insights about Trudeau. I am grateful to those who offered their experiences and assessments of Trudeau, and who steered me toward fruitful avenues of inquiry. This includes Derek Burney, Graham Fraser, Conrad Black,

Peter Russell, David Zussman, Bill Pristanski, Elizabeth May, François Bregha, Jim MacNeill, Adam Daifalah, James Anderson, Rob Collins, Chris Vivone, Tom Velk, Brian Lee Crowley, Marjorie Lebreton, David Angus, Scott Reid, Arthur Milnes, Regan Watts, David Frum, and Harry Near. My faithful friend Johnny Usborne was always the first person to see my rough work and steer me in the right direction. Those right honourable gentlemen, Brian Mulroney and John Turner, provided their views on a range of issues, bringing perspectives to bear that only a member of the prime minister's club could muster.

Barely a day has gone by over the past few years when I did not explore my subject with a member of the Parliamentary Press Gallery. The names of those who offered insight and encouragement are simply too numerous to mention. Anyone who believes that no one in Ottawa works hard or knows real dedication is unaware of the heroic efforts made by the fourth estate. They provide a vital check and balance on the power exercised by our parliamentarians and government officials, and do so at a pay grade that is rarely above that of a mid-level public servant.

I appreciate the fact that I may be introducing Trudeau to a new generation of Canadians. That's why I am particularly grateful to have insights from those who were born well after Trudeau left office. In particular, Ted Cousins, a brilliant and aspiring writer and adventurer, helped to give this book a contemporary perspective. Daniel Horovitz, who did yeoman's work on my previous book, stepped up to the plate once again to make sure every page had punch and polish. My two oldest children, Nathaniel and Charlotte, pitched in with editing help, as did my sisters, who, incidentally, look particularly good when wearing red.

The relationship between an author and editor is often fraught with stress and conflict. My good fortune was to work with the best editor on the planet. Tasha Kheiriddin — author, columnist, broadcaster, teacher, political activist — certainly has the historical knowledge and political background necessary to take on this project in spades. But she is also an exceptionally talented writer who took my raw material and brought it to an altogether different level.

To describe Kel Pero as the copyeditor does not do the job description justice. She has the trained eye of an accomplished academic, but also the brilliance and good judgment to pick up flaws that only the most exceptional among us might discern. She was pure joy to work with, and her exceptional talents are beyond my powers to describe properly.

The presentation of the book — including the cover and pages — was given exceptional treatment by Carole McLachlin. With over 900 endnotes, and graphs and charts of various styles, this was a challenge of the highest order, even for a creative genius. Carole delivered a beautiful book and never missed a deadline.

I was fortunate to have a number of vociferous Trudeau defenders critique my manuscript. Their work ensured that any observation not supported by solid evidence was purged from the final text. I took heed of their suggestions — including their wishes not to be named in the acknowledgements.

In the age of social media and downloadable everything, the Canadian publishing world is shrinking in almost every way imaginable. But there are a few success stories out there, like Great River Media (GRM), which is growing by leaps and bounds by filling in the gaps left by traditional publishers and struggling media companies. When I took this project to GRM CEO Mark Sutcliffe, he conjectured that this would likely be the most important literary effort I would ever embark upon. When it was suggested that the book be accelerated in 2010 to follow the John English biography as quickly as possible, Mark told me to take my time, dig deep into the archives, and make my work the most authoritative book on the record of a prime minister that had ever been written. Mark has been my partner in this project every step of the way. Donna Neil and Michael Curran manage the day-to-day operations of GRM, which they do with great ability and commitment. Donna was the hands-on publisher of this book, and she navigated every technical, production, and business issue that arose with great joy and much acumen. I always knew I was in good hands with Donna in the lead.

On a personal level, I am blessed with a large and beautiful family. My mother Jeanette, a sprightly 86, continues to be my inspiration. My siblings Sue, Tom, Kathy, and Steve are with me in every moment. My mother-in-law and father-in law, Jim and June Coke, do nothing but contribute to the quality of life for everyone around them, especially me. My wife, Marian Coke, inspires me with her healthy ways and devotion to living an enjoyable life. And my children — Nathaniel, Charlotte, Megan and Michael — well, you are the joy of my life. This book is dedicated to you.

INDEX

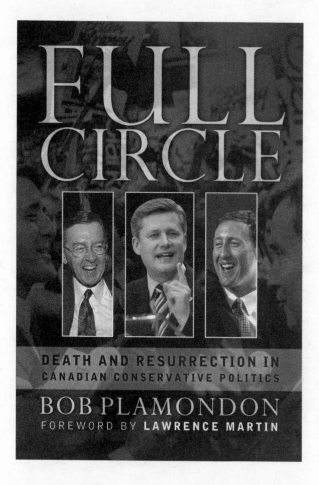

ACCOLADES FOR THE 2006 MONTREAL GAZETTE BESTSELLER:

Full Circle: Death and Resurrection in Canadian Conservative Politics

"Masterful ... enthralling ... Plamondon offers so many insights into recent
Canadian politics, this book reads like a thriller ... This should be read by
every Canadian. Or, at least, every Canadian who votes."
Paul Jackson — Calgary Sun

"(Full Circle) is a solid, detailed chronicle of the players and the events
surrounding some stormy years for the Tories. Describing it as 'meticulous,'
however, doesn't do it justice — it's thorough and highly readable to boot ..."
Susan Delacourt — Toronto Star

Available at the usual online sources.

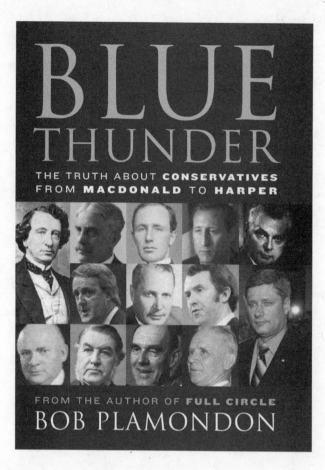

ACCOLADES FOR THE 2009 GLOBE AND MAIL BESTSELLER:

Blue Thunder: The Truth about Conservatives from Macdonald to Harper

"Aptly and ably summarizes ... *The Truth About Conservatives*. The 500-page tome takes on the unenviable task of trying to make political reactionaries interesting. It succeeds admirably ... a valuable contribution to the thin shelf of authoritative texts on the right wing of Canadian politics. If truth were the sum of all the ascertainable facts, Plamondon's œuvre would be it."
Peter C. Newman — for the Globe and Mail

"This book is a major contribution to Canadian political history and science; a page-turner usefully revealing much more about the present governing federal party, how it wins and loses and is distinguishable from its opponents, than is known by all but a studious few ..."
— Conrad Black

Available at the usual online sources.

BOB PLAMONDON

Hay West

A STORY OF CANADIANS HELPING CANADIANS

Praise for Hay West

"A compelling story with vivid detail that brings the Hay West story to life. The detail is what is important in understanding the struggles and motivations of real lives. It absolutely makes me proud to be a Canadian. Good hearts and true decency are words that describe the folks in this story and Canadians at their best."
— *Robert Bateman*

"This book presents a wonderful opportunity to celebrate the tremendous generosity of countless volunteers, donors and sponsors who worked so hard and selflessly on behalf of their fellow Canadians."
— *Rt. Hon Jean Chrétien*

Available at the usual online sources.